Rome and the Anglicans

J. C. H. Aveling · D. M. Loades
H. R. McAdoo

Rome
and the Anglicans

Historical and Doctrinal Aspects
of Anglican – Roman Catholic Relations

edited with a postscript
by
Wolfgang Haase

Walter de Gruyter · Berlin · New York
1982

CIP-Kurztitelaufnahme der Deutschen Bibliothek

Rome and the Anglicans : histor. and doctrinal aspects of Anglican − Roman Cathol. relations / J. C. H. Aveling ; D. M. Loades ; H. R. McAdoo. Ed. with a postscript by Wolfgang Haase. − Berlin ; New York : de Gruyter, 1982.
  ISBN 3-11-008267-5
NE: Aveling, J. C. H. [Mitverf.]; Loades, D. M. [Mitverf.]; McAdoo, H. R. [Mitverf.]; Haase, Wolfgang [Hrsg.]

Contents

Relations between the Anglican and Roman Catholic Churches in the 16th and 17th Centuries

by David M. Loades, Bangor

Contents

I. Introduction

In this brief paper I do not intend to discuss doctrinal controversies, nor the work of protestant evangelists or catholic missionaries at the parochial level. My intention is to examine the political and diplomatic relationship between the two churches as represented by their respective heads — successive Popes and English monarchs. Unlike the social history of puritanism and catholic recusancy, this has not been a popular subject for research in recent years. The most

considerable monograph specifically devoted to Anglo-Papal relations, W. E.
Wilkie's 'The Cardinal Protectors of England' (1974) deals only with the period
1492—1534, and the substantial output of recusant historians has included only
one work on the later period since 1955, a reprint in 1968 of C. G. Bayne's
'Anglo Roman relations 1558—1565', first published in 1913. At the same time
many books and articles have appeared dealing with English catholicism in
general, or with particular aspects of it, which have discussed Anglo-Papal
relations incidentally or as a matter of context. The most directly relevant are by
G. de C. Parmiter and H. A. Kelly on Henry VIII's divorce, C. de Frede on the
catholic restoration under Mary Tudor, and P. McGrath on the political
problems of the Elizabethan catholics. These, and many other contributions are
listed in the bibliographical appendix to this paper, and mention only need be
made here of the work of Leo Hicks, T. H. Clancy, J. P. Crehan and R. H.
Pogson in printed articles,[1] and of T. P. Bostick and J. V. Gifford in unpublished
theses.[2] English attitudes towards the Papacy, both official and popular, have
received rather more attention — from Elton, Scarisbrick and McConica on the
reign of Henry VIII;[3] from myself on Mary Tudor;[4] from Bossy, Cross and
Trimble on the later sixteenth century;[5] and from Hill, Caraman, Kenyon and
Miller,[6] to name but a few of those who have written on the seventeenth century.
The most important recent book on post-reformation English catholicism, J. A.
Bossy's 'The English Catholic Community, 1570—1850' (1975), while not
ignoring the continuous significance of the Roman authority, is primarily concerned with the internal evolution of the church, and particularly with the role of
the gentry in that process. Papal policy towards England has received no treatment as a coherent theme over a long period, and older works, such as P. Hughes,
'Rome and the Counter Reformation in England' (1942) or G. Albion, 'Charles I
and the Court of Rome' (1935) have not been superseded. The Curia was seldom
well informed about English affairs. The country was in any case distant, and

---

[1] Each of these authors has written numerous articles, and other works over a period of
years; only the more recent and directly relevant are listed in the bibliography, below
pp. 49—53.

[2] T. P. BOSTICK, English Foreign Policy, the Diplomacy of the Divorce, 1528—1534, Illinois
Ph.D., 1967; J. V. GIFFORD, The Controversy over the Oath of Allegiance in 1606, Oxford B.Litt., 1971.

[3] G. R. ELTON, Policy and Police, Cambridge, 1972; J. J. SCARISBRICK, Henry VIII, London 1968; J. K. McCONICA, English Humanists and Reformation Politics, Oxford, 1965.

[4] D. M. LOADES, Two Tudor Conspiracies, Cambridge, 1965; IDEM, The Oxford Martyrs,
London, 1970; IDEM, The Enforcement of Reaction, 1553—1558, Journal of Ecclesiastical
History, 1965, XVI (i), 59—66.

[5] J. A. BOSSY, The Character of Elizabethan Catholicism, Past and Present, 1962, XXI; C.
CROSS, The Puritan Earl; Henry Hastings, Third Earl of Huntingdon 1536—1595,
London, 1966; W. R. TRIMBLE, The Catholic Laity in Elizabethan England, Cambridge,
Mass., 1964.

[6] C. HILL, AntiChrist in Seventeenth Century England, London, 1971; P. CARAMAN, The
Years of Seige; Catholic Life from James I to Cromwell, London, 1966; J. P. KENYON,
The Popish Plot, London, 1972; J. MILLER, Popery and Politics in England, 1660—1688,
Cambridge, 1973.

during the years of schism information was received mainly through exiles and third parties who were frequently biased, and often themselves ignorant. Also, virtually from the beginning of the schism the Papacy showed an inveterate tendency to pursue two conflicting policies simultaneously. Until the end of the sixteenth century successive Popes strove to foster and support the English catholics by propaganda and missionary activity of a purely spiritual nature, while at the same time entertaining with scanty concealment schemes for the forcible reconversion of the country by a mixture of political assassination and foreign invasion. It is not surprising that Englishmen of the seventeenth century associated the propagation of the catholic faith with violence and deception long after the Papacy had abandoned such schemes as unworthy and unreal. Later Popes continued to be plagued by a double policy, although of a less obviously contradictory nature. The shadow of political conversion lingered, although it was now embodied in hopes for the personal conversion of the monarch. In fact this way to reunion was as much the result of unreal political calculations as that of a victorious catholic uprising, and almost equally damaging to the welfare and interests of the English catholics. Not until James II began to make serious moves to implement such a policy did the Papacy finally shed its illusions about the English situation, and concentrate its attention upon ministering to those Englishmen who continued, at whatever cost to themselves, to acknowledge its spiritual authority.

II. The situation at the beginning of the sixteenth century

In the opening years of the sixteenth century relations between Rome and England were calm and amicable. Those relics of ancient warfare, the statutes of Provisors and Praemunire remained unrepealed, but no attempt was made to invoke them as long as Henry VII lived.[7] Henry was conventionally pious, and the three Popes with whom he had to deal, Innocent VIII (1484—1492), Alexander VI (1492—1503) and Julius II (1503—1513), were all anxious to secure his political support. Consequently he was able to invoke the sanction of excommunication against his enemies in Ireland, to restrict benefit of clergy, to reduce the immunities of sanctuary, and to nominate to the episcopal bench at his own discretion. In return Henry gave a certain amount of diplomatic support, persecuted heretics, and supported the jubilee indulgence of 1501. The situation was one of unwritten *Concordat*; apparently stable, but in fact at the mercy of changing circumstances and personalities. The development of the office of Cardinal Protector between 1492 and 1514, although appearing to provide a guarantee of continuity and good communications, was itself at the mercy of personal ambitions

---

[7] These statutes, designed to submit papal jurisdiction in England to royal limitation, had culminated in an Act of 1393. For a brief but pertinent comment on Henry's relations with the papacy, see S. B. CHRIMES, Henry VII, London, 1972, 240—241.

and animosities, as was demonstrated by the fortunes of Christopher Bainbridge and Adriano Castellesi.[7a]

Anti-clericalism had been strong in England for many years, and fierce intellectual criticism of the church (already common in other parts of Europe) began to appear soon after 1500.[8] The church was an extremely useful institution from the king's point of view. It gave sanctity to his office and weight to his laws. It provided him with a career structure for his civil servants, and with tangible evidence of that Divine favour which was so important in preserving the loyalty of his subjects. But the church also needed the king. Its wealth and complex landed endowments presented a standing temptation to lay harrassment, and without royal backing the jurisdiction of its courts lacked substance. Both lay anti-clericalism and clerical humanism presented the monarchy with weapons of sharp correction against the church within its dominions should that church draw back from the political and administrative alliance to which it seemed committed before 1509. The church was thus in the classic position of a man serving two masters, and the closer the agreement between those masters the more tenuous did its autonomy become. Consequently one of the chief results of the goodwill which prevailed between England and Rome from 1485 to 1509 was that the English church became virtually a hostage for papal acquiescence in the policies of the English Crown. This was not in itself unprecedented, but continuous warfare in Italy and the addition of the powerful Lutheran challenge to existing criticism also contributed to the weakening of Papal authority in England. These factors combined to make the English church uniquely vulnerable to royal pressure when Henry VIII's matrimonial crisis developed in the late 1520s.

III. Henry VIII; the matrimonial crisis

The circumstances of that crisis are too well known to need recounting, but it is worth remembering that to Clement VII it came as a bolt from a clear sky. The diligence and cordiality of English communications with Rome had waned after the old king's death, and both Leo X and Adrian VI had complained occasionally of unfilial negligance, but there had certainly been no breakdown of relations.[8a] Some years ago Professor A. F. Pollard represented English policy between 1514 and 1525 as being harnessed to Papal aims by the ambitions of

---

[7a] W. E. WILKIE, The Cardinal Protectors of England, Cambridge, 1974, 40–52, 105–110.

[8] For example: Oratio habita ad clerum in Convocatione, by JOHN COLET, London, 1511.

[8a] It was not until Henry and Wolsey began to move away from a pro-Imperial alliance in 1525 that there was any noticeable cooling of relations, and that seems to have been caused more by Wolsey's complicated intrigues in the curia than by any deliberate intention. WILKIE, op. cit., 141–149.

Thomas Wolsey.[9] This view has now been effectively challenged,[10] but Wolsey's double position as Chancellor and Papal Legate must have seemed to provide a guarantee against fundamental divergence, and King Henry had taken the trouble to enter the theological lists against Luther with his 'Assertio Septem Sacramentorum', a work which had contained, among other things, an unequivocal assertion of Papal authority. At the same time, because of the way in which Wolsey had monopolised English business, Clement was unaware of the strength of the anti-clericalism which the Cardinal was stirring up in England, and uninformed of Henry's state of mind. More important, England's established contacts in the Curia, proved inadequate to manipulate its more intimate politics. This fact was to be of critical importance in the tense and dramatic conditions created by the sack of Rome, Clement's imprisonment in the Castel Sant' Angelo, and his escape to Orvieto in December 1527. For a time the Curia was shattered, the Pope unnerved and thoroughly alienated from the Emperor. When the first English envoy, William Knight, made contact with Clement a few days before his escape, he found him almost pathetically anxious to win friends; but by the time that Knight had followed him to Orvieto, he was already less amenable. A man more familiar with Clement's character, or better provided with confidential information might still have gained his point had he been prepared to offer prompt and generous relief of the poverty which was the Pope's most pressing anxiety. This Knight was unable to do, and his mission was already well on the way to failure when he was replaced by Gregory Casale with new instructions from Wolsey in January 1528.

Casale was a more skilful diplomat than Knight, and had the advantage of being an Italian, but he was never given adequate powers, and acted mainly as resident host to successive special missions which followed him in rapid succession over the next four years.[11] English importunity was the least of Clement's worries in the early months of 1528. He was quite willing to do the Emperor any injury within his power, but understandably nervous of the possible consequences; and neither he nor his advisers, such as Cardinal Pucci, could understand why Wolsey was making such a fuss. In their eyes the sensible course would have been for the English Cardinal to have judged the matter himself, and only brought the case to Rome should the validity of the King's second marriage be challenged.[12] To Wolsey such a course was a mere waste of time, since opposition to the Boleyn marriage was so strong that a challenge was inevitable. He was quite willing to judge the case, but only by virtue of a Decretal Commission which would have made his decision final, and not subject to appeal. This Clement adamantly refused to grant, although he was prepared to issue a general commission, and to make an informal undertaking to confirm the commissioners' decision.

---

[9] A. F. POLLARD, Wolsey, London, 1929.

[10] By SCARISBRICK, op. cit., and others. It is more likely that Wolsey's diplomacy was motivated chiefly by the desire to gratify Henry and keep England at the centre of European affairs. R. B. WERNHAM, Before the Armada, London, 1966, 89—110.

[11] SCARISBRICK, op. cit., 205—224.

[12] Letters and Papers of the Reign of Henry VIII, ed. BREWER et al., London 1862—1910, IV, 3802.

This unsatisfactory compromise, reached in April 1528, was the nearest that any of the English missions came to diplomatic success. By the summer of that year the Imperial forces had withdrawn from the Papal states, and by October the Curia was back in Rome. Clement's animosity against the Emperor was waning, and with it any remaining chance that he would take resolute action in defiance of Charles' wishes.

Meanwhile Wolsey and his agents in Rome, principally Stephen Gardiner, kept up a feverish activity.[13] Cardinal Campeggio was to be joined with Wolsey in commission to hear the King of England's case, and part of this activity was directed towards overcoming his gout and his reluctance. The rest was fruitlessly expended upon renewed attempts to secure a Decretal Commission. Campeggio eventually reached England at the end of September, secretly instructed by Clement to use every possible pretext for delay, to find Wolsey and Henry consumed with impatience. By November, in an agony of exasperation the English Cardinal was repeating over and over again that if Clement did not gratify his master swiftly it would be the end of Papal authority in England.[14] Campeggio was unmoved by such extravagance. He was in an extremely difficult position, and saw only one real hope of satisfying the conflicting demands being made upon him — to persuade Catherine into a graceful withdrawal. While the Legate pursued his hopeless quest, a series of developments further weakened Henry's position. A papal brief confirming the dispensation for his original marriage turned up in Spain, undermining the little that his diplomacy had achieved. In February and March of 1529 rumours of Clement's death, and his actual illness, caused further confusion and delay, while at the end of April the Emperor's agents in Rome made a formal protest against the King of England's suit, and petitioned the Pope to revoke the case to the Curia. In these circumstances Henry's agents in Rome could accomplish nothing in the direction of amplifying the commission which had already been granted, and the king's only hope lay in getting a favourable verdict from Campeggio and Wolsey as quickly as possible. The Legates began work at length on 18 June, but it is clear that Campeggio never had any intention of giving judgement. Following Clement's instructions, and no doubt his own inclinations, he found a technical pretext to adjourn the court on 31 July, and soon after the case was revoked to Rome.[15]

Henry had been totally defeated by a mixture of his own incompetence and Imperial pressure. Furious and humiliated, he now needed a scapegoat and a new policy. The former was easier to find than the latter, and predictably the weight of his displeasure fell upon Wolsey. The story of the Chancellor's fall is too well known to need repetition, but it is important to realise that more was involved than the disgrace of a once trusted minister. Wolsey was a prince of the Church,

---

[13] Ibid., 4167 etc. See also STEFAN EHSES, Römische Dokumente zur Geschichte der Ehescheidung Heinrichs VIII von England, 1527–1534, Paderborn, 1893, 23ff.; H. A. KELLY, The Matrimonial Trials of Henry VIII, Stanford, Calif., 1976, 54–74.

[14] EHSES, op. cit., 48ff., 54. Quoted in SCARISBRICK, op. cit., 213.

[15] By the Roman Calendar, term ended on that day, and since the court was technically a papal one Campeggio seized this opportunity to adjourn for the summer vacation.

and the manner in which he was handled was of the gravest significance for the Papacy which he theoretically represented. On 21 September, after several weeks of tension and uncertainty, he was deprived of the Great Seal; and on 9 October he was charged with offences against the Statutes of Praemunire, and speedily convicted. Objectively, the charges were absurd, since they involved the exercise of Papal jurisdiction without the king's consent; but Wolsey put up no serious resistance, and no protest was forthcoming from Rome. Shortly after, Henry pardoned his old servant's praemunire, and by keeping him for some months in a demoralising limbo between hope and fear was able to take from him the temporalities of several of his benefices, and sundry ecclesiastical properties which were not Wolsey's to give.[16] Encouraged by intermittent gestures of renewed favour, in April 1530 the Cardinal withdrew towards his province of York, and apparently began to entertain hopes of recovering his position with Papal assistance. If these intrigues were real at all they can hardly have been substantial; but they provided sufficient pretext for the king to order his arrest upon a charge of treason at the beginning of November. Wolsey died without coming to trial, but not before his fate had demonstrated that, to a man in his position, the panoply of Legatine authority was at best a worthless protection and at worst a disastrous liability. Wolsey fell, not because he was a symbol of papal jurisdiction but because he had failed the king. Nevertheless, by the time he died his disgrace had become an integral part of that policy of ecclesiastical blackmail which marked the second stage of Henry's search for a solution to his 'great matter'.

The king's principal ally in this policy was the parliament which met in November 1529 — particularly the House of Commons.[17] In acting as they did the Commons were doing no more than picking up the threads of an ancient controversy, a controversy which had blazed up fiercely as recently as 1514. On that occasion, true to the existing spirit of concordat, Henry had damped down the fires of anti-clericalism;[18] now he fanned them. There is no space here to discuss the proceedings of the so-called Reformation Parliament, but it is quite clear that by 1530 the king was strongly sympathetic to demands for ecclesiastical reform. He was also beginning to express new and disquieting opinions about the extent of his own role in that reform. Professor Scarisbrick has recently argued that the appearance of these ideas was not simply the result of Henry's desire to coerce the Pope, and his views carry weight.[19] Nevertheless, by the summer of 1530, when the English king had spent much time, effort and money endeavouring to strengthen his case at Rome, the bishops of his own realm were thoroughly alarmed by the pressure building up against them in parliament. Bitterly as he disliked the idea, up to this point Henry had accepted the prospect of having to

[16] For example, Durham Place, in the Strand, which remained in the king's hands although it properly belonged to the see of Durham. C. STURGE, Cuthbert Tunstall, London, 1938.

[17] S. E. LEHMBERG, The Reformation Parliament, 1529—1536, Cambridge, 1970, 76—182.

[18] Over the notorious case of Richard Hunne, the London merchant who had been found murdered in the bishop's prison, see E. J. DAVIS, The Authorities for the Case of Richard Hunne, 1514—15, English Historical Review, 1915, XXX, 477—488; also A. OGLE, The Tragedy of the Lollards Tower, Oxford, 1949.

[19] SCARISBRICK, op. cit., 241—250.

plead his cause at Rome, and had concentrated his attention on obtaining a favourable verdict. This phase culminated in early June with the despatch to Clement of a petition bearing the seals of nearly a hundred English dignitaries, begging him to find for Henry, and dropping ominous (but vague) hints about alternative solutions. There was no chance of a favourable response. Emperor and Pope were by this time the closest of friends, and Charles's agents were committed to frustrating English efforts at every turn. In the face of this, by August 1530, Henry's attitude had undergone a critical change. Loud importunity had been replaced by a cool denial that the Pope had any jurisdiction to pronounce upon the King of England's marriage. The ancient privileges and customs of the realm, he declared, exempted Englishmen from being cited before foreign courts; the Pope's authority in England extended only to matters of heresy. Consequently there was no reason why the marriage question should not be committed to the Archbishop of Canterbury, in spite of the fact that Clement had inhibited all further discussion pending the outcome of Catherine's appeal. The Pope was in any case both a bastard and a simoniac, Henry alleged, and if the manifest justice of his claim was not admitted, he was fully prepared to appeal in his turn — to a General Council.[20]

IV. Henry VIII; the royal supremacy

By the end of 1530 the king's thinking was more radical than that of any of his known advisers, and a source of acute embarrassment to his envoys in Rome.[20a] When challenged by an indignant Pope to substantiate the claims which Henry insisted that they should make on his behalf, they could find nothing. Neither England's jurisdictional immunity, nor the king's vaguer claim to 'Imperial' dignity could be supported by evidence from the Vatican archives. For the next fifteen months these envoys (principally William Benet and Edward Carne) strove by a variety of arguments, inducements and threats to get the king's case heard in England. They were unsuccessful, and Henry's own position lacked both logic and consistency. In spite of his belligerent claims, he was not yet fully committed to the doctrine of English autonomy, as the continued efforts of his envoys testified. At the same time a sweeping attack upon the English clergy, culminating in charges of Praemunire against both Convocations, was allowed

[20] The idea of appealing to a General Council of the church against a papal decision was not a new one, and Luther had recently done the same. The renaissance Popes generally were nervous of a Council, remembering the anti-papal record of the Councils of Constance and Basle. Clement was thought to be especially apprehensive of a Council because of irregularities in his own election — and no papal initiative in that direction was taken until after his death, in spite of pressure from all sides. H. JEDIN, Geschichte des Konzils von Trient, I, Freiburg im Breisgau, 1949.

[20a] Recent research has indicated that the source of the King's views at this time was a composite document ('Collectanea satis copiosa') in process of compilation by a group of divines supporting the divorce. J. A. GUY, The Public Career of Sir Thomas More, London, 1980, p. 131.

to peter out in a royal pardon and an equivocal submission.[21] Henry was certainly feeling his way towards a fully fledged concept of Royal Supremacy — all the elements of which were present in his mind — but both emotionally and intellectually he was irresolute. It was still possible as late as the beginning of 1532 that a change of heart on Clement's part could simply have restored the *status quo*; but Clement, understandably, took Henry's threats and blandishments with a large pinch of salt. He saw no reason, either political or canonical, to change his mind. The king thereupon moved from threats to action. How far the dramatic events of 1532 and 1533 were brought about by this stalemate over the 'great matter', and how far they were the result of long brooding about ecclesiastical jurisdiction, is hard to tell. The traditional thesis of a complete causal relationship between the 'divorce' and the break with Rome is no longer adequate. Henry held some views of a Caesaro-Papist kind in the early 1520s, and it is quite probable that England would have come to a position similar to extreme Gallicanism even if there had been no matrimonial issue. On the other hand it would be unreal to maintain that the royal ultimatum based upon the Commons 'Supplication against the Ordinaries', or the Act in Restraint of Annates,[22] were not part of a campaign to force the Pope's hand. Henry was reaching the end of his resources. His attempts to secure a favourable nomination to the College of Cardinals had failed, and his ostentatious *entente* with Francis I, reached in late October 1532, provided no real guarantee of adequate political backing in the Curia. In the three years since the failure of the Blackfriars court he had battered the English church into a submission which would, in itself, have seriously disrupted Anglo-Papal relations, but he had made not the slightest progress towards obtaining a favourable judgement of his case. All he had to show for his efforts was the fact that no definitive sentence had been pronounced against him.

This *impasse* was finally broken at the beginning of 1533, ostensibly by Henry's discovery of the fact that Anne Boleyn was pregnant. In reality that pregnancy was a symptom rather than the cause of the crucial decision. The death of Archbishop Warham on 22 August 1532, and the emergence of Thomas Cromwell as Henry's leading adviser in the last months of the year, are more likely to have been the decisive factors. The way was now open for the king to act upon the ideas which he had been voicing for some time, and by appointing an amenable Archbishop to settle his 'great matter' in England without further reference to Pope or Curia. Professor Elton has argued convincingly that Cromwell was the man who finally steeled the king's resolution,[23] and it was certainly

[21] D. WILKINS, Concilia Magnae Britanniae et Hiberniae, London, 1737, III, 725ff.; G. R. ELTON, The Commons supplication of 1532, English Historical Review, 1951, LXVI; J. P. COOPER, The Supplication against the Ordinaries Reconsidered, English Historical Review, 1957, LXXII; M. KELLY, The Submission of the Clergy, Transactions of the Royal Historical Society, 5 series, 15, 1965, 97—119.

[22] 23 Henry VIII c. 20. LEHMBERG, op. cit., 135—138.

[23] G. R. ELTON, The Tudor Revolution in Government, Cambridge, 1953; IDEM, King or Minister? The Man Behind the Henrician Reformation, History, 1954, XXXIX; IDEM, Thomas Cromwell, Reform and Renewal, Cambridge, 1972.

he who organised the subsequent campaign which translated Henry's aspirations into legal and political realities. The progress of that campaign is familiar to all students of the period, and only certain features call for comment here. Clement was warned that new and dangerous moves were afoot in England, but Henry had been crying 'wolf' for years, and the Pope was not wholly without sympathy for his problems. Consequently he made no difficulty about confirming Thomas Cranmer's appointment as Archbishop of Canterbury, which, as things were to turn out, was to be the last effective act of papal authority relating to England for more than twenty years. At the same time, Henry refrained from burning his boats immediately. His excusators continued to plead in the Curia, even after Anne Boleyn had been crowned as his Queen, and it was not to be until 1534 that Papal jurisdiction was unequivocally excluded from England by Parliament and Convocation. By that time, of course, the initiative did not lay entirely with the king. Clement responded to the English defiance with some moderation, but he could not ignore it. In Consistory on 11 July Henry's marriage to Anne was solemnly condemned, and he was ordered to take back Catherine, who was still his lawful wife pending the outcome of her appeal. He was given until September to do so, under pain of excommunication.

The king took up the guage by cancelling the commissions of his agents in Rome, and by sending Gardiner and Edmund Bonner to defy the Pope to his face by appealing to a General Council. By the end of 1533 Henry stood excommunicate (although the sentence had not been formally promulgated), and all direct communication between England and the Curia had ceased. For the remainder of his pontificate (until September 1534), Clement's attitude was remarkably supine. He gave no lead or encouragement to those Englishmen who wished to resist the royal supremacy, and played into the hands of that important and persuasive group who were arguing that only the king could cleanse the Augean stables of the English church.[24] Apart from Cromwell, John Fisher and Sir Thomas More, it seems that very few people either in England or in Rome understood the true significance of what was happening. Popes and English kings had quarrelled before; sooner or later, many must have thought, a negotiated settlement would be reached and all the high principled language of the royal supremacy would be quietly forgotten. The new Pope, Paul III, was anxious for an accommodation, and spoke of re-opening the king's matrimonial case.[25] Both Francis and Charles V were sympathetic towards an agreement which would have relieved them of the embarrassment of having to do business with a colleague who was under the ban of the church. Henry, however, would accept nothing less than a complete surrender to his claims; and the executions of Fisher and More in the summer of 1535 put an abrupt, if temporary, end to all talk of reconciliation. A second excommunication was pronounced against

---

[24] This was a line which had been taken as early as 1529 by the radical SIMON FISH in his 'A Supplication for the Beggars'; by 1534 it had been taken up by less extreme publicists, such as Robert Crowley, Christopher St. German and Richard Sampson.

[25] Letters and Papers, VIII, 806—807. SCARISBRICK, op. cit., 333—334.

him, and Bulls prepared absolving his subjects of their allegiance and declaring him deposed from his throne. By the summer of 1536, however, the pendulum had swung back again. Both Catherine and Anne were dead, and the Pope was willing to make sweeping concessions. The Emperor was openly enthusiastic, and the shrewdest observers in Rome believed that a settlement would come in a matter of weeks.[25a] Had the royal supremacy been nothing more than a device to secure the anullment of the king's first marriage, these expectations would have been justified. By this time, however, Henry was deeply convinced that all Papal jurisdiction was wrongful and usurped; and his only interest in negotiation was to forstall the possibility that either the Emperor or the King of France might be prevailed upon to execute the Papal sentence against him.

This never seemed a very likely eventuality, but could not be altogether discounted, and Henry remained acutely suspicious of papal intentions. His suspicions were confirmed by Paul's reaction to the news of rebellion in England towards the end of 1536. The king's remote kinsman and arch-enemy, Reginald Pole,[26] was created a Cardinal and despatched northwards for the purpose of activating the Bull of excommunication. Hopefully, this was to be done by the strength of the rebels themselves; but should that fail Pole was empowered to do his utmost to invoke the aid of other Christian princes. Pole arrived in the Low Countries only after the rebellion was over, and it is extremely uncertain that he would have been able to enlist any substantial support had he arrived earlier. Henry was furious over what he regarded as the treason of one of his own subjects, and Pole was fortunate to escape either abduction or assassination. Within a few years those members of his family who remained in England were to pay the price of his zeal in the papal cause.[27] For the time being the Pope's animosity had been frustrated, but there was no more talk of an amicable settlement. For at least as long as Henry lived the English schism would continue, unless it could be broken by armed invasion. Thus by the end of 1537 he was competing directly with the Pope for friendship and alliance, and a second polarity had been added to the existing Franco-Habsburg rivalry. Consequently, English security depended upon the preservation of this pattern, and English diplomacy was consistently directed against any sign of a *rapprochement* between Francis and Charles, as well as against the ever present threat of a General Council of the church. Towards the end of 1538, Henry appeared to be facing defeat on both fronts, and Pope Paul, now fully determined on his overthrow, prepared again to promulgate the Bull of deposition

---

[25a] For a full discussion of this abortive negotiation which involved Campeggio and his brother Marcantonio, see WILKIE, op. cit., 226—233.

[26] A son of Margaret, Countess of Salisbury, and thus a grandson of George, Duke of Clarence, the younger brother of Edward IV. Having at first co-operated in the king's plan to obtain the opinions of the universities concerning the marriage, POLE became increasingly hostile to Henry's actions, and withdrew to Italy in 1530. There, in 1535 he wrote 'Pro Ecclesiasticae unitatis defensione', a manuscript of which he sent to the king. It was published in Rome, without his consent, in 1537.

[27] In the aftermath of the so-called 'Exeter conspiracy' of 1538. His mother, his brother, Lord Montague and his cousin the Marquis of Exeter were all beheaded for treason.

against him. Just before the New Year Pole set out on another crusading mission, and in January 1539 the Emperor and the King of France concluded a formal treaty at Toledo. England was seized by an invasion panic which probably placed the king in a stronger position than he had occupied at any time during the previous ten years, but the threat came to nothing. Disillusioned, Pole returned to Rome, and as the European balance returned to equilibrium, Henry drew back from his flirtations with the German Lutherans.[28] Within England his own peculiar brand of orthodoxy was re-asserted and protestant reformers passed under a cloud with the fall of their patron, Thomas Cromwell. An uncompromising erastianism, which seemed to need no doctrinal support, was the unprecedented outcome of a decade of crisis at home and abroad.

V. The end of conservative erastianism

By 1545, England again stood in peril of a Franco-Habsburg alliance, but in that situation the Pope had played no significant part. In December of the same year the long awaited General Council began its work at Trent, but that assembly did not bring the danger which had been anticipated. On the contrary it resulted in a final, and somewhat mysterious, gesture of reconciliation from Rome. Paul was apparently so anxious to secure some English representation at Trent that in August 1546 he sent a secret emissary to Henry — one Guron Bertano — offering almost total endorsement of all that had been done in return for a formal submission. Nothing came of this overture, and very little is known about its reception. When the king died five months later, the political and religious situation which he left in England was uniquely unfavourable to reconciliation. Whether by his own intention or not, the tutors and councillors of his young successor were predominantly men sympathetic to doctrinal protestantism;[29] from the Papacy's point of view heretics as well as schismatics. For the next six years the religious history of England was to be one of legislated reformation, and the issues of controversy were between the protestants and the conservative Henricians. During this period the authority of the Pope was principally a propaganda weapon which each side used against the other as occasion served. Stephen Gardiner, whose 'De vera obedientia oratio' was the principal intellectual defence of the royal supremacy, was also throughout the leader of the conservative group. Arguing against the introduction of religious

---

[28] In January 1539 Christopher Mont had been sent as envoy to the Duke of Saxony and the Landgrave of Hesse, to negotiate both for a relationship with the Schmalkaldic League and for the Cleves marriage. The marriage was completed by January 1540, and repudiated within six months. Letters and Papers, XIII (i) 1189; XIV (i) 103; SCARISBRICK, op. cit., 368–375.

[29] Notably Richard Coxe and John Cheke. For a full discussion of the composition of this household and its significance, see McCONICA, op. cit., 214–234.

innovations at the beginning of the new reign, he claimed that such changes played into the Pope's hands, since he ". . wanteth not wit to beat into other princes' ears that where his authority is abolished, there at every change of governors shall be change of religion." This was a substantial point, but of course his opponents were quick to reply that the surest way to exclude Papal authority was to remove popish doctrine and ceremonies. If papal jurisdiction had been grounded upon human custom rather than Divine law, the same was true of the sacrifice of the mass. To the reformers there did not seem to be any logical reason to reject one catholic tradition and retain others which were equally unscriptural in origin.

After striving for about four years to preserve his vision of a conservative royal supremacy, Gardiner eventually succumbed to the logic of this argument, and concluded that catholic doctrine and papal authority were inseperable. Without unity of jurisdiction there could be no unity of faith.[30] The majority of his friends and followers, such as Cuthbert Tunstall and Edmund Bonner, came to the same conclusion, although they made no public announcement of their conversion and thus avoided facing charges of treason or praemunire. Their change of heart was to become fully apparent only in the following reign. Meanwhile it had become clear that many years of anti-papal propaganda, coming on top of a long tradition of anticlericalism, had left the Pope with few friends among the English people. Even those who disliked protestantism sufficiently to rebel against the introduction of the Prayer Book in 1549 had nothing to say in his defence — although they did ask for the rehabilitation of Reginald Pole.[31] Insofar as the papacy entered into the political calculations of Edward VI and his mentors, it was purely as an external threat. Neither Paul III, nor Julius III who succeeded him in 1550 made any further move against England; partly because they had other things to think about and partly, perhaps, because of the king's minority. On the other hand, neither would have objected had the Emperor or King Henry II of France used the crusading pretext to make war on England for their own purposes. Henry VIII's excommunication had died with him, but his realm was now subjected to both schism and heresy — a position increasingly difficult to distinguish from that of the kingdoms of Scandinavia or the Lutheran principalities of Germany. In the event religion was not made an excuse for war, because as usual neither of the major powers wished to drive England into the arms of the other. Charles V maintained persistent diplomatic pressure to protect Princess Mary from the Council's attempts to deprive her of the mass,[32] but otherwise religion played a negligible part in England's relations with her neighbours during this period — and the Papacy none at all.

---

[30] D. M. Loades, The Oxford Martyrs, London, 1970, 55—57. Gardiner set out his arguments against the protestant trend of ecclesiastical policy in a series of letters to Protector Somerset. J. A. Muller, The Letters of Stephen Gardiner, Cambridge, 1933, 316, 379, 405, etc.

[31] Articles of the western rebels, no. 12, in: A Copy of a Letter, London, 1549.

[32] W. K. Jordan Edward VI; the Young King, London, 1968, 206—9; Idem, Edward VI; the Threshold of Power, London, 1970, 256—265.

   This situation was dramatically transformed by the death of King Edward, still under age, at the beginning of July 1553. John Dudley, Duke of Northumberland, the President of the Council, who had embraced protestantism in order to obtain the maximum advantage from the young king's personal convictions, was left to face the prospect of a catholic successor. Unfortunately for his attempt to alter the succession, the papalist convictions of the lawful heir were not generally appreciated. In the dark days after her mother's death Mary had yielded to her father's pressure and accepted the royal supremacy.[33] Only a few of her intimates realised what anguish this surrender has subsequently caused her, or how strong was her determination to repudiate it. In the crisis of 1553 Dudley and his friends conspicuously failed to mobilize anti-papal emotions against Mary; and since most of the protestants were unwilling to support him on the grounds that he was a time server and an exploiter of the gospel, his position quickly collapsed. Mary was almost universally acclaimed, on the mistaken assumption that she would restore her father's conservative erastianism; "religion as King Henry left it". The Queen and some of her less discreet supporters jumped to the opposite conclusion, and assumed that her easy victory was intended to be a mandate for a policy of full reaction. "A miracle wrought by God for none other purpose . . ." as Reginald Pole was soon to express it.[34] Mary had spent her adult life far from the centre of power, and had been subjected to much humiliation and unhappiness. In this situation her two consolations had been her religion, and the friendship of her cousin Charles V. Now, in her time of triumph, conscience and loyalty spoke with different voices. The Emperor was firmly convinced that the best interests of the catholic church in England would be served by caution in ecclesiastical matters, and by a marriage between Mary and his own son Philip which would hopefully guarantee a catholic succession and bring England permanently within the orbit of Habsburg orthodoxy. Such a marriage would also have the advantage of strengthening Philip's position in the Netherlands, and giving him the main credit for any reconciliation which might subsequently be negotiated between England and Rome.[34a] He was therefore strongly opposed to any declaration of religious policy which might arouse powerful opposition in England until such time as the marriage alliance had been completed and Philip placed in a sufficiently strong position to ensure that such a policy could be successfully carried through.[35] At the same time Mary was desperately eager to restore England to the catholic fold, and was urged in the same direction by letters from Reginald Pole, which not only represented this as the clear path of duty, but alleged that the whole legitimacy of her regime depended upon it.[36] Caution, ably represented by the Emperor's ambassador Simon Renard, at first presented the more persuasive arguments, and Mary wisely

[33] Letters and Papers, X, 1137.
[34] Calendar of State Papers, Spanish, XI, 419.
[34a] D. M. LOADES, The Reign of Mary Tudor, London, 1979, 112—114.
[35] Calendar of State Papers, Spanish, XI, 194.
[36] Calendar of State Papers, Venetian, V, 398.

refrained from making any public pronouncement on the subject of the royal supremacy.

Pope Julius III was well aware that the conservatism of the new English Queen embraced the Roman jurisdiction as well as the mass. He was also aware of Reginald Pole's extreme enthusiasm for the reconciliation of his native land. On 5 August 1553 Bulls were issued giving Pole the necessary powers to negotiate, and the messengers bearing them to Viterbo were met on the road by Pole's own messengers, hastening to Rome to request the mission. Such expedition was almost unprecedented, and, as it turned out, mistaken. Julius knew better than to suppose that the reconciliation of England was simply a matter of despatching a Cardinal Legate. There was other work for Pole to do in the north which happily coincided with a possible mission to England; the perpetual problem of peace negotiations between the Emperor and the French.[37] Pole's commission embraced both tasks, thus bringing England back into the centre of Papal diplomacy; but such a dual policy turned out to be a grave disadvantage to the English mission. Certainly Pole was, from the Pope's point of view, profitably employed during the months which he was forced to wait for admission to England; but he became increasingly distracted and disillusioned. Even when he was safely installed, his energies were to be constantly diverted to international diplomacy, and many of the intractable problems of the English church received less attention than was necessary. In the short term, Pole's hopes were raised too quickly, and his passionate advocacy of immediate submission went unheeded. Mary's surrender to 'wordly prudence' drove him to a despair which is only comprehensible in terms of his own experience and convictions. The nature of his original quarrel with Henry VIII, and even more his intellectual and spiritual struggles over the doctrine of Justification, had left him convinced of the absolute centrality of the Roman obedience to the catholic faith.[38] For the English conservatives the Papacy might be a necessary prop and safeguard; for Pole it was very much more. Without Rome there could be no salvation, no law and no morality.

"I say", he wrote to Mary on 27 August, "that the establishment of this obedience is a greater establishment of your right to the Crown than any confederacy whatever which might be formed with any foreign Prince, or than the goodwill of your people at home, both which things are unstable and . . . may fail."[39] In this frame of mind, Pole could not be expected to appreciate the strategic considerations which dominated the Emperor and influenced the Queen; but the Pope was more sympathetic. His personal envoy, Gian Francesco Commendone, visited England secretly in August 1553, and talked to Mary at some length. To him she confessed the warmth of her affection for the Holy See, and her desire to make open submission on behalf of the realm; but

---

[37] R. H. POGSON, Cardinal Pole, Papal Legate to England, Cambridge Ph.D, 1972, 105—110.

[38] D. FENLON, Heresy and Obedience in Tridentine Italy, Cambridge, 1972, 100—115.

[39] Cal.Ven. V, 398.

she also explained the difficulties in her path.[40] Commendone was so far convinced as to recommend his master to be guided by the wishes of the Queen, and to do everything in his power to smooth her chosen path. Consequently, Julius did not share his Legate's indignant frustration, but patiently reassured Pole with his confidence of ultimate success.

VI. Queen Mary and the legatine mission of Cardinal Pole

Within six months of her succession Mary had successfully dismantled the protestant establishment of her brother's reign, negotiated a marriage alliance with Philip of Spain, and defeated all organised opposition. She had not, however, rid herself of the title of Supreme Head of the Church; and it had become abundantly clear that she would not be able to do so until the question of the secularised ecclesiastical lands had been settled. These were the lands of the dissolved religious foundations, taken by the Crown and subsequently sold. By 1553 they were widely distributed in the possession of gentlemen and noblemen who had bought them at fair market prices, and were determined to resist any attempt at resumption, either by force or spiritual blackmail. Apart from the Queen herself, and those senior clergy who had been recently 'reconverted', there was in any case little enthusiasm for the Papacy in England — and much deeply engrained distrust. In order to overcome this distrust and make reconciliation a political possibility, more was needed than the restoration of the mass and traditional ceremonies. The Pope would have to be prepared to 'write off' the monastic and other lands, and to hope that in due course the piety of subsequent generations would re-endow the church to its former level. Naturally Julius found the prospect of bargaining with recalcitrant schismatics extremely distasteful, but by the summer of 1554 he was convinced that there was no other way, and on 28 June he wrote to Pole authorising him to make concessions. At the same time he instructed the Legate to give the English reconciliation priority over all his other commitments.[41]

This was the first significant step forward since the Bull of the previous August, but Pole did not welcome it unreservedly. On an issue of this kind compromise was not in his nature; nor was he convinced that concessions were necessary. Despite its lack of outward success, his mission had not been altogether fruitless. Julius had authorised him to exercise his Legatine authority from outside England, and he had in fact absolved a number of individual penitents, confirmed several episcopal appointments, and issued a steady trickle of dispensations — all in defiance of English law.[42] This evidence of goodwill, both

[40] Ibid., 429.
[41] British Museum, Additional MS 25 425 ff. 285—286.
[42] Pole opened his Legatine Register in March 1554, six months before he landed in England. C. H. GARRETT, The Legatine Register of Cardinal Pole, Journal of Modern History, 1941, XIII, 189—94; LOADES, Oxford Martyrs, 113—116.

on the part of the Queen and of the private individuals concerned, Pole had taken to indicate that the extreme caution of Mary's policies was unjustified, and that Englishmen were much less averse to the Pope than was commonly represented. He was therefore extremely reluctant to give any undertaking on the question of church lands, and the negotiations hung fire — despite the abrupt withdrawal of all Imperial opposition to his mission following upon the final celebration of Mary's marriage to Philip in July 1554. Philip was a warm supporter of reconciliation. Like his father, he believed that the church lands would have to be guaranteed and was prepared to take the initiative in such a negotiation himself. Between August and October pressure from all sides wore down Pole's resistance, and he agreed at length to accept a new brief which would give him explicit instructions to make the required surrender. The way was then sufficiently clear for him to be admitted to England as Legate. The new brief, despatched from Rome on 7 November, reached Pole on the eve of his meeting with parliament; it was judged sufficient by all parties, and an impressive ceremony of reconciliation followed. The emotions generated by that occasion moved both Mary and Pole deeply, but political rocks still lay beneath the calm surface. Within a few weeks sharp disagreements had arisen over the exact nature of the guarantees which had been given to the 'possessioners', as they were significantly called. In the Pope's name Pole had waived all ecclesiastical censures, and agreed that the church would make no attempt to disturb the *status quo*. He had not acknowledged that the statutes dissolving the religious houses had given to the Crown a legal title which could be transmitted to the purchasers. The security of the latter thus depended upon the papal dispensation itself, and no Pope could irrevocably commit his successors.[43] In the event the bargain was not disrupted; parliament duly repealed the royal supremacy, and the Bull of Plenary Indulgence followed in January 1555. Nevertheless suspicions lingered, and were soon to be sharpened into fear by the twists and turns of papal policy.

Julius III died on 23 March 1555, and his death had a most unsettling effect, both upon Pole and upon the English situation in general. At first it was widely expected that Pole would himself be elected, and although he professed complete indifference, he knew perfectly well that such an advancement would put an end to his work in England almost as soon as it had begun. On the other hand, if he was not elected the new Pope might take a quite different view of the English mission, and the harmony between Pope and Legate which was essential for success would disappear. The news of Cardinal Cervini's election as Marcellus II was consequently greeted with relief in England. Cervini was an old friend of Pole's, and immediately confirmed the Legate's powers. However, within three weeks he also died, and uncertainty once more prevailed. This time the outcome was less fortunate. Cardinal Caraffa, who became Pope Paul IV, was not only a man of invincible obstinacy, but a lifelong enemy of the Habsburgs and a long standing opponent of that school of liberal catholic theology which

---

[43] British Museum, Add. MS 41577 f. 161. CREHAN, op. cit.

Pole had led in the 1540s.[44] In spite of his high standing, the orthodoxy of the English Cardinal has always been suspect in certain parts of the Curia, and Pole had never been completely free from the fear that his position was being steadily undermined during his long absence in the north. This fear was greatly intensified by Caraffa's election, and problems soon began to multiply. Like Marcellus, the new Pope confirmed Pole's commission, but he also issued a Bull condemning the alienation of ecclesiastical property which seemed to threaten the whole foundation of the English settlement. After a great effort, Pole managed to persuade him to exempt England, and to confirm Julius' dispensation, but by the summer of 1555 the omens for future co-operation were not good. At this juncture the main difficulty was that Paul was not interested in the English situation as such, but only as an aspect of the general European crisis. He saw Pole primarily as a resident ambassador in England, and agent at large in North Western Europe.[45] In other words he reverted to Julius' original conception of the mission, before its priorities had been re-organised in June 1554. Pole, who was inclined to be daunted by the problems he faced in England and to seek escape by contemplating the pleasures of Italy, could ill afford this massive additional distraction. He was only too ready to agree with the broad interpretation of the crisis, and to divert his own energies, and those of his subordinates, away from the English church. Both he and Gardiner spent considerable time at the peace negotiations at La Marque during 1555; and in August of the same year Thomas Goldwell, one of the most zealous and effective agents of catholicism in England, was sent on a prolonged mission to Rome in connection with the same negotiations.

The catholic restoration in England had turned out to be a more difficult business than either Mary or Pole had anticipated. Neither had taken seriously the possibility of deeply convinced protestant opposition, or had made plans for a campaign of orthodox evangelisation. Consequently they relied very heavily upon jurisdictional weapons. Pole, as we have seen, placed the Roman obedience at the centre of his faith, and believed that his main task was the re-imposition of discipline. This priority was clearly reflected in the decrees of the Legatine Synod which he called during the winter of 1555/6,[46] and in the inflexible policy of persecution which was to bequeath such a disastrous legacy to subsequent generations of English catholics. At least one recent scholar has argued that the Cardinal's reasoning was sound; and that for the vast majority of Englishmen the restoration of orthodox customs and habits was the most effective way to restore sound doctrine. Failure was not so much the result of a misconceived policy as of Mary's untimely death and Elizabeth's refusal to continue in the

---

[44] For a full discussion of this attitude, see FENLON, Heresy and Obedience.

[45] POGSON, Cardinal Pole, 116ff.

[46] J. P. MARMION, The London Synod of Reginald, Cardinal Pole, Keele M.A., 1974. The decrees are printed in WILKINS, Concilia, IV, 126ff. An expanded version of these decrees was published in Rome in 1564, under the title 'Reformatio Angliae ex decretis Reginaldi Poli Cardinalis'.

catholic church.[47] There is some evidence to support such an hypothesis, but more to indicate that the self-conscious papalism of these years was a mistake. Conservative writers who rejoiced at the return of the mass studiously avoided reference to the Pope, and the development of Paul IV's own policies made him a disastrous liability to a church so orientated. Had the English mission concentrated upon evangelisation, and had the restored catholic church adopted a more Gallican attitude, it would certainly have been in a better position to survive the crisis which Paul brought upon it in 1557. If Pole calculated that explicit ultramontanism would preserve the English church from too close an association with England's political subordination to Spain, then he was disappointed. Ironically enough, the Roman obedience was becoming firmly linked with Spain in the minds of many Englishmen at precisely that time when the breakdown of relations between Paul and Philip threatened to bring the whole English mission to a grinding halt.

Sir Edward Carne, Mary's ambassador in Rome, had many occasions to complain of the Pope's neglect of his sovereign's affairs. In June 1556 he reported in despair that he had repeatedly failed to persuade Paul to deal with the episcopal vacancies at Winchester and Chester, both of which sees had been unfilled since the previous year.[48] Chichester, Lincoln, Peterborough and Carlisle all stood vacant for more than twelve months between 1556 and 1557; while Salisbury and Oxford, vacated in the latter year, were still unfilled at the end of the reign. The fault may not have lain entirely with Paul, but his lack of concern is manifest, and did no good to the English church. Finally, in April 1557, Carne wrote to say that the long threatened blow had fallen. The Pope had decided to break off diplomatic relations with Philip for political reasons, and had ". . . revoked all his ministers and legates within the realms and dominions of . . . the king." Worse was to follow. On 31 May 1557, Cardinal Morone was arrested on charges of heresy. Morone was Pole's closest friend within the Curia, and had been entrusted by Julius III with the special oversight of English affairs. Since the beginning of the mission he had acted as advocate and protector, encouraging Pole, keeping him supplied with news of Italian affairs, and making good some of his deficiencies as a politician. The arrest of Morone not only cut an exceedingly valuable line of communication between England and Rome, but gave an additional and sinister significance to the termination of Pole's commission. This was made more apparent by the Pope's reaction to Mary's indignant protests and expostulation. He was prepared to recognise the special needs of the English church, but no amount of intercession would persuade him to continue Pole in office. Instead, the Cardinal was to return to Rome to answer "certain religious suspicions", being replaced in England by an octogenarian Friar, William Peto, whose only qualification for the post was that he had once been a confessor to Catherine of Aragon! Mary was appalled and insulted. On 14 June Pole's recall was published in Rome, and a few days

---

[47] POGSON, op. cit., and IDEM, Reginald Pole and the Priorities of Government in Mary Tudor's Church, Historical Journal, 1975, XVIII, 3—20.

[48] Public Record Office, SP 69/10 f. 57.

later he laid down his office, but the Queen would not admit to England the nuncio who bore the actual letters of revocation. Nor would she accept Peto in his place.[49] If there were charges of heresy to be laid against Pole, she declared in an astonishing echo of her father's spirit, ". . . she would, in observance of the laws and privileges of her realm, refer them to the cognisance and decision of her own ecclesiastical courts."

For the English Cardinal these were months of acute misery. In spite of the obvious danger to himself and the threat to his work in England, his conscience prompted him to obey the Pope's wishes; but Philip and Mary were determined that he should not leave the country. As Archbishop of Canterbury (a position which he had held since Cranmer's execution in 1556), he still had sufficient authority to sustain the English mission. The king and queen insisted that they had confidence in him, and in no one else, for this work. Pole replied unhappily that he must perforce obey their wishes, but that he could have no direct dealings with princes who were at war with the Pope. He withdrew from the Court and retired to Canterbury. By the autumn the worst was over. Peace was patched up between Paul and Philip, and formal diplomatic relations were resumed. But the deadlock over the English mission was never broken. The Pope persisted in his desire to send Peto, but Mary was unrelenting in her refusal, and Peto himself declined to accept the office on the grounds of his age and unsuitability. Sir Edward Carne gave up the fruitless negotiation, and Pole continued to run the English church as *legatus natus* until his death in November 1558. In doing so, however, he compromised one of his deepest principles; and although in fact Paul accepted defeat with a bad grace and took no further action either against Pole or England, during the last year of his life Pole was a sick and despondent man. Instead of relieving the political gloom of 1558 with the courage of faith, he rather contributed to it. Military defeat abroad, and hunger and disease at home contributed to a vague but powerful feeling that God had testified against the catholic Queen and the church in which she so intensely believed.[50]

VII. Elizabeth I; the sheltered years

Ironically enough, the simultaneous deaths of Pole and Mary were greeted with almost equal relief in England and in Rome. In spite of her doubtful birth, Paul seems at first to have regarded Elizabeth as an improvement on her obstinate half-sister.[51] She was not tied to Spanish policy, and she was free from the insidious influence of the half-heretical Cardinal. Rumours quickly spread that

[49] D. M. LOADES, Reign of Mary, 428—439.
[50] D. M. LOADES, Oxford Martyrs, 256—258. RICHARD SAMPSON to Bullinger, Original Letters, I, 177.
[51] BAYNE, Anglo-Roman relations, 10.

the French were moving heaven and earth to persuade Paul to declare her a bastard, and to pronounce in favour of the title of Mary of Scotland. He may have considered doing so, but in fact Henry II made no formal move in that direction; and when Paul did begin to change his mind about the English Queen it was not on account of French prompting. There is neither need nor space here to describe the development of Elizabeth's religious policy, which had been the subject of frequent scholarly re-appraisals.[52] During the first few weeks of her reign she gave no more than a series of ambiguous hints, which worried the English catholics but passed unnoticed in Rome. However, early in February 1559 the situation began to clarify. Sir Edward Carne was recalled, thus effectively breaking off diplomatic relations with the Holy See,[53] and a Bill for the resurrection of the royal supremacy was introduced into parliament. Elizabeth's intention at this stage is uncertain, but it seems likely that she contemplated a protestant settlement from the first, and was initially frustrated by catholic opposition in the Lords. Despite this hitch in her plans, Paul was substantially correct when, in March 1559, he described Elizabeth as "being revolted from his obedience and this see." Considering his choleric temperament, the Pope's reaction to these developments seems to have been surprisingly mild – almost indifferent. He may have been imperfectly informed, and his mind was certainly on other things, but the expected storm never came.

Between February and May Elizabeth was driven further into the arms of the English protestants by the absolute refusal of the catholic clergy, high and low, to have anything to do with the royal supremacy. She was caught between the recalcitrance of the Convocations,[54] and the great weight of lay opinion which demanded a return to national policies and a national church. The result was a settlement which was effectively a bargain between the Queen and those protestants who still upheld the erastian principles of Cranmer and the other Edwardian leaders. However much Elizabeth might endeavour to cloud the issue in conversation with catholic diplomats, she had effectively reverted to the situation of 1552. She was able to do this because, like her father and brother, she was protected by the European balance of power. Philip, mindful of his exposed position in the Netherlands, needed English support, or at least neutrality. He was haunted by the fear that the French, who were already strongly entrenched in Scotland, might seize any opportunity created by a papal initiative against Elizabeth to invade England in the cause of Mary Stewart. Consequently

---

[52] Notably by J. E. NEALE, The Elizabethan Acts of Supremacy and Uniformity, English Historical Review, 1950, LXV, 304–332; and W. P. HAUGAARD, Elizabeth and the English Reformation, Cambridge, 1968. More recently N. L. JONES, in a work as yet unpublished, has extensively and convincingly challenged certain aspects of Neale's interpretation. N. L. JONES, Faith by statute, Cambridge Ph.D., 1977.

[53] In fact Carne remained in Italy, protesting that he was detained against his will, but it later transpired that he had arranged his own 'detention' in order to avoid subscribing to the changes in England. BAYNE, op. cit.

[54] The Convocations which assembled in January 1559 unequivocally re-asserted catholic doctrine and the papal authority, and the depleted bench of bishops consistently opposed the royal supremacy in the House of Lords. HAUGAARD, op. cit., 87–88.

he swallowed his mounting dislike of Elisabeth's religious policy, and set out to prevent any open rupture between England and Rome. In a series of letters to his agents in Rome during May 1559, Philip urged them to inform the Pope that the position of the heretical party in England was by no means as strong as it appeared; the great majority of the population were good catholics; and hopes were entertained of the Queen's own conversion.[55] These latter hopes, of course, were based upon her marriage to a catholic prince — hopes which Elizabeth assiduously kept alive, to the intense alarm and annoyance of her protestant councillors. These urgent representations seem to have had the desired effect. Paul was much less hostile to Philip than he had been two years previously, and was consequently inclined to allow him to apply his own remedies to the English situation. By July the Pope was strongly incensed against Elizabeth, describing her as a heretic and a bastard, but he took no formal action against her. Instead, he urged Philip to call upon the aid of the English catholics, and to launch his own invasion from the Netherlands. Such a drastic course formed no part of Philip's plans, but his agents in Rome could hardly say so openly, and neither party took any further steps before Paul died on 18 August.

The new Pope, Pius IV, was not elected until the end of December, and being a statesman rather than a zealot, was not inclined to resort to sanctions until all the resources of diplomacy had been exhausted. Philip was therefore spared the necessity to make any difficult decisions about his relations with England for a long time. He could continue to make indignant noises about Elizabeth's heresy without having to withdraw his ambassador, and gradually came to terms with the fact that she was not going to marry a catholic prince. But Pius, although cautious, was not neglectful of his responsibilities, and decided early in 1560 to send a mission to England in the hope of re-opening direct communications. In one sense the moment was opportune, since Elizabeth was becoming increasingly involved in the revolt of the Scottish Lords of the Congregation, and her relations with France were correspondingly strained. She heard the news of the proposed mission with ill-concealed alarm, and the English council stepped up its activities against religious non-conformists. Although ostensibly conceived in a friendly and conciliatory spirit, the Pope's action was a calculated threat, and this was emphasised by the choice of Parpaglia, titular Abbot of San Saluto, to lead the mission. As an ex-member of Pole's household, Parpaglia was obnoxious to Elizabeth, and as a French sympathiser unacceptable to Philip. It was largely for this latter reason that the mission came to nothing. Philip's diplomacy first managed to get Parpaglia stopped, and then recalled, without Elizabeth having been forced to refuse him admission. English successes in Scotland, culminating in the treaty of Edinburgh in July 1560, and the steady weakening of French influence under the pressure of mounting domestic tension also contributing to this outcome.

These early years were critical for the stability of Elizabeth's new religious settlement. It was extremely important to her that the fragile alliance between protestant nationalists like Cecil and Knollys, and conservative erastians such as

[55] BAYNE, op. cit.

Arundel and Shrewsbury should hold together. This harmony was threatened alike by zealous puritans and by conscientious papalists. At first the former seemed to her to present the greater threat, since their enthusiasm for the destruction of traditional worship endangered that general acquiescence upon which the regime depended. Hence the apparent paradox of a protestant Queen curbing the puritans, while turning a blind eye to the continuance of catholic practices.[56] Clandestine masses were neither here nor there, unless they became linked to a revival of papalism — in which case the Queen's tolerance abruptly disappeared. From Elizabeth's point of view one of the principal dangers of missions such as that of Parpaglia was that they might provide just that element of leadership and inspiration which catholic opposition in England had so far conspicuously lacked. Consequently the Pope's decision, towards the end of 1560, to reconvene the Council of Trent, spelled a new threat to the fragile English church. Although Philip again attempted to dissuade him, Pius was determined to try a second time to get a nuncio into England, and an invitation to send emissaries to the Council provided an ideal pretext. This time the man chosen was the unexceptionable protonotary Martinengo. Martinengo arrived in the Low Countries in April 1561, bearing letters of friendly greeting to the English Queen, in which the schism and heresy of her realm were blandly ignored. Pius's hope, clearly derived from misinformation about the English situation, seems to have been to detach the Queen from her heretical advisers, and to persuade her by offers of friendship and support to revert to the policies and personnel of her sister's reign. Although he was thoroughly sceptical about this approach, Philip reluctantly supported it through his ambassador in London, De Quadra. Support of a kind also came from an unexpected quarter. Lord Robert Dudley, the Queen's favourite, seeing his hopes of matrimony diminishing, was prepared to add his voice to De Quadra's in return for the latter's support of his pretensions to the Crown matrimonial.[57]

This unlikely diplomatic combination turned out to be no match for Cecil and his allies. About the middle of April De Quadra was hopeful of securing the necessary safeconduct for Martinengo, but by the end of the month his expectations had been completely dashed by a series of apparently fortuitous events.[58] A priest by the name of Coxe was arrested at Gravesend, and an investigation of his baggage produced evidence of very widespread evasion and defiance of the Acts of Supremacy and Uniformity; the trail led to several survivors of Mary's Privy Council, and several ex-bishops. Rumours of the appearance of a miraculous cross in Glamorganshire sparked off another investigation, and fresh evidence of extensive catholic sympathies. A Jesuit named David Wolf turned up

---

[56] Several bishops and other reformed clergy expressed their unease in letters to Bullinger, which form one of our chief sources for the interpretation of this period. Zurich Letters, ed. H. ROBINSON, Parker Society, 1842.

[57] W. MACCAFFREY, The Shaping of the Elizabethan Regime, London, 1969, 75–80.

[58] It is clear that Cecil planned this stroke carefully for the purpose of frustrating the negotiations, or, as he put it "for the rebating of the papists humours, which by the Queen's lenity grow too rank . . .". Public Record Office, SP 12/16/55, 66–68; SP 12/18/7, 8, 19.

most opportunely in Ireland, in the middle of Shaun O'Neill's rebellious prepar-
ations. Full publicity was given to all these discoveries, and protestant opinion
became thoroughly alarmed. The Queen herself took fright at such appearances
of catholic conspiracy, and on 1 May the Privy Council unanimously agreed to
refuse Martinengo admittance. If there had ever been any possibility that Elizabeth would voluntarily reverse her religious policy, it vanished with this decision,
and the Pope was left to digest the rebuff as best he could.

Pius made no further attempt at direct communication with England, and
although hope of the Queen's conversion still lingered in some quarters, it ceased
to be a major political factor. For the remainder of his pontificate, until 1565, he
sought ways and means to apply effective sanctions against Eizabeth and to
ameliorate the position of the English catholics. Pius was wise enough to realise
that a sentence of excommunication and deposition would be futile without the
willing support of the catholic powers, and might serve only to stimulate the
English government to the kind of fierce persecution from which it had hitherto
refrained. Twice did the Pope contemplate such action, in 1561 and 1563, and
both times drew back in the face of Spanish opposition and French weakness.
Nor did his efforts on behalf of the English catholics enjoy much more success.
A petition from them, forwarded by De Quadra in 1562, sought guidance on
the question of occasional conformity. To have permitted such a practice would
have been to encourage that drift into Anglicanism which was already very
marked, and which was a prime object of Elizabeth's gentle policy. On the
other hand to prohibit it entirely would have meant forcing all substantial
catholics to make a specific choice between their religion and their wordly prospects. Pius dealt with the petition obliquely by referring it to the Inquisition as
an hypothetical case. The Inquisition, as might be expected, issued a flat pro-
hibition, which was subsequently transmitted to De Quadra, but not as a Papal
sentence. At the same time De Quadra himself was authorised to make good the
lack of Apostolic authority in England by delegating to suitable priests those
powers of absolution normally reserved to the hierarchy. These devices satisfied
nobody, increasing the burden on catholic consciences without providing any
real leadership or pastoral care. However, in 1563 the first of a long series of
patched up religious compromises in France seemed to offer a hopeful precedent
for England, and a new approach to Elizabeth was decided upon. This was to
come, not from the Pope but from the Emperor and Philip in the form of a
suggestion that English catholics might be accorded a recognised minority status
similar to that accorded to the French protestants. In the event it was Ferdinand
alone who wrote, in September 1563, and his request was categorically rejected.
Pius did not entirely give up at this point, but his subsequent efforts were no more
than hopeful intrigues of little significance. Coercion was politically impossible,
so persuasion only remained, unless the papacy was to neglect its duty and abandon the English church altogether. The vitality of English catholicism was at a
low ebb by 1565, in spite of the prevailing preference for traditional religious
practices. In addition to the three hundred or so Marian priests who had refused
the oath of supremacy and been deprived, numerous clergy continued to celebrate
the old rites when opportunities presented themselves, but this kind of 'sur-

vivalism' hardly offered a dynamic alternative to the established church.[59] On the other hand a small number of dedicated academic exiles had settled in the Low Countries and turned themselves into effective and voluminous propagandists.[60] It was these men who first became convinced that the catholic church in England was simply dying of inanition, and that the natural instinct to avoid persecution lay at the root of the trouble. They were ready to urge militant action of all kinds, and some were also ready to take part in such action at the risk of their lives. In the new Pope, Pius V, elected in January 1566, they found a man willing to listen, and respond, to their urgings. Consequently the period of his pontificate, from 1566 to 1572 transformed relations between England and the Papacy for the remainder of the century. Pius V was a zealot with nothing of the politician in his make up, and Elizabeth found herself faced for the first time by a Pope who had already decided that her conservative sympathies were humbug, and that her removal by any available means was essential to the spiritual welfare of her subjects.

VIII. 'Regnans in Excelsis'; the years of total conflict

Even Pius was not so optimistic as to suppose, however, that God would act in England without substantial human agents. Should Elizabeth be either killed or deposed, Mary Stewart would almost inevitably succeed her, and at first the Pope was by no means convinced that this would be an improvement. Mary had scandalised the Curia by her behaviour in Scotland, and in 1566 would not have been acceptable to either Pius or Philip as Queen of England. Two years later this situation was dramatically changed by her flight to England, and imprisonment there. The loss of her Scottish throne, and effectively of her Scottish husband made her a much more promising instrument for Spanish policy, at a time when Anglo-Spanish relations had been strained almost to breaking point by Elizabeth's confiscation of a large supply of bullion on its way to pay the Spanish forces in the Netherlands.[61] Also, by the beginning of 1569 Mary had made her peace with the papacy, and was already beginning to acquire something of the aura of a catholic martyr. More important still, there

---

[59] Opinions differ as to the effectiveness of these Marian priests. Bossy (English Catholic Community) regards them as little more than an appendix to the history of the medieval church, but Haigh (The Fall of a Church or the Rise of a Sect? Post Reformation Catholicism in England, Historical Journal 1978, XXI, 181—186) argues that they represented a real element of continuity, and that their effectiveness has been much under-rated.

[60] Notably Thomas Stapleton, Thomas Harding, Richard Smith, William Soane and Richard White. See A. C. Southern, Elizabethan Recusant Prose, London, 1950; and P. Mc-Grath, Papists and Puritans under Elizabeth I, London, 1967, 57—65.

[61] This money still technically belonged to the Genoese bankers when the ships carrying it were driven to seek shelter in Southampton. Cecil, with the Queen's approval, borrowed it for English purposes. MacCaffrey, op. cit., 183—195.

was strong feeling among the conservative aristocracy in England against Cecil and his allies on the Council, who were thought to be endangering the country by reckless protestant policies. Consequently two separate but overlapping conspiracies developed during 1568 and 1569. The greater was designed to over-throw Cecil, to secure Mary's recognition as Elizabeth's heir, and to marry her to the Duke of Norfolk. The lesser (in terms of support) intended to depose Elizabeth and to place Mary on her throne, hopefully with Spanish and Papal backing. The religious aspect of the former was conservative, but probably looked no further than a modification of the 1559 settlement; the latter was ex-plicitly catholic and ultramontane. It is difficult for the historian to distinguish between these two movements of opposition, and many contemporaries found it impossible, but the distinction was nevertheless of critical importance.[62] The great majority of those who were sympathetic to the first conspiracy were loyal to Elizabeth and would not have contemplated armed resistance under any circumstances. Those who were sympathetic to the second were quite prepared to fight, but were few and ill-equipped.

Thus it happened that the rebellion which actually occurred in 1569 was more the result of muddle and panic than of deliberate intention. The Earls of Northumberland and Westmorland were discontented conservatives who allowed themselves to be manoevered into open treason by followers and kins-men who were more resolute and clear sighted. Having set out to make a massive conservative demonstration on the lines of the Pilgrimage of Grace, they ended up controlling a small part of North East England, and appealing to the Pope and the Duke of Alva for immediate aid.[63] When this appeal reached Rome, Pius was understandably convinced that the long expected moment of truth had come. An agent of his own, one Nicholas Morton, had reported the great strength of the English catholics, and he had interpreted this to mean a willingness to respond to a suitable papal initiative. Nicholas Sander, one of the most energetic of the English exiles, had also convinced him that many English-men would rise against Elizabeth if they could be re-assured that they were not committing mortal sin in doing so. Consequently he replied almost immediately to the rebel's plea, assuring them of his moral and financial support. A few days later he signed the Bull 'Regnans in Excelsis', excommunicating Elizabeth, and releasing her subjects from their allegiance. In spite of the exemplary speed of his reaction, Pius was too late. The Earls' letter had taken from 7 November to 16 February to reach him; Alva had done nothing, and by the time the Bull of deposition was issued, the rebellion had long since collapsed. Philip, although much less sympathetic to Elizabeth than he had been ten years before, was indignant at what he considered to be the Pope's precipitate and irresponsible action; and the English catholics were impaled upon the horns of a cruel dilemma.

---

[62] The best recent accounts are in MacCaffrey, op. cit., 221–246; Anthony Fletcher, Tudor Rebellions, London, 1968, 91–106; and M. E. James, The Concept of Order and the Northern Rising of 1569, Past and Present, 1973, LX, 49–83.
[63] Calendar of State Papers, Spanish, 1568–79, 186, 217, 224. MacCaffrey, op. cit. 232–233.

'Regnans in Excelsis' was a declaration of war. For the first time men and women were required to choose between their religion and their allegiance, and the mass became a symbol of treason. There was no longer any room for Henrician compromise. Loyalty to the Crown meant acceptance of protestant doctrine. Had the papacy taken this unequivocal stand in 1559, Elizabeth might well have been forced to submit, but in ten years she had established herself securely, and catholic loyalties had become confused and eroded. Nevertheless, the Bull was not without positive results. It re-affirmed the Pope's leadership of the English catholics, and helped to stop the slide into conformity. In other words it laid the foundations for that tough and resiliant recusancy which was to be English catholicism for the next two hundred and fifty years. But this result would not have been achieved had it not been for the less dramatic but more constructive work of the English exiles, particularly the foundation of the English college at Douai by William Allen in 1568. Douai was specifically designed to train young Englishmen for the priesthood in order that they should return as missionaries to their native land. The training was long and rigorous, so that it was not until 1573 that the first students were ordained, and 1574 when the first missionary priests returned to England. By that time, their task was a great deal more dangerous than Allen had originally intended. They were treated not merely as religious dissidents but as the spies and emissaries of a hostile foreign power. Labouring under the greatest difficulties, they achieved considerable success; not so much in the conversion of protestants as in the strengthening of those who had never given up their loyalty to the old faith. Under the twin pressures of persecution and missionary evangelism the religious conservatives split. The majority conformed to the established church, while the remainder became increasingly resolute and identifiable recusants. Aided by the Douai priests, and later by Jesuit missionaries, Pius had succeeded in preserving a remnant of the English church in full communion with Rome; but in both human and political terms the price was extremely high.[63a]

That price was paid mainly by the missionary priests themselves, many of whom suffered torture and death after the execution of the first seminarian, Cuthbert Mayne, in 1576.[64] To a lesser extent it was paid by the English catholic laity, who suffered fines, imprisonment, civil disabilities, and imputations of treason which most of them were desperately anxious to refute. It was also paid in a different way by the Papacy, which became to protestant Englishmen not merely a symbol of cruelty and oppression (which it had been before), but of diabolical pride and hypocricy. Pius V and the Popes who followed him, Gregory XIII (1572–1585) and Sixtus V (1585–1590) considered

---

[63a] This is the normally accepted view, expressed most recently and fully by BOSSY. HAIGH, both in 'The Fall of a Church?' and in a paper as yet unpublished, has argued that the missionaries did a major disservice to English catholicism by abandoning the geographical areas where the old faith was strong, and converting it into a 'seigneurial religion' of aristocratic households to suit their own convenience.

[64] RICHARD CHALLONER, Memoirs of Missionary Priests, London, 1741–1742, part i, 12 ff. A. L. ROWSE, Tudor Cornwall, London, 1941, 344–354. MCGRATH, op. cit., 117–118.

it to be their manifest duty to regain England for the catholic church, and saw no contradiction in the simultaneous use of spiritual and political weapons. Gregory, for instance, founded the English college in Rome, launched the Jesuit mission, and in 1580 issued an 'explanation' of 'Regnans in Excelsis' which mitigated some of its starkness.[65] But at the same time he was repeatedly and deliberately involved in plots against Elizabeth's life, and in attempts to stimulate invasion, or rebellion in Ireland. In 1579 James FitzGerald was sent with his blessing to stir up his kinfolk in Munster, and in the following year was joined by a force of 1500 Spanish troops under the Papal banner. Under these circumstances it is not surprising that the English government treated priests as fifth columnists; yet their disavowals of political intentions were undoubtedly sincere. "My charge", declared Edmund Campion in 1580, "is . . . to preach the Gospel . . . (and) to cry alarm spiritual against proud vice and foul ignorance . . . I never had mind, and am strictly forbidden by our fathers that sent me, to deal in any respect with matters of state or policy of the realm, as things which appertain not to my calling."[66] The tragedy of the English mission is contained in this contradiction.

To the modern mind it must seem that both sides were as confused in their values as they were vehement in their protestations. When Sir William Cecil claimed, in his 'Execution of Justice',[67] that papists were not being punished for their religion but for treason, William Allen was quite correct to point out that since catholicism was being treated as treason *per se*, this statement was meaningless.[68] At the same time Allen's own avowals of pure religious motivation accord ill with his known advocacy of military attack on England, and with the letters which he wrote to Philip of Spain urging such a course upon him. As long as catholics believed that the Pope had the power to depose an heretical sovereign, then their acceptance of papal authority made them potential traitors. It was to demonstrate this point rather than to provide evidence of actual treason that the so called 'Bloody questions' were put to captured priests, and the propaganda value of the answers was considerable. In fact only a handful of catholics within England, either clergy or laity, were involved in political intrigues, but many of the exiles were deeply committed, and the English government was fully justified in taking the threat which they represented seriously.

The climax of these dangers came in the 1580s. In December 1580 the Cardinal Secretary of State privately but unequivocally sanctioned Elizabeth's

---

[65] This declared that the sentence against Elizabeth ". . . in no way bound the catholics, things being as they are, but then only when the public execution of the said Bull can be carried out." In other words catholics were not necessarily bound, in all circumstances, to seek to carry the sentence into effect. A. O. MEYER, England and the Catholic Church under Queen Elizabeth, London, 1913, 246.

[66] MEYER, op. cit., 143–144.

[67] The Execution of Justice in England, by William Cecil, London, 1584; a propaganda work intended to justify the severe measures which the government was then taking against catholics.

[68] A True, Sincere and Modest Defence of English Catholics, by William Allen, (probably Rouen), 1584.

murder: ". . . whoever removes her from this life", he wrote, "with the due end of God's service, not only would not sin, but would even be doing a meritorious deed . . ."[69] The assassination of William of Orange in 1584 proved how immediate this peril was, and in 1586 the discovery of Babington's plot fulfilled Englishmen's worst suspicions. A number of young men from catholic gentry families were involved, and the conspiracy not only cost Mary Stewart her life, but struck a very heavy blow against catholic evangelism in England. "That wicked and ill-fated conspiracy", wrote the Jesuit Robert Southwell in December 1586, ". . . did to the catholic cause so great mischief that even our enemies, had they the choice, could never have chosen ought more mischievous to us . . ."[70] By the time this happened England was openly at war with Spain, Philip's deep reluctance having been gradually overcome by a mixture of English provocation and religious conviction. The old association between the Papacy and Spain in English minds, forged in the reign of Mary, had been refurbished and was by this time stronger than ever.[71] For the first time since Henry VIII's excommunication over fifty years before a catholic power was ready and willing to impose the sanctions of the church upon an English monarch. William Allen and his fellow exiles were delighted. "I think there can be very few indeed", Allen wrote to Philip in 1587, "who love their country and religion who do not from their hearts desire to be once more subject to your most clement rule."[72] If this letter was sincere, it was a measure of the immense distance which separated the militant exiles from their co-religionists in England, most of whom regarded the prospect of a Spanish invasion with almost as much fear and horror as did their protestant fellow countrymen. The new Pope, Sixtus V, although not as enthusiastic as might have been expected and suspicious of Philip's motives, could hardly fail to lend public support to the Enterprise. He made William Allen a Cardinal and agreed to contribute a million ducats to the cost of the campaign. He did not, however, pronounce any additional sentence against Elizabeth and the 'Declaration' which appeared renewing her excommunication and explaining the pious intentions of the King of Spain bore Allen's name alone.[73]

IX. Clement VIII; diplomatic stalement and catholic divisions

The complete failure of Philip's 'Armada' left Allen in a very exposed position, and paved the way for those deep and bitter divisions which were to afflict the English catholics over the next decade. It was not clear for several years

[69] P. Hughes, Rome and the Counter Reformation in England, London, 1942, 214.

[70] J. H. Pollen, English Martyrs, 1584—1603, Catholic Record Society, 1908, V, 314.

[71] W. S. Maltby, The Black Legend in England, Duke University Press, 1971.

[72] Letters and Memorials of Cardinal Allen, ed. T. F. Knox, London, 1882, 272ff. McGrath, op. cit., 200.

[73] This 'Declaration' was printed by M. A. Tierney, Dodd's Church History of England, London, 1839—42, III, Appendix XII.

that the Spanish danger had really been averted, and there was little improvement
in the lot of the recusants. Nevertheless a sharp and explicit reaction took place
against the views which Allen had expressed, both in his 'Declaration' and in his
unpublished 'Admonition to the Nobility and People of England'. A number of
catholic works appeared, including Robert Southwell's 'Humble Supplication to
Her Majesty', which expressed the warmest loyalty to Elizabeth in temporal
matters, and rejected all association with Spain. It was, perhaps, fortunate that
the English Cardinal, who was the official ruler as well as the natural leader of
the English mission, died in 1594. Thereafter the leadership of what might be
called 'political' catholicism devolved upon the Jesuit Robert Parsons, who was
a less authoratative and prestigious figure. This, combined with the fact that the
English province was without any canonically appointed head for four years,
enabled a little progress to be made towards a *modus vivendi* between the
catholics and the government. At the same time both the Papacy and the English
Crown began to move cautiously away from the entrenched positions which had
been taken up over twenty years before. In 1589 Sir Christopher Hatton had
made a passionate attack upon the Pope in parliament, and as late as 1593 the
Council was still sponsoring strong anti-catholic legislation; but by 1601 the
government was quietly facilitating negotiations between English catholics and
the Curia. Similarly Clement VIII (1592—1605) was not a crusader in the mold
of Pius V or Gregory XIII. He was prepared to consider reopening relations
with the heretical Queen, and saw no reason why he should be intractable for
the sake of implementing Spanish policy.

The thirteen years of his pontificate saw a number of important changes in
the situation of the English catholics. Until Allen's elevation to the Cardinalate
the catholic church in England had had neither structure nor discipline; ". . . no
man subject to his fellows, no way to call disorders to accompt, no common
conference, no sovereignty nor subjection; but every one lying severally and
secretly by himself . . ." as Allen himself had written.[74] During the seven years
between his elevation and his death, the Cardinal had not been able to do much
to remedy this situation, and the 'Cardinal Protectors of England' remained
shadowy figures whose main function was to see that judicial proceedings involving Englishmen were brought to the attention of the correct officials in
Rome. Consequently disciplinary problems were endemic, and were aggravated
both by political activism and by the fact that the Jesuit missionaries were
subject to no authority save that of their own superiors. The story of the
'Wisbech stirs' is too familiar to need repetition, but it was to be particularly
unfortunate that the quarrel between the Jesuits and the secular priests should
have become linked to political disagreements through the activities of Parsons.
In 1595 the latter was instrumental in producing 'A Conference about the next
succession to the Crown of England', which proposed a religious 'test' and
argued strongly in favour of the claim of the Spanish Infanta. This document
was in every sense provocative, and the storm which it aroused did more than
anything else to bring the divisions among the catholics to the attention of the

---

[74] Letters and Memorials of Cardinal Allen, 378. McGRATH, op. cit., 276.

rest of the country. Even this scandal, which seriously weakened the church in the face of continued pressure from the English government, failed to arouse the Pope to action. Both Parsons and his secular enemies put forward plans for a new ecclesiastical organisation in 1597, but neither was adopted. Finally, in March 1598 the Cardinal Protector issued a brief setting up an Archpriest with limited authority over secular priests working in England and Scotland, but no jurisdiction over either the laity or the Jesuits.[75] This scheme itself was both clumsy and insufficient, since it made no provision for episcopal functions, and the appointment of George Blackwell as the first Archpriest ensured disaster. Blackwell, although a secular was strongly sympathetic to the Jesuits. "All catholics must hereafter depend upon Blackwell", wrote one of the anti-Jesuit faction, "and he upon Garnet (the Jesuit superior), and Garnet upon Parsons, and Parsons upon the Devil who is the author of all rebellions, treasons, murders, disobedience and all such designments as this wicked Jesuit hath hitherto designed against her majesty, her crown, her safety and her life."[76] The Archpriest's abrasive personality quickly stimulated his opponents to action, and before the end of 1598 two representative secular priests had been despatched to Rome to petition the Pope for a canonically elected bishop to rule the English province. They also sought to obtain an inhibition against the political propaganda of Parsons and other Jesuits, which they represented as doing untold harm to the catholic cause. They represented a substantial and responsible body of English clerical opinion, but they were no match for Parsons' international influence.

As soon as he was aware of their mission, Garnet wrote direct to the Pope, alleging that Blackwell's opponents in England were merely a handful of troublesome malcontents who should not be accorded a hearing. Consequently when they reached Rome at the end of 1598, the two emissaries were arrested, subjected to a form of trial and expelled from the city without being given any chance to discharge their mission. In April 1599 Blackwell's position and authority were confirmed by Papal letter. Although the inexplicable injustice of Clement's action caused much indignation in England, there could be no question of defying his explicit command, and the quarrel might well have retreated again beneath the surface of public life. It did not do so because Blackwell, not content with receiving his opponents' submissions, demanded that they should acknowledge themselves to have been guilty of schism in their original defiance. In this he was supported by Garnet and other Jesuits, who published a justification of his attitude.[77] In January 1600 Blackwell forbade his opponents to reply to this work under threat of ecclesiastical penalties, and in October suspended two of his leading critics from their priestly functions. Such high handed action invited a

---

[75] The brief is printed in Dodd's Church History, III, cxix ff. See also J. H. POLLEN, The Institution of the Archpriest Blackwell, London, 1916.

[76] WILLIAM WATSON, A sparing discoverie of our English Iesuits and of Fa. Parsons proceedings under pretence of promoting the Catholick faith in England, 1601. Quoted in McGRATH, op. cit., 286.

[77] THOMAS LISTER, Adversus factiosos in ecclesia, 1599.

renewal of conflict, and within a month a petition against Blackwell's misgovern-
ment was despatched to the Pope bearing the signatures of 33 secular priests. So
bitter were some of the Archpriest's enemies that they entered into secret negotiations with the English government. There had been isolated instances before of
catholics who had denounced their co-religionists for lending themselves to
treasonable conspiracy, but this was a more deliberate and more constructive
approach. The details of the discussions are not known, but probably the
'appellants' as they were soon to be called agreed to work for the recall of the
Jesuits from England, and perhaps the re-opening of direct relations between
England and Rome. In return they were certainly provided with money and other
material assistance in forwarding their petition.[78]

This time, for a variety of reasons, their protest fared better. Clement
responded to the petition of November 1600 by rebuking Blackwell, ordering
him to withdraw his accusations of schism, and imposing silence upon both sides.
The Appellant representatives were then received in Rome, and prolonged negotiations ensued, lasting from February to July 1602. Although they had compromised themselves by their relations with an heretical government, the Appellants
were strongly supported by French diplomatic influence. The Jesuits had
committed themselves to a Spanish candidate for the English succession, and
Henry IV naturally regarded such a prospect with deep disfavour. The outcome, a
Holy Office decree of 20 July 1602, was not really a victory for either side. Blackwell was placed under the direct supervision of the Pope and the Cardinal
Protector of England, and was explicitly forbidden to consult with the Jesuits.[79]
On the other hand he was continued in his existing office, and the appellants were
sharply called to heel for ". . . dealings and communications with heretics to the
prejudice of catholics." In spite of some persuasive pleading, Clement had
decided not to countenance negotiations with Elizabeth, and the possibility of
reaching some *modus vivendi* on the basis of a limited toleration did not
materialise. However, the situation did not remain altogether unchanged. An
important Royal proclamation of November 1602, while reaffirming in unequivocal words the policy of a single established religion, and making conventionally
hostile noises against the Pope, nevertheless recognised that catholics could, in a
sense, be loyal subjects.[80] The laws against the Jesuits and their adherents were to
be strictly enforced, but other priests (equally in danger of the law) were to be
allowed two months to leave the realm. Moreover any who explicitly acknowledged the Queen's temporal authority were to be given some special but unspeci-
fied immunity. No doubt the government hoped to split the catholic clergy along
the line of the existing dispute, but the outcome was rather less dramatic. In
January 1603 thirteen secular priests signed a declaration of temporal allegiance to

[78] Meyer, op. cit., 426; McGrath, op. cit., 291. The agent was Richard Bancroft, Bishop of
London.
[79] Meyer, op. cit., 446; McGrath, op. cit., 293. See also T. G. Law, The Archpriest Controversy, II; A Historical Sketch, Introduction, 7.
[80] P. L. Hughes and J. F. Larkin, Tudor Royal Proclamations, III, Yale University Press,
1969, 250—255.

Elizabeth, acknowledging themselves bound to obey her civil laws, as being ". . . so grounded upon the word of God, as that no authority, no cause . . . can or ought . . . to be a sufficient warrant, more unto us than to any protestant, to disobey her majesty in any civil or temporal matter."[81] This repudiation of the papal deposing power represented the *de facto* attitude taken by the catholic laity for years, but it commanded the assent of only a handful of the four hundred or so priests working in England. Weakened as they were by divisions, they saw this declaration as a mere device to divide them further and to cut them off from the Papacy. The government, understandably, regarded their refusal to adhere as evidence of continued attachment to the deposing power. Had the Queen not been visibly declining to her end the consequences might have been serious, both for those who signed the declaration and for those who refused. But in fact Clement took no action against the dissidents, and Elizabeth's death created new possibilities for a political and religious *rapprochement*.

In one sense the peaceful accession of the protestant James was a death blow to catholic hopes. The major catholic powers, particularly Spain, finally concluded that English catholicism was a broken reed for their political purposes, and lost all interest in forcible conversion. The Anglo-Spanish peace of 1604 was partly a reflection of this change of attitude. So, too, was the Gunpowder Plot, which probably represented a last despairing flicker of that political activism which had been expressed in theory by Allen and Parsons and in practice by Babington and Norton. In another sense, however, the new king could be looked to with hope and expectation. His Queen, Anne of Denmark, was a catholic convert, albeit of a rather feeble and ambiguous kind;[82] and he had given some assurances to his future catholic subjects in the process of building up support in England. Clement seems to have entertained hopes of James's own conversion, and communicated with him through Sir James Lindsay, a Scottish catholic exile. The king's response was courteous, but verbal and non-committal. In the summer of 1603, after his accession, the Pope tried again, this time through the agency of Sir Anthony Standen who was in Italy on a diplomatic errand from James to the Doge.[83] His intention was to use Standen to carry private letters and devotional objects to the Queen, in the hope that her response might lead to an exchange of courtesies which would develop into a formal relationship. However, by the time Standen reached England again the irresponsible activities of the disillusioned appellant William Watson had revived fears of popish conspiracy. Standen's 'innocent plot' was detected and he was imprisoned in the Tower. James's position at this stage seems to have been that he was willing to extend considerable relief to the catholic laity, including the remission of recusancy fines, but was determined to keep up his predecessor's pressure

---

[81] Dodd's Church History, III, clxxxviii ff. MEYER, op. cit., 456 ff.

[82] There is no doubt about her conversion, but her persistence in the faith is still a matter of some doubt. A. W. WARD, James VI and the Papacy, Scottish Historical Review, 1905, II, 249–252; A. O. MEYER, Clemens VIII und Jacob I von England, Rome, 1904; G. ALBION, Charles I and the Court of Rome, London, 1935, 194.

[83] L. HICKS, The Embassy of Sir Anthony Standen in 1603, Recusant History, 1963, VII, 50–81.

against the clergy. This illogical attitude may have originated in a misunderstanding of the declaration of January 1603. The signatories never had any intention of abandoning their priestly vocation, but the king may not have understood this, concentrating too exclusively upon their protestations of allegiance.[84] Mutual misunderstanding led to mutual disillusionment, and Watson's conspiracy convinced him that all priests were tarred with the same brush. Nevertheless the Pope's tentative overtures had given James some hope that Clement might prove an ally in resolving the problems of double allegiance. Towards the end of 1603 he had therefore dropped a hint to the papal Nuncio in Paris that a willingness on Clement's part to excommunicate those clergy who sought to use their priestly functions for political purposes would help in to take a more lenient view of the catholic church in England. The Nuncio, Del Bufalo, forwarded this suggestion with some enthusiasm, but it met with a chilly response and the first year of the new reign ended without any significant progress towards a resumption of relations.

X. Progress towards a new Papal policy

Nevertheless the slight thaw discernable before Elizabeth's death had continued, and was accompanied by a gradual but marked change in the attitude of many of the leading clergy. After James's accession the deposing power became an increasingly academic issue. Clement had no intention of launching a new 'Regnans in Excelsis' against the English king, and most of the political activists of the previous years began to move towards that sectarian view of English catholicism which the recusant gentry had been anxious to see accepted for some time. Opinion in the Curia also moved noticeably against political activism, although not for the same reasons:

"With the English heretics one must proceed dextrously, but honestly and in good faith", a correspondant wrote to Cardinal Aldobrandini in December 1603, "putting patriotism only second to the love of God, and if Father Parsons and his followers in Rome and elsewhere had acted on these principles perhaps, and indeed without a 'perhaps', England by now would have been converted to the faith."[85]

This attitude was hardly fair to Parsons, effectively using him as a scapegoat for the relative failure of the mission, but it was symptomatic of a very important change. Only by breaking that association between the Papacy and England's political enemies which successive Popes had built up over forty years could the church hope to regain the ground which it had lost. Before his death

---

[84] J. A. Bossy, The English Catholic Community, 1603–1625, in: The Reign of James VI and I, ed. A. G. R. Smith, London, 93–94.

[85] Tornello to Cardinal Aldobrandini, 3 December 1603; quoted by K. M. Lea, Sir Anthony Standen and Some Anglo-Italian Letters, English Historical Review, 1932, XLVII, 461 ff.

in 1610 Parsons himself had abandoned many of his earlier opinions and become reconciled to the permanence of the Anglican establishment, at least for the foreseeable future. This movement of opinion did not, however, make the English clergy any more willing to negotiate a settlement with the government at the Pope's expense. When, in the aftermath of the Gunpowder Plot, James attempted to exploit the apparent division created by the declarations of 1603, he met with little success.

The statute 3 & 4 James I c.iv set out an oath of allegiance which explicitly rejected the deposing power as "impious and heretical". This was much too strong, even for those priests who had previously professed temporal allegiance to Elizabeth, and hardly any of the surviving appellants could be persuaded to accept it. The oath certainly stirred up controversy, but if it was designed to identify and isolate the diminishing minority of political activists, then it failed completely. Those who attacked the oath, such as John Mush, Garnet, and Parsons, were by this time no more committed to political action than those who defended it, such as Thomas Preston[86] and Blackwell. Indeed, their practical view of the English situation did not much differ, but the objectors were far more acutely aware of the dangers inherent in making theoretical attacks upon the papal authority. Pope Paul V lost no time in condemning the oath, and since several priests including Garnet were swiftly apprehended and executed for refusing it, it seemed for a time that the Elizabethan confrontation was to be resumed. Blackwell did his best to alleviate this situation by producing a modified version of the oath, which he declared on his own authority to be acceptable, and which he took himself after his arrest in June 1607. His efforts were denounced by the Pope, and found little favour among the English clergy, but he persisted in his attitude and was deprived of his office by a Papal brief dated February 1 1608.

The new Archpriest, George Birkhead, took stock of the situation in England and found that only about twenty of the five hundred priests working in the country had taken the oath.[87] Debate and controversy continued for some time, but Birkhead was strict in maintaining the official line, and the discussion soon ceased to have any real significance. During the years in which Birkhead and his successor, William Harrison, held office (1608—1621) the main interest of the English catholics lay in their own efforts to secure the appointment of a bishop, and in the efforts which others made on their behalf to secure a relaxation of the penal laws. The latter were closely bound up with James's negotiations for a Spanish marriage.[88] These protracted and ultimately futile exchanges lie out-

---

[86] A Benedictine who wrote under the name of ROGER WIDDRINGTON, A Theological Disputation Concerning the Oath of Allegiance, 1613.

[87] W. M. BRADY, Annals of the Catholic Hierarchy in England and Scotland, London, 1883, 65.

[88] S. R. GARDINER, Prince Charles and the Spanish Marriage, London, 1872, is still the fullest and most detailed account of these negotiations. The intention was to marry Prince Henry, and after his death (1612) Prince Charles to the Spanish Infanta as part of a general scheme for the pacification of Europe. It was James's preoccupation with this scheme which gave the Spanish ambassador, Count Gondomar, so much influence over him.

side the scope of this paper, save for the fact that a papal dispensation would have been required, and Paul V showed no willingness to abandon the attitude of passive hostility which he had shown towards the English government since 1606. In response to enquiries from Philip III he insisted upon the conversion of Prince Charles and full legal toleration for English catholics as the minimum conditions for his approval. Impossible as these conditions were, they were still a long way from 'Regnans in Excelsis' and Stukeley's expedition to Ireland. Paul never ceased to regard it as his duty to recover England for the catholic faith, but his long Pontificate, from 1605 to 1621, saw the final abandonment of coercion as a possible means to that end. Aristocratic, and above all royal conversions, preferably under the cover of legal toleration, came to be seen as the most promising policy. By 1630 direct relations, albeit of a discreet (not to say clandestine) nature had been resumed.

Meanwhile the long standing hostility between the secular and regular clergy had taken on another aspect, reflecting two contrasting attitudes towards the church in England. The Jesuits, who increased greatly in numbers between 1600 and 1620, and the Benedictines tended to see England as a true mission field, analagous to Japan.[89] They therefore rejected institutional continuity with the pre-reformation church, and consequently opposed episcopal jurisdiction and the introduction of parochial organisation. In their view the relationship between priest and layman was not one of government, and they were quite prepared to allow catholic communities in England to choose their own pastors. They could afford to take this line because they were subject to the authority and control of their own superiors, so that they ran no risk of lacking either supervision or authoritative support. The secular clergy, understandably, did not appreciate this view of the church, although it appealed to many of the recusant gentry. Without some sort of an hierarchical structure they felt that discipline could not be preserved. The powers of the Archpriest were quite inadequate. Nor did they see why they should abandon all claim to being the true, historical *Ecclesia Anglicana*, a claim which could be seen as essential to the ultimate success of their missionary efforts. William Harrison, Archpriest from 1615 to 1621, fully endorsed the opinion of the seculars and made strenuous efforts to persuade the Curia of the necessity to appoint a bishop for England, with the full powers of an Ordinary. His arguments carried sufficient weight for the office of Archpriest to be kept vacant for two years after his death. Finally in March 1623 William Bishop, one of the original appellants, was consecrated Bishop of Chalcedon and sent to England as Vicar Apostolic – thus triggering off a new conflict which was not to be finally resolved for over half a century.

Bishop occupied his position for less than a year, since he did not land in England until July 1623 and died in the following April, but in that short time he instituted a complete reorganisation of the church. In place of the existing *ad hoc* arrangements he divided the country into Archdeaconries and Rural Deaneries, appointing suitable priests to the offices thus created, and set up in addition five

[89] BOSSY, The English catholic community, 1603–1625 (see above, n. 84).

Vicars General.[90] These officials together he constituted into a Chapter, and appointed one John Colleton as Dean. In this way he not merely demonstrated his status as an Ordinary, but provided for the future orderly government of the church should the Papacy fail to maintain the episcopal succession. These proceedings, as might be expected, caused the strongest resentment amongst the regulars, as did Bishop's attempt to invoke the decrees of the Council of Trent and restrict the hearing of confessions to those whom he had himself licenced. Had Bishop not died so soon a serious conflict would almost certainly have developed before the end of 1624. In the event it was to be three more years before the issue came to a head. Richard Smith, his successor as Bishop of Chalcedon, bore himself with a high hand, not merely continuing Bishop's policy over confessions but setting up a network of new officers such as notaries and registrars. His purpose seems to have been to subject the laity, as far as circumstances permitted, to the full jurisdiction of the catholic church, including the payment of dues and taxes for the support of himself, his officers and the parish priests. This course of action naturally bred quarrels and protests, which the regulars hastened to bring to the attention of the Curia, with the result that in December 1627 a decree of the Holy Office, confirmed by the Pope, cut the ground from under Smith's feet by pronouncing that, as a bishop *in partibus*, he did not have the standing of Ordinary in England, but was merely a delegate whose authority was revocable at the pleasure of the Pope.[91] This decision, so explicitly hostile to the secular clergy, did nothing to quieten the furious controversy which was by this time raging among the English catholics, reopening the split between regulars and seculars which had never really healed since the quarrels of the 1590s. Smith was placed in an impossible position by this decree, which was soon after followed by a Papal brief ordering him to allow the regulars to exercise full faculties, as they had done before Bishop's reorganisation. He went to France and lodged a protest with the Nuncio in Paris, claiming that the Pope's action had made his continued service in England useless. In 1632 he resigned his office and remained in France. No successor was appointed, and the burden of administering the church in England devolved upon the Dean and Chapter, which remained in existance without any form of Papal recognition, constantly challenged by the regulars who refused to accept its jurisdiction.

XI. Henrietta Maria and the years of personal diplomacy

The English catholics were thus left for many years without any adequate system of government or discipline, although frequent representations were made to Rome. Paradoxically, one of the chief reasons for this apparent neglect

[90] BRADY, Annals, 71–73.
[91] Ibid., 77–80.

seems to have been the improved political relationship between the Papacy and the English government which followed upon Charles's marriage to Henrietta Maria of France. The negotiations for this marriage, which occupied part of 1623 and the whole of 1624, had been three cornered between England, France and the Papacy. Pope Urban VIII was less inflexible than his predecessor Paul V over the necessary dispensation, but he drove a hard bargain, which included the suspension of the penal laws and an extensive ecclesiastical establishment for the Princess. When Henrietta arrived in England in June 1625 she brought with her the Bishop of Mende as her Almoner, and upwards of twenty priests in a household of over one hundred.[92] The short term consequences of this were disastrous. English catholics flocked to the Queen's chapel in St. James's, and provocations from both sides resulted in furious quarrels. Charles, who had succeeded to the throne in the interval between the completion of the treaty and his bride's arrival in England, could now see the full political significance of this situation, and reacted sharply. The relaxation of the penal laws was rescinded, and in July 1626 the Queen's entire French entourage — by this time numbering almost four hundred — was expelled. Only her private confessor Fr. Philip was allowed to remain. For this and other reasons relations between England and France became increasingly tense during the latter part of 1626. Attempts to negotiate a much diminished household for Henrietta broke down, and early in the following year the two countries drifted into open war.

Urban had clearly hoped to use the French princess and her household clergy as a means of bringing relief and support to the English catholics, but he had not made sufficient allowance either for the strength of English protestant resentment or for the indiscretion of the French themselves. Henrietta was willing enough to play the role assigned to her, but was extremely young and guilessly arrogant. It is not surprising that by 1627 the recusants were complaining that their situation was worse than at any time since Elizabeth's death. Not only had they been cheated of the hopes of relief held out by the marriage treaty, but they now found themselves again associated with foreign enemies. The Pope was equally indignant at the frustration of his hopes, and in September 1626 issued a series of fiercely worded briefs denouncing the perfidious king of England, and urging both Louis XIII and Philip IV to avenge the wrongs of the church.[93] At first he was enthusiastic for a Franco-Spanish league against the heretical island, and it seemed that the days of Pius V had returned. But Urban swiftly repented of his rashness, realising that in a sense the English catholics were hostages for his behaviour. No canonical sentence was pronounced against Charles, and Richelieu's attempts to persuade him in 1627 to contribute to the French war effort were completely fruitless. Consequently when the war came to an end in April 1629 the Pope was well placed diplomatically to resume his efforts, and since personal relations between Henrietta and Charles had improved dramatically after the assassination of the Duke of Buckingham in 1628, the omens for success were more favourable than

[92] ALBION, op. cit., 80.
[93] Arch. Vat., Epistolae ad Principes, XL, 409—417; ALBION, op. cit., 92 n. 2.

at any time since 1624. Two other factors also contributed an element of hope. Charles's quarrel with the opposition forces in parliament, which had been developing steadily since his accession, culminated on 2 March 1629 in that celebrated demonstration in which the Speaker was forcibly detained in his chair. Mistakenly, but understandably the king dissolved parliament with the firm intention of not meeting it again. Thus for the time being the most powerful focus of anti-catholic feeling was removed, and Charles managed to convince himself that Sir John Eliot and his allies did not really speak for a significant sector of English opinion.[94] The second factor was the appointment of the crypto-catholic Sir Richard Weston as Lord Treasurer. Weston speedily established contact with Richelieu's confidant Père Joseph, and through him arranged for the staff of the Queen's private chapel to be replenished – this time with a team of nine French Capuchins. Consequently, when full diplomatic relations with France were restored in February 1630, the influence of the Queen and her household was rapidly increasing, and the prospects for the English catholics looked better than at any time since the origin of the schism.

Henrietta had to some extent learned the lesson of her earlier failure. Although she was completely devoid of political intelligence, she did now appreciate the crucial importance of retaining her husband's sympathy and indulgence, no longer relying even by implication upon her own status as a French royal princess. One of the most important consequences of this was that there was no resumption of the gratuitous intrigue and provocation which had done so much to incense Charles against her first household. His refusal to accept a Grand Almoner of episcopal rank was quietly accepted,[95] and the Capuchins proved a useful reinforcement to the English mission without causing significant political controversy. Urban was speedily satisfied that his earlier restraint had been rewarded, and began to look cautiously for a way ahead. Charles, who few years earlier had been denounced in the Curia as "a heretic of the worst type" was now regarded as being ripe for conversion. This hope was based partly upon the king's genuine willingness to gratify his wife, partly upon the appearance of such catholic sympathisers as Cottington[96] and Weston in high office, and partly upon a misunderstanding of the position of the Arminians who were now so high in Charles's favour. Even Duperron, the Queen's Almoner, who was normally an accurate observer, at first made the mistake of thinking that Laud was an ally.[97] In spite of this, Urban was better informed about English affairs than any of his predecessors for many years. Quite apart from the information which he derived from the French clergy in England, he also had the benefit of a series of reports from Padre Allessandro, who visited England secretly on missions from the Cardinal Protector in 1623, 1630 and 1632. The last and most important of these reports was sent to

---

[94] P. ZAGORIN, Court and Country, London, 1969, 79–85.

[95] ALBION, op. cit., 107–108. The Bishop of Bazas had been designated for the appointment.

[96] Sir Francis (later Lord) Cottington, Chancellor or the Exchequer and Master of the Court of Wards, see M. J. HAVRAN, Caroline Courtier: the life of Lord Cottington, London, 1973.

[97] This impression was shared by Panzani and other agents. ALBION, op. cit., 109, 148.

Barberini in January 1633, and covered the whole state of the church in England following the departure of the Bishop of Chalcedon.[98] Allessandro was emphatic that a Papal envoy with full authority should be sent. In the favourable climate of opinion then prevailing such an envoy could be accredited to the Queen, and would have some hope of being well received by the king, at least in private.

Duperron endorsed these opinions, but in the event the next move came not from Urban but from a small group of Scottish catholics, aided and abetted by Henrietta. In the summer of 1633 Sir Robert Douglas went to Rome bearing credentials from the Queen to Cardinal Barberini and a proposal for which the Cardinal Protector was totally unprepared. This was no less than a suggestion that the time was now ripe for the creation of a British Cardinal. No Englishman or Scot had been raised to the purple since the death of William Allen, and Douglas's backers were convinced that such a promotion would not only go a long way towards settling the feuds within the English catholic community, but would also gratify the king and draw him nearer to the faith. The candidate put forward was George Con, a Scot of noble birth who was already in the household of the Cardinal Secretary of State.[99] Barberini kept Douglas at arms length. Lengthy and inconsequential negotiations followed, in which Douglas pleaded the loyal services of the English queen and greatly exaggerated Charles's sympathy. It was February 1634 before the envoy was vouchsafed any real answer, and then the question of a British Cardinal was quietly skirted. Barberini, who seems to have acted throughout with Urban's full approval, agreed to send a Papal Agent to resolve the quarrels between the Regulars and Seculars, and also consented on the Pope's behalf to an exchange of Residents with the English queen. Thus, although Douglas's mission could hardly be described as a success, the outcome was gratifying to Henrietta, and brought England nearer to diplomatic relations with the Curia than at any time since the recall of Sir Edward Carne in 1559.

Many catholics were by this time impatient at the Pope's caution, writing enthusiastically of the freedom accorded to their worship in England, and making the most optimistic prognostications about the king's conversion and the re-union of the churches. Urban was not to be drawn. In 1634 he reacted sharply to a suggestion from the Prior of Douai that he ought to authorise concessions over the oath of allegiance and open a direct correspondence with Charles. With the advantage of historical perspective it seems clear that the Pope was right. In spite of its fashionable following at court, and the steady trickle of conversions accredited to the French Capuchins, the political base of English catholicism was small. The absence of parliament with its perpetual puritan clamour created something of a fool's paradise, in which it was possible to forget the deep anti-

---

[98] Allesandro to Barberini, 7 January 1633; Codex Barberini Latin. 7049, ff. 4—7. Quoted ALBION, op. cit., 111 ff.

[99] Son of Patrick Con, Laird of Auchry, near Turriff. Educated at Douai, and at the Scots colleges in Paris and Rome. Entered the household of Cardinal Montalto in 1623, and subsequently that of Cardinal Barberini.

Roman prejudice which was such an important element in English national feeling. Moreover there is no real evidence that Charles ever contemplated conversion. His interest in theology, his pleasure in the company of urbane and cultivated men, and his increasingly uncritical affection for Henrietta misled those who wanted to be misled. The person whose influence with the king was greatest in this connection was William Laud, and Laud was strongly opposed to Rome and all its works, realising how damaging the 'papist' label was to his own ecclesiastical programme. Charles did not commit himself to a forlorn policy in his relations with Rome, but he did unwittingly create misunderstandings which stirred up a hornet's nest against himself and resulted in bitter disillusionment for the English catholics.

Urban could not, however, afford to neglect the wishes of his English and Scottish subjects entirely. He honoured Barberini's undertaking to send an Agent with exemplary speed, and Gregorio Panzani landed in England on 15 December 1634, presenting his credentials to the Queen the following day. Officially Panzani was concerned only with the internal affairs of the English church, but unofficially he soon established contact with such sympathetic politicians as Windebank and Cottington, and through them persuaded Charles to sanction the despatch of a Resident to Rome in the queen's name. The man eventually selected to go from England was Sir William Hamilton, and the care with which he was briefly by the king makes it clear that he was in substance, although not in name, an English Ambassador.[100] Similarly the corresponding Resident sent from Rome to England, none other than that George Con whose name had earlier been raised as a candidate for the purple, was expected to do business with Charles although not accredited to him. Hamilton reached Rome in June 1636, and Con arrived in England the following month. Optimists in both places spoke of speedy negotiations for reconciliation, but in reality the missions were exploratory, and neither Charles nor Urban hoped for more than a limited agreement over the Oath of Allegiance and some sort of understanding about the Palatinate.[101] In the event even that measure of success was not achieved. Con was lionised at the English court, and had great personal success with the king, but his mission made little progress. The private initiative of the catholic convert Christopher Davenport, who had published a very mild commentary on the Thirty Nine Articles in hope of furthering the cause of reconciliation was an acute embarrassment to him.[102] Davenport's book had made a

---

[100] The man originally chosen, Sir Arthur Brett, died early in 1636, before he could set out. Hamilton received the instructions which had originally been drawn up for Brett. ALBION, op. cit., 157.

[101] Charles's brother-in-law, Frederick V had been deprived of his Electoral title and estates following his abortive attempt to secure the throne of Bohemia in 1618–20. This had been one of the root causes of the thirty years war, and both James and Charles had attempted for several years to secure the return of the Palatinate through the good offices of the catholic powers.

[102] This commentary appeared as an appendix to his Deus, natura, gratia, Lyons, 1634. For its effects, see ERMIN KLAUS, Christopher Davenport, Munster, 1938; also R. I. BRADLEY, Christopher Davenport and the Thirty Nine Articles, Archiv für Reformationsgeschichte, 1961, LII, 205–228.

very favourable impression at the English court, and had been unequivocally condemned in Rome. Con spent much time and energy smoothing over this conflict, but could not alter the basic intransigence of the Roman theologians, which had always made real negotiation impossible. He was hampered, too, by Henrietta's well intentioned importunity for his elevation to the Cardinalate, which was interpreted by some in Rome to be the product of his own ambition. After a little more than three years, defeated by ill-health and the implacable hostility of Archbishop Laud, he was withdrawn and replaced by Carlo Rosetti. At the beginning of 1640 he died in Rome.

XII. Urban VIII and the failure of the ʿconversion policyʾ

During his stay in England, Con had conducted endless complex negotiations, and his failure was not due to any lack of skill or persistence on his part. He had also brought a short period of unprecedented relief to the English catholics. His own chapel and the Queen's were open almost without limitation, and priests were able to move about and conduct their ministry openly. Unfortunately many of them reacted with more enthusiasm than discretion. A series of spectacular aristocratic conversions alienated the court still further from the majority of the ruling class, and there was much extravagant talk of the imminence of reconciliation.[103] Protestant fears were needlessly aroused, and Con himself driven to exasperation. *"Prudentiores sunt filii tenebrarum"*, he commented. By the time he left England, in the autumn of 1639, the king's affairs were at a low ebb, and he had been constrained to meet the threat from Scotland by seeking a special financial contribution from the catholics. Con assisted in this to the best of his ability and £ 10,000 had been raised before his departure; but the political price was heavy. Rosetti, in spite of the warm welcome which he received from the queen, had inherited a fruitless and dangerous mission. Cautiously, he diminished the publicity of catholic worship and instructed the superiors of the religious orders to make sure that their members behaved with more discretion. But after the failure of the prolonged negotiations over the Oath of Allegiance there was little immediate prospect of an improvement in Anglo-Papal relations, and the queen's continued pressure for an English Cardinal (this time Walter Montague) merely reflected her lack of political grasp. Urban was quite willing to keep open his channels of communication, but he had no intention of making any concessions; and Charles's bargaining position grew steadily weaker as his power to defend the catholics against their enemies became more suspect. The Short Parliament of April 1640 was accompanied by a great increase in violent anti-papal demonstrations. The houses of several prominent catholics were sacked, and the king was under

---

[103] Panzani was particularly prone to optimism in this direction. ALBION, op. cit., 167–215.

severe pressure to redeem his political credit by re-activating the penal laws.[104] To his honour, he refused. Instead he celebrated the birth of his third son in July by ordering the release of all those catholics whom his zealous officials had imprisoned. In the circumstances this was foolish, and accomplished nothing but to add fury to the anti-papal storm which was to break irresistably with the meeting of the Long Parliament.

To the leaders of the House of Commons, particularly John Pym, the presence of a Papal Agent in England and the recent ostentatious behaviour of the catholics presented a useful political armoury. Arminianism and prerogative government could both with some plausibility be represented as tending to subject the realm to Popery. The still glowing embers of 'Regnans in Excelsis' and the Gunpowder Plot were fanned into vigorous life. Wild stories were told, even within the House itself, that ". . . many thousands (of papists) were in pay to be ready to cut all the protestant throats."[105] By the summer of 1641 a nation-wide atmosphere of panic had been created and the king's authority was crumbling away. Rumours reached the court that Parliament was contemplating a capital charge against Rosetti under an unrepealed Elizabethan law, as a servant of the Pope. On the 8 July he crossed to Dunkirk. Several prominent English catholics had already fled, including Windebank, and others were to follow. Bay the autumn of 1641 Charles was powerless to prevent an extensive resumption of persecution, and several priests were executed. It was already widely believed that there existed "a grand conspiracy of the Pope and his Jesuited instruments, to extirpate the protestant religion, re-establish popery, subvert laws, liberties, peace, parliaments, by kindling a civil war in . . . all his majesties realms . . ."[106] and in the latter part of October these fears were suddenly substantiated by the outbreak of rebellion in Ireland. The stages by which this situation was transformed into Civil War lie outside the scope of this paper, but the English catholics were naturally among the first to choose sides, and it is a moot point whether their vigorous partisanship was more an asset than a liability to the king.[106a] At first the parliamentary leaders were scrupulously careful to represent Charles as having been led astray by plausible papists (among whom the queen figured prominently), but as the struggle continued they became increasingly convinced that he was a willing dupe — a party to the conspiracy rather than one of its victims.

As the situation in England deteriorated, first Windebank and then Henrietta tried to presuade Urban, through his agents in northern Europe to provide funds for the hard pressed king. They cited his goodwill to the church, and the implacable anti-catholicism of his enemies, but the Pope was unmoved. Charles was not a catholic and could not be represented as defending the true faith; even

---

[104] Ibid, 338—339.
[105] The Journal of Sir Symonds D'Ewes, ed. WALLACE NOTESTEIN, New Haven, 1923, 25.
[106] W. PRYNNE, Romes Master Peece, quoted ALBION, op. cit., 343.
[106a] P. R. NEWMAN, Catholic royalist activists in the north, 1642—6, Recusant History, XIV, 1977, 26—38.

if the Pope had possessed the necessary resources he could not have hazarded them in such a cause. Unless the king announced his conversion he could not even count upon the good offices of the Pope with other catholic princes. In effect Charles had compromised himself in the eyes of his subjects and contributed to his own downfall for nothing. As the figurehead of a crumbling government, and later as a prisoner, he was useless to a Pope whose concern was with the English church. It was by no means clear to Urban at the end of his life that it was in his interest to prop up the collapsing English monarchy, even in return for that full toleration which Charles was at last prepared to grant. He died in July 1644, and his successor, Innocent X, after a series of somewhat unreal negotiations with Charles's envoys also came to accept the futility of further efforts. By 1647 the government of England was in the hands of men who regarded the Pope as Anti-Christ and the tentative relationship of the previous fifteen years finally came to an end.

The persecution of catholics was at its fiercest between 1641 and 1646. In those five years twenty one priests were executed and innumberable lay people imprisoned.[107] Thereafter, somewhat unexpectedly, the situation began to improve. There could be no question of diplomatic contact, however indirect, between the Papacy and the successive governments of the Commonwealth and Protectorate, but Cromwell was a man of remarkable tolerance. Although he never accorded any formal indulgence to the catholics, in practice like the Anglicans they enjoyed extensive freedom of worship provided that they were discreet.[108] Only two priests were executed during the nine years that Cromwell was in power, and one of those he tried unsuccessfully to save. Once the monarchs of Europe had learned to stomach a regicide government, and normal diplomatic relations had been resumed, Embassy chapels in London were again open to English catholics, although they enjoyed nothing like the popularity of the 1630s. In 1657 parliament endeavoured to impose a new anti-papal oath, but the Protector never allowed it to be enforced, and could claim with justice that he had ". . . plucked many out of the fire, the raging fire of persecution, which did tyrannise over their consciences, and encroached by an arbitrariness of power upon their estates."[109] The Protector's reluctance to allow any coercive ecclesiastical establishment to tamper with men's vision of God gave relief when it was least looked for, and caused many catholics to look back with something like regret after the return of the Laudian church at the Restoration.

---

[107] C. Cross, The Church in England, 1646—1660, in: The Interregnum, ed. G. E. Aylmer, London, 1972, 114—115.

[108] Ibid. William Prynne deduced from this as early as 1648 that the Army had been infiltrated and taken over by papists and Jesuits. J. Miller, Popery and Politics in England 1660—1688, Cambridge, 1973, 85. R. Clifton, The Popular Fear of Catholicism During the English Revolution, Past and Present, 1971, LII, 23—55.

[109] W. C Abbott, The Writings and Speeches of Oliver Cromwell, Cambridge (Mass.) 1937—1947, IV, 368.

XIII. Blacklo and the revival of intolerant Anglicanism

During the interregnum, in 1655, Richard Smith, Bishop of Chalcedon died in Paris at the age of 88. No steps were taken to replace him, or to provide any other form of papally approved government for the English catholic community, by this time about quarter of a million strong.[110] It is hardly surprising, therefore that these years saw the appearance of a new 'Gallican' movement among the English clergy. This movement took its name from a secular priest, Thomas Blacklo, who in 1647 had opened negotiations with the army leaders, promising comprehensive allegiance to the regime in power in return for a guarantee of toleration. Threatened as the catholics were at that time by the intolerance of the presbyterian parliament this had seemed a reasonable course of action. Blacklo had enjoyed considerable support within England, and cautious acquiescence from Rome. His initial efforts had been abruptly terminated by the second Civil war, and when he and his followers such as Sir Kenelm Digby attempted to resume negotiations with the Protector, they found themselves isolated from the bulk of catholic opinion. This was partly because the concessions which the Blackloites were prepared to make no longer seemed necessary in view of Cromwell's indulgent attitude, and partly because in the interval their opinions had produced a sharp reaction from Rome. Not only were they prepared to renounce the deposing power altogether, but they also upheld the complete validity of the Chapter originally established by William Bishop, and claimed that it possessed full power to elect a new Bishop for England irrespective of the wishes of the Pope. Blackloism was the extreme wing of that movement among the English clergy which represented the seventeenth century catholic church as the true heir of the medieval *Ecclesia Anglicana*, and which wished to repudiate the powerful centralising tendencies of the Counter Reformation. "This hath been the practice heretofore in catholic times in England", wrote Henry Holden, one of their number, "is now in France and in all other catholic states and kingdoms."[111] The Blackloites were anxious above all to remove the aspersion that it was impossible to be a good catholic and a good Englishman. Inevitably they were bitterly hostile to the Jesuits, and endeavoured to secure their complete excluson.

Because of its extremism, and because Blacklo's writings were condemned at Rome, Blackloism never gained the full adherence of more than a small minority of the English clergy, although many were sympathetic to it in varying degrees. It proved a serious embarrassment to the Chapter, the position of which was already sufficiently ambiguous, and laid it open to charges of

---

[110] Scholarly estimates of the size of the catholic community vary enormously, from 60,000 (MILLER, 11—12) to 540,000 (BRYAN MAGEE, The English Recusants, 115—117). This figure is based on that given by KENYON, Popish Plot, 24—5, and is probably accurate if 'church papists' are included.

[111] R. PUGH, Blacklo's Cabal, 1680, 33. Quoted MILLER, op.cit., 44.

Gallicanism and Jansenism. In 1661 and again in 1667 the Chapter condemned Blacklo, and endeavoured to silence his adherents. These pronouncements did not alleviate Papal suspicions, and indeed the Chapter maintained its independent attitude towards Rome, continuing to press for the appointment of an ordinary and continuing to exercise its own authority in spite of the refusal of successive Popes to confirm it. This quasi-autonomy was entirely justified in practical terms, because in spite of constant negotiations the problem of providing an acceptable alternative government for the catholic church in England was not to be resolved for twenty five years after the Restoration. In 1661 catholic hopes were naturally high. Charles was known to be sympathetic to the faith, so that a measure of toleration and a resumption of the gentlemanly unofficial relationship of the 1630s seemed a reasonable expectation. Up to a point this was satisfied, but Charles lacked his father's conscientiousness and there was no resumption of the earnest, albeit inconclusive, negotiations for a formal *entente* based upon an agreed oath of allegiance. The king was willing to tolerate the catholics — indeed anxious to do so — but unwilling to take the political risks which any formal steps in that direction would have entailed. Between 1660 and 1669 the penal laws were slackly enforced, but neither the legal nor the political position of the catholics underwent any significant change. Thereafter for about three years the success of Charles's pro-French policy seemed to promise a brighter future, but such hopes were dashed by the sharp protestant and anti-French reaction, in parliament and outside it, which began in 1673. In that year the 'Test Act' swept all conscientious catholics out of public office,[112] and the Council was obliged to take a much stricter line with recusants. Five years later the Popish Plot re-created the panic-stricken atmosphere of 1641, and thanks to the conversion of James Duke of York, the heir to the throne, 'Popery' became a leading political and constitutional issue until the Revolution of 1688.

XIV. The Duke of York and Exclusion; catholicism as a political issue

The Pope himself, however, played but a small part in these developments. Just as Clement VIII had come to see the impossibility of overthrowing English protestantism by rebellion or invasion, and had abandoned the militant stance of Pius V; so Alexander VII and his successors appreciated that the personal conversion of the English king would not effect the conversion of the realm, and abandoned the pressurising diplomacy of Urban VIII. After the experiences of his youth and early manhood Charles also knew perfectly well that he could not enforce toleration — let alone conversion; and with this degree of realism on

[112] By this Act it became necessary for the holder of any office, civil or military, to take the sacrament of the eucharist according to the rite of the church of England, to take the oaths of supremacy and allegiance, and to make a declaration against transubstantion. The eucharistic test was one which had been urged by parliament upon Elizabeth and James I, but rejected by them.

both sides, the relationship ceased to be of first rate political importance. At first Charles was primarily concerned to secure the red hat for his kinsman D'Aubigny, and secondarily to persuade the Pope to provide some suitable government for the English catholic community; but neither of these aims were pursued with much energy. Probably the king would have preferred an ordinary to the appointment of a new Vicar Apostolic, but in 1664 when it was suggested to him that D'Aubigny might become Cardinal and Vicar Apostolic at the same time, he was happy to agree to the proposal.[113] However D'Aubigny died in 1665 before his elevation could be confirmed, and Charles showed no anxiety to resume negotiations. Although there was no formal diplomatic relationship, Charles sent informal agents to Rome whenever he felt inclined, for example Richard Bellings in 1663, and received the Internuncio in Brussels whenever he visited England on the business of the mission. Also, like his father, he married a catholic wife and her household provided a ready means of communication with Rome should an indirect approach be deemed more advisable. Catherine possessed nothing like the influence which Henrietta Maria had come to enjoy in England, but her establishment did provide a useful lodging place for promising catholic clergy. The most conspicuous example of this is provided by Philip Howard (3rd son of Henry Earl of Arundel), who succeeded D'Aubigny as the Queen's Grand Almoner in 1665. Howard was regarded – and regarded himself – as an obvious episcopal candidate, but his promotion was delayed, and eventually frustrated by political considerations. Clement IX, for reasons which we have already noticed, was not anxious to erect an ordinary in England, but he also regarded the king's approval as essential for any appointment, and after 1665 Charles could not be persuaded to accept a Vicar Apostolic. The negotiations which went on from 1668 to 1672 were therefore inconclusive. Visits to England in 1669 and 1670 by the Internuncios Agretti and Airoldi revealed that the Chapter was more co-operative than had been supposed, and the new Pope, Clement X, decided to ignore the king's unhelpful attitude. A congregation for English affairs in April 1672 produced a compromise solution by nominating Howard as Vicar Apostolic with the title of Bishop; a return to the position of 1623 but without ambiguity or room for misrepresentation. By the time it was made this decision had been overtaken by events, first the Anglo-Dutch war and second the upsurge of anti-catholic feeling. In 1675 Howard was forced to leave the country, and it was considered too dangerous and provocative to go ahead with any plan to erect a fresh ecclesiatical authority in England.

XV. The Papacy and the last years of 'political catholicism'

During the Exclusion crisis and its aftermath, particularly between 1678 and 1683, the catholic church in England was once again reaping a harvest of

---

[113] MILLER, op. cit., 46.

popular mythology, in which the key figures were Louis XIV, Pius V and 'Bloody Mary'. In this case the fear of savage 'popish' rebellion and the massacre of the god-fearing, although very evident on the surface, was probably less important than the more rational connection between 'popery' and arbitrary government. The contemporary situation in France, and Charles II's well known admiration for Louis gave substance to these fears, which were reinforced by a propagandist interpretation of the 1630s when, it was believed, England had last stood in peril of arbitrary rule inspired and dominated by catholics. Just as the determination of late sixteenth century popes to remove Elizabeth contributed so largely to the indentification of English national feeling with protestantism, so the attempts of the early seventeenth century to bring about conversion or toleration by the unfettered use of the royal prerogative played a considerable part in that association between constitutionalism and reformed religion which brought about the Revolution and the Act of Settlement. It would be unjust to blame Alexander VII or Clement X for welcoming Charles II's Declarations of Indulgence, but the fact that these so quickly ran into serious parliamentary opposition was symptomatic of the problems which the popes of this period faced in their dealings with England.

These problems came to a head in the person of Charles's brother and heir, James, Duke of York. A recent scholar has written "Without James's conversion there would have been little persecution of catholics in the 1670s, no Popish Plot and no Exclusion Crisis."[114] Charles fought a bitter and successful battle to preserve his brother's inheritance, but he could not transmit to James the discretion or political skill needed to retain it for long. Innocent XI realised perfectly well that James had brought the English catholics into danger and undesired political prominence, and while he could not fail to respond sympathetically to his overtures when he ascended the throne in 1685, he regarded the new king's headlong course with the greatest alarm. There is no reason to believe that James really intended the restoration of England to the Roman obedience by the use of arbitrary power. Even his limited intelligence was sufficient to see the impossibility of such a course, and until 1687 he can have had little expectation of an heir to continue his work. His true aim was certainly more limited; to extend to his catholic subjects full liberty of worship and civil rights, and to base that tolerance firmly upon valid legislation.[115] It is possible that James, in common with catholic optimists of earlier periods, may have believed that the removal of penal laws would have resulted in such a flood of conversions that the country would soon have become catholic again of its own freewill. If such was his belief, his strong determination to repeal the laws is understandable, but it becomes still more unlikely that he entertained any intentions of enforcing catholicism.

---

[114] Ibid, 180.
[115] The struggle to obtain such legislation underlay most of the controversial policies of the reign, such as the attacks upon the corporations. MILLER, op. cit.; D. OGG, England in the reigns of James II and William III, Oxford, 1955; J. R. JONES, County and Court; England 1658—1714, London, 1978.

As might be expected in the changed circumstances, the government of the church was soon resolved, and in August 1685 John Leyburne was appointed Vicar Apostolic, with the title of Bishop of Adrametum. A papal Nuncio was also sent to England, and full diplomatic relations were restored. Leyburne lived at court, and was able to work openly, but his advice seems to have carried little weight with the king. Wherever possible Leyburne seems to have urged James to moderation, and his efforts in this direction were seconded not only by the nuncio, D'Adda, but also by Philip Howard – a Cardinal since 1675 and Cardinal Protector of England since 1679. Howard was deeply distrustful of the king's policies, having a more realistic appreciation of the strength of English protestant resentment, and fearing that his aggressiveness would once again expose ordinary catholics to the full weight of that resentment. James's attitude towards the papacy was also tactless and high handed, so that relations were frequently strained and Innocent was given a good opportunity to appreciate the reasons for the king's mounting political difficulties at home. For over two years he tried to bully the Pope into granting a red hat to Edward Petre SJ, the Dean of his Chapel, refusing to take 'no' for an answer and threatening to withdraw his ambassador from Rome.[116] He also attempted to force Innocent into elevating his wife's kinsman, Rainaldo D'Este, by demanding that he be appointed Cardinal Protector – ignoring the fact that Howard already held that post. Altogether James's policy towards the Curia was clumsy, self defeating, and insufficiently mindful of the welfare of the church. It was not until 1688, a few months before his fall, that he asked for, and was swiftly granted, three extra Vicars Apostolic so that the country could be more conveniently divided into four districts. Consequently, when he was overtaken by political disaster, the Pope was neither particularly surprised, nor as distressed as might have been expected. Innocent owed James no debt of gratitude for embracing the faith and little for his handling of the English church. Such an obstinate and arrogant disciple of Louis XIV was more a liability than an asset, and his fall was an anticlimax in Anglo-Papal relations which left subsequent popes free to concentrate upon an English church now finally, and not unwillingly, relegated to minority status.

Bibliographical Appendix of works published since 1955

ALBION, G., The Old Chapter and Brotherhood, 1623–1973, Clergy Review, 1973, LVIII, 679–688.

ALEXANDER, G., Bonner and the Marian Persecutions, History, 1975, LX, 374–91.

ALEXANDER, M. V. C., Charles I's Lord Treasurer; Sir Richard Weston Earl of Portland, 1577–1635, London, 1975.

ANSTRUTHER, G., Cardinal Howard and the English Court, Archivum Fratrum Praedicatorum, 1958, XXVIII.

IDEM, The Seminary Priests, 1558–1603, Ushaw College, Durham, 1969.

AYLMER, G. E., St. Patrick's Day 1628 in Witham, Essex. Past and Present, 1973, LXI, 139–148.

[116] British Museum, Lansdowne MS 1152 B, ff. 260–261. MILLER, op. cit., 233.

BARCHARD, F. V., Reginald, Cardinal Pole, 1553–1558, unpublished Tulane University Ph. D. thesis, 1971.
BAYNE, C. G., Anglo-Roman Relations, 1558–1565, Oxford, 1913 (reprinted 1968).
BASSETT, B., The English Jesuits from Campion to Martindale, London, 1967.
BIRRELL, T. A., English Catholics without a Bishop 1655–1672, Recusant History, 1958, IV, 142–180.
BON, J. D., The English Reformation, Product of King or Minister', Church History, 1972, XLI, 186–197.
BOSSY, J. A., The Character of Elizabethan Catholicism, Past and Present, 1962, XXI, 39–59.
IDEM, Rome and the Elizabethan Catholics, Historical Journal, 1964, VII (i), 135–142.
IDEM, Henry IV, the Appellants and the Jesuits, Recusant History, 1965, VIII (ii), 80–122.
IDEM, The English Catholic Community, 1603–1625, in: The Reign of James VI and I, ed. A. G. R. SMITH, London, 1973.
IDEM, The English Catholic Community, 1570–1850, London, 1975.
BOSTICK, T. P., English Foreign Policy, the Diplomacy of the Divorce 1528–1534, unpublished Illinois Ph. D. thesis, 1967.
BOWKER, M., The Supremacy and the Episcopate; the Struggle for Control, 1534–1540, Historical Journal, 1975, XVIII, 227–43.
BRADLEY, R. I., Blacklo and the Counter Reformation, in: From the Renaissance to the Counter Reformation. Essays in Honor of Garrett H. Mattingly, ed. C. H. CARTER, New York, 1965.
IDEM, Christopher Davenport and the Thirty Nine Articles, Archiv für Reformationsgeschichte, 1961, LII, 205–228.
BRESLOW, M. A., English Puritan Views of Foreign Nations, 1618–1640, Harvard University Press, 1970.

CANNING, D. and HANLEY, J., The Anglican World. A: During the Pontificates of Urban VIII and Innocent X (1623–1655) [by D.C.]. B: From Alexander VII to Alexander VIII (1655–91) [by J. H.], Sacrae Congregationis de Propaganda fide memoria verum, 1622–1972, 1, 2: 1622–1700. Rome, 1972, 149–76, 176–200.
CLANCY, T. H., Pamphlets and Politics under Elizabeth I, The Month, 1960, XXIII, 283–290.
IDEM, English Catholics and the Papal Deposing Power, Recusant History, 1961–3, VI (iii, v) VII (i); 114–140, 205–227, 2–10.
IDEM, Papist Pamphleteers; the Allen-Parsons Party, 1572–1615, Loyola University Press, Chicago, 1964.
IDEM, The Jesuits and the Independants, 1647, Archivum Historicum Societatis Iesu, 1971, XL, 67–70.
IDEM, Papist-Protestant-Puritan; English Religious Taxonomy 1565–1665, Recusant History, 1976, XIII, 227–53.
CLIFTON, R., The Popular Fear of Catholics During the English Revolution, Past and Present, 1971, LII, 23–55.
CREHAN, J. H., St. Ignatius and Cardinal Pole, Archivum Historicum Societatis Iesu, 1956, XXV, 72–98.
IDEM, The Return to Obedience; New Judgement on Cardinal Pole, The Month, 1955, new series XIV, 221–229.
CROSS, C., The Royal Supremacy in the Elizabethan Church, London, 1969.
IDEM, Church and People, 1450–1660, London, 1977.
IDEM, The Church in England 1646–1660, in: The Interregnum, ed. G. E. AYLMER, London, 1972.

DAYRAS, S. and D'HAUSSY, C., Le catholicisme en Angleterre, Paris, 1970.
DICKENS, A. G., The English Reformation, London, 1964.
DOCKERY, J. B., Christopher Davenport, Friar and Diplomat, London, 1960.
DODWELL, C. R., The English Church and the Continent, London, 1959.

DURST, P., Intended Treason; what Really Happened in the Gunpowder Plot, London, 1971.

DWYER, C. R., Pole's Defence of the Unity of the Church, edited, with introduction, Westminster, 1965.

EDWARDS, F., Henry More, S. J., Administrator and Historian, 1586–1661, Archivum Historicum Societatis Iesu, 1972, XLI, 233–281.

ELTON, G. R., Reform and Reformation, 1509–1558, London, 1977.

FREDE, C. DE, La restaurazione cattolica in Inghilterra sotto Maria Tudor, Naples, 1971.

GIFFORD, J. V., The Controversy Over the Oath of Allegiance in 1606, unpublished Oxford B. Litt. thesis, 1971.

GREEN, I. M., The Re-establishment of the Church of England 1660–1663, Oxford, 1978.

GROSVENOR, I. D., Catholics and Politics; the Worcestershire Election of 1604, Recusant History, 1978, XIV, 149–162.

GUILDAY, P., The English Catholic Refugees on the Continent, 1558–1795, London, 1914 (reprinted 1969).

HAIGH, C., Reformation and Resistance in Tudor Lancashire, Oxford, 1975.

IDEM, The Fall of a Church or the Rise of a Sect? Post Reformation Catholicism in England, Historical Journal, 1978, XXI, 181–186.

HALLER, W., Foxe's Book of Martyrs and the Elect Nation, London, 1963.

HANLON, SISTER JOSEPH D., The Effects of the Counter Reformation upon the English Catholics, 1603–1630, unpublished Columbia Ph. D. thesis, 1959.

HAVRAN, M. J., The Catholics in Caroline England, Oxford, 1962.

IDEM, Caroline Courtier: the Life of Lord Cottington, London, 1973.

HICKS, L., An Elizabethan Problem; Some Aspects of the Careers of Two Exile Adventurers, London, 1964.

IDEM, The Embassy of Sir Anthony Standen in 1603, Recusant History, 1963, VII, 50–81.

HILL, C., God's Englishman, London, 1970.

IDEM, AntiChrist in Seventeenth Century England, London, 1971.

JAMES, M. E., The Concept of Order and the Northern Rising of 1569, Past and Present, 1973, LX, 49–83.

JONES, H. L., Faith by Statute; the Elizabethan Settlement of 1559, unpublished Cambridge Ph. D. thesis, 1977.

JONES, J. R., Country and Court; England 1658–1714, London, 1978.

KELLY, H. A., The Matrimonial Trials of Henry VIII, Stanford, California, 1976.

KELLY, M., The Submission of the Clergy, Transaction of the Royal Historical Society, 1965, 5 series XV, 97–119.

KENYON, J. P., The Popish Plot, London, 1972.

KINGDON, R. M., The Execution of Justice by William Cecil and A, True, Sincere and Modest Defence of the English Catholics by William Allen, New York, 1965.

LEROY, A., Le Grand Schisme d'Angleterre, Paris, 1967.

LEVINE, M., Henry VIII's Use of his Spiritual and Temporal Jurisdiction, Historical Journal, 1967, X (i), 3–11.

LINDLEY, K. J., The Part Played by Catholics in the English Civil War, unpublished Manchester Ph. D. thesis, 1968.

IDEM, The Lay Catholics of England in the Reign of Charles I, Journal of Ecclesiastical History, 1971, XXII, 199–221.

LOADES, D. M., The Oxford Martyrs, London, 1970.

IDEM, The Reign of Mary Tudor, 1553–58, London, 1979.

LOOMIE, A. J., The Spanish Elizabethans: the English exiles at the Court of Philip II., New York, 1963.

IDEM, Toleration and Diplomacy; the Religious Issue in Anglo-Spanish Relations, 1603–1605, Transactions of the American Philosophical Society, 1963, LIII (vi).

IDEM, Guy Fawkes in Spain, Bulletin of the Institute of Historical Research, Supplement 8, 1971.

IDEM, Richard Berry, Gondomar's English Catholic Adviser, Recusant History, 1971–2, XI, 47–57.

IDEM, Gondomar's Selection of English Officers, 1622, English Historical Review, 1973, LXXXVIII, 574–581.

IDEM, Spain and the Jacobean Catholics, 1603–1612, Catholic Record Society, London, 1973.

IDEM, The Armadas and the Catholics of England, Catholic Historical Review, 1973–4, LIX, 385–403.

IDEM, Spain and the Jacobean Catholics, 1613–1624, Catholic Record Society, London, 1978.

LUNN, M., Benedictine Opposition to Bishop Richard Smith, 1625–1629, Recusant History, 1971–2, XI, 1–20.

IDEM, The Origins and Early Development of the Revived English Benedictine Congregation, Cambridge Ph. D. thesis, 1970.

MARMION, J. P., The London Synod of Reginald, Cardinal Pole, 1555–6, unpublished Keele M. A. thesis, 1974.

IDEM, Cardinal Pole in Recent Studies, Recusant History, 1975, XIII, 56–61.

MARTIN, F. X., Friar Nugent 1569–1635, Rome, Capuchin Historical Institute, 1962.

McGRATH, P., Papists and Puritans under Elizabeth I, London, 1967.

MEYER, A. O., England and the Catholic Church under Queen Elizabeth, translated by J. R. McKee, London, 1915 (reprinted 1967).

MILLER, J., Popery and Politics in England, 1660–1688, Cambridge, 1973.

IDEM, Catholic Officers in the Later Stuart Army, English Historical Review, 1973, LXXXVIII.

IDEM, James II: a Study in Kingship, Hove, 1978.

MOREY, A., The Catholic Subjects of Elizabeth I, London, 1978.

MURRAY, R. H., The Political Consequences of the Reformation, New York, 1960.

MURPHY, M., St. Oliver Plunkett and Downside, Downside, 1975.

NEWMAN, P. R., Catholic Royalist Activists in the North, 1642–6, Recusant History, 1977, XIV, 26–38.

O'CONNELL, M. R., Thomas Stapleton and the Counter Reformation, Yale University Press, 1964.

OLSEN, V. N., John Foxe and the Elizabethan Church, California University Press, 1973.

OWEN, D., The Enforcement of the Reformation in the Diocese of Ely, in: Miscellanea Historiae Ecclesiasticae, III, Louvain, 1970, 167–174.

PARMITER, G. DE C., The King's Great Matter, London, 1967.

IDEM, A Note on Some Aspects of the Royal Supremacy of Henry VIII, Recusant History, 1969–70, X, 183–192.

IDEM, Elizabethan Popish Recusants in the Inns of Court, Bulletin of the Institute of Historical Research, Supplement 9, 1976.

IDEM, Plowden, Englefield and Sandford; 1, 1558–1585; 2, 1585–1609, Recusant History, 1976, XIII, 159–77; 1977, XIV, 9–25.

PETERS, R., Some Catholic Opinions of King James VI and I, Recusant History, 1969–70, X, 292–303.

PETTI, A. G. R., Letters and Despatches of Richard Verstegan, Catholic Record Society, London, 1959.

PHILLIPS, J., The Reformation of Images. Destruction of Art in England, 1535–1660, Berkeley, California, 1974.

POGSON, R. H., Cardinal Pole; Papal Legate to England, unpublished Cambridge Ph. D. thesis, 1972.

IDEM, Revival and Reform in Mary Tudor's Church, Journal of Ecclesiastical History, 1974, XXV, 249–65.

IDEM, Reginald Pole and the Priorities of Government in Mary Tudor's Church, Historical Journal, 1975, XVIII, 3–20.

IDEM, The Legacy of the Schism; Confusion, continuity, and change in the Marian Clergy, in: The Mid-Tudor Polity, 1540–1560, ed. J. LOACH and R. TITTLER, London, 1980, 116–136.

RENOLD, P., The Wisbech Stirs, 1595–1598, Catholic Record Society, London, 1958.

REYNOLDS, E. E., The Roman Catholic Church in England and Wales, London, 1973.

ROGERS, D. M., and ALLISON, A. F., A Catalogue of Catholic Books in English Printed Abroad or Secretly in England, 1558–1640, Bognor Regis, 1956.

ROSE, ELIOT, Cases of Conscience; Alternatives Open to Recusants and Puritans under Elizabeth and James I, Cambridge 1975.

ROSTENBURG, L., The Minority Press and the English Crown, 1558–1625, Nieuwkoop, 1971.

SCARISBRICK, J., Henry VIII, London, 1968.

SHRIVER, F., Orthodoxy and Diplomacy; James I and the Vorstius Affair, English Historical Review, 1970, LXXXV, 449–474.

SILKE, J. J., Kinsale; the Spanish Intervention in Ireland, Liverpool University Press, 1970.

SIMONS, J., Robert Parson's Certamen Ecclesiae Anglicanae, Assen, 1965.

STEER, F. W., The Life of St. Philip Howard, London, 1971.

SYKES, N., Old Priest and New Presbyter, Cambridge, 1956.

TELLECHEA IDIGORAS, J. I., Bartolomé Carranza y la restauración católica inglesa, Anthalogia Annua, 1964, XII, 159–282.

THOMAS, R., Comprehension and Indulgence, in: G. F. NUTTALL and O. CHADWICK, eds., From Uniformity to Unity 1662–1962, London, 1962.

VAN DER ESSEN, A., Les catholiques Londoniens et l'ambassade d'Espagne, 1633–1637, in: Scrinium Lovoniense, Louvain, 1961, 475–485.

WATKIN, E. I., Roman Catholicism in England From the Reformation to 1950, London, 1957.

WEINER, C. Z., The Beleaguered Isle; a Study of Elizabethan and Early Jacobean Anticatholicism, Past and Present, 1971, LXI, 27–62.

WHITE, G. L., Anglican Reactions to the Council of Trent in the Reign of Elizabeth I, unpublished Vanderbilt University Ph.D. thesis, 1975.

WILKIE, W. E., The Cardinal Protectors of England. Rome and the Tudors before the Reformation, Cambridge, 1974.

ZINNHOBLER, R., Heinrich VIII und die Reformation in England, Theologisch-praktische Quartalschrift, 1970, CXVIII, 241–248.

The English Clergy, Catholic and Protestant, in the 16th and 17th Centuries

by J. C. H. Aveling, Bracknell

Contents

I. Introduction: the main problem — how far was clerical life modernised at this period?

This is an attempt to discuss some of the questions and problems confronting the historian of the 16th and 17th century English clergy. It concentrates mainly on their educational formation, professional methods and intellectual activity. Catholic and Protestant clergy are dealt with equally and in juxtaposition, not, as has been traditional, completely separately for all the world as if they were entirely different species. This treatment has no oecumenical overtones, but is simply an effort to study more effectively the degree to which both clergies faced similar problems, found similar solutions, and were influenced positively by each other's efforts.

The discussion must surely be dominated by one major question: when did the distinctively modern pattern of clerical life (the Churches as voluntary, self-organising bodies, separate from the State and society at large; the clergy as *bourgeois* members of the professional class) come into being? To medievalists like Professors Powicke and Southern it happened decisively in the early 16th century. To them the medieval ecclesiastical and clerical set-up, with all its internal contradictions and tensions, and its intermittent reformist tendencies in a 'modern' direction, was solely given meaning and unity as a system by "the identification of the Church with the whole of organised society". On such a view the medieval set-up stood or fell with Papal supremacy, the mastery of Pope and clergy over States and lay society: it was a system in which the clerical 'order' was the *only* real profession and performed all professional functions in society, and yet in which the (very numerous) clergy were an 'order' and not a class, a very heterogeneous mass of persons ranging from aristocrats and the highly educated to proletarian *illiterati*. On such a view the medieval set-up was clearly fast collapsing from the later 14th century: the *coup de grâce* was given by Luther and Henry VIII. Once the Papal supremacy and clerical mastery were gone, the survival down to the 19th century or even later of many of the outer forms of the medieval ecclesiastical order was meaningless. The medieval order's forms had been largely dictated by the social and economic conditions of a primitive, preindustrial society. Hence, outside the exceptional urban and industrial areas, the ecclesiastical forms could not change substantially until the advent of the industrial age. The idea of unity in religion as a prime basis of social order and morality — another overhang from the middle ages — might die very hard down even to the early 19th century, and be sustained by State establishment of religion. But from the 16th century, on this view, it was equally doomed. The ecclesiastical conservatism of Henry VIII, Hooker, Coleridge, Peel and the young Gladstone was a nostalgia as sentimental as the antiquarian conservatism of Aubrey and Spelman. Logically also, on such a view, the 'seminary' movement of 1570—1640 amongst Catholics and Protestants to professionalise the bulk of the clergy, minimally successful as it was, belongs to the modern professionalisation of the clergy and not to the medieval era of the Gregorian Reform and 12th century Renaissance university movement.

There is obviously a great deal of room for discussion here. In a real sense indeed it began inside the bosom of the medieval Church, and was resurrected inside the Church of England from the 1590s between those who saw the Reformation as a revolution, and those who saw it as a spring-clean of the medieval system. At least one modern Church historian sees the watershed between modern and medieval as coming in the last decades of the 17th century, while there are modern medievalists who place it in the late 14th and 15th centuries. We may perhaps wonder whether the question at issue, however intellectually interesting, is of much practical historical importance. 'Medieval' and 'modern' may be, as categories, altogether too grand and vague.

II. 1500—1534: the twilight of the medieval clergy?

The debate to some extent governed traditional treatment of the Church history of this period. To some — evangelical Protestants, but also a Catholic historian like Professor David Knowles — it was a static and stagnant period for the clergy when the medieval system was bankrupt and the clergy incapable of giving birth to a different system, either the medieval one restored to its supposed pristine splendour, or a new one. To others the clergy were basically sound and in process of adapting themselves to the changing standards of society — though perhaps not fast enough. Due to scarcity of sources new research work on 1400—1534 has long been in very short supply. But lately things have changed: studies on the 15th century are multiplying; there is recent work on the 15th century higher clergy and religious, on English prehumanism and Erasmianism, on religious dissent, especially of the Lollards and early English Protestants, and two studies of the pastoral clergy of 1500—1534. To what extent do they illuminate the period and give new life and direction to discussion of it?[1]

---

[1] THOMPSON, A. H., The English Clergy and their Organization in the Later Middle Ages, London, 1947; ASTON, M., The Fifteenth Century, London, 1968; RAPP, F., L'Eglise et la Vie Religieuse en Occident à la Fin du Moyen Age, Paris, 1971; OWEN, D. M., Church and Society in Medieval Lincolnshire, Lincoln, 1971; HALE, J. R., England and the Italian Renaissance, London, 1954; CASPARI, F., Humanism and Social Order in Tudor England, London, 1954; McCONICA, J. K., English Humanists and Reformation Politics under

1. The state of the episcopate and diocesan staffs

   As a class, or even mostly as individuals, the English episcopate of the period still lacks research work and reassessment. The standard view of them bases itself on the ideal of a bishop as spiritual father to his diocese, totally dedicated to spiritual concerns, and sees the episcopate of 1500—1534 as falling short of the ideal very badly: as civil servants with a legal professional training, rewarded by the Crown with episcopal rank and revenues, their dioceses run in their absence by 'officials' in a merely legal fashion: none of the bishops of much spiritual or intellectual stature, and Wolsey a phenomenon who ostensibly raised the medieval ecclesiastical system to its highest peak, but who really depressed and subjugated it and the episcopate more than ever before to secular power. We may legitimately wonder — pending more solid information — whether this estimate does justice to the episcopate. In the first place, none of the classical definitions of the office (the New Testament, Gratian and the Canons, St. Gregory's 'Cura Pastoralis,' the consecration rites of the 'Pontificale' and Anglican 'Ordinal', the prayers of Hooper and Becon for 'chief pastors', or the canons for the archdiocese of Milan of St. Charles Borromeo) really defines it in more than vague, almost moralistic terms; the Council of Trent certainly defined it no more closely. In practice, in the immensely long history of the office, it has from the start, like a chameleon, taken its form and style from the social and economic situation around it, and this has varied greatly. At very few periods and places has a bishop ever been principally a glorified parish priest. In any case such a function would have been quite impossible at any time in the middle ages or in 1500—1534 or long afterwards, since dioceses commonly consisted of very large areas of thinly scattered agrarian communities connected by a vile road system. By long tradition a bishop in England was a member of an 'order' devoted to a multiplicity of tasks — defending the rights of the clerical order, defending papal and royal authority, binding together Church and State in one *plebs Christiana*. As an individual he was a magnate with a responsibility for the good order of his 'country' in conjunction with, and with a watching brief on, the lay magnates and gentry of the area, and as a *literatus* he was a natural counsellor, secretary and ambassador to the King. Bishops could be acknowledged as holy men (like Fisher), or as theologians (like Robert Aldrich, bishop of Carlisle, long a don and Eton schoolmaster, a friend of Erasmus), but those were generally qualifications which made them indifferent bishops. The bishops of 1500—34 who probably did most for the Church were Wolsey and Fox — neither of them particularly holy or noted theologians. Holy men, like Hugh of Lincoln or Fisher (for all that Fisher was a noted university administrator) tended to be poor diocesans, and theologians (like Cranmer, who spent four-

Henry VIII and Edward VI, Oxford, 1965; SIMON, J., Education and Society in Tudor England, Cambridge, 1966; CHARLTON, K., Education in Renaissance England, London, 1965; DICKENS, A. G., The English Reformation, London, 1967; BOWKER, M., The Secular Clergy in the Diocese of Lincoln, 1495—1520, Cambridge, 1968; HEATH, P., The English Parish Clergy on the Eve of the Reformation, London, 1968.

fifths of his episcopal time studying his books) even worse. There was much to be said for a university course in civil law (or 'both laws') for an aspirant to the episcopate. It was a real test of both practical and intellectual ability. It did not — contrary to a widely-repeated view — make a man especially servile to authority. Gardiner, who is usually cited as a perfect example of a servile, theologically uneducated civilian bishop, was long imprisoned for his resolute disobedience to the government in Edward VI's reign, and produced a competent book, 'De Vera Obedientia'. It would also be wrong to imagine that most bishops were active 'civil servants' (in an almost modern sense): a substantial minority were religious or university dons; of the majority who were lawyers by training, few were permanently occupied full-time in central royal administration during the most part of their episcopate. We don't yet know much about their periods of residence in their sees. But it is likely that few of them absented themselves totally, and that most resided a good deal more than we have been led to imagine. Again, it seems unrealistic to charge the bishops with not being spiritual leaders and prophets. In history that role has comparatively rarely fallen to bishops, and those who have fulfilled it in some degree have generally done so in virtue of abilities and a reputation which preceded, and had little to do with, their episcopate. (Cranmer, Ridley, Latimer and other episcopal Reformers certainly owed their spiritual and doctrinal leadership to their university careers and to coincidental features of the situation they were in — the political situation, their circles of bookish friends and patrons.) As for Wolsey, his ecclesiastical administration is still slightly documented and less studied, and we are in no position as yet to judge it. In general we may not be far from the truth if we see the episcopate, with all its faults and the near-anonymity of many of its members, as still a crucial and powerful feature (though one amongst many) in the English scene.

It is hard to generalise about diocesan administration in 1500—1534, since episcopal court books have rarely survived, and episcopal registers mostly remain unpublished. But it is surely unjust to condemn it out of hand as merely a legal machine. Traditionally administration of every kind used legalistic forms, visitations and inquisitions, prosecutions and law-suits, and administrative progress invariably meant more courts and more refined legal methods. We carp at this at our peril, since the system fitted like a glove a social and religious system remote from anything we experience — a society consisting of very many tight, isolated communities, a very unruly and violent people, the absence of resources to pay large numbers of trained officials, an ecclesiastical administration dealing with the whole of society. In any case the surviving records hardly inform us at all of the vast web of family and tenantry relationships within which the legal administration worked and which formed the flesh on its bones.

It is also surely unfair to judge the English cathedrals and their staffs of 1500—1534 by some vague ideal of 'the pastoral heart of the diocese'. The secular cathedrals certainly abounded in anomalies and untidinesses, masses of non-resident prebendaries (university dons, career administrators), services performed by substitutes of lower degree, colleges of chantry priests apparently very underemployed, and fabrics often ill-maintained. But cathedrals have very rarely,

at any period in history, served much of a pastoral purpose. Medievals had long
tried to justify their existence by thinking of them as large collegiate churches
devoted to intercession and good works — a rather thin justification, which had
worn very thin by 1500. In fact the posts and revenues of cathedrals were increasingly used — and justified — on less exalted principles: maintaining scholarship at large in the Church by supporting university teachers, maintaining
diocesan administration (in which the small resident prebendal staffs and even a
good many vicars-choral and chantry priests were employed at least part-time),
providing good preaching and parochial curates in parishes in the vicinity under
the control of the Chapter or cathedral colleges, and even serving as an economic support to the often rather precarious finances of cathedral city corporations. No efforts at cathedral reform, either Catholic (Cardinal Pole's reform
decrees) or Protestant (intermittent Edwardine and Elizabethan injunctions to
prune the number of non-residents, start cathedral courses of sermons), after
1534, were going to effect much change.

2. 'University clerks'

The 'university clerks' of 1500—1534 seem especially odd to us, who are
used to a strong general homogeneity of all clergy as professional men, and to a
sharp line of division between clergy and laity. What are we to make of Dr.
Caius of Cambridge — layman or clergy-man? or of Reginald Pole, an undoubtedly pious cleric who positively resisted entry into major Orders until
necessity drove him late in life; or Cranmer as a perfectly legitimately married
university clerk in minor Orders? Indeed, the history of 16th century 'laicisation' of the civil service, the law (secular and ecclesiastical), the universities,
schools and medical profession is still a subject full of obscurities and traps for
the unwary. Throughout the later middle ages and 16th century the canonical
line of division between layman and clerk by no means coincided with the real
(though often vague) line of division between ecclesiastical and secular avoca-
tions. It is possible that this 'laicisation' was only an accentuation of one already
well-established feature of the ancient, complex interpenetration of clergy and
laity, and of the technically lay and clerical spheres in society: that is, the
performance of functions within the canonically ecclesiastical sphere by men
who were canonically layman (or, at least to 1559, clerks who never went
beyond tonsure or minor Orders). Such functions were: matriculated students
or teachers of Arts at universities, students of theology, schoolmasters, cathedral
prebendaries, absentee incumbents of benefices, rectors of parishes, judges or
advocates in ecclesiastical courts, medical practitioners, choirmen, parish clerks,
churchwardens and 'honest men' of parishes. The invasion of the universities by
lay students from the early 16th century (and consequent increase in the number
of lay 'clerks'), the apparent sharp decline in the numbers of clergy by the mid-
century, the passage into lay landowners' hands of many advowsons and rectories after the Dissolution were at least some of the accumulation of causes of an
increased lay penetration of the ecclesiastical sphere. But it was merely a change

in degree. The framework of laws, institutions and ideas within which this increase operated remained itself largely unchanged in 1600. All laymen, as in the later middle ages, remained subject to clerical jurisdiction in multiple ways. All education had a clerical flavour to it. Medicine was subject to episcopal licences; so was printing and publishing. The obverse of the interpenetration of spheres was the involvement of clergy in the lay sphere, as royal civil servants, ambassadors, stewards and men of affairs (sometimes doubling with chaplaincies) to lay landowners, as (generally under a cloud of illicitness) farmers, tradesmen, craftsmen, professional musicians. Eventually, but equally slowly, this feature was to decline as the century wore on. But in 1534 such changes, of both kinds, cannot have been very far advanced, and they represented a tendency with roots far back in the middle ages. We are hardly in a position to judge the 'university clerks', a very variegated group who spanned the interpenetration of ecclesiastical and secular. In society as it was then still constituted 'the Church' was a term with grades of meaning: the hierarchs or 'possessioners'; the whole clerical order (with its tentacle-like arms stretching far into the secular world); the ecclesiastical sphere of jurisdiction (which covered everyone); all society under God. 'Anticlericalism' could similarly have grades of meaning. Perhaps it was traditionally fiercest against the hierarchs, and rooted amongst their closest dependents, the lower clergy and the laity most immediately subject to hierarchs. So also entry into major Orders or the vows of religion could be, and officially always ought to have been, a high personal vocation. Yet most often it was thought of in a matter-of-fact way, decided by superiors, landlords or parents, fitness for elementary education, availability of job-prospects. As with arranged marriages, it was expected and presumed that love and a sense of vocation would normally automatically follow assumption of the state. This antique ultra-objectivity was, as we shall see, to die very hard. Protestantism, with its stress on prophetic vocation, hardly dinted it, and only the advent of industrial society and the modern relation of society and religion destroyed it. On the other hand objections to it in part existed all through the middle ages – and, for instance, led to modifications in the system of oblation of children to the cloister. Considerations of this kind should give us pause before we accept the customary condemnation of early 16th century mass ordinations with little or no examination of the candidates.

3. The pastoral clergy

The traditional picture of the pastoral clergy of 1500–1534 is a depressing one of hordes of miserably poor, superstitious illiterates. It goes back to the well-known generalisations of the Humanists, Thomas More, Starkey and Archbishop Edward Lee, relieved only by More's judgment that things were even worse on the Continent. In the main the picture has been endorsed, with picturesque examples of superstition, by the author of the best recent general study of the English Reformation, Professor A. G. Dickens. A more hopeful and tolerant picture has been sketched by medievalists – particularly W. A. Pantin.

They have emphasised that the pastoral clergy were an order but hardly a homogeneous class of society. There were wide differences in types of parishes and jobs, between town and country, and even within large towns, between fashionable parishes (often endowed by patrician merchants) and small suburban enclaves, and between priests of well-endowed chantries and jobbing priests 'singing for souls' or supplying for sick curates. The medievalists also point out that it is unrealistic to regard pastoral priests as the teachers and props of a superstitious folk-religion. As the Protestant evangelists were to discover, a largely illiterate rustic (or town labouring pauper) population was impervious to a religion of the printed book, and the pastoral clergy were more the products of the folk-religion than its upholders, its assistants more than its directors. As for preaching and confessing, the popularity of friars' churches and indulgenced pilgrimages most probably stemmed from the fact that the bulk of these services was provided by religious. Educational opportunities for ordinands steadily improved in the late 14th and 15th centuries. The line between university clerks proper and *illiterati* (those unlearned in Latin) was not hard and fast. There were probably more university 'drop-outs' after a year or two than students who graduated. There could be reasonably well-educated pastoral priests who (like Robert Parkyn of Adwick-le-Street) were apparently only the products of grammar schools, or petty schools and the help of good tutors and friends who were university clerks. There was an English, home-bred version of the Continental 'devotio Moderna', manifested in the statutes of the new Oxbridge colleges and linked grammar schools, in the existence of the Humanist monk Robert Joseph of Evesham's circle of university clerk, monk and pastoral incumbent pen-friends, in the modest spate of MS and printed instruction manuals for priests, 'Dormi Secures' (sermon outlines) and guides for confessors, in the scattered evidence that some religious houses were fostering the education of secular clerks destined for their benefices.[2]

The two recent studies of this subject are forced to admit that the matter can only be decided by the production of a much greater weight of factual evidence than is yet available. The cases of both traditionalists and medievalists rest alike on thin evidence. Thus, for instance, the record of the pastoral clergy of the small but lively fenland port of Yaxley, Huntingdonshire may well be fairly typical. From at least the 12th century the benefice was appropriated to the abbot and convent of Thorney, and a vicarage was ordained by 1250. Ostensibly the monastery held the rectory, and appointed by private treaty a succession of vicars, whose names and details rarely if ever appear in the diocesan (Lincoln) records. In practice, from the late 14th century to the dissolution of the monastery, the Crown set aside Thorney's rights and appointed a series of royal clerks (absentees) to the rectory, which was a valuable one. One or two vicars or curates of Yaxley or its parochial chapel appear as mere names in court records of trespass or violence down the years. From the 1480s Huntingdonshire wills survive, though from 1485 to 1522 there are no wills of Yaxley priests and only one mention of (an otherwise unknown) priest as present at the

[2] PANTIN, W. A., The English Clergy in the Fourteenth Century, Oxford, 1955.

making of a parishioner's will. From 1522 every Yaxley will mentions a priest or priests, and from 1529 to 1548 we are on much firmer ground with an active (though apparently *illiteratus*) vicar and a succession of equally illiterate curates, some of whom were 'jobbers' round neighbouring parishes. After the dissolution of Thorney Abbey the benefice and rectory became Crown property until sold off by Charles I, and the Crown appointed a succession of vicars in rapid succession. None were resident until 1583 and the parish continued to be served, to all appearances, by jobbing illiterate curates. From 1583 to 1623 the parish enjoyed its very first, totally resident literate (only just) vicar, who was not licenced to preach. The value of the vicarage was then estimated at £11 gross, and the incumbent — a very popular man in the parish — was several times in arrears with his subsidy payments and complaining of dire poverty quite genuinely, as his will shows.[3]

Mrs. Bowker suggests that clerical educational standards and achievements were most probably rising slowly but steadily long before 1500 — but not fast enough to keep pace with the expectations of the Humanists or the standards of the better-educated clergy. It is possible (though we cannot prove it) that even though there was now a greater number of university places (or did the closure of the university halls temporarily *decrease* the supply of cheap places?) and grammar schools, in the rush to occupy them better-provided ordinands and lay boys elbowed out of the way poor ordinands, who may now relatively have had worse educational opportunities than in the early 15th century. If this were true, then a gap was opening between educational clerical 'possessioners' and 'have-nots' which could lead to bad blood and rancour. In such a situation the rather academic satire directed at 'superstition' and 'barbarism' by the Humanists might have appealed to the better-educated clerics for purely circumstantial reasons. Also by 1520 prices were some 50% higher than in 1495, and the weight of royal taxation of the clergy increasing. As in education, so in economics, it is possible that a wider gulf appeared between better-off and poor pastoral clergy. Rectors (generally university clerks) and some vicars (whose sources of income might include a piece of glebe and lesser tithes) may have been at least partially cushioned against the inflation, whereas the merely stipendiary priests were not. There are two particularly obscure points. The first concerns the very large number of ordinands who occur in ordination registers of this period as ordained to a vague title supplied by a religious house — with which they otherwise appear to have had no connection whatever. Possibly at least a third of benefices was appropriated to religious houses. Were these titles a mere legal formality for ordinands really ordained without jobs to go to?

---

[3] COXE, T., The Topographical, Ecclesiastical and Natural History of Huntingdonshire, London, 1700; His Majesty's Stationery Office, in: Calendars of Patent Rolls, London, 1906 ff. passim; Calendars of Papal Registers, London 1930 ff.; Calendars of Papal Letters, London 1945 ff. passim; Lincoln Record Society, Bishop Sutton's Register, IV, vol. 52, Lincoln, 1930; ibid., Lincolnshire Visitations, 1517–31, vol. 33, Lincoln, 1922; ibid., Bishop Cooper's Register, vol. 2, 1911; ibid., The State of the Church, vol. 23, 1920: Huntingdonshire County Record Office, Huntingdonshire Wills, vols. 6–15, passim.

Possibly a large number of the ordinands did begin by serving as (unrecorded) stipendiary curates on short contracts in monastic parishes. Possible some were *alumni* of grammar or petty schools maintained by religious houses — a subject on which we are very ill-informed. The second obscurity concerns clerical celibacy. Was it really a serious problem? University clerks, often long or always in minor Orders, could and did marry legitimately, or at least contract 'common law marriages' to avoid losing fellowships or creating a legal barrier to further advancement. The few surviving episcopal visitation records indicate that only a small percentage of pastoral priests were charged with 'moral' offences. Yet it was a commonplace of early Protestant polemic that fornication or 'common law' marriage was extremely common and winked at by the authorities largely for this reason (so, for instance, Hooper and Becon). More says expressly that the English clergy were more law-abiding in this matter than their Continental colleagues. The surviving wills of the clergy of this period reveal a scattering of illegitimate children (though we do not know when in their father's career they were conceived), but none in most cases. Medievalists show that Gregorian legislation on celibacy never had more than a limited success — though their examples are mostly drawn from the Continent or from university clerks. On the other hand historical demographers point out that the "European pattern of marriage" established in the later middle ages as a painful means of economic advance involved late marriage and the exaltation of celibacy even outside the priesthood and the cloister. When clerical marriage became legal in England, the rush into matrimony, especially amongst older priests (probably by then a higher proportion of the profession than had earlier been normal), was surprisingly moderate and gradual. Even extreme Protestants continued to regard clerical celibacy as "the better way."[4]

We might also speculate whether the pastoral clergy shared in some degree the 'crisis of identity' of the religious. They had been pushed along in the later middle ages by a strong current of 'secularisation', an increasing general standard of living and comfort, educational standard and administrative and economic sophistication. They had made piecemeal, *de facto* adaptations of their way of living, but perhaps never come to terms mentally with the pace and direction of the changes. Hence, while steadily moving in the direction of becoming *bourgeois*, they may have felt alienated from the primitive, severer, more ascetic and spiritually exalted clerical ideal of past ages. Hence, perhaps, may have come that 'earthiness' and yet inner discontent which some historians think they can detect in the early Tudor clergy, the results of a 'loss of identity' well-established before the cataclysms of 1534—59. But did the pre-Tridentine priest ever have a clear public 'image'? Was it not, indeed, a major difficulty for the clergy that, like the episcopate, they fulfilled a good many practical functions in society which, however, was heavily permeated by other religious influences, so that the clergy must have seemed only one strand in a complex weave?

[4] BOWKER, op.cit., pp. 136ff.; see IDEM, An Episcopal Court Book for the Diocese of Lincoln, 1514—20, Lincoln, 1967.

4. Religious involved in pastoral care

In this essay we are concerned with the 'secular Church', and so not directly with the religious Orders, another strand in the religious weave. But although tradition drew as firm a line between the secular clergy and religious as it did between clergy and laity, the two lines were equally blurred in practice: there was considerable interpenetration both ways across the lines. Unfortunately this topic still awaits its historian. It is largely omitted from consideration by Professor David Knowles' recent thorough study of Tudor religious. In the first place the religious state, though clearly within the narrowest sphere of ecclesiastical jurisdiction, was traditionally 'lay' in essence. But by the later middle ages it had become heavily 'clericalised'; lay brothers and nuns were relatively few. Perhaps over a third of the pastoral clergy were employees, directly and indirectly, of religious communities, a quarter of whose gross income was drawn from appropriated secular churches. A considerable amount of pastoral work was done by religious. The Canons regular served parishes; friars' churches commonly acted as preaching and confessional centres; even monks occasionally served churches and their churches pilgrims. Professor Dickens has unearthed the commonplace book of John Gysborn, a Premonstratensian Canon serving a Lincolnshire parish between 1520 and 1531. A sizeable proportion of cathedrals was served by monastic communities. Some of the bigger monasteries controlled archdeaconries and had monk-archdeacons. In 1500—1534 the religious supplied seven diocesan, and over thirty suffragan, bishops — indeed they seem to have provided most of the suffragans and so performed most episcopal liturgical functions. Religious had a sizeable stake in the universities, with their own *studia* and colleges there. At this period a few religious were even students at Inns of Court. On the other hand secular clergy and laity penetrated the world of the religious fairly extensively, as chantry priests in monastic churches and cathedrals, masters in almonry and grammar schools maintained by religious, choirmasters, choirmen and boys, organists, masters and students in religious university colleges (Cranmer taught in such a college at Cambridge for a time), curates of religious benefices, lodgers in religious houses or oblates or conventual servants. The secular clergy of ordinary cathedrals (resident prebendaries, vicars choral, chantry priests) and collegiate institutions, though canonically distinct from religious, in reality at this period lived under much the same rules and conditions. Historians of monasticism have been rather inclined to see this blurring of the line of distinction as a perversion of the purity of the religious life. Medievalists, on the contrary, have been inclined to stress its good effects. The clash of views was ancient amongst the religious themselves; it arose again during the Catholic Counter-Reformation, which, however, generally in practice continued the customary interpenetration of worlds. It is hard to see how things could be otherwise in a society constituted as it was[5].

---

[5] DICKENS, op. cit., pp. 16—20; PANTIN, W. A. and AVELING, H., eds., The Letter-Book of Robert Joseph of Evesham, Oxford Historical Society, New Series, vol. 19, Oxford,

In conclusion, we might be tempted to think of the English clergy of 1500—1534 that their basic trouble was their inability to adapt themselves positively and decisively to changes in society — the slow crumbling of a folk-religion of observances, based on a primitive social and economic order and minimal literacy, before the inroads of a new, more sophisticated and literate order. We might see modern parallels. But we may wonder whether the clerical dilemma then was different in kind (and not just in degree) from that of both Catholic and Protestant clergy between 1534 and the later 19th century.

III. 1534—1559: the impact of the Reformation on the clergy

There has been relatively little modern work on the clergy of these years: it has concentrated mainly on the political, administrative, liturgical and economic aspects of Church history, with a notable lack of interest in the Marian Catholic restoration. There certainly have been studies in detail of a number of small but prominent groupings of university clerks: the early Protestant divines and trans-lators of the Bible; the Henrician conservative bishops; the Humanists; the Marian exiles; the martyrologist Foxe and his associates; Reginald Pole and his circle at Padua and Rome. But, even when added together, these groups formed only a small minority of the university clerks, and a tiny proportion of the whole clergy — of whom only one group, the ex-religious, have received special attention.

1. The episcopate under stress

The episcopate clearly went through a traumatic quarter of a century. There were large-scale deprivations, and, apparently for political reasons, a quite unusual amount of translations from see to see: the total turnover of bishops was very high. There were repeated and short-lived changes in the legal status of the episcopate. In rapid succession they were removed from papal and legatine control and their ordinary jurisdiction subjected (apparently without legal limit) to the authority of statute law and also first of a Vicegerent in Spirituals and then the royal Council; then their old legal status was briefly abolished and replaced by a limited jurisdiction granted by letters patent (as if they were royal commissioners or civil servants); then they were returned to subjection to papal and legatine control, mixed oddly with statute and royal ecclesiastical commissions; in 1559 they were back under statute and the Council. Between 1547 and 1553 there was always a very real threat that episcopacy would either

1967; DICKENS, A. G., ed., Clifford Letters of the Sixteenth Century, Surtees Society, vol. 172, Durham, 1962; KNOWLES, D., The Religious Orders in England, III: The Tudor Age, Cambridge, 1959.

be radically refashioned or even abolished. Dioceses were split and new ones created by Henry VIII; under Northumberland some were abolished and others amalgamated. Episcopal revenues and estates took a severe beating. During these years of even intenser inflation, bishops' estates suffered wholesale disadvantageous 'exchanges' with Crown properties. In 1551−3 it was seriously proposed to take all their estates and, in return, make them royal stipendiaries. Also the frequent *interregna* of bishops meant that most of their estates were several times in the Crown's hands and duly mulcted. By 1554 all bishops were making ends meet by holding *in commendam* numerous canonries and even benefices. The canon law faculties at the universities were abolished and not restored, and down to 1554 the whole machinery of ecclesiastical courts was threatened with closure. Monastic communities and chantry priests were cleared out of cathedrals, as it turned out finally. Things could hardly have been more insecure for bishops and their staffs, and the end was not yet. In 1559−60 came by far the biggest crop of deprivations. We know that the episcopal order was going to survive. But that cannot have been evident to contemporaries, and the order was to remain more or less insecure down to the 1660s.

Yet, like the whole clerical order, the universities and schools, the episcopate survived the blast. It was shaken to its very foundations and left shaky there. The medieval Church had an unresolved dispute about the basis of episcopal jurisdiction: was ordinary jurisdiction *iure divino* and so in itself illimitable by the superior power of the Pope (albeit the bishops on such a view were still in general subject to the Pope, and their ordinary jurisdiction in practice much supplemented by delegated papal authority), or were bishops vicars of the Pope, and so their jurisdiction without any essential stability or shape? The dispute raged without theoretical issue throughout the sessions of the Council of Trent during these years. In the Church of England, as Gardiner pointed out in his 'De Vera Obedientia', the Crown took over Papal powers and championship of the second of the two views in dispute. It is true that there appears to have been no counterpart in England amongst divines and common lawyers of the Tridentine arguments and, in spite of Gardiner, a legal haze remained over the problem. Sometimes the Crown acted as if there was nothing sacred about episcopal ordinary jurisdiction; sometimes *de facto* it seemed to treat it as basically sacred. As for divines, none defended the *iure divino* theory in writing; yet also none, even most extreme Protestants, absolutely and explicitly denied it or asserted that the episcopate was merely an accident of history. In practice episcopacy survived extraordinarily intact, possibly because, with all its gross anomalies and pastoral inefficiency, it fitted like a glove the social, economic and administrative realities of the age, and anyway Tudor policy was always to retain old institutions and pile new duties on to them. The changes of legal status made little practical difference to the workings of the system, which was wedged into place in the national scene by a host of long-established arrangements. It is true that there was now some decline in the number of active or retired civil servants in the episcopate, and a notable increase in the number of university dons and ex-superiors of religious houses (no less than 33 appointments to diocesan bishoprics in 25 years for the latter.) But, as we have seen, active civil service bishops had never been very numerous on the bench, and the increasing frequency and importance of Parliaments and multiplication of royal commissions imposing jobs on bishops tended to make them more 'official' than ever. Moreover bishops were still mostly chosen for their administrative ability. The exceptions to this rule during this period were political choices made hurriedly to fit a change in government religious policy. Pending research into the subject, we may suspect that bishops now resided in their sees neither more nor less than before 1534. In spite of threats of extinction (and made all the more necessary by the unusually large number of episcopal *interregna*) the self-running legal episcopal administrations functioned much as usual. There may have been a shortage of trained canonists, but certainly at York the courts were not crippled, and made do with civilians and even vicars-choral. Suffragan bishops functioned as before. Only three bishops during these years — Holgate, Hooper and Latimer — seem to have attempted to give a 'new look' to administration and a directly personal touch. Their experiments were short-lived and superficial and it is notable that, in those years of fairly vigorous Convocation activity and frequent colloquies and theological committees, none of the three made use of diocesan councils of priests. Deaneries, prebends and arch-deaconries appear to have remained just as much the maintenance of absentee ambassadors, university dons, students and aristocratic pluralists (some still not in Orders.) The newly created ex-monastic secular cathedral Chapters appear to have conformed swiftly to the established pattern, usually with ex-religious as bishops, deans and resident prebendaries. Changes of official faith and cathedral liturgy tended to make astonishingly little difference to the character or personnel of the institutions. Thus at York Minster the Dean (1544—67) was a totally absentee clerical ambassador; the Chancellor (1537—61) was a resident theologian and administrator with two other prebends elsewhere in England; the Precentor was an aristocratic canonist who combined the post of diocesan 'official' to the Protestant Archbishop Holgate and the Catholic Heath with constant service as Vice-President of the Council of the North; the Subdean (1548—70) was an aristocratic resident theologian administrator; the Succentor (1546—60) an ex-superior of a religious house; the Archdeacon of York (1536—60) an aristocratic lawyer with six benefices in plurality; the Archdeacon of Cleveland (1547—65) a physician, Warden of All Souls, Oxford and also Dean of Winchester in plurality, probably not in major Orders; the Arch-deacon of Nottingham (at York 1538—1560) another ex-religious superior and suffragan bishop actively deputising for Archbishops Lee, Holgate and Heath in steady succession. At York the college of chantry priests in the Minster was dissolved with a minimum of disturbance of its members: some were already also vicars choral; others soon became vicars choral or acquired curacies in York. John Thorne, the Minster organist and choirmaster from 1541 to 1573 without break, was certainly a university clerk famed as a logician, and so probably a part-time tutor to university entrants. He functioned as an organist under Archbishops Lee, Holgate, Heath and Young, occupied a prebendal house, farmed prebendal properties, and, during the period when Holgate silenced the Minster organ, held an office concerned with the cathedral fabric.

Wherever we look in the ecclesiastical establishment at the Minster — major offices, minor liturgical offices, court officials, schoolmasters (both the Protestant Holgate and the Catholic Heath refounded Minster schools) — we get a strong impression of a complex practical system, rooted in property rights, so tenacious as to find ways of surviving any sort of cataclysm. Bishops' estates and households have been little studied at this (or any) period. But we may reasonably guess that the same tenacity applied here. In some cases the royal 'exchanges' of lands may only have meant the loss by the see of lands which, in the customary fashion of bishops, were always on long leases at very low rents and high entry fines, and which may have been less valuable in the long run in an age of inflation than the impropriated rectories and tithes gained from the Crown in compensation. In Edward VI's reign married bishops appeared on the scene so briefly that it is very doubtful whether the fact made any significant impact. Nepotism, an undoubted consequence of episcopal marriage, was, after all, well-known amongst high ecclesiastics long before 1534.[6]

2. 'University clerks', the crisis of the universities, and clerical parties

There is little sign that university clerks came to bulk less in the ecclesiastical scene, or that they became, to any notable extent, detached from their monopolistic hold on the most lucrative Church jobs. The revolutionary changes were obviously liable to disturb them almost as much as bishops: there is evidence that numerous individuals were disturbed, but most of them eventually resumed their places on the ladder of promotion, and their system and manner of life remained unchanged. Long before 1534 they must have been well accustomed to "crosses to the main chance" — hot competition for office frequently produced rival claimants and lawsuits which could go amiss; a new bishop, a new head of a college, a change of patrons could lead to the loss of jobs to make way for favourites and relations; anyway the climb of the ladder of a clerical career inevitably meant swapping jobs. The lists of known deprivees and exiles amongst university clerks in three waves (the 1530s, 1554 and 1559 onwards) is impressive — thus, for example, in 1554 44 fellows of Cambridge colleges were deprived and went abroad, and 46 other graduates; St. John's College alone lost over 20 fellows by deprivation, and 9 of them went overseas. But to keep the picture in proportion we need to remember that those deprived were only a small fraction of the whole class of university clerks, that their jobs were rapidly filled, and that the great majority of the deprived were far from inactive or starving thereafter and back safely and profitably on the ladder of preferment a few years later. Some of the extruded, like the dispossessed religious, had property rights to pensions; others retained prebends or benefices originally held in plurality with their lost offices. If they went abroad they were

---

[6] DICKENS, op. cit., passim; on York Minster see AVELING, J. C. H., Catholic Recusancy in the City of York, 1558—1791, Appendix II: The Early Elizabethan Ecclesiastical Establishment at York, London, 1970, pp. 293—327.

treading a familiar and well-beaten academic road, and the ablest could hope to get studentships or teaching posts in foreign universities; Catholics could get benefices, and Protestants chaplaincies and tutorships to English mercantile or exile communities. Padua, a centre for English Catholic exiles in Henry VIII's reign, and always (as the best medical school in Europe) a draw for English medical students, became a home for Protestant Marian exiles. Some of them profited by the chance to read for a medical degree. If the extruded stayed in England and had no benefices, they could (like Thomas Cartwright) fill in the time usefully by reading for the Bar at an Inn of Court, or (like Becon) take a tutorship in the country. Private chaplaincies and tutorships then formed an extremely important set of aids to success in a clerical career, neglected by very few of the able and successful clerics of the century.[7]

The universities were certainly going through a disturbed period, though, due to scarcity of records, it is difficult to see much more than the outlines of the crisis. In part it had roots far back into the 14th century in a process of slow and sometimes painful adaptation to social, economic and ideological changes in society at large. These, and later, changes were perhaps made all the more crucial for university clerks because England did not share in the European university-foundation movement of the later middle ages, and university openings were still restricted to Oxford and Cambridge. By 1500 the many private halls or hospices were fast closing, and their places being supplied (perhaps too slowly) by the foundation of much more regimented colleges; the regency system of teaching was collapsing and being replaced by college lecturing. Humanism, with its fairly revolutionary educational theories, was gaining *droit de cité* alongside the old syllabus and teaching organisation. Between 1500 and 1534 the process advanced further, and lay students began to arrive. One overall effect of these changes was perhaps much hotter competition for university studentships and fellowships, and increasing difficulties for poor clerical students. Inflation added to the difficulties. Then, starting with Cromwell's university Injunctions of 1535 came government planning, inspired partly by Humanist theories, partly by Protestant idealism, and perhaps mostly by hard-headed administrative interest. The dissolution of religious houses and chantries, the consequent dissolution of monastic *studia* and colleges, the threat to academic institutions based on chantry endowments, the disturbance in bene-fice patronage — on which so many students depended for financial support — then made the enduring crisis really severe. Indeed it may well have threatened the universities with ruin. The State interfered again with new Statutes in 1549 and 1555, ostensibly to try to stabilise, and enforce standards on, the shaken and rather fluid teaching organisation and syllabus, to encourage first Protestant then Catholic divinity studies, and to rescue smaller colleges, teachers and

[7] On exiles see: PORTER, H. C., Reformation and Reaction in Tudor Cambridge, Cambridge, 1958; SCHILLINGS, A., Matricule de l'Université de Louvain, vol. 4: 1528—69, Louvain, 1934; FENLON, D., Heresy and Obedience in Tridentine Italy: Cardinal Pole and the Counter-Reformation, Cambridge, 1972; GARRETT, C. H., The Marian Exiles, Cambridge, 1938; CLEBSCH, W. A., England's Earliest Protestants, 1520—35, Yale, 1964.

students in financial difficulties. The flow of lay students smartly increased, and by 1560 could be called a flood. Monastic colleges were rescued and refounded by the Crown and property speculators who had made money out of the inflation — which was now spiralling. By 1547—9 expert witnesses could draw very different conclusions from the state of the universities. One judged that they had never been so affluent and thronged. Another, more discerning, judged them to be near ruin, crowded with the lay sons of the gentry who pushed worthy poor clerical students out of college places and accommodation, drove up the cost of living in the town, and captured the market in available teachers by drawing them from small classes and starvation stipends in official faculty or college lectureships to lucrative extra-curricular tutorships which proliferated, even to the point of the refoundation of small tutorial establishments. In 1549 Latimer echoed this condemnation, and reported that many good clerical bachelors were forced by economic and institutional pressures — as well as sometimes religious persecution — to quit the universities early. For lack of divinity students sure that they could stay the course, the divinity faculty was declining. If things went much further this way, it would perish, and only "a little English divinity" for lay and clerical Arts students would be left, and that extra-curricular.[8]

From such evidence we can dimly perceive the universities' 'crisis of adaptation'. That they survived and that the crisis was more or less successfully surmounted after 1560 was remarkable. In organisation and administration the adaptation retained the traditional pattern while incorporating large new features into it. Like the episcopate, universities remained basically self-operating ecclesiastical jurisdictions. Also like the episcopate they had now to accept powerful Crown control which had an ambiguity about it. It might mean that university self-government and liberty depended merely on royal grace and could at any time be radically set aside and the institution transformed; or it could mean the Crown recognised an almost *iure divino* freedom of universities as pillars of Church and Commonwealth. At times during 1534—1559 the Crown behaved as if the first view were true, more often as if it accepted tacitly the second. The ambiguity lasted on after 1560 and cast a veil of doubt over university arrangements; dissidents could always appeal to secular authority. Moreover the secular functions of the universities as educators of a lay clericature were now greatly increasing. An ambiguity hung over this feature also, as Latimer saw. Would the universities become progressively secularised, or would university and clerical tradition and the general permeation of society by religious forces roll back the tide and secure the future of the universities as ecclesiastical bodies and of their lay education as basically clerical? Latimer believed that extra strong help was needed from clerical pressure groups. As for discipline, the rise of large colleges with a tightly paternalistic structure and the new power of the informal council of Heads of Houses in concert with a

---

[8] PANTIN, W. A., The Conception of the Universities in England in the Period of the Renaissance, in: Les Universités Européennes du XIVe au XVIIIe Siècle, Aspects et Problèmes, Actes du Colloque International à l'Occasion du VIe Centenaire de l'Université Jagellone de Cracovie, 1964, Geneva, 1967, pp. 60 ff.; SIMON and CHARLTON, op. cit.

Chancellor (usually with Cabinet rank) pretty exactly replaced the old medieval Chancellor and Council of Regent Masters; the 'democracy' and rebelliousness of younger college fellows and lay student fellow-commoners and pensioners replaced the ancient turbulence of young regent masters and the mob of clerical students in halls or lodgings. The lay-out was new, but the situation as always. Problems of supply of students were solved by circumstances and the pressing of new methods to old uses. The old system of maintaining clerical students, graduates or not, out of benefices must have fallen into decay. The distinction at canon law between clerical and lay students made by tonsure and minor Orders must have remained, since it was only disused in 1550—3, but, as we shall see, there were very few ordinations between 1535 and 1560 and benefices seem to have been in short supply, and there are signs that authority was setting its face against the holding of benefices by students and fellows except in cases where exceptional influence could be brought to bear. (Dr. John Clement's son was, as a university student, specially licenced by Queen Mary to hold a York prebend.) A new system of sizarships, bursaries and scholarships began to grow up. It had always existed in a shadowy and unofficial way: now it became official and vital. As far as poor clerical students were concerned the new system, precarious and unsatisfactory as it often was, could hardly have been a harder bandwaggon to climb on than the old system.[9]

There remains the difficult, technical problem of the adaptation of the curriculum and teaching methods. It is now often presumed that 'scholasticism' died in the universities by 1535 of its own long-standing ailments, of the onset of Humanism, and of a *coup-de-grâce* administered by Cromwell's Injunctions. It is also presumed that a Humanistic, non-metaphysical course prevailed through a Ramist fashion in the 1570s until the last decades of the century when, rather like bastard feudalism, 'scholasticism' had a sinister resurrection. The theory holds water provided that we take 'scholasticism' in a very narrow sense indeed which is hardly the usually accepted one. The old 'scholasticism' was one in which the Arts course (and therefore higher studies) were dominated by the study of logic and 'philosophy'. 'Grammar' (the Latin language and authors) was largely confined to pre-university studies, only dealt with nominally at university, and rigidly treated as a preliminary to logic. 'Philosophy' was the reading of standard medieval texts: it would probably be true to say that these were eclectic, drawing matter from Seneca, St. Augustine, the Thomists, Scotists and Nominalists, and that although a student would get an easy familiarity with metaphysics, the treatise on logic would still dominate the treatment by texts and the masters. The holes and corners of the Arts course were filled with subsidiary subjects: arithmetic, geometry, cosmography, astronomy and perhaps even music, all dealt with in a peculiar way which owed everything to early medieval tradition. The theology course by tradition had the Bible as its basic text, with lectures on its books; the treatment was generally

[9] CURTIS, M. H., Oxford and Cambridge in Transition, 1558—1642, Oxford, 1959; KEARNEY, H. F., Scholars and Gentlemen: Universities and Society, 1500—1700, London, 1970.

more or less by logical analysis and exposition of traditional doctrinal interpretations from *catenae* of Patristic texts. But much more energy and time were spent on the public reading and commenting of a standard, systematic exposition of theology – Peter Lombard, Thomas Aquinas, Scotus or Biel. Teaching in both courses would generally proceed by the giving out of dictated summaries ('dictates'), then explained and learned by the students for 'repetition'; the matter was then driven home by formal disputations of set theses, which could be highly competitive[10].

We have the detailed injunctions to the universities of 1535, 1549 and 1555 and a number of new college statutes. It is not easy to piece together from these how the new curricula differed from the old – especially since we have little guarantee that they were exactly followed in practice. The impression we get is that the new Arts course had precisely the same structure as its predecessor. Grammar was totally banished, since it was presumed that no student could now attempt the Arts course unless he had a pre-university thorough grounding in Ciceronian Latin. It is likely that extra-curricular short courses of grammar existed, and that a proportion of lay students got stuck there and never even matriculated in Arts. The logic section still held pride of place, though its 'flavour' must have been greatly changed by the use of totally new, Humanistic texts, with large doses of Aristotle in new translations from Greek, and a great deal of linguistic analysis of Cicero's orations. 'Philosophy' also had entirely new, Humanistic texts, mostly eclectic ones based on Aristotle and Plato. The customary subsidiary subjects remained, but with a 'new Humanistic look' in the texts. In the divinity course the old structure was retained. The Biblical lectures were given a lion's share of the available time, and the treatment presumed to be of a far higher standard of linguistic scholarship and mastery of the Patristic sources in new, full texts. The systematic theological lectures would doubtless, if officially Protestant, use Melancthon's 'Loci Communes' or something similar, or if officially Catholic, Aquinas, Lombard or Cano. It was now presumed that students of Arts and Divinity knew enough Greek to cope with Greek texts and references, and courses in Greek were laid on – but it is not clear how seriously this condition was ever pressed. Teaching methods throughout the courses were still by 'lectures' with 'dictates' and repetition and disputations.

It would require immensely close and expert examination of all this to determine exactly the real effects of the changes. We could imagine that academics bred under the old system were intensely shocked by the Latin style, tone, and demise of cherished texts. However the old system had never been changeless, Humanism had slipped into the universities slowly over many years past, and there is slight evidence of any academic battles over its rise in England. As for the Humanists, there is just as little evidence that they trumpeted their victory. The popular opinion – mostly amongst *illiterati* – that 'the new learning' was a fair omnibus term since Humanism and Protestantism were two sides of the same coin was only partly true. Hooper probably spoke for most academic Protestants

---

[10] KEARNEY, op. cit.

when, as a considerable adept of the new academic style, he both praised it as the historical midwife of the Gospel and for its clarity, *elegantia* and accurate handling of Scripture, and yet condemned it for 'latinae orationis pompam, fucum et calamistra'. Historians will marvel at the conservatism of the academic revolutionaries. The components of the new style were, like Thomism, Scotism and Nominalism before them, born in a medieval setting; old habits of mind and approach easily modified new ideas in execution, and the mental limitations of students and masters all down the history of education have speedily falsified the idealism of innovators. It is notable that at least three accomplished 'scholastic' divines, Thomas Cartwright, John Whitgift and Thomas Stapleton, were trained in the Edwardine universities under the new system, and their 'scholasticism' long preceded the supposed 'resurrection of scholasticism' in the last years of the century. It would also be unwise to make hasty judgments about university divinity in 1534–59 from the (apparently accidental) extreme shortage of surviving Latin academic texts and 'dictates', and the dominance of 'English divinity' (aimed at the educated layman and *illiteratus* clerks) in the printers' lists. [11]

It is a commonplace that English university clerks reacted sluggishly to the doctrinal crisis of these years. We should have expected them to play a leading part in the debate, the 'possessioner' divines (heads of houses, faculties, bishops) to defend the established order, the younger divines (regent masters reading for B. D., bachelors, younger college fellows) to champion extremer courses. On the whole it is surprising how *piano* the reaction of even these groups were in the 1520s and 1530s. The Establishment divines appear to have produced little anti-Lutheran literature or judgments; there was no English Sorbonne or Louvain. On the other hand Cambridge, even in 1550–3, never became remotely another Wittenburg. The first generation of English Protestant divines was a very small group, containing men of real ability but no leading theologian (not even of the academic stature of Wycliffe) or potential intellectual leader. It is significant that, as the movement began to gain wider support amongst young fellows and masters, they perforce had to idolise men who sometimes had charm and great mental vigour (like Latimer and Hooper) but never consummate creative minds. We get very dim glimpses of the rise of an anti-Protestant group of young academics, probably associated with Worcestershire and Winchester (Richard Smith, John Howman als. Feckenham, the Harpsfields, Thomas Watson, John Morwen, Thomas Stapleton, Richard Pates, John Sapcot – under the patronage of the conservative bishops, Gardiner, Bonner and Heath). Though Smith and Stapleton were, later in life, to become considerable Catholic academics on the Continent, there were no really outstanding theologians in the group. From 1534 official pressures on the debate, by censorship, the Oaths of Succession and Supremacy, the statute of the Six Articles, and, eventually, the demand to accept the new English liturgy and ordinal multiplied. But it was remarkable that, apart from the oaths, there was still, in 1553, no new, compulsory formulary of faith

---

[11] Later Writings of Bishop Hooper, Parker Society, Cambridge, 1852, pp. 382 ff.

or religious test for academics and incumbents. A good many, even of the 'Catholic' group, remained in their ecclesiastical posts steadily throughout these years, and even on through Edward VI's reign. In 1547–50 the bishops of the Catholic group were deprived of office. This was not for rejection of any Protestant formulary of faith, since there was none with statutory authority by 1553, but for suspicion of treason or refusal to enforce the new Ordinal in their dioceses. The university clerks of the group, as prebendaries, absentee incumbents, or academics seem to have been untroubled: since they usually had no direct parish responsibility they would be untouched by the enforcement of the Prayer Book, and as absentees by the purely local diocesan injunctions and formularies of faith of the few Protestant bishops who attempted such intensive action. When Hooper did attempt to pin down two 'Catholic' canons in his diocese, Johnson and Joliffe, they evaded his efforts by claiming that he lacked authority. The attitude of the Catholic group during this period was apparently declared by Gardiner and Bonner, who made no effort to flee abroad, but stoutly insisted that their deprivations were illegal so long as Edward VI was a minor. Relatively few of the group did take refuge abroad. In Mary's reign it was the turn of the Protestants to face stress. Few of them dared to maintain that Mary had no right to the throne, or to engage in armed rebellion. From 1554, unlike the Catholics in 1547–53, they had to face a statutorily based imposition of formularies, and the resurrection of the old heresy laws. Deprivation made very heavy inroads indeed into their ranks and quite large-scale emigration. But still a fair number of the group, though deprived, managed to live unmolested in England. The Marian persecution fell heavily on the leaders of the group, and on extremists amongst the laity; but no persevering effort seems to have been made against the clerical rank and file if they lived quietly after deprivation. In any case the Catholic group was even smaller, and less equipped with ability, than the Protestants, and the Marian government was quite unable to staff the chief places in the Church solidly with them. It appears that, by 1558, the Catholics had been able to gain an increasing – but still definitely minority – following amongst junior university clerks.

Hence in 1558–9 there was a clear impression of *déjà vu* about the situation of Elizabeth's officially Catholic government. The Protestant group, facing its second triumph, and now overwhelmingly a second-generation party, was still a relatively small minority of university clerks. It was also sharply divided on doctrinal issues. For political and prudential reasons the government was bound – like their Edwardine and Marian precedessors – to hope that the number of necessary deprivations of their opponents would be relatively limited. In any case, also like their predecessors, they would have to rely heavily on university clerks who did not belong really to either group. These clerks had, ever since 1534, been in a large majority in their class. We know far less about them than we do of the Catholics and Protestants – though they made up quite half of Elizabeth's episcopal appointments in 1559–60. It is obviously important that we should find out more about them, because of their numerical importance, and because they are the key to the explanation of the sluggish reaction of their class to the Reformation. But perhaps also the mentality of these 'middlemen' may be the key to some puzzling features of the behaviour and mental processes of the Catholics and Protestants.[12]

There is evidence of a good deal of genuine hesitation and variation of opinion, even within the bounds of the definite religious groups. Thomas Stapleton went up to New College, Oxford from the very conservative atmosphere of Winchester in Edward VI's reign, into the full impact of the academic revolution, and accepted a fellowship shortly before the end of the reign. He remained an Oxford divine throughout Mary's reign, becoming a prebendary (absentee) of Chichester in 1558. In 1559 he went to Louvain university, but retained his prebend for some years, revisited England and (apparently) hesitated before committing himself to permanent exile. Richard Smith was a prominent Humanist and Henrician divine. In 1537, as Master of Whittington College, he contributed to the making of 'The Institution of a Christian Man' and was Regius Professor of Divinity at Oxford. In 1547 he published a defence of transubstantiation, repudiated it under pressure in 1549, and then went to Louvain to teach theology. He returned to academic preferment in England in Mary's reign, and then back to Louvain to teach in 1560. Henry Cole was probably the ablest mind in the 'Catholic' group. He was a fellow of New College, Oxford from 1521 to 1540, though he had sabbatical leave to continue his civil law studies at Padua and Paris between 1530 and 1539. Then he returned to Oxford and acquired in rapid succession a doctorate of law, two prebends and the Wardenship of New College. He appears to have practiced as an advocate in the Court of the Arches, managed his college and read theology for a B.D. simultaneously. In Edward VI's reign he showed clear signs of hesitation: first he became friendly with Peter Martyr and accepted the government religious policy of 1549, then he resigned his Wardenship in 1551 and accepted the Catholic restoration of 1554 vigorously — he was Pole's vicar-general, Provost of Eton, Dean of St. Paul's and archdeacon of Ely. Though he stuck to his Catholicism in 1559 and endured imprisonment and deprivation, there is evidence that thereafter he was no ultramontane. The pamphlets which passed backwards and forwards between England and Louvain during the Jewel-Harding controversy in the 1560s reveal first-hand evidence of Cole's earlier doubts and equally those of both Jewel and Harding. Both men had lived together at school and at Oxford; both were absentee academic prebendaries of Salisbury, both were convinced Henricians, and then, after 1547, passed over to Protestantism — Jewel with more hesitation than Harding. Then Jewel came closely under the influence of Peter Martyr and was a leading young Protestant divine in 1554. Yet he then recanted most of his Protestantism, hesitated again and fled abroad to return in 1559 as a trusted Protestant destined for the episcopate. Harding's evidence (perhaps onesided) is that the two men met at Salisbury in 1559 and Jewel professed that he could not accept a Royal Supremacy: yet in a few years time he was a moderate. For his part, Harding admitted his own staunch Protestantism in Edward VI's reign, and wrote that he only made a Catholic subscription in 1553 after hesitation, swayed ultimately by the thought that

---

[12] HAUGAARD, W. P., Elizabeth and the English Reformation, Cambridge, 1968; PORTER, op. cit.

Edward VI's death must be a sign from Providence. Thereafter he went on to be a strong ultramontane Catholic and Louvain apologist. Nicholas Sander belonged to the same Winchester and New College background as so many of these 'Catholics'. Yet he accepted a fellowship in 1548 and remained at Oxford through the rest of Edward VI's reign and Mary's, teaching law. He left for Rome in 1560, and a long career as a virulent ultramontane apologist.[13]

There is fairly conclusive evidence that other prominent 'Catholics' — like the two Harpsfield brothers, abbot John Feckenham, Thomas Watson, bishop Pursglove and Alban Langdale remained basically 'Henrician' from 1534 to their deaths in the 1580s, though their attitudes to Edwardine Protestantism ranged from outright rejection to quite thorough-going episcopal cooperation. Their Catholicism was humanist, 'Conciliarist', and they saw little attraction in a life of exile or in totally aggressive polemical recusancy.[14]

On the Protestant group's side the evidences of doubts and variations certainly exist and our impression that they were distinctly less than amongst the 'Catholics' probably stems from the degree to which we have to depend on devoutly Protestant martyrologists. We have seen the cases of Jewel and Harding. Three Protestant bishops, Shaxton, Bird and Holgate, eventually recanted and cooperated with Marian Catholicism. Holgate had, all along, been a doctrinal moderate. Of Elizabeth's 25 appointments to the episcopal bench in 1559—60 four had received ecclesiastical preferment in Mary's reign, and a fifth, Scory, had then done penance for his marriage and been restored to priestly functions as a Catholic — before quitting England to join the Marian Protestant exiles. Winchester and New College had their Protestants, John Lowth, one of them and a protegé of the Marian Protestant martyr Winchester archdeacon, John Philpot, was an 'artist' fellow of New College to 1545, and then migrated to Cambridge and, during Mary's reign, retained two benefices and took a degree in civil law. Later he tried to persuade Foxe to include a highly-coloured story of his sufferings for Protestantism in the 'Acts and Monuments'.[15]

Information about genuine 'middlemen' amongst the university clerks is very scanty indeed. There are the cases of two Elizabethan bishops of 1559, both pillars of Anglo-Catholic legend. Richard Cheyney is celebrated because he was a

---

[13] RICHARDS, M., Thomas Stapleton, Journal of Ecclesiastical History, vol. 18, 1967, pp. 187—199; O'CONNELL, M. R., Thomas Stapleton and the Counter-Reformation, Yale, 1964; on Richard Smith, see SCHILLINGS, op. cit., passim; SOUTHERN, A. C., Elizabethan Recusant Prose, 1559—82, London, 1950; LECHAT, R., Refugiés Anglais dans les Pays Bas, 1558—1603, Louvain, 1914. On Cole: SOUTHERN, op.cit. On Jewel and Harding: BOOTY, J. E., John Jewel as an Apologist of the Church of England, London, 1963. On Sander: VEECH, T. M., Dr. Nicholas Sanders and the English Reformation, Louvain, 1935.

[14] GOLDAST, M., Monarchiae S. Romani Imperii, Cologne, 1613, vol. iii, p. 66; AVELING, H., John Howman als. Feckenham, in: Dictionnaire d'Histoire et de Géographie Ecclési-astiques, vol. 16, Paris, 1967, col. 803—809; MEREDITH, R., The Eyres of Hassop, 1470—1640, Derbyshire Archaeological Journal, vol. 85, 1965, pp. 52—54 (on Pursglove); SOUTHERN, op. cit.

[15] DICKENS, A. G., Robert Holgate, St. Anthony's Hall Publications, vol. 8, York, 1955; HAUGAARD, op. cit.

Cambridge academic protegé of the Catholic leader Heath, beneficed throughout Edward VI's reign and Mary's, refusing in 1553 to accept transubstantiation and yet confirmed in his archdeaconry by the Catholic authorities (Hereford diocese) after a profession of near-Lutheran views on the eucharist; an Elizabethan diocesan bishop who refused to subscribe to the sacramental and eucharistic sections of the 39 Articles in 1563 because he held more right-wing views; an anti-Calvinist and patron of the young Edmund Campion. We know relatively little about him and there are considerable gaps in his record. He certainly was a Humanist and competent in both Patristic and scholastic theology. We do not know how he occupied his time between 1540 (when he graduated B.D.) and 1559: there seems to be no record of a continuing academic career of any distinction, yet he was clearly set forward by the Protestant party in Canterbury Convocation in 1553, and as a candidate for the episcopate in 1559, largely because of a reputation for great learning. Edmund Guest was an Edwardine academic of equally mysterious distinction. He apparently lived in retirement in Mary's reign. As an Elizabethan bishop he was Cheyney's ally against the Calvinists. Then there are cases like that of John Rokeby, the very active Chancellor of the diocese of York from the 1530s to his death in 1570, serving Lee, Holgate, Heath and Young as Archbishops with equal devotion and expertise. He was a civilian who served as Henry VIII's counsel at the Blackfriars divorce suit. He had a wide reputation as an honest man. Such evidence of him as we have makes it hard to see him as merely a time-server. He had both Protestant and Catholic connections. Such cases, together with material from the papers of Archbishops Cranmer and Matthew Parker, have often been used to buttress a theory that there was a strong native English current of academic 'dissent' — Conciliarist or even anti-Papal, symbolist and 'occasional' in its sacramental and eucharistic theology. The theory is that this current provided the real intellectual stimulus and basis for the ideas of men who were also incidentally to some degree attracted, and affected, by Humanist and Protestant influences. Hence (if this be true) the English academic field from the 1520s was dominated by a 'central', 'reformist' and moderate temper, liable to reject alike extreme evangelical Protestantism and ultramontane, extreme conservative Catholicism. We should thus account for the moderation and hesitations of the majority of university clerks, for their acceptance, to a degree, of early Edwardine Protestantism, their rejection of its later extremism, their acceptance of the Marian restored Catholicism in expectation of reform, their doubts about its actualities, and their provisional acceptance of the Elizabethan settlement but not Calvinism.

This is an attractive theory. Modern research has cast much doubt on the idea that medieval academic theology was a monolithic system built on a 'golden tradition' of Thomistic Realism, sapped away in the later middle ages by totally sceptical and fideist Nominalism, and by anti-scholastic and anti-metaphysical Humanism. We are now content to see the medieval theological scene as far more complex, shifting and full of eclecticism, and with, so as to speak, an inbuilt current of 'dissent' which was at once radical and yet conservative. This research is clearing the way for what must inevitably be a very long-term, technical and cooperative new study of 16th century theology set firmly on its true medieval background. Such a study will need a developed discipline of textual criticism and analysis, a 'diplomatic' of a kind which medievalists have long had, but which historians of the 16th century have been slow to approach. It is only in this way that we can hope to solve the problems underlying 16th century theological texts. For example: to what extent are Cranmer's writings his own or part of that 'committee theology' so common in the 16th century? To what extent was his thinking a slow, cautious lowering of conservative and scholarly defences before a flood of Continental 'instant gospelling', or an eclectic and highly individual creation, drawing alike on an English medieval theological tradition, on Humanism, on his own Patristic studies, and on many varieties of Continental Protestant thinking? A clever and determined Protestant like Hooper habitually omits reference to contemporary Protestant writings, and sets out his polemics in three parallel sections (in descending order of importance), Scriptural proofs, Patristic proofs, 'dialectical' arguments — the last overtly *ad hominem* for Catholic opponents. This arrangement was already becoming standard amongst Catholics and Protestants as the three theologies, Scriptural, 'positive', and scholastic were born. Did Hooper simply lift the framework and arguments wholesale from some Continental textbook — say Melancthon's 'Loci Communes Theologorum'; or was the whole exercise an academic formality in the current fashion? Was he a formalist, or was he stating in formal terms trains of his own independent thought — and if so, was Scriptural theology the basis of his thinking? The case for a 'central' or 'reformist' English current of thought hangs on the solution of such problems, and on the discovery of a great many more 'dictates' and theological texts, especially from the lesser figures amongst the English university clerks.[16]

3. The pastoral clergy

a) Decline in numbers?

When we move over to consider the great mass of the 'pastoral clergy' of 1534—1559, we must first look at the problem of numbers. For reasons not yet fully investigated, the numbers of men ordained in the country at large declined very sharply and suddenly from 1535 and only began to pick up again in the 1560s and 1570s. No doubt this was due in part to the contemporary sharp declines in the numbers of pastoral posts available and to sharp increases in the numbers of priests in the clerical labour-market. The dissolution of the religious houses from 1536 threw some thousands of their priests into the market with 'capacities' to hold benefices, chantries or curacies. Up to the dissolution also many secular clergy were ordained to titles (apparently promised stipendiary

---

[16] On Cheyney: HAUGAARD, op. cit.; Dictionary of National Biography, Oxford, 1948, p. 234. On Rokeby: DICKENS, A. G., The Marian Reaction in the Diocese of York, Pt. 1: The Clergy, York, 1957, pp. 6—7; BROOKS, P., Thomas Cranmer's Doctrine of the Eucharist, London, 1965; compare DUGMORE, C. W., The Mass and the English Reformers, London-New York, 1958.

curacies) supplied by religious houses, and a good many of those ordained to minor Orders were 'presented' by religious houses. The dissolution put an end to this, and perhaps the new owners of ex-monastic cures (the Crown, landowners, bishops) now deliberately and systematically refused to grant 'titles' wholesale — it may be for economic or 'reformist' reasons. (There seem to be no evidences of express injunctions ordering such a restriction.) The university clerks amongst religious appear generally to have obtained benefices and preferment readily, or, if old, to have lived on their fairly substantial pensions. But the rank and file ex-religious priests appear to have had difficulty in finding employment. This can be inferred, but not proved, from Court of Augmentations pensions records, from the relatively scanty diocesan records of curacies, from clerical wills, and from occasional evidence that, immediately before the dissolution, some superiors took care to place a few of their subjects in cures belonging to the houses, and that some university clerk ex-religious with benefices habitually employed their rank and file fellows as curates. It is not easy to estimate how far the deficiencies of training for ordination within religious houses handicapped this rank and file for pastoral jobs. After 1547 the dissolution of the chantries removed many posts and unloaded a further sizeable body of priests (perhaps some 2000) on to the labour market. Admittedly ex-chantry priests were normally pensioned off, though their pensions, like those of ex-religious, were subject to inflation and taxation. A good many of them had combined service of a chantry with (ostensibly officially unpaid) parochial work as curates. This work was now no longer available to most of them — unless they chose to do it without payment — since private Masses and Mass stipends now ceased (though they were revived in 1553—8).[17]

No doubt there were other general reasons for the shortage of ordinands. The insecurity of most ecclesiastical institutions and the disarray of, and shortage of places at, schools and universities possibly discouraged applicants for ordination. Religious reasons must also have played a part. There was a very noticeable slowness amongst university clerks to take more than minor Orders, or, when they ceased (1550—3), to be ordained to the diaconate.

It is generally said that this radical and startlingly rapid reduction in clerical jobs and personnel was inevitable in a changeover from a traditional Catholic order to a Protestant one, and that in any case the old order had (probably because of the shortage of secular jobs in the slowly increasing population of the pre-industrial England of 1400—1534) far too many clerics for its real needs. Thus, on these grounds alone, the reduction would be healthy, if painful for the clergy. It is usual to cite Thomas More's saying that fewer and better priests were needed, or the Council of Trent's stricture on the 'unbridled flood' of ordinations. But More was only making a very general, spiritual judgment, and

---

[17] KNOWLES, op. cit., p. 409; for the decline in ordinations from 1535 see: Borthwick Institute, York, Registers Lee, Holgate, Heath and Sede Vacante (York diocese); ROPER, M., The Secular Clergy of the Diocese of Lincoln, Oxford B. Litt. thesis, 1962; BARRATT, D. M., The Condition of the Parochial Clergy from the Reformation to 1660 with Special Reference to the Dioceses of Oxford, Worcester and Gloucester, Oxford Ph. D. thesis, 1953.

the fathers of Trent were thinking mainly of the lack of effective ordination examinations. We do not know, and probably never will, whether there was really a surplus of clergy to needs in 1500–1534. It may well be that, amongst the secular clergy, as certainly was true amongst religious, numbers were at a relatively high peak in the early 14th century, dropped very heavily thereafter (as did the population as a whole), and then picked up slowly throughout the 15th and first decades of the 16th, but by 1534 stood well below the peak level of 1320–30. To what extent, before 1535, did the insistence of the canons on titles or a proved patrimony as a condition for ordination to major Orders really act as an effective tieing of supply to demand? There was certainly then a 'pool of labour' of jobbing Mass-priests. But we know little of its real size. Its existence (and continued existence under Protestantism) was a necessary corollary of the benefice and plurality system and served a real need. An artificial bottleneck in clerical preferment, with a consequent artificial surplus of junior or less socially-privileged clergy, has been a pretty constant feature of Church history, and even exists to some extent today alike in Catholic Eire and the Church of England. As for the argument that in medieval society men had special economic reasons for seeking ordination, it is hard to see that these suddenly ceased to be operative around 1535. The 'proletarian' pastoral clergy of 1535–59 were most likely often economically depressed, but probably not more so than wide classes of the laity. In the 1560s, when the economic position of the pastoral clergy cannot have been much improved, we know that, at least in some dioceses, tradesmen were seeking and obtaining ordination in some numbers. Another factor is variations in the supply of cures up to 1534. There is far too little available detailed evidence to allow of statistics. But the late 14th and the 15th centuries saw extensive rebuilding of churches, foundation of chantries and colleges, and (possibly) increase in parochial and private chapels, chaplaincies, tutorials and teaching posts. But, simultaneously, plague, enclosures, depopulation and shifts of population led to the ruin or abandonment of a good many churches and chapels, and some chantries lapsed. By the early decades of the 16th century cities commonly had on their hands a surprisingly large number of derelict, or near-disused, urban churches.

The job-situation of the pastoral clergy cannot have been appreciably affected by deprivations for religious reasons, since these seem to have been relatively few. In 1553–8 married curates were fairly systematically subjected to canonical processes. The records of this which have been printed and contemporary visitations appear to show that most readily accepted correction, the formal break-up of their families, and reintegration into pastoral service. In the diocese of Canterbury, at least, such men were allowed usually to stay in their cures. By 1559 in Yorkshire the general problem of vagrancy embraced a fairly substantial number of 'runagate', unemployed or jobbing clergy, Scots as well as English. But it cannot be established that most of these had been deprived for religious reasons.[18]

[18] DICKENS, A. G., The Marian Reaction in the Diocese of York, York, 1957; FRERE, W. H., The Marian Reaction, London, 1903; WHATMORE, L. E., ed., Archdeacon Harpsfield's

It has been suggested that by 1553–9 the job-situation was radically altered, and that, due to the cumulative effects of twenty years of small ordination lists, and to deaths and retirements on pensions, there was now a considerable dearth of clergy. Thus of 150 cures in Kent in 1557 22 were without resident clergy. But again the available evidence is small and difficult to interpret. Some of the empty Kentish parishes were chapelries fast dying economically; others were enduring quite normal *interregna* or perhaps also long-disputed quarrels over advowsons; others were so small and poorly-endowed that the patron or rector or vicar could reasonably claim inability to pay a curate a living wage – in such cases it seems to have been normal practice to arrange for a neighbouring curate to give part of his time to the parish. When we have made generous allowances for exceptional features in the situation (the accumulated ecclesiastical disorder from the Edwardine period, and a long *interregnum* in the Archiepiscopate), it still seems true that the records reveal a long-standing acute problem of administrative mismanagement and grossly inadequate payment of curates.[19] It is very likely that the average age of the clergy was rising markedly. This must have some bearing on the well-established fact that the vast majority of pastoral clergy stayed put in their cures throughout the great changes of official religious policy. For most historians this fact is readily explainable: the clergy were the product of a folk-religion which was only minimally a religion of personal, doctrinal choice and book-learning; the rapid succession of changes must have confused them and bred a prudential decision to await further change back to normal, or, alternatively, a disgust with, and indisposition to listen to, governments and officially-inspired divines; unlike university clerks, pastoral clergy were men with deep local roots; galloping inflation must have obsessed them with job-security. One could add that apparent indifference to official religious policy was always a trait of the pastoral clergy. In the 11th and 12th centuries they seem to have 'worn' the changes imposed by the Gregorian Reform. During the Interdict in John's reign 'hardly a mouse squeaked in England.' In 1642–60 the parish clergy mostly stayed in their cures, accepting all changes of Westminster policy. Although some clergy took part in every Tudor rebellion and parish clergy directed the Western rising of 1549, the overwhelming majority always steered clear of involvement. It is considerations of this kind which have led most modern historians to charge the parish clergy with almost gross corporate selfishness and timidity. A recent specialist has tried to prove that they gave less monetary help to the poor by far than any other class in the 16th century. But were they really guilty of a *trahison des clercs*, an "incapacity for sustained conviction"? As *illiterati* or semi-literate they were very unlikely to leave behind them written traces of their opinions, other than 'commonplace books', and marginal jottings in printed books or MSS or parish registers. The only contemporaries liable to record their sayings were notaries in ecclesiastical court cases in which they might occasionally be in-

Canterbury Visitations, 1556–8, Catholic Record Society Record Series, vols. 45, 46, London, 1950–1951.

[19] WHATMORE, op. cit.

volved. The 'catch' of these sorts of evidence is never likely to be more than slight.[20]

b) The impact of liturgical change

Perhaps the most astonishing feature of their record is their mass-acceptance of the huge liturgical changes of 1534—59. In general in Church history even relatively small disturbances of the liturgical habits of curates and parishioners have created violent demonstrations: it was true in St. Augustine's day in Hippo, and is again today. Yet, to all appearances, no other liturgical changes have ever been as revolutionary as those in England in 1534—59. Archdeacon Harpsfield's 1557 visitation records of the diocese of Canterbury show that by then the great majority of its churches had disused, wrecked chancels, belfries broken and one bell left, naves littered with the broken rubbish of removed side-altars and screens, nave windows broken or daubed over with neutral paint, church plate and valuables vanished. The gutted naves were, we should imagine, from 1550—3, the unlovely setting for an academic, revolutionary liturgical experiment for which neither priests nor people had been really prepared in mind, and in the organisation of which they received extremely little positive, detailed guidance. Cranmer's answers to the Western rebels in 1549 and Bishop Hooper's diocesan injunctions of 1552 give us glimpses into what appear to be two entirely different mental worlds in conflict — the old one, where an esoteric mystery is murmured fast or sung by clergy and songmen in the chancel while the congregation outside the screen 'hears', says their beads, cons a book of devotion or 'walks and talks'; the new one, where the normal Sunday service is psalmody and Scripture read slowly and loudly to edify, instruct and convince the congregation of sin, leading up to quarterly 'Communion days' round a bare table, where intending communicants have to pass an examination by the curate in what they have learned from Sunday Mattins, sermon and catechising. In the old order, we should imagine, the pastoral clergy are the 'presidents' merely of a rich and complex traditional folk-religion of many different colourful observances covering not only the church and Sundays, but family life, foodstuffs, folk-customs, the agricultural round and most week-days. Religious instruction in such an order mainly occurs through the elder members of families in the home, and the curate merely (like the archdeacon automatically receiving ordinands prepared by the folk-religion) receives those so instructed to first Confession and first Holy Communion. Preaching, in such an order, is an extra: 'exhortations' are common and accompany most priestly actions. But in the new order we must presume the folk-religion suppressed: the curate is now an evangelist and missioner, and all his work, liturgical or not, is preaching the Gospel of Justification by Faith alone. Also the old order was obligatory, in a loose and communal way; the new order is obligatory in a more sharp, governmentally-imposed way. The curate's liturgical and teaching duties (and even observance of rubrics) now have a statutory basis. Civil authorities,

---

[20] JORDAN, W. K., Philanthropy in England, London, 1959, pp. 385—387.

Catholic as well as Protestant, are increasingly concerned with church
attendance and frequentation of the sacraments. The curate is expected to keep a
parish register, adding lists of communicants. At visitations he is increasingly
subjected to compulsory reading and examinations by repetition of his school
tasks and pressed to undertake the reading of homilies or preaching and
catechesis following detailed directives. Episcopal authority is beginning to
interfere in a rigid and paternalistic fashion in the running of parishes. In 1557,
for instance, Archdeacon Harpsfield in Kent enjoined that Easter duties be performed by families assigned to a succession of weekly shifts, that attendance at
processions be equally made compulsory, that men with good voices be
compelled to choir duties, that curates serving two parishes be responsible for
escorting parishioners with them. Over and above this there was a markedly
increasing tendency for Crown and Parliament to load on to curates and churchwardens local governmental duties such as poor relief, the supply of arms and
armour, and the care of roads and bridges.

We could, considering all this, well imagine that such Copernican changes
must have gravely upset a very large proportion of the pastoral clergy, especially
the most rustic and illiterate. Although the greatest shock came briefly in
1550–3, it had been preceded by a long series of severe changes from 1534–6.
The Marian Catholic restoration hardly provided a rest and secure return to
medieval normality. The heritage of destruction of the folk-religion, both
material and mental, was so great by 1553 that the brief and politically insecure
Marian interlude provided little real relief. Due to spiralling inflation and
poverty, small parishes could not afford the high cessments needed for essential
repairs and Catholic fittings. Even larger parishes had generally only achieved a
bare minimum of liturgical restoration by the end of 1558. Outside England,
especially in Calvinist areas, it proved quite impossible to adapt and reeducate
existing ex-Catholic pastoral clergy in large numbers for service as Protestant
ministers. Must we explain the continuance in office of the great majority of
their English counterparts as due to the far more gradual and wavering onset of
Protestantism in England? Or was it due to some hypothetical gift of the
English for pragmatism and compromise? Or did the widespread incidence in
England of dirt and delapidation in churches, slapdash performance of the
liturgy, extremely infrequent Communion, careless church attendance and
heterodox opinions well before 1534 witness to the early decay of the grip of a
formal folk-religion of observances amongst a great many curates and parishioners? The truth is that we are largely in the dark about the state of mind of
most curates before 1534 and from 1534 to 1559. The accidental survival of the
papers of Robert Parkyn, curate of Adwick-le-Street, Yorkshire and the letter-
book of Robert Joseph, monk of Evesham casts a flood of light into the dark.
We see devout yeoman families producing a multiplicity of priests and religious,
of priests sufficiently educated to appreciate, albeit dimly, fashionable currents
of 'Devotio Moderna' mysticism, humanism and Protestantism, passed on to
them by university clerk patrons and friends. We see such curates willing to
serve in ill-paid pastoral cures, supported by a love of books and study and by
supplies of money and books from relations and friends. We see in them a

mainly deep conservatism, which does not prevent most of them conforming to every successive change of government policy. But we have no idea how representative of their class such men were.[21]

IV. 1559–1600: the Elizabethan clergy

Until recently this was a very stagnant area of the field of English Church history studies. But it has now been vigorously stirred up by a mass of new work: by Neale and Haugaard on the 1559 settlement; by Davies and Cross on the episcopate's relations with the Crown; by Porter, Curtis, Simon, Charlton, Fletcher, Stone and Kearney on the universities and university clerks; by Knappen and Collinson on the Puritan movement; by New, Booty, Southgate, Morgan, Breward and the Georges on the theological constitutents and tensions of nascent Anglicanism; by Christopher Hill on the economic position of the clergy, and by Dickens and Brooks on their social standing; by Tyler and Marchant on the ecclesiastical courts; by Sisson on Hooker and Peel and Babbage on Bancroft; by McGrath, Bossy, Renold, Kenny, O'Connell and Loomie on the Catholic seminary priest movement. As we should expect, this new work has tended to revise hitherto established views, produce a mass of unexpected complexities and new problems, and make very clear our continuing great lack of information and research on many crucial features of the clerical scene.[22]

1. The traditional interpretation

The broad general traditional picture of clerical development after 1559 was fairly clear. It was agreed that the period of decaying medievalism, unsettlement and insecurity lasted to the mid-1570s, and then gave place to great changes. In the first place there was a considerable shift in the proportions of the spectrum of clerical opinion on doctrine. The original majority of more or less

---

[21] PANTIN and AVELING, op. cit. (Robert Joseph); DICKENS, A. G., Aspects of Intellectual Transition among the English Parish Clergy of the Reformation Period, in: Archiv für Reformationsgeschichte, Freiburg im Breisgau, 1952, pp. 54–59 (Parkyn).

[22] DICKENS, A. G., The English Reformation, London, 1972, pp. 464, 487–489 for most of these references; CROSS, C., The Royal Supremacy in the Elizabethan Church, London, 1969; DAVIES, E. T., Episcopacy and the Royal Supremacy in the Church of England in the 16th Century, Oxford, 1950; FLETCHER, H. F., The Intellectual Development of John Milton, vol. 2: The Cambridge Period, Yale, 1950; STONE, L., The Educational Revolution in England, 1540–1640, Past and Present, vol. 8 (fasc. 28), 1964, pp. 41–80; MORGAN, I., The Godly Preachers of the Elizabethan Church, London, 1965.

conservative or undecided 'middlemen' was largely extinguished by death. In their place appeared a great majority of solidly Protestant clergy, mostly the result of a crash-programme of ordinations in the the 1560s and 1570s. By then also the original Protestant group had lost its coherence and largely died out. In the later 1570s a new wave of extreme Protestantism, the Puritans, appeared in the universities: this movement was bred out of discontent with the poor quality of the hastily-collected 'new clergy' and with the studied moderation and lack of respect for spiritual values of the government, and was inspired positively by Calvinist doctrine. In spite of government pressure, the Puritans captured control of the seats of influence in the universities and some key bishoprics, and thereby a sizeable minority of pastoral clergy. Thus by the 1580s it could be said that the theological temper of the Church was mainly Calvinist. This, in turn, led in the 1590s to a small, but significant university-based theological reaction towards 'Arminianism' and anti-Presbyterianism, a reaction however which had not yet, by 1600, made many recruits amongst the parish clergy. Meanwhile the 1559 settlement produced a relatively small, but intellectually distinguished body of Marian Catholic university clerks who settled abroad as exiles and there embraced the full reactionary principles of ultramontane, Counter-Reformation Catholicism. The ferment of discontent with the Anglican Establishment in the 1570s at Oxford and Cambridge produced not only Puritanism, but a second, smaller but equally intellectually distinguished movement of reaction towards Catholicism. This carried abroad another small wave of university clerks and led to the foundation by the old, Marian Catholic exiles of English seminaries and the English mission, an aggressive missionary enterprise to rescue the remnant of 'survivalist' Catholics, convert them to ultra-montane Catholicism, and, if possible, recover England by force.

The second feature of the clerical picture, according to the older view, was a revolution in clerical training both before and after ordination, amongst both Protestants and Catholics. On the Protestant side it was the work of the university clerk Puritans, who, by diocesan 'prophesyings' for curates and incumbents, and by devout college tutorships and parsonage 'reading parties' for ordinands created a positively new type of Protestant clergyman, an instructed evangelist and mission preacher of the Calvinist version of the gospel. The steady flow of these young, well-trained cergymen into parishes and 'lecture-ships' and the effects of 'prophesyings' and 'exercises' on existing, older curates brought near the demise of the medieval ignorant liturgical functionary. It was, however, generally admitted that, even by 1600, very substantial numbers of such 'unconverted' clergy still existed, particularly in backward areas of the country. Simultaneously the new Catholic seminary priests were trained by Jesuits to be far different from the old 'Mass-priests' or secular-minded univers-ity clerks; they were elaborately trained missionary auxiliaries of the Jesuits, converted men, freed of the ecclesiastical trappings of the benefice system. The Marian Catholic rustic priests recruited into the mission were quite often put through refresher courses abroad in the seminaries: the odd few who evaded this experience and survived to the 1590s were rare museum pieces. Hence, on both sides of the religious fence, it certainly seemed that the medieval clerical set-up was fast dying, and the new image of the highly professional pastoral clergy established.

Another feature of the accepted picture dovetailed neatly in with this professionalisation – a distinct social and economic upgrading of the pastoral clergy. Amongst the Protestant clergy the decline in the number of secular or administrative posts open to university clerks, the retention of pluralism, and the new association of pastoral duty with a university education sent a much higher proportion of university clerks into pastoral cures. From the 1570s the Puritan movement helped to recruit for ordination an increasing number of distinctly middle class university students and to provide for them reasonably good stipends by 'lectureships', aristocratic patronage or otherwise. Thus by 1600 the Church of England was apparently well-advanced along the road towards a pastorate composed in the main of comfortably-off minor gentry or bourgeois men, with an enduring minority of plebeian, ill-educated poor curates. Simultaneously Robert Southwell's judgment that the Catholic seminary priests were mainly gentry, and Henry Garnet's defensive remark that no Jesuit missioner ever had more than two servants were often quoted to prove that the Catholic clergy had moved even further along the road to modernity.

The episcopate figured very little in the accepted picture of the Elizabethan clergy. It was generally agreed that the Protestant bishops were so tightly enmeshed in government control that the few of them who were prophets (like Grindal) were forcibly silenced, the few with real learning or administrative gifts (like Jewel, Whitgift and Bancroft) turned into obedient defenders of Crown policy, and the rest left to immerse themselves in obscurity and economic and family cares. As for the Catholic bishops, the deprived Marian diocesans lapsed into silence in England or obscurity abroad, and the new English mission functioned, on Jesuit 'presbyterian' and 'Curial' principles, without ordinary episcopal organisation. It was surmised that the two most vigorous English religious movements of the age, the Puritan and seminary priest organisations, both owed exceedingly little to episcopal leadership. On both sides of the fence 'episcopal Gallicanism' was moribund until the 1590s, when it enjoyed a small revival – through Bishops Bancroft and Bilson, and the university clerks, Matthew Sutcliffe and Hooker on the Anglican side, and through the 'Appellant' priests on the Catholic side, in both cases without making much significant impression by 1600. On the whole this was establishing an 'episcopal image' which was to endure to the 19th century.

2. The nature of Elizabethan Anglicanism

Recent work on the Protestant side of the clerical doctrinal spectrum of opinion has tended to be vigorous, controversial and confusing. This is partly due to a healthy questioning of old assumptions, and partly the result of the weakness of Church history studies in England and the absence of anything really comparable with the highly experienced and technically competent specialist school of studies of medieval theology and philosophy. This is not only an English weakness. In spite of a recent revival of interest on the Continent in Reformation and Counter-Reformation theology and of challenges to long-accepted defensive and denominational interpretations, the work of analysis, reconstruction of the textual, social and academic background and reinterpretation is still generally sketchy, superficial and timid. There does seem to be a sense in which, after 1559, and particularly from the 1570s, 'Anglicanism' came into existence as a fairly homogeneous Protestantism of the whole 'established' clergy. But this hardening and simplification of the religious spectrum, due to many factors, political, propagandist as well as ideological, appears to have been very partial in its effects. The Protestant homogeneity enclosed a considerable and shifting complexity of opinions, attitudes and emphases. This has been made clear, if not much illuminated, by the recent sharp debate amongst historians on the nature of Elizabethan Puritanism. Elizabethan 'Anglicanism' has a real continuity with the Protestant founding fathers, the Edwardian Protestant clerical group and the Marian exiles, yet it manifestly, from the 1570s, owed far more to a vastly bigger new generation of selfmade converts, tributaries to other Protestant influences. It appears to have been very strongly permeated from end to end, from Horne and Jewel to Whitgift, Bilson and Bancroft, by Calvinist influences, yet these were in practice apparently much refracted and moderated by a multiplicity of other influences deriving from many quarters – from Lutheranism, from the practical piety and Patristic studies and 'primitive Church' idealism of the 'Devotio Moderna' and Humanism, from late medieval eclectic Nominalism, Thomism and 'Augustinianism', and even from foreign Catholic manuals of 'positive theology', philosophy and 'cases of conscience'. For that matter we may well wonder exactly how homogeneous, simple and monolithic contemporary Calvinism and Lutheranism really were. Modern reinterpretations of them are beginning to hint at a quite different picture. Again, Elizabethan Anglicanism appears to have both insular and in the stream of Continental developments, to judge alone from the older sections of college libraries and the marginal notes in Elizabethan Anglican works of divinity. 'Anglicanism' seems to have shared with both Calvinism and Counter-Reformation Catholicism a complex blend of influences. There was (for lack of a better word) a strong 'moral Augustinianism', a 'Puritan' or 'Jansenistic' pessimism, *Angst*, evangelicalism, fascinated interest in practical casuistry, the spiritual comfort and direction of 'weak consciences', and the manifold determination of our lives by 'traductions' of original sin, heredity, bad breeding, education, mixtures of 'humours'. These preoccupations were shared by men as otherwise diverse as Joseph Hall, William Perkins, Augustine Baker and Benet Canfield. There was 'devout Humanism' with its enthusiasm for the primitive Church and classical past, its Patristic studies and sense of history and tradition mixed with radical anti-medievalism, its attack on 'questionary divinity' mixed with its own academicism and scholasticism – in itself a bundle of contradictions. A close study of the divinity of Anglicans like Jewel, Whittaker, Perkins and Hooker seems to show how tributary they all were to these complex influences, and how difficult it is to put them into pigeonholes labelled 'Anglican', 'Puritan'. In particular, William Perkins has not yet received the close attention his massive theological

achievement deserves. In many ways he simply does not fit into the established
'Puritan' pigeonhole. In opening his volumes we turn automatically to the
(obviously prominent) sections on Predestination and Reprobation, and to the
now famous folding inset diagram of the workings of Predestination. But the
diagram was the outcome of his *expertise* in tutoring divinity students at Cambridge, and no part of his pastoral teaching. His doctrine on these famous points
possibly owed something to Calvin, but Perkins never quotes or refers to the
'Institutes' or Keckermann (the standard Calvinist manual). His main acknowledged sources are St. Augustine, St. Bernard, the Greek Fathers, Anselm, Biel
and Aquinas. His preoccupation with these doctrines was not academic or meta-
physical but pastoral, as he faced what he saw as massive popular religious
ignorance, Pelagianism and the remnants of Catholic folk-religion. Moreover
this opposition was not merely passive: evangelistic preaching produced, alongside genuine conversions of heart, a much larger mass of outright rejection or
lapsing from apparent conversion. The doctrine of Galatians and St. Augustine
seemed to be the Christian interpetation of such a situation. Moreover for
Perkins Predestination is rooted in the love of God in Christ. His treatise on
Election is, in effect, one on the Incarnation and sanctification in Christ — a
magnificent section, relying heavily on the Fathers. He accepts Hell and the
terrible doctrine of Reprobation, but firmly and humanely rejects any idea that
its signs are evident. As he says, those who die raving against religion may well
mostly be merely crazed with pain. As for Papists, he cheerfully presumes that
many have been and are saved even in the Roman Church. His treatment of the
signs of Election is 'Puritan' at first sight; but its approach can be mostly paral-
lelled from late medieval theology or even Counter-Reformation Catholic divines,
and it and his treatise on 'The Combat of Flesh and Spirit' might well have
been written by Kempis or Luis of Granada. In 'The Reformed Catholike,'
while ostensibly confuting the many English Protestant 'politics' who asserted
that there was no fundamental difference between Rome and Canterbury, he
produces a close analysis, based on a sound reading of Catholic divines of the
day, tending to show that there was much common ground, and, on some vital
points, no really essential difference. His issue was really with Rome as a practical system. He was inclined to accept the perpetual virginity of Mary and made
much of her status as *Theotokos*. His views of the Sacraments and their causality
were sharply opposed to Bellarmine's but still in the general line of medieval 'Augustinian' tradition. His doctrine of the Eucharist is Patristic and 'high' if patently
not Roman. He takes issue with Roman 'case-divinity' as too legal and astray in the
treatment of venial sin; but he is a firm believer in the practical necessity of
private Confession for many, and of the study of Cases. On Church order and
ceremonies he is uncontroversial, and says the only issue amongst Anglicans is
about 'persons and the manner of putting the government into execution'. As
for Sabbatarianism, he says recreation on Sundays is a very necessary help to
godliness for most; 'I take it we are not denied to rejoice and solace ourselves
upon this day.' He disapproved of the vows of religion and its medieval,
canonical structure, but clearly approved of the calling of individuals or groups
to an informal life of the Little Gidding kind. He even held that relics of the

saints (proved) should be "kept privately and in honour." His views on Tradition, while firmly unTridentine, were largely Patristic and discerning.[23]

3. The nature of Elizabethan Catholicism

It is not easy to penetrate behind the apparently monolithic and heavily defensive unity of Tridentine theology of the English Elizabethan Catholics. John Bossy has suggested that the laity continued throughout the period to cling to a 'survivalist', almost Henrician Catholicism, while the bulk of the seminary priests tended to be stiffly Ultramontane. Late in the century 'Henrician' views took root amongst a substantial minority of the priests, the Appellants. It certainly seems true that denial of the Pope's deposing power and refusal to regard 'Church papistry' and *communicatio in sacris* with Anglicans as gravely sinful were common in England. Even Nicholas Sanders, a Louvain canonist and apologist given to very sweeping pronouncements on the God-given unity and infallibility of the Catholic Church under the Papacy, displayed some surprising Conciliarist tendencies. These politico-religious tensions and disputes within the English Catholic community, and even amongst the clergy, have been pretty throughly explored, but we still know relatively little about deeper theological tensions. It is possible to identify a diversity of strands in English Catholic theological writing of this period. The 'Devotio Moderna' quest for reformation of the Church by individual and group self-conversion, by prayer and steering very clear of academic divinity and involvement in ecclesiastical power clearly remained strong amongst the English Catholics; it produced 'the Lady Matins lot' in devout recusant families, the English Jesuits and equally the revolt against Jesuit direction which carried a good many seminarists into Benedictine monasteries, 'the foundation movement' of English convents from the 1590s, and two remarkable spiritual guides and writers, Benet Canfield and Augustine Baker. Then there was Humanism, with its quest for Biblical and Patristic scholarship to make clear the splendour of primitive Christianity, and so bring about a radical simplification and purification of clerical life and education and of Catholicism in general, alike degraded and stifled by legalism, bureaucracy, sterile academicism and folk superstition. The diffused influence of the purely academic side of Humanism on the English Catholic clergy was obviously huge and practically universal. It moulded the literary forms and style used by the Louvain apologists, the teaching methods used in the seminaries and by the English Jesuits, who recruited the two Rastell brothers, members of Thomas More's family circle which edited his works at Louvain. They also recruited Campion and Southwell and competent humanist teachers like Richard Gibbons (who taught Scripture and Hebrew and produced editions of a huge Patristic concordance and of Harpsfield's works.) Another strand in English Catholic clerical thought was a reaction towards the extremist medieval clerical

---

[23] The Workes of that Famous and Worthy Minister of Christ in the University of Cambridge, Mr. Wm. Perkins, Cambridge, 1616.

claims to be a privileged order censoring lay society, reinforced by a highly aggressive assertion of the *iure divino* authority of the Papacy and the infallible truth of traditional Catholic theological opinions and devotional practices. This was evident enough in the apologetics of Dorman, Harding, Sanders and their Louvain colleagues, in the writing of Allen and Persons, and the training courses of the seminaries and Jesuits. Another strand was 'moral Augustinianism', a pre-occupation, both on the broad scale of human history and in introspection and spiritual direction, with Predestination and Election, the sovereignty of Grace, casuistry and the search for purity of motive. This also clearly was very diffused, and evident alike in Allen, Persons, Stapleton, Sanders, Augustine Baker and Benet Canfield. It had its typical productions, such as the Jesuit John Gibbons' 'Concertatio Ecclesiae Anglicanae,' Richard Bristow's 'Tabulae' used at Douai, Thomas Stapleton's 'Vera Admiranda seu de Magnitudine Romanae Ecclesiae' and his 'Orationes', 'Cur cum Haeresi creverit Magia' and 'An Politici horum Temporum in Numero Christianorum sint Habendi', and the extraordinary spiritual writings of Augustine Baker and Benet Canfield.[24]

These strands did not combine easily or smoothly. While the broad academic programme of Humanism was accepted without question by the English Catholic clergy, there seems to have been a very strong move by the 1580s and 1590s to counteract the 'paganism' of its authors (particularly Aristotle and Cicero) by substituting 'Christianised' or bowdlerised texts. This was certainly the opinion of Persons and of Allen's Jesuit academic adviser, Possevinus. Also Erasmus' writings were pretty generally proscribed as far too radical and Pelagian, alike by Persons and Augustine Baker. For that matter Thomas More's radicalism and Conciliarism were censored by Rastell's and Stapleton's editions and biographies of him. Persons' 'A Memorial of the Reformation of England' reveals a mind in which Humanist ideas jostle very uneasily with ultra-clericalism and 'moral Augustinianism'. For him Trent was hardly a reformation of the Church at all; what is needed is a thorough return to 'the purity of the primitive Church'. But this means 'the perfect restitution of Ecclesiastical Discipline that was in use in the ancient Christian Church', with the Inquisition and strait censorship of morals and literature. Indeed Persons' whole remarkable career abroad seems to have been full of internal tensions and contradictions. In the spirit of the 'Devotio Moderna' and Humanism he was genuinely seeking to promote an English Catholicism free of superstitious traditionalism, legalism and bureaucratic interference by both Curial officials and secular authorities; he was a genuine radical and believer in the ideal of Scriptural primitive Christianity. In 'The Three Conversions' and 'The Christian Directory' he shows a genuine belief that it is prayer and 'pious affection' which alone procure individual and mass conversions. We may even suspect that he himself was what he accused the English of being by nature, resentful of authority, and that his exaltation of

---

[24] BOSSY, J., The Character of Elizabethan Catholicism, Past and Present, vol. 6 (fasc. 21), 1962, pp. 39—59; VEECH, op. cit.; KNOX, T. F., The First and Second Diaries of the English College, Douai, London, 1878, p. 154; STAPLETON, THOMAS, Opera Omnia, Paris, 1620, vol. 2, pp. 501ff., 677ff.

Papal and princely authority and obedience *ad nutum* was given its force by his knowledge that only direct application to the highest authority could overcome bureaucratic obstruction and red tape, and by his very personal pessimism about human power to obey law. It is ironical that the Appellants detested a Jesuit domination which was only imposed on them because the sole alternative was chaos in the seminaries and mission field, and yet themselves largely shared Persons' outlook.[25]

We know little of the impact on the English Catholic clergy of Baianism. In 1587 Leonard Lessius S.J. challenged the 'moral' and theological Augustinianism of Le Bay and the Louvain theological faculty, and was condemned by them for semi-Pelagianism. The condemnation was confirmed by the University of Douai. At that time the English College had moved from Douai to Rheims, but some seminarists were kept at the Jesuit College in Douai. The English 'colleges' of writers at Louvain had faded out in 1575. Apparently only one English divine figured in the Baian dispute. This was Thomas Stapleton, the only English Catholic with a wide reputation as a theologian. At the time of Lessius' condemnation Stapleton was leaving a Jesuit noviciate. He returned to Douai and was expelled from the university for supporting Lessius. Yet in 1590 he was nominated by Philip II to a regius professorship of theology (Le Bay's own post) in Louvain, and actually occupied the chair until his death in 1598. Opinion in the faculty there remained 'Augustinian'. Did Stapleton continue to defend Lessius' views? He certainly now accused two eminent Catholic theologians, Pighius and Dominic Soto of near-Pelagianism. His lectures on Justification date from this period. They are expressly anti-Lutheran, but Stapleton's line of argument perhaps indicates his final attitude to quarrels about Predestination and Grace inside or outside the Catholic Church. He appears to insist (in agreement with Lessius and contrary to Le Bay) that it is dangerous to try to base theology on 'the literal sense' of Scripture or the Fathers alone. In such profound and ultimately inexpressible mysteries one must expect to rely on the authority of the Church, which will accept equally, and hold together in one unity, apparently contradictory viewpoints. The fault of the Protestants, and of Catholic Augustinians and Pelagians was to rely on private textual interpretations and partial views.[26]

4. Common ground shared by Elizabethan Anglicans and Catholics

It therefore does seem tenable that both Elizabethan Anglicanism and Catholicism were relatively homogeneous bodies by the 1580s, though doctrinal opinion within each was compounded of very diverse influences which could

[25] KNOX, op.cit., p. 256 (Possevinus); PERSONS, R., A Memorial of the Reformation of England, ed. GEE, E., London, 1690; McCANN, J., ed., Memorials of Fr. Augustine Baker, Catholic Record Society, vol. 33, London, 1933, p. 47; PERSONS, R. The Christian Directory, (no place), 1583; The Three Conversions, (no place), 1603.

[26] O'CONNELL and RICHARDS, opp. citt.

clash within individuals or produce noisy collisions between groups of clergy, especially between zealots and their cooler opponents. We still await a close exploration of what the two denominations had in common and what really divided them. Once the line of division seemed final, the temper of the apologists on both sides was to assume that it must coincide with the ancient line between the true Church and the Kingdom of Darkness, and that there must, *a priori*, be some simple and evident principle accounting for the division. To Protestants the favourite principle was the division between the position of St. Paul in 'Galatians' or St. Augustine and the Jews and Pelagians. Thus at the end of the century Archbishop Mathew of York was using a vivid statement of this principle in the form with which he received seminary priests into the Church of England. To such a view it followed logically that Papists must be idolaters and incapable of truly Christian prayer. Catholic priests could not be ministers of the Gospel, since they had, by definition, neither a Divine calling to preach untruth nor a calling from true ecclesiastical authority. To Catholics the favourite principle was the authority of the Church and Papacy; reject that and you were bound to fall into 'private judgment' and every possible kind of heresy in the end. With logic as close as the Protestants' — usually learned from the same textbooks — this meant that Anglicans could have no priesthood and, according to Persons, no prayer-life, since they could not believe in habitual grace and were determinists. This attitude of mind undoubtedly accounts for the fact that there was never any effort at a Catholic authoritative decision on the validity of Anglican Orders. Some Catholic clergy believed that Anglican ordination was 'the mark of the Beast', and essentially indelible even in converts to Catholicism. However there were clergy on both sides who showed more discernment. It was certainly the commoner opinion amongst Protestants that the Papacy was Antichrist, but some divines — by no means all anti-Puritans — were not quite so sure of this; to them the power of Evil was embodied to some extent in Popery, but perhaps more in the Turk, in witchcraft, and in atheism and religious indifference or popular 'Protestant' Pelagianism. Thus to William Perkins the line between the true Church and outer darkness by no means coincides with the denominational line. Formally Protestant England was full of "the blind divinity of the world" and even slipping steadily back into its pre-Reformation vomit of Pelagianism and legalism. In Popery 'a remnant there has always served God in some measure truly' and many of our pre-Reformation ancestors were saved in it. Joseph Hall, a very firm Protestant, admitted freely that he learned to pray with 'more light from one obscure nameless Moncke which wrote some 112 years ago than from the directions of all other writers', and lamented that prayer could not be kept up continually 'as the old Monkes knew'. In 1578—9 Thomas Stapleton propounded in Douai some *quaestiones quodlibetales* on the relation of contemporary Protestantism to Antichrist. The contrary arguments are that Protestants do not accept the old, fundamental heresies, and that they are, in intention, very Christian. He disposes of these to his satisfaction by arguing that as Christ's Body is one, so is the body of Antichrist, so all heresies are connected; contract one and you virtually contract all. Indeed there is an obvious pattern in history indicating that the second coming of Christ is near: the East has fallen to

Islam, the abomination (Queen Elizabeth) sits in the Temple, a Christian *dia-spora* has appeared (the American Indian converts), and Protestantism is logically the ultimate heresy (since the earliest heresies were about the nature of the Father, the next about the Son, Protestantism about the Church and sacraments). Heretics cannot have 'religio' because they deny the reality of Grace and reject Catholic worship. Protestantism, by its doctrine of Justification, deprives men of Grace, the spring of moral effort, and so produces libertines; libertines are the seed bed of the immense growth of witchcraft, itself a clear sign of the Second Coming. But the same year Stapleton was arguing ferociously that Catholic 'schismatics' and 'politici', anticlerical and tolerant of Protestantism, were worse than heretics and Turks. In 'De Quinque Sacrae Scientiae Abusibus' he equated with heretics Catholic humanists who flood the divinity course with 'polite literature', pestiferous vanities and uselessnesses. But by 1582 it is evident from his 'De universa Justificationis Doctrina' that his original polemical principles were letting him down. He had once assumed that the literal sense of Scripture and the Fathers must confirm current Catholic teaching, so that Protestant interpretations must inevitably be malicious misreadings, easily refuted by textual research. He had also assumed that 'once certain doctrinal problems have been reduced to their principles, then men may hope for a final end to this vast controversial chaos'. Now he was driven back on a more pragmatic argument: that Scripture and the Fathers speak in metaphors which are irreducible to scholastic abstractions. The fault of Protestants is to want an 'instant', simple, onesided interpretation, whereas the Church wisely insists on holding all the contradictions together in balance. He was willing now to admit that Protestants had some partial truth and Christian baptism, that they had Durandus and Biel on their side (whom he thought to have been condemned by the Church,) and that Catholic thinkers like Scotus, Eck, Pighius and Dominic Soto were far from the balance of Catholic truth.[27]

It is, moreover, clear that at this period Anglicans were using Catholic books exensively. The devotional and academic literature of the day derived in the main from late medieval originals, constantly recast, pirated across national and denominational boundaries, and thinly disguised with Catholic or Protestant terms and polemic. Thus the 'Imitation of Christ' was very widely used by Elizabethan Protestants and Catholics; so were traditional manuals of prayers and meditations ascribed to St. Bernard or St. Augustine. Luis of Granada's devotional works were probably more used amongst Anglicans than Catholics. Persons' 'Christian Directory', a work by Gaspar Loate recast, was pirated by the Puritan, Edmund Bunney, and very widely used by Anglicans, to Person's fury. In the schools and universities Protestants came to prefer the logic texts of the Catholic exiles, Seton and Sanderson (dedicated to Cardinal Allen) to all others for brevity, and Suarez' 'Christianised' philosophy manual to that of the Calvinist Keckermann — the latter itself only a recasting of a manual by Ramon Lull. Perkins noted that Cambridge divinity students in the 1590s were abandon-

[27] Borthwick Institute, York, Chancery Book, 1613—1618, f. 41v. (Archbishop Mathew); STAPLETON, op. cit., vol. 2, pp. 501ff.

ing Melanchthon's 'Loci Communes' for Peter Lombard and Aquinas, Continental texts of the Fathers and Biblical commentaries by both German Protestants and Jesuits.[28]

A close reading of at least some of the devotional manuals and arts and theology texts of both sides leaves an impression of a strong 'family likeness' and the common impact of such forces as a preoccupation with Predestination and grace, a presumption that there must be a single absolute authority in religion, that a 'pluralist' society must be a monstrosity, 'moral Augustinianism', a profound distrust of humanism (even while its methods were being taken for granted), a division between clerical zealots and the 'politici', between clerical 'establishment men' and activists and, on the other hand, clerics devoted to 'the theoretical life' of prayer and meditation. By the end of the century pamphleteers amongst both moderate Catholics and Anglicans were agreed that Jesuits and Puritans were tarred with the same brush. Hooker's real attitudes and sympathies (witness his reflections in the Preface to the first Book of his 'Ecclesiastical Polity' on the religious attitudes of the English) were not far removed from those of Appellants like William Watson (witness his 'Decachordon').

5. A revolution in Anglican and Catholic methods of clerical training?

The second feature of the traditional picture of Elizabethan clerical life is the rise and considerable measure of success amongst both Protestants and Catholics of professional training schemes and seminaries, and the consequent blurring of the old sharp distinction between university clerks and pastoral clergy. The evidence for this 'academic revolution' amongst Anglicans, at least up to 1600, is thin and unconvincing. There are now available in print sufficient, though very incomplete, statistics from diocesan records to make it pretty certain that between 1560 and 1600, at least in the South-East and Midlands, the proportion of parish clergy with some sort of university degree rose very strikingly. But what exactly does this increase signify? Fuller statistics, and a careful analysis of these graduate incumbents and their benefices, may well establish that the change simply reflects the remarkable increase in the numbers of university students after 1560 (itself apparently largely caused by a number of quite secular social and economic pressures) and the consequent hotter competition for jobs suitable for university clerks; inevitably many of the new graduates could not find higher ecclesiastical posts or fellowships, so they would turn to the idea of ordination and finding good benefices. The better qualified and connected graduate ordinands would become pluralist incumbents: this had happened occasionally before 1559, but now it may well have happened much more often. The less qualified and well-connected would have to be content with single benefices of the better kind, in the hope of later finding patronage

[28] See the older sections of Sidney Sussex College Library, Cambridge; PERKINS, op. cit., vol. 2, p. 153.

and promotion. Moreover there is little evidence that the graduates made more effective Protestant clergymen than their non-graduate colleagues. In the 1590s it seems that a very high proportion of the pastoral clergy, graduates included, were not considered capable of preaching by their bishops. Thus in Lincolnshire in 1603 of some 580 parish clergy 220 were graduates and only 130 were licenced to preach. This is not surprising if, as we have just seen, it is possible that many of the graduates' entry into the Ministry was not due to any special sense of 'calling', and if their university course had given them little or no professional clerical training. The vast majority of the graduates who entered parochial work were 'artists', not divines. The often-cited evidence for Puritan 'seminaries' run within colleges by devout tutors, or in parsonages, for graduate ordinands or undergraduates on vacation 'reading-parties', by devout graduate incumbents is scanty indeed before 1600. The little solid evidence we have as yet on university arts courses and tutorial methods in 1560—1600 shows little trace of any desire to pass on any more 'clerical' *expertise* than had existed before 1559. The now automatically accepted humanistic flavour of the textbooks and the 'Christian' arts manuals in use (sometimes Ramus, but more often Keckermann or even Suarez) and the traditional setting of college chapel services and clerical tutors certainly provided a clerical atmosphere to the course for lay-students and ordinands alike (though most probably before ordination these classes of students were undistinguishable). But it was surely a very traditional atmosphere. It would be wrong to imagine that Humanism and the Reformation had no real effect on Oxbridge: but they exploded within an exceedingly tightly enclosed and thick-walled academic chamber of a traditional shape. The scathing comments of the Puritans, in detail, on the professional standards of the parish clergy and on the lack of interest in professional training amongst university dons, the very existence of a scattering of Puritan 'parsonage seminaries' and the foundation of two new colleges at Cambridge expressly as seminaries witness to the unlikelihood that mere graduation produced a trained parish clergy. The Puritans saw the bulk of the parish clergy as 'dumb dogs' — liturgical functionaries of the traditional kind. William Perkins, himself significantly long an extra-collegiate evangelist in Cambridge and unofficial guide to undergraduates, in the 1590s sketched out an ideal of 'schools of the Prophets' which he clearly thought was in no way being fulfilled by existing college teaching. The existence of 'prophesyings' over wide areas in the 1570s and deanery 'exercises' for clergy thereafter is certain. But the efficacy of them as post-ordination or post-graduate training is in doubt. It is interesting that the bishops always included Arts graduates in these schemes.

The foundation Statutes of Sidney Sussex College, Cambridge are explicit in their criticism of collegiate life around them. The college was not to be 'amplissimum campum' in which 'iuvenes apum more de omnigenis flosculis pro libito libent', but 'seminarium angustum et conclusum', a select seed-bed in which carefully selected scholars, all committed in advance to be ordinands, may be nurtured apart by fellows who are all to be divines and then, when mature transferred to the wide field of the Church 'quae eorum fructu opipare crescat in plenitudinem Christi.' There were to be a limited number (the buildings were very small) of lay fellow-commoners and pensioners subjected to the same seminary discipline, with safeguards to ensure that they did not infect the scholars with a secular spirit.[29]

A recent volume of studies of clerical training in Europe in the later 16th century has put these Anglican efforts in a perspective which is new to English readers. 'Prophezei' were standard form throughout Protestant Europe wherever it was necessary to try to 'recondition' ex-Catholic pastoral clergy as Protestant ministers. They seem to have been pretty uniformly unsuccessful. Calvinists on the continent and in Scotland generally relied on the recruitment of ordinands young from parishes and sent them as scholarship boys to specially-created Academies; relatively few became university graduates, partly because the universities were felt to be stubbornly traditionalist and secular. On the other hand the Lutherans of Saxony and Württemburg had, in theory at least, a highly-organised system of ordinand training through scholarships to Academies and on to universities. However it is still not clear that this in practice produced an effective professional training: in the United Provinces it certainly did not.[30]

If Anglican professional training left much to be desired, we might well imagine that the same could not be true of Catholics, who, surely, had brand new seminaries founded expressly for an intense training of missioners and far from the corrupting influence of Oxbridge. But here too there is evidence that the realities fell far short of reformers' ideals. Relatively little has so far been published on the Catholic seminary movement in Europe, and even less about 16th century universities in Catholic countries and theological courses. But two recent short studies contain new material. They suggest that Catholic tradition and the Canons had no clear 'image' of the pastoral priest, other than as a technically competent 'liturgical functionary'. The 'image' of spiritual fathers did exist, but in tradition was associated with religious and bishops. In the middle ages reformers, usually themselves religious, tended to want to assimilate parochial clergy to the 'ordo' of religious. One method was the episcopal school or 'seminarium', where, under a quasi-religious discipline, a carefully-chosen élite of boy-ordinands was trained specially to serve in key-benefices in dioceses and act as a leaven amongst the rustic curates. The decree on seminaries 'Cum adolescentium aetas' of the Council of Trent in 1563 was purely in this tradition. It proposed that poor boys of 12 should be trained by bishops at the latters' expense. The duller ones, after a utility course of a very medieval kind (grammar, chant, computus, ceremonies) should be used as a pool to supply the service of churches — presumably vacant in some Catholic countries due to Protestant irruptions. The brighter ordinands should be retained for 'further

[29] BARRATT, op. cit.; FOSTER, C. W., The State of the Church in the Reigns of Elizabeth and James I, Lincoln Record Society, vol. 23, Lincoln, 1926; KEARNEY, op. cit.; Sidney Sussex College Library, Cambridge, Statutes, 1598.

[30] BAKER, D., ed., Miscellanea Historiae Ecclesiasticae, vol. 3, Bibliothèque de la Revue d'Histoire Ecclésiastique, Fasc. 50, Louvain, 1970; HAWS, C. H., The Scottish Parish Clergy at the Reformation, 1540–74, Scottish Record Society, New Series, vol. 3, Edinburgh, 1972, pp. V–XV.

studies', though it is not specified what these might be. Perhaps it was a way of providing future teachers in the seminary. It is also implied that such seminaries will merely provide a small leaven of celibate curates, an episcopal *familia* in his service, in the midst of a great mass of clergy likely always to be educated in a quite different, but just as traditional way, either as rustics from parsonage-apprenticeships or petty schools, or as secular-minded university clerks. The bulk of the benefices of any value would continue to be monopolised, *in absentia*, by the university clerks. Anyway to get a benefice required patronage and probably a private income to ensure a title for ordination. The 'Tridentine seminary' was thus a very limited period-piece. But it was not the only Catholic model for training establishments. The 'Devotio Moderna' had already, long before Trent, provided the "linked school and university college", Winchester and New College, Eton and King's College, Deventer and Zwolle and their colleges, the Montaigu at Paris. The Jesuits — perhaps with an eye on the Lutherans' linked academies and university hostels for ordinands — produced their own equivalents, especially the Germanicum at Rome in 1552. The Germanicum was an expressly missionary college to educate episcopally-sponsored students to act, back in the Empire, as élite secular priests and Jesuit auxiliaries. It is a fact that a great many episcopal seminaries later copied the Statutes of the Germanicum, and that the Jesuits were invited to staff some of them. Under the influence of these 'non-Tridentine' models, and, no doubt, social and economic pressures of the later 16th century and the absolute need that seminary priests should be of sufficient social standing and educational qualifications to secure benefices, most Catholic seminaries by 1600 were filled with middle class, not poor, students, and those sufficiently intelligent to take it urged on to university courses. However our authors consider that the intellectual level attained even so by the average Catholic seminarist was lower than that of Protestant ordinands formed in Academies.[31]

These studies form a good perspective for the English Colleges founded by Allen and Persons. William Allen was an Oxford don and 'artist' university clerk of the old school: he was not ordained to major Orders until after he had settled in exile. Perhaps his later remark that before his day men had feared ordination refers to university clerks and his own attitude of mind before the 1560s — since there is no sign whatever that rustic curates had ever feared or held back from ordination: quite the reverse. Allen arrived abroad to find there a small but academically distinguished body of English university dons and clerks whose attitudes were typical of their kind. They attempted automatically to gravitate to university teaching posts or to canonries or major benefices. Missionary work especially in an England where there could be no assured stable income from benefices was not their *métier*: it was associated with friars or Jesuits who were organised and paid for by their superiors and so who could operate without benefices. Moreover Allen and the English exiled clerks could hardly

---

[31] BAKER, op. cit., pp. 109 ff. HALKIN, L. E., La Formation du Clergé Catholique après le Concile de Trente, and pp. 151 ff.; VAN LAARHOVEN, J., La Formation des Prêtres dans la Première Moitié du XVIe. siècle.

accept the idea of living 'under the cross', the life of a sect outside the Establishment and the law. To them the Church *was* the nation and the ecclesiastical establishment. They could only wait, and work for, the political revolution which would (as in 1553) restore the Catholic establishment in England. Hence the exiles had already formed small 'colleges' or hostels at Louvain university, and settled in them to try for university posts and fill in time by writing polemical works. In 1568 Allen raised money to found a similar English College in the newly set-up university of Douai. By 1573—4 money was running short and university posts not forthcoming for most of the exiles. In the succeeding years the College gradually changed its character and became a seminary. The change does not seem to have been the result of any decisive single act by Allen. In 1578—80 he was still insisting that the primary purpose of the college was to build up and sustain a band of university clerks qualified to take over major ecclesiastical posts in England when Catholicism was restored there by political action. But a variety of circumstances forced him to accept into his originally select little establishment (of six or eight English divines and a few Belgian divines as paying boarders) up to 120 English visitors, scholars and pensioners. The ferment at Oxbridge in the 1570s caused by rapidly rising student numbers, a shortage of teaching posts for graduates and religious dissensions brought a flow of graduates and students to Flanders and to Douai. As Allen frankly admitted the motives of many of these visitors were very mixed; some were genuinely turning to Catholicism, but others were merely discontented with their job-prospects as university clerks in England, anxious to avoid being driven to Anglican ordination and parochial life, and confused about their religion. Allen received subsidies from Philip II, the Pope and benefactors to provide scholarships for ordinands on a very limited scale. Benefices and university teaching posts for Englishmen in Flanders were in very short supply. In 1578 the growing hostility of the Douai townspeople to these developments, the political situation in Flanders, and the hostility of other English clerical and lay pensioners of Philip II living scattered over Flanders to this diversion of subsidies to the college forced Allen to move the establishment. The 'artists' were moved to Jesuit colleges, the staff and divines to Rheims in France, and Persons helped out by gradually providing makeshift accomodation for some divines in new colleges at Rome, Valladolid, Seville, San Lucar, finding staff (often foreign Jesuits), Papal subsidies and benefactors. Thus by the 1590s, when the college at Rheims was able to return to Douai, the English seminaries ostensibly formed an impressive training complex. The numbers of students in training fluctuated greatly, but probably at times rose to upwards of 250. The numbers despatched as priests to the English mission also fluctuated wildly from year to year, but in the 1580s and 1590s most probably averaged 25—30 a year. By 1600 it is likely that there were upwards of 300 seminary priests in England.[32]

---

[32] KNOX, T. F., Letters and Memorials of Cardinal Allen, London, 1882; RENOLD, P., ed., Letters of Allen and Barret, Catholic Record Society, vol. 53, London, 1970, pp. xv—xvi and Letters 25—27; CLANCY, T. H., Political Thought of the Counter-Reformation in England, 1572—1615, London Univ. Ph. D. thesis, 1960; PARISH, J. E., Robert Persons

Allen in his polemical treatises, and in letters to the Pope begging for increased subsidies, habitually spoke of the college's missionary work as a conversion of England on the scale of the mission of St. Augustine. To his mind however this can hardly have meant a hope that such a very small number of clergy could convert to Catholicism the English population person by person. As a man of his day he imagined fondly (at any rate in his earlier years) that huge numbers in England were Catholics as heart and real Protestants few, and he expected that there would be mass reconciliations of the dependents and tenants of the magnates when their masters were induced to declare for a Catholic revolution. The missioners were to go to England to be on the spot when that revolution came. Meanwhile they could hold the committed openly Catholic gentry to the faith, attempt to convert 'schismatics', and collect funds and recruits for the seminaries. To Allen the 'mission' was never more than subsidiary to the main, political and revolutionary enterprise. Also he and others (particularly Robert Southwell) habitually spoke of the seminary divines as far better educated than Anglican divines. This was partly polemical rhetoric, and partly an inevitable conclusion from the Catholic premiss that Protestants could only have opinions, not real theology. The realities of the training in the seminaries were far otherwise. The methods used seem to have differed in no way from those obtaining everywhere in Europe in Catholic seminaries and colleges, though the peculiar form of house-discipline used seems to have been borrowed from that of the Jesuit university hostels for ordinands. Some students arrived already graduated in Arts. Allen did not question these qualifications, though some Catholics thought them useless, partly because they argued that Protestant belief vitiated even the Oxbridge Arts courses, and partly because the taking of a degree there meant acceptance of the Oath of Supremacy. However the Douai Diary of the 1580s admits that the Puritan Whittaker was a good grammarian, even if he was no real *theologus*. Most students arrived only partly qualified in Arts. The college sometimes supplied an Arts course, taught mainly by the abler theology students; at other times it sent the 'artists' to a nearby Jesuit college. Those qualified in Arts were graded by ability. A small number of the ablest were set to 'Scholastic Theology' courses. The college endeavoured as far as its teaching resources allowed to supply this course in the house, but divines seem often to have attended university lectures, at Douai university when the college was there, and at the universities of Paris and Pont-à-Mousson when it was at Rheims. Some divines were sent to the English College, Rome where they could attend the Papal university or lectures at the Jesuit Germanicum. We get an impression that the level of attainment of the divines was not high. Whenever possible, at Douai college, the course was based on St. Thomas, using dictated commentaries of Robert Italus, published in Louvain. More often the lectures

and the English Counter-Reformation, Rice Univ. Studies, vol. 52/1, Winter, 1966, New York; MEYER, A. O., England and the Catholic Church under Queen Elizabeth, ed. BOSSY, J., London, 1970, pp. 492ff.; ANSTRUTHER, G., The Seminary Priests, vol. 1: Elizabethan, Ware, 1968; KENNY, A., From Hospice to College, 1559–1579, Venerabile Sexcentenary Issue, Exeter, 1962, pp. 218–273.

used Peter Lombard. There were difficulties about the 'horridior et spinosior' sections in St. Thomas in 1587 — possibly because of the modest standard of the college teachers and divines, but also possibly because that year the Baian controversy in Louvain made theological problems of Predestination and Grace red-hot issues. Some divines were ordained long before their course was finished. Others managed to attain bachelorates ot even doctorates exceedingly rapidly and easily. Allen was very critical of these degrees, and the knowing called them 'entes rationis'.

The great majority of the ordinands took a short course, averaging two years, in 'Positive Theology'. This meant 'Controversies', rubrics and ceremonies, and 'Cases' (or 'Moral Theology.') 'Controversies' included a run through the 'Catechism of the Council of Trent', brief dictates on Scripture (that is, strings of proof texts to be used in controversy), and 'exercises' to drive the matter home. There were also dictated lectures on St. Augustine's 'De catechizandis rudibus', and, if time, a run through Peter Canisius' 'Short Catechism' with explanations by the teacher from his longer version. 'Cases' meant a run through a manual. In 1578—80 this was Martin Azpilcueta's 'Enchiridion sive Manuale Confessariorum et Poenitentium', very recently published in Spanish in Rome. This manual (usually known as 'Navarrus') has an honourable place in the long line of descent from late medieval manuals for confessors to 19th century 'Moral Theology' manuals. It attempted to combine, briefly and clearly, an introduction taken from the sections in the scholastic theology course on the soul, free will, Grace, beatitude, merit and sin with a purely practical instruction on confessional technique. The 'doctrinal' section is 'Augustinian' and firmly sets aside Aristotle and St. Thomas; on the dangerous topics of Predestination, Grace and merit it is exceedingly brief and simple. The tone of the practical section is traditional and full of 'moral Augustinian' severity. The only indication we have of the efficacy of this teaching is the complaint of the Appellants that seminary priests were left incapable of supplying the real moral and spiritual needs of serious-minded English people. Finally the whole syllabus of seminary studies made only a minimal provision of instruction in Greek and Hebrew and in History. If there was time portions of Eusebius' 'Ecclesiastical History' and of Bede might be read at meals.[33]

Allen's attitude to the training was pragmatic. His own theological course at Louvain must have been short; his Regius Professorship of Divinity at Douai was due to Philip II, and he never revealed any very profound interest in, or ability for, the subject. He explained to the Carthusian Prior Chauncy that the missioners must be a cut above the old Mass-priests; on the other hand *docti* priests were not required on the mission, and so a brief, practical course was all that was needed. Traditional 'manual' theology sufficed. For scholastic divines a short course based on St. Thomas or Peter Lombard was best, to produce *solide docti et acuti disputatores*. This, plus "a perfect hatred of heresy", was needed to armour his men against apostasy. In theory he was all assurance about the essen-

---

[33] KNOX, opp. citt.; I used the Sidney Sussex College, Cambridge library copy of Navarrus (q/4/26).

tial superiority of Catholic theology; in practice he was far from being so sanguine. To his mind a close study of Scripture was unnecessary and dangerous, but the practical needs of disputation with heretics demanded the use of the Douai English Biblical text, carefully armoured with Catholic explanations, and some drilling in proof-texts. If possible a little brushing of Greek and Hebrew could help 'to avoid the traps of the heretics'. His attitude towards clerical higher studies was ambivalent. On the one hand, as a traditionalist university clerk, he sympathised with that class' professional pride and feeling that society owed them respect and a suitable living, and with their lack of desire to embrace pastoral life. He thought it highly desirable that, as the first generation of exiled dons and canonists died out, their place should be supplied, against the day when their services would be needed in a Catholic England. In fact, in the 1580s, there was a thin sprinkling of English university clerks, mostly canonists or civilians but with some theologians, occupying posts as canons, penitentiaries, ecclesiastical administrators and university teachers in Louvain, Douai, Cambrai, Milan and Rome. There were even two English bishops employed in foreign dioceses. Allen himself passed on to a Cardinalate and service in the Roman Curia. On the other hand he noted with disapproval the way in which a good many well-qualified Oxbridge convert graduates bribed or pushed their way to higher degrees on the Continent and stayed there, competing frantically for a share in the (all too scanty) supply of Papal and royal pension money and angling for benefices and university posts. He felt that such men put the colleges' finances in peril and lowered the estimation of foreigners for English university clerks. Robert Persons also had a past as an Oxford don, and he shared Allen's feelings. Both men had considerable doubts about the rush of seminary students and unemployed university clerks into religious Orders in the 1590s. With reason they suspected that the motive was often a desire to avoid going on the mission and to secure an easy, bookish life appropriate to their privileged status. Allen seems to have sought the help of the Jesuits largely because they were the ablest available practitioners of short, practical, carefully dictated courses, and because their very strict house discipline and insistence on general Confessions and the taking of the 'Spiritual Exercises' by ordinands helped to weed out the unmotivated and cope with the seminaries' severe disciplinary problems. He was always frank in saying that, apart from such a tough conditioning, no priest (especially those under thirty years of age) could hope to avoid apostasy or compromise with heresy in a mission area where there was no Catholic Establishment ("no discipline or censures") and no Catholic government ("no form of external commonwealth".) It would be wrong to think that Allen and Persons never spoke hopefully of the English mission. But the whole context of their thought about it was 'Augustinian' and far from triumphalist (at least when they were not writing polemics.) To their minds a disaster had fallen on England by the just judgment of God *propter peccata nostra*. The whole scene was a desperate one, with massive heresies without, and *politici*, compromisers, 'schismatics', careerists and Pelagian Catholics within the fold. One could only pray, struggle and consult "the signs of the times" in the books of Daniel and the Apocalypse. Such a mentality was medieval. It is difficult to see that it, or indeed the mentality of Catholic missioners to America or the East, had anything distinctively new or 'modern'. As in the later middle ages, rationalism and openness of mind to new situations existed, but cocooned within an 'Augustinian' outlook.

Their pessimism was reinforced by their experiences with ordinands and seminary priests. The undoubted heroism of a good proportion of them was a flower which bloomed in very unpromising soil. The seminaries of Douai-Rheims, Rome and Valladolid were all regularly convulsed by student unrest, dissidence and even outright rebellion from as early as 1578–9. To the minds of the superiors the causes were multiple. In the first place the English were then regarded as (perhaps the Welsh excepted) the most unruly and temperamental of all nations. The officials of the Roman Curia thought them mostly madmen. In spite of increasingly strong efforts to exclude, head-off or eject unsuitable candidates (or even priests) the 'screened' remained a very mixed bag. The superiors had very practical reasons for sharing in one of the great preoccupations of the age, a puzzled enquiry into human destiny and the interaction of nature ('humours', temperament, heredity, education) and Grace, mingling shrewd realism and psychological insight with a dogmatic pattern derived from 'Augustinian' theology and scholastic 'psychology'. It was noted that some ordinands arrived at the seminary burning with zeal for the mission and even martyrdom (sometimes before they had been reconciled to the Church), but, after exposure to house-discipline, the 'Exercises' and routine studies, lost their zeal and departed or reached ordination and tried to stay abroad. Others left for England as priests apparently full of zeal and lapsed in England. Contrariwise, not infrequently it was the troublesome students, or even the timid ones, who, in the event, became martyrs. The superiors were upset by this proof of the inefficacy of their training methods, but comforted by evidence which fitted in with their view of the interaction of nature and Grace. In 1597 Persons remarked that the Pope and Curia openly questioned the motives of English students and even martyrs, thinking it likely the martyrs' constancy was due to the well-known English 'choller and obstinate will to contradict the magistrate' and not to supernatural motives. Cardinal Baronius had said 'your youths brag of martyrdom, but are Refractarii and have no part of martyrs' spirit which is humility and obedience'. Persons himself thought most English Catholics *carnales*, seekers of God and the Church for self-interested reasons. In the 1580s Barret, the second President of Douai college, said that an increasing number of students arrived in their teens as the boorish and ill-educated, ill-instructed sons of rustic country gentry, coming more at the behest of their parents or missioners or from a desire to escape the Anglican ministry or to get travel and adventure than for spiritual reasons. Robert Southwell, when prefect of studies at the Rome college, thought it necessary to try to 'break their wills'. The discipline caused rebellions by students of all ages, and especially graduates, who resented being treated as children. It was difficult to decide whether the restive should be dismissed (since their *viaticums* were expensive, and without them they tended to stay in the town as university students and make trouble in the college) or hurried on to ordination. It was even harder to know what to do with unsatisfactory deacons or priests. Efforts to found sodalities or foster delation confused the distinction between confessional and house discipline and roused worse resentments. The growing tendency to recruit Jesuits or 'Ignatians' ('those wonderfully well affected to ours' and either privately vowed to enter the Society or retained as auxiliaries) especially in Rome divided the clergy and undoubtedly created both the Appellant movement and the rush of students into Italian and Spanish Benedictine monasteries. Since, even in 1600, the English Jesuits were few and had no Province or novitiate of their own, the students who joined the Society and persevered commonly spent years teaching in foreign Jesuit houses (for instance in Prague, Vilna, Gratz, Olmutz or Naples) before being released to serve on the English mission. Many never reached the mission, or desired to do so. The English Jesuits were clearly exercised in conscience about this unhappy situation. Persons saw that the college most under Jesuit influence (Rome) had the worst reputation for student rebellion. He blamed the fact on to the intrigues of the enemies of the Society, the climate in Rome (of 175 students admitted to the college in 1579—85 18 died in college and 14 were dismissed for ill-health, of whom two died at Rheims on the way to England), the worldliness of the Curia, and (to Persons' mind) the over-liberal atmosphere of the Italian system of education.[34]

The realities of seminary life must account to some extent for the troubles and stresses of the priests' lives on the mission. It has often been supposed that they lived a cloak-and-dagger existence round ingenious hiding-holes in aristocratic country houses, reaping an easy and rich harvest of souls from a mostly 'schismatic' population, and faced prison and execution with unfailingly heroic constancy. This, it is imagined, was the result of superb training backed by a Napoleonic secret mission organisation. A careful reading of the material on which this picture has been based (autobiographical or biographical accounts by John Gerard, Edmund Campion, Persons, Robert Southwell, Morse and Garnet, and Bishop Challoner's 'Memoirs of Missionary Priests') suggests strongly that the picture has been oversimplified. The correspondence of Allen, Persons and Barret, the scraps of evidence of the missioners, and the literature of the Wisbech 'Stirs' and Appellant controversy reinforce the impression strongly. The seminary priests' mission was a very small and inchoate affair of a few seminarists and a majority of largely rootless 'Marian' priests until 1585—90, when it began to take a more definite shape. Just as the beginnings of the mission in 1574—80 had been almost unplanned, so the 'jelling' seems to have been far more the result of social and economic forces and the will and prejudices of conservative, 'survivalist' country gentry than of masterful clerkly planning. There were clerical types with which we are already familiar: the martyrs, the almost free-lance Jesuit missioners with their little bands of auxiliary 'Ignatians' and their plans to organise the apostolate in certain areas, the Appellant group. The Appellants, often the better-educated graduates and convert clergymen,

[34] KENNY, A., ed., The Responsa Scholarum of the English College, Rome, Pt. 1: 1598—1621, Catholic Record Society, vol. 54, 1962; FOLEY, H., Records of the English Province, S. J., London, 1877—1883.

prisoners in Wisbech or London for most of their mission careers, planned to organise the missioners into a tight clerical 'Trades Union' under a Bishop, so that they could effectively resist domination by both Jesuits and gentry patrons. Each of these three clerical types left behind it a literature: the 'short lives' and formal, hortatory last letters of martyrs; the memoirs of the Jesuits; the correspondence and pamphlets of the Appellants. They are so well-known that we inevitably tend to think of them as the normal missioners of the period. In fact they seem to have been atypical, minority groups. The largely silent majority of the missioners included martyrs who were undistinguished, apparently unemployed, and without any desire for, or cult of, martyrdom: such were chance victims of a political storm of the moment. Quite a large proportion of the missioners were caught and spent years in confinement as 'confessors' in boredom, often easy relations with their captors and no great danger. Especially after 1590 there was an increasing number of undistinguished Jesuit missioners who served run-of-the-mill 'stations' and who probably had more sympathy with the Appellants than they did with their own superiors. There were even Appellants, like John Mush, who had been protegés of the Jesuits, had sympathy for their problems, and counselled moderation. So far as we can judge the ordinary missioner, after a period of unsettlement and unemployment on first landing, gravitated to his home country and there settled down to a hum-drum existence on a 'station'. The organisation of the 'stations', serving the households of minor gentry and well-to-do yeomen, was the result of a mass of haphazard arrangements made by patrons with particular priests and subject to much change due to the death of patrons or the removal of priests. They were hardly tidy 'parishes'. It is unlikely that the average priest resided in aristocratic houses, or any patron's house. The missioners' work was that of 'Mass priests'. There are indications that they did little (and were capable of little) in the way of systematic catechising, instruction or preaching, and that the converts whom they received were influenced far more by innate conservatism, fear of death, acute anxiety about salvation, family pressures and private reading than by any words or influence of priests. The Catholicism of an area like Yorkshire in 1600 appears to have been an odd phenomenon, at once stubborn and very precarious, a 'survivalism' amongst rustic gentry and their immediate tenants, shot through with much conformism and 'Church Papistry', and kept in existence by factors of every kind, of which clerical leadership was only one. The rival (and relatively unsuccessful) clerical pressure groups seeking to reform this inchoate system described it in terms reminiscent of those used by the Puritans. Thus the Appellant, William Watson, in his 'Decachordon of Ten Quodlibeticall Questions Concerning Religion and State' bewails a decline in lay estimation of the Catholic clergy, because 'every gentleman of reckoning' has his servant-chaplain and familiarity breeds contempt, because ordinary 'stations' are generally served by unlearned, 'dumb dog' poor clergy, and because there is, especially in London, a crowd of priest 'wanderers' without steady employment, begging the laity for patronage.[35]

---

[35] Decachordon, (no place), 1602; AVELING, H., Northern Catholics, London, 1967.

6. Changes in the economic and social status of the clergy?

Thus by 1600 the English Catholic laity most probably judged their clergy much as the literate Anglican laity did theirs, as very familiar, uninspiring but necessary takers of services and (very infrequent) dispensers of sacraments. Outside the very exceptional surroundings in which Byrd conducted his Masses, Elizabethan Catholic services must have been as simple and rustic affairs as those of Anglicans, without vestments, music or preaching. On both sides the laity thought their clergy too preoccupied with status and incomes, and the 'evangelistic' and 'clericalist' minority of clergy dangerous fanatics. Added to this the canonical situation for Catholics must have been hair-raising to simple priests, with countless — especially marital — anomalies and scandals. The minority of devout laity on both sides (containing a significantly large number of women) were severely critical of the 'dumb dogs' and sought teaching, confession and spiritual direction from the more learned and evangelistic minorities of the clergy, the great Puritan divines and the more able Jesuits. On both sides also there was a distinct tendency by 1600 for the devout laity to form, on their own initiative, pious societies, households or informal groups, associating with, and supporting, clergy of their own choice. It was such groupings which founded Sidney Sussex and Emmanuel Colleges, supported 'lecturers', and provided the vocations and financial backing for the 'foundation movement' of Catholic monasteries and convents in Flanders and France from 1598.

The third feature in the traditional picture of the Elizabethan clergy was a rise in their social and economic standing in the community. For the Anglican clergy this is still accepted in the main by modern specialists. It is pointed out that, in spite of a good deal of evidence of poverty amongst stipendiary curates and the holders of small vicarages, there are clear signs of moderate prosperity amongst incumbents who were cushioned against inflation by control of tithe and glebe lands; that clerical marriage probably helped; and that there is evidence of a fair sprinkling of pastoral priests with intellectual tastes and writing ability. Unfortunately we are still very ill-informed about university clerks as dons and ecclesiastical administrators. The evidence for distinctly middle class graduate incumbents clearly only relates to a type of man who, before 1559, would have been a university clerk not actively in pastoral service. Below them in the social and economic scale lay the great majority of pastoral clergy. For them the evidence seems largely lacking and, where it exists, hardly implying any significant change in status, social or economic. The evidence from their wills about their books is quite inconclusive: perhaps they possessed more books than their pre-1559 brethren, but the increase is modest and implies no more than they were keeping level with developments in society at large. A good many tried (we do not know how successfully) to augment their incomes by teaching or tutoring, by (at least in Yorkshire) keeping alehouses in their parsonages, or by themselves farming glebe land (a practice which was probably not as common as historians seem to think.) None of these practices were new. We know that Elizabethan society was under economic stress and that, while a great many individuals or families rose or fell in class status, the main pattern and structure of the classes and orders remained remarkably stable. It is likely that the clergy, on the whole, retained tenaciously, and were, by the other orders, kept in, their traditional place. They remained socially and legally an order apart from lay society — witness, for instance, the way their professional unity defeated all efforts by the Elizabethan government and landowners to throw clerical contributions in 'armour' and military manpower into a common county pool. On the other hand the clergy remained an order and by 1600 were still far from being a single homogeneous class, even though Harrison's statistical table attempts to treat them as one. As an order apart from lay society they were still regarded by the laity basically with a medieval kind of suspicion, sometimes near contempt and hostility, sometimes a rather baffled respect. Thomas Fuller's remark about the clergy belongs to the mid-17th century but is surely true of 1600. In 'Mixt Contemplations in Better Times' he saw English society as a human body; the head was the Crown, the neck the nobility, the chest the gentry, the loins the merchants and citizens, the thighs the yeomanry, the legs and feet artificers and day-labourers. "As for the clergy (here by me purposely omitted) what place soever shall be assigned them: if low, God grant patience; if high, give humility unto them."[36]

No one has yet attempted to study the social and economic status of the Catholic clergy. Whereas, in spite of the Reformation spoliations, the endowed income of the Anglican clergy was altogether vast, the official income of the Catholic clergy was very small. Papal and Spanish governmental subsidies, private benefactions from foreigners and money collected in England for the seminaries left them always in debt and occasionally in danger of closure. A strong reason for the admission of lay convictors to Douai college and Persons' foundation of a boys' preparatory school was an effort to raise funds for the seminary. It appears that a fairly substantial number of students and ordinands had private means. On the English mission the Jesuit missioners made a practice, from around 1585, of supporting their 'auxiliaries' initially until they could be 'found a place'. In general the incomes of missioners came from their own private resources if any ('child's portions', rent charges, legacies), stipends paid by gentry they served or collections from the faithful. It is possible that a few, like Augustine Baker in the 1620s and 1630s, made money as agents for landowners, tutors or lawyers. Some mission 'stations' were stable enough to have endowments in the hands of lay trustees by the 1620s; it is possible that this was true in 1600, though evidence is still lacking. Thus is seems that the missioners depended just as much as their Anglican colleagues on birth, patronage and ambition to make a tolerable living. Those missioners who lacked, or neglected, such helps fared at least as badly as the poorer Anglican curates, eking out an insecure existence alternately serving poorly-paid temporary 'places' and then unemployed, and usually drifting to London. The well-connected and vigorous missioners appear to have been relatively prosperous, even when in gaol, and to

---

[36] HILL, C., Economic Problems of the Church, London, 1956; DICKENS, Aspects of Intellectual Transition, op. cit.; FULLER, T., Mixt Contemplations in Better Times, London, 1660, 1st series, 2.

have had property to leave in their wills. No doubt the majority occupied an intermediate position, with steady but fairly poorly-paid work, secured only by humiliating dependence on gentry patrons, yeoman congregations or Jesuit superiors. This situation is sketched in the Appellant literature. Henry Garnet answered on behalf of the Jesuits that they were themselves caught up into the same difficulties, and were only attempting to secure an equitable distribution of the available 'places' and funds. Certainly by 1600 we get an impression that the mission was overstocked with clergy. In a flight of polemical rhetoric Robert Southwell asserted that most seminary priests were gentlemen and socially superior to the Anglican clergy. The seminary records, supplemented by some local studies in the genealogical and social background of missioners, do not bear out his assertion. It seems that seminarists were generally drawn from much the same 'mix' as Anglican clergy: there was a small minority drawn from the better-off gentry, and an equally small proletarian group. The majority came from poor gentry or yeoman stock, which is why it is so often hard or impossible to trace in any detail the family background of priest martyrs. This is undoubtedly the reason why the majority of the missioners felt themselves despised or treated as servants by the Catholic gentry.[37]

7. The eclipse of the episcopate?

The last feature of the traditional picture of the Elizabethan clergy is the eclipse of the episcopate. Very little recent work on the Elizabethan Anglican episcopate has seen the light. But it is surely unwise to underrate the bishops. In spite of their apparently antiquated, feudal estate policies and royal spoliation of their property by forced 'exchanges' and prolonged *interregna*, they most probably maintained their relative economic status in society fairly successfully to 1600. The 'exchanges' were most probably often of lands (which were economically not very profitable within the traditional episcopal estate policies) for advowsons and impropriated rectories and tithes (much more profitable if carefully administered, and increasing bishops' control over a proportion of incumbencies in the diocese). The bishops clearly had immense difficulties in controlling their dioceses. The latter were often far too large, the machinery of diocesan administration legalistic and cumbrous, parish boundaries often unreal and out of date. The aristocracy and gentry and Crown had a massive control of advowsons, impropriated rectories and tithes. It required litigation to get churches and chancels kept in adequate repair. There was a very strong pressure to reduce the bishops to the status of subordinate managers of a government-run department of State, and parish clergy into unpaid local civil servants controlled by secular

37 BROOKS, F. W., The Social Position of the Parson in the 16th Century, Journal of the Archaeological Association, 3rd series, vol. 10, London, 1945–7; LOOMIE, A. J., The Spanish Elizabethans: the English Exiles at the Court of Philip II, New York, 1963; TIERNEY, M. A., ed., Dodd's Church History of England, Wolverhampton, 1839–1843; SOUTHWELL, R., An Humble Supplication to her Matie., ed. BALD, R. C., London, 1953.

authorities. In a good many dioceses substantial minorities of the landed gentry were Puritans and Catholic recusants or 'Church Papists'. The Puritans concentrated their criticisms of the state of the Church on the episcopate, and a militant wing constantly sought to build up a vigorous 'near-presbyterian' lay and clerical organisation independent of bishops. Added to all this the bishops were not immune from the all-pervading miasma of jobbery, careerism and corruption. It is remarkable that the bench of bishops had four successive leaders of remarkable courage and character, Parker, Grindal, Whitgift and Bancroft, independent-minded fighters for a strong, reformed and modernised episcopal and clerical order capable of standing up to lay pressures. Increased episcopal control of advowsons and the higher number of university clerks residing in benefices made it possible for vigorous bishops like Horne, Cox, Sandys, Chaderton and Cooper to try to establish more effective examination of ordinands, more positive episcopal visitations, and an educational policy for the clergy through rural deanery 'exercises' and diocesan synods. The results may well have been very modest, but the very full surviving diocesan records of a good many Elizabethan dioceses represent something more than reactionary ecclesiastical bureaucracy.[38]

V. 1600—1700: the 17th century clergy

1. The mass of writing on this period leaves many features of it obscure

Someone beginning to study modern Church history could be pardoned for imagining that, in leaving the 16th century for the 17th, he will be emerging from a dark, rather medieval tunnel to run easily through a sunlit landscape relatively modern in character. A prodigious amount has been written about 17th century English religion. The century itself abounded in writers of memoirs, diaries, 'short lives', 'sufferings', formal histories and collections of documents. The contemporary urge for introspection, self-justification and speculation about personalities affected almost every field of writing from sermons to verse, theology, apologetics and even law and science. A second deposit of literature about the 17th century, even more massive, was laid by a mixture of antiquarianism, romanticism and desire to trace the pedigrees of parties by 18th and 19th century writers. There were Scott, Shorthouse and Isaac D'Israeli, the Tractarians' interest in the Laudians, Principal Tulloch's 'Rational Theology and Christian Philosophy in England in the 17th Century', the Tory revivalists, the New Whigs, Carlyle and Cromwelliana, the publication of Strype's collections. The 20th century has laid on top of all this a third, and even vaster deposit of literature and published documents, a broad river of interpretation with many unexpected tributaries. There are economic and social historians (Tawney and

---

[38] HILL, op. cit., chapters 1,2; HEMBRY, P. M., The Bishops of Bath and Wells, 1540—1640, Oxford, 1967.

Christopher Hill, following Marx and Engels' fascinated interest in 17th century England, Stone) who now regard the parson as 'the key-figure in the struggles of the time.' There are historical demographers of the 17th century as a pre-industrial society, for whom parish records form a main source. There are historians of education (W. S. Howell, Curtis, Stone, Charlton, Simon, Beales, Kearney, Costello) for whom the university clerks are of crucial importance. There are historiographers (Butterfield and Wormald) for whom Augustinianism and apocalyptic are vital. There are historians of science (Westfall, Wolf, Rabb and Kearney), intensely interested in clerical reactions. There are historians of the study of theology in Europe (Congar, Amann, Deman), of Anglican moral theology (McAdoo, Mortimer), of Biblical criticism (Congar, Tavard), of mystical theology (Knowles, Veghel, Kinloch), of Milleniarism (Thrupp, Lamond, Cohn, Tuveson, Solt), of culture (Hazard), of liturgy in England (Addleshaw, Horton Davies), of ideas of toleration (Lecler, Jordan), of Jansenism (Abercrombie, R. Clark, Cognet), of the Laudians (Trevor Roper, Bosher), of the Puritans and Dissenters (Cragg, Whiting), of 'official' Anglicanism from 1660 (Sykes, Nuttall and Chadwick), on ecclesiastical courts (Marchant), the Cambridge Platonists (Powicke, Colie, de Pauley), on English sermon literature (Mitchell). There are modern, revised editions of Walker and Calamy, and modern lives of Laud, Andrewes, Richard Baxter, Nicholas Ferrar, Goodman, Archbishop Abbot, George Herbert, Jeremy Taylor, Bishop Williams, and a good many lesser clerical figures.

Enormous as this literature is, it has two great limitations. The first is that it leaves huge gaps almost uncovered. Thus, for instance, the diocesan records of the 17th century, particularly after 1660 (when, admittedly, they become much scantier and more formal) remain largely unstudied — which is why Miss Barratt's Oxford thesis (unpublished) on the diocesan clergy of the dioceses of Oxford, Worcester and Gloucester, 1559—1660 and Canon Foster's 'State of the Church' (Lincoln diocesan records, 1571—1625) are so repeatedly quoted in books. Hence the only two (both recent) studies of the 17th century Anglican clergy (Christopher Hill and A. Tindal Hart) are brave forays into largely unknown territory, using a multitude of scraps of information culled from printed sources of very diverse kinds. The Puritans after 1603 have not yet been dealt with with anything like the thoroughness devoted by Patrick Collinson to their Elizabethan colleagues. The Laudians remain still almost totally unstudied before 1642. The bishops of the century, especially before 1642, are even less studied that the Elizabethan episcopate. There has recently been a considerable concentration by historians on varous features of Anglican theology and religious thought during the century (especially to 1642) — on apocalyptic, politico-religious theories, ideas on toleration, on science, casuistry, Ramism, historiography, 'Covenant theology'. But the 'main road' of Anglican divinity remains unstudied. The universities have been recently studied up to 1660 but very lightly after that date, and the work has made relatively little use of MS evidence. Anglican ecclesiastical administration after 1642 is virtually an untouched field. The second limitation of recent work on 17th century Anglicanism is its theological amateurism. There is no English equivalent of the 'Dictionnaire de Théologie Catholique' (later volumes and supplements) or the well-established 'school' of Continental historians of dogma which lies behind it. In England 'secular' historians, and English Literature and Modern Languages specialists (the only book on the English and Irish supporters of Jansenism is by a Modern Linguist) have been compelled to venture deep into technically difficult ecclesiastical territory because English Church historians are too few, too little trained and too preoccupied with other periods.

If anything the situation is worse in the field of studies of 17th century history of the English Catholics. Godfrey Anstruther has begun to publish a very detailed dictionary of 'The Seminary Priests' – a kind of 'Namierisation' of them as a class. There is a recent similar volume on the English Dominicans by W. Gumbley (though they were late on the scene and few), but the 'Necrology' of the English Benedictines, by H. Birt is badly in need of revision, and there is nothing similar for the Franciscans and only the extraordinary and massive jumble of documents published long ago by Br. Foley for the English Jesuits. Most of the surviving registers of the seminaries abroad appear to have been published, but they are much in need of efforts to fill the gaps and provide a modern and expert backing of other documents and notes. For lack of this they are only of very limited use. Very little has been printed on the Archpriest controversy since Law, or on the quarrels of Jesuits and seculars, the Bishop Smith affair and the Old Chapter since Sergeant's 'Old Chapter' and the incomplete Dodd-Tierney 'Church History' and Panzani's life by Berington. Brady's 'Episcopal Succession' is in great need of revision, correction and supplementing, as is Gillow's 'Biographical Dictionary of English Catholics'. Philip Hughes' 'Rome and the Counter-Reformation in England' is still useful but rather ex parte and unfinished. Similarly Gordon Albion's 'Charles I and the Court of Rome' is a valuable expanded thesis which the author was never able to supplement by necessary further researches. There is a little new material in Havran's 'Catholics in Caroline England', in P. Hardacre's 'Royalists during the Puritan Revolution', J. Kenyon's 'The Popish Plot' and J. Miller's 'Popery and Politics in England, 1660–1688'. There are very recent essays by J. Bossy on Jacobean Catholicism, and by K. Lindley on the part played by Catholics in the Civil Wars. As for biographies there is copious material for one of Augustine Baker, and printed lives of Benet Canfield, Henry Garnet, William Weston and Christopher Davenport. The volumes of records published by the Catholic Records Society, its monograph series (on recusancy in York from 1558 to 1791 by Aveling, and in Wiltshire from 1660 by Williams), a few other detailed studies of local recusant history (for Yorkshire by Aveling, Monmouthshire by Pugh, Essex, Staffordshire and Worcestershire by local research teams) and articles in 'Recusant History' provide a very dense but patchy store of regional information. In general published work on 17th century English Catholicism is so small-scale and patchy that it is still impossible to get a sketchy, but accurate, overall picture of the complexities of its development. There are immense gaps: for instance information on the training of the clergy in seminaries and religious houses, English Catholic theological and polemical writing and its connections with, and place in, the controversies then raging in France and elsewhere on the

Continent; the detailed history of the English religious houses and Provinces; the full complexities of anti-Jesuit movements and 'Brotherhoods' amongst the secular clergy after 1620; ecclesiastical organisation (mission and episcopal); English Catholic schools in England and abroad; the connection between the English and Dutch anti-Jesuit movements (noted by Professor Birrell, but still unexplored in detail.)

2. The problem of clerical numbers

Historians have lately taken up and accepted a view which was apparently current in the 17th century, that the overall numbers of clergy increased considerably, so that by 1640—1700 there was a surplus of them, clerical unemployment and underemployment, and a mounting unrest in the younger members of the profession. The main reason suggested by contemporaries was the substantial increase in numbers of students at Oxford and Cambridge up to the Civil Wars and again in the 1660s: this was supposed to have produced a surplus of graduates over available suitable jobs: hence many graduates sought ordination merely as a way out, or even became Puritans (to get in on the inner circle of Puritan patronage) or Catholics (to get to seminaries). Today historians suggest other contributory reasons: the establishment of clerical families and mass recruitment into the profession of the sons of the clergy (due to social acceptance of clerical marriage by 1600 and the build-up of scholarship places for their children); the recruiting efforts amongst undergraduates and graduates of devout Puritan and 'Arminian' tutors; the provision of more clerical jobs (fellowships, 'lecturers', chaplaincies, clerical schoolmasterships, even the deprivations of Puritan clergy in 1606—7, the 1630s, 1642—60 and 1662.) It has been suggested that perhaps the clerical establishment was undermanned up to 1600 and so there was slack to be taken up. It is possible that there was a transient general improvement in the real incomes of Anglican pastoral clergy in the economic booms of 1603—12 and the 1630s, or even after 1670. Thus, if these speculations are true, the overall numbers of the Anglican clergy would have reached a peak (and also perhaps their average age) by the 1690s.[39]

Oddly enough such theorists have so far ignored evidence that numbers of non-Anglican clergy increased substantially during the century. The modern authority on the Dissenting clergy of 1662—1700 ventures no definite opinion on their statistics. But some 1200—1400 clergy were ejected from benefices in 1662. Their leaders, up to 1672, were unwilling to compromise chances of 'comprehension' within the Church of England by conducting non-episcopal ordinations. However from 1672 Dissenting ordinations began, and academies produced ordinands on such a scale (for instance Frankland's academy produced 110 ministers by 1700) that by the 1680s there were signs of overproduction,

---

[39] HILL, op. cit.; CURTIS, M. H., The Alienated Intellectuals of Early Stuart England, Past and Present, vol. 6 (fasc. 23), 1962, pp. 25—43; STONE, L., The Educational Revolution in England, 1540—1640, ibid., vol. 8 (fasc. 28), 1964, pp. 41—80.

and ministers began to take to schoolmastering. No historian has yet shown more than very passing and casual interest in English Catholic clerical statisticals. But there is enough published material to support a theory that there were far more Catholic clergy in 1700 than in 1600. The 'foundation movement' and opening of English Provinces and novitiates of religious Orders from the later 1590s obviously produced very fast an extra body of regular clergy alongside the seminary priests. Recusant numbers seem to have increased considerably up to 1642; endowments for 'places' and missions increased, the supply of 'places' increased, the establishment of a securer and safer congregational organisation and of schools facilitated recruitment of ordinands; seminaries even began to acquire bursaries. It is possible that the Catholic clergy continued to receive small but useful accessions from convert graduates and Anglican clergymen, especially in the 1630s, 1650s and James II's reign. Thus we could imagine that whereas in 1600 the English clerical scene was overwhelmingly Anglican, with a very small contingent of Catholic priests and a handful of Protestant sectary ministers, by 1700 the non-Anglican minister of religion was a well-known feature, and the Catholic and Dissenting clergy substantial minorities − even if Gregory King in 1688 ignored them in his economic table.[40]

The suggestions are backed by a good weight of suggestive evidence and probabilities. But we still lack solid statistical evidence. Statistical judgments by 17th century observers have to be treated with caution. A string of writers, from Perkins to Defoe, judged that the country needed fewer, but better, clergy: but such judgments are perennial and have no statistical importance. Detailed efforts at statistics were then invariably crippled by the absence of reliable basic material and the extreme complexity of administration. The Catholic 'Old Chapter' habitually made wild and contradictory estimates as to the number of Catholic missioners. The Dissenting leaders seem to have had no machinery for collecting reliable statistics. No two authorities up to 1700 ever succeeded in agreeing on the tally of Anglican benefices, and no one even tried to count curates, lecturers and chaplains. As for observers' general impressions: they were to a large extent governed by the special conditions of 17th century English society. In a pre-industrial society there could be frequent, sudden, and quite strangely localised increases or decreases in population, usually caused by natural disasters such as famine, plague or 'sweating sickness' (influenza), by 'depopulation' (of town centres or of villages by emparking), or (amongst clergy) by deprivations (often with very patchy regional differences). English society consisted of many relatively small communities which were long habituated to adjusting to such rapid changes, and yet very allergic to discrepancies between local supply and demand caused by them. Thus it appears that in 1600−42 observers tended to think the country overpopulated because of high prices and 'dearth' and unemployment: after 1660 they thought it under-populated because prices were static or even falling. Ecclesiastical institutions

[40] CRAGG, G. R., Puritanism in the Period of the Great Persecution, 1660−88, Cambridge, 1957; AVELING, H., The Education of 18th Century English Monks, Downside Review, Spring, 1961.

and the clergy had a rough passage during the century. There was a good deal of intermittent but sharp persecution or disturbance of clerical minorities, very possibly more deprivation of benefices than in 1534–1600, and more political and economic pressure on colleges and seminaries. Hence – over and above problems of supply and demand of clergy caused by natural disasters – the clergy seem to have had an unusual amount of adjusting to do to political upsets in their organisation, recruitment and employment prospects.

We should probably be safe in taking Gregory King's rough 1688 estimate of Anglican clergy at 10,000. We are told by various authorities that there were, around 1603, 8,600 or 9,200 benefices, possibly 2,500 of which were held by pluralists. We do not know how many stipendiary curates, chaplains, lecturers, clerical schoolmasters without cures, university dons and unemployed clergy there were, nor how many benefices were currently unoccupied. We certainly have no means of estimating exact clerical numbers in 1680–1700. As for statistical evidence of clerical undermanning amongst Anglicans up to 1600, we only know that Lincoln diocese had 1285 clergy in 1585 and 1184 in 1603. Our sources of information on Catholic clerical numbers teem with gaps and pitfalls, but it seems reasonable to think that there were about 400 priests in 1600 (about 300–250 of them seculars – in England, the rest overseas) and 1200 in 1700 (about 550–250 seculars, 300 regulars – in England, and 650 overseas – in the great majority regulars). By 1700 we may guess there were 1000–1200 Dissenting ministers, and so 2200–2400 non-Anglican clergy to 10,000 Anglicans.[41]

Judging the extent to which, if at all, the clerical element bulked larger in society in 1700 than in 1600 statistically is a highly speculative enterprise. In the first place we are hazy about the population figures, both absolutely and in religious groups. Moreover, as historical demographers point out, many English churches in the 17th century cannot have had enough 'sittings' to accommodate all parishioners, and there were most probably a great many who rarely attended church. Observers in the later 16th century noted large numbers of 'atheists', 'mislikers of religion' and 'neuters'. In the first years of the 17th century Sarmiento thought that, in a total population he estimated at 3.6 million, 600,000 were mere 'conformists' and another 900,000 'atheists'. It was a commonplace amongst observers like Greenham, Perkins, George Herbert, Jeremy Taylor and Aubrey that many of the lower orders, and an alarming number of educated people had no real religion. In a well-known passage Bindoff accepts the guess of the medievalists that in 1500–34 the English clergy formed up to 1 in 50 of the adult population – possibly 15,000. In 1688 Gregory King estimated the total population at 5½ million, possibly a 50–60% increase since 1534, and if there were then some 12,000–13,000 clergy of all denominations, they formed about 1 in 130–140 of the adult population – compared with Bindoff's rough estimate of 1 in 1400 today. The relative decrease (1534–1700) was to be expected, considering the vanishing of most religious and chantry priests, and the extreme slowness of the administrative machine to

---

[41] FOSTER, op. cit.; ANSTRUTHER, op. cit.

adjust parish boundaries to increases and shifts in population (though private enterprise did something in this direction, through 'lecturers', 'augmentations' by parishioners, private chaplaincies and Catholic and Dissenting 'gathered congregations.') Still the relative decrease was small, and clergy thick on the ground throughout the 17th century.

The overall increase in clerical numbers owed much to religious devotion, but at least as much again to more material causes: the multiplication of denominations, and, within denominations, of competing ecclesiastical establishments; the relative shortage of non-clerical professional jobs for graduates; and even wasteful ill-deployment of clergy. Amongst Anglicans there was always a shortage of graduates, or clergy of any kind, to man stipendiary curacies and poor benefices. The much-increased inflow of graduates into pastoral cures probably increased the number of pluralities and so the problem of finding enough poor clergy. In poor dioceses, especially in Wales and the north, and everywhere in periods when demand for clergy suddenly soared, Anglican bishops were hard put to it to find ordinands of sufficient quality and numbers. Down to 1700 there were more than twice as many Catholic missioners, secular and regular, in the south than in the north − a relative proportion which much exceeded that of overall population between the two areas. The reason was clear: the poverty of the north. But quite apart from this, Anglican bishops, with the best will in the world, could often exercise little control over the admission of ordinands or the coming and going of clergy since these were bound up with private contracts made by patrons. Patronage was an all-pervasive spider's web of quasi-contractual relationships in which bishops, as well as clergy, were caught: violence done to it by a bishop could rebound on his own head in many unforeseen and unpleasant ways. Also contemporary ideas about divine vocations by no means excluded a variety of very ancient and mundane pressures which still brought many into clerical life: this fact inevitably made examination of candidates for ordination difficult. So, for instance, John Strype took Orders because it had been his dying father's wish. John Aubrey was pressed hard by his eminent friends (including a bishop) to take Orders as a way of escaping bankruptcy. Catholic seminary Presidents had their own acute problems about ordinands and the supply of priests. The English mission and the funds of seminaries were tightly enclosed within the gentry patronage system. The placing of missioners could only be very partially negotiated by secular priest superiors: such placing was by private treaty between missioner and patron. Priests after ordination could hang about the Continent for years, seeking benefices or acquiring higher university degrees. The problem as to whether the student son of a gentry benefactor and secular mission patron should be dismissed the seminary or not for insufficient motivation, or whether he should be ordained was sometimes painful. Religious superiors were caught in similar dilemmas. Sometimes they refused entrants for lack of funds and places: at other times they were desperate for subjects to man the impressive plant of houses founded enthusiastically during the expansive early years of the century. In 1615 the Jesuit General Vitelleschi ordered a pruning of the Provinces, the harder screening of candidates for admission, the limitation of novitiate numbers, and the closure of redundant houses. The Appellants accused the Orders of sacrificing the good of the mission to the welfare of the houses abroad by sending missioners simply to collect funds, patronage and recruits for the religious' schools and novitiates. Even religious had to be allowed to keep *peculium* (their patrimony) on the mission and this caused much heart-searching, a good many breaches of discipline and even some litigation.[42]

There were other factors increasing the great complexity of clerical staffing problems. The Anglicans received a dribble of ex-Catholic priest converts (including an Italian archbishop of Spalato) and foreign Protestants (du Moulin, Saravia, Peter Baro), which was probably balanced by their loss of clergy to the Catholics or (like Cartwright and William Ames) to foreign Protestantism. As a large proportion of Catholic priests lived and worked abroad (including the English Jesuit mission in Maryland and Jesuits lent to the Dutch mission in the 1650s) so the Anglicans had clergy going to the colonies, or as embassy chaplains and chaplains to merchant communities. There were Anglican clergy who abandoned clerical life for secular occupations in part or whole – even William Perkins conceded that there might be good reasons for such a course. Lastly the Catholic clergy suffered a substantial toll of losses by apostasy, mental and physical breakdown, and the relatively high death-rate in epidemics in the seminaries and religious houses.[43]

3. The prima facie case for a great improvement in clerical education and intellectual vigour in this period

It has generally been assumed that the 17th century English clergy, particularly the Anglican clergy, were, on the whole, more earnest, better educated and professionally trained, and even more prolific of fine poets, mathematicians and scientists than either their 16th century predecessors or 18th century successors. There is a good deal of *prima facie* evidence in support of this view. As we have seen, the proportion of graduates amongst the Anglican pastoral clergy grew remarkably during the century. French observers are reputed to have called the Anglican clergy *stupor mundi*, and far more learned than their Continental counterparts. 17th century Anglican theological literature forms a *corpus* a good deal larger in quantity, and more solid and systematic than the writings

[42] DICK, O., ed., Aubrey's Brief Lives, London, 1972, p. 118; AVELING, H., Northern Catholics, op. cit.; Douai Diaries, 1598–1654, Catholic Record Society, vol. 10, London, 1924; LAMALLE, E., Catalogues des Provinces S. J., in: Archivum Historicum Societatis Jesu, vol. 13, Rome, 1944; ALLANSON, A., Biographies of English Benedictines, Ampleforth Abbey Library, York.

[43] PERKINS, Workes, op. cit., vol. 2, p. 763; like St. Paul and the Patriarchs, for some good reason such as poverty "I doubt not but the ministers of the Gospel now may take unto them other callings provided they are no hindrance to their principal calling nor offence to men."

of the Reformation and Elizabethan divines, more modern in language and outlook, and certainly more influential on the development of Anglican thought in the 18th and 19th centuries. This *corpus* was remarkably comprehensive: Scriptural scholarship (Walton, Usher and their collaborators in the 'Biblia Polyglotta'), Patristics (Young, Usher, Montague, and Laud's impetus to the study of the Oriental languages), Church history (Heylyn, Hacket, Fuller, Stillingfleet, Burnet, Strype), systematic divinity (Field, Leigh, Francis Mason, Thorndike, Beveridge, South, Jeremy Taylor), 'experimental divinity' (Perkins, Preston, Sibbes), moral theology and 'cases' (Ames, Bramhall, Sanderson, Davenant, Jeremy Taylor, Richard Baxter), apologetics (Chillingworth, Montague and a host of others), 'mystical divinity' (Law, Ken, Joseph Hall). It was an age of scholarly liturgical studies, of the Scottish Prayer Book of 1638 and the Non-Juring liturgy, of a widespread cult of 'retirement', meditation and 'contemplation' (Nicholas Ferrar and Little Gidding, Andrewes, Cosin), and of clerical religious verse (Donne, Herbert). The sheer volume of all this religious book-production implies (even when generous allowances have been made for the pressures towards publication of careerism, patronage and fashion, and the smallness of editions) a much increased theologically literate reading public. As for Anglican clerical earnestness, this was an age when writers of all groups were obsessed with the idea of vocation, the age (to 1642, at least) of the greatest Puritan pastors and college tutors, of Herbert, Baxter and George Fox. It seems even more obvious that the Dissenting clergy, the bitter critics of clerical ignorance and laxity, must have been model pastors. Amongst Catholic missioners surely the remarkable increase in recusant numbers to 1642 implies an apostolate more effective than that of the Elizabethan missioners. Although Catholic university clerks produced no single theologian with the stature in Catholic Europe of Stapleton, they had a serried array of very able manualists (Holden, Kellison, Broughton, Bishop, Champney, Davenport) of a kind lacking before 1600, much abler controversialists (Knott, Letchmere, Leyburn), remarkable historians (Cressy, Benet Weldon, Augustine Baker). They had two quite remarkably acute (if eccentric) speculative theologians (Thomas White als. Blacklo and John Barnes), and two very influential writers of 'mystical divinity' (Baker and Canfield) heading the array of devotional manuals produced by the reflowering of English religious houses. They even had a major clerical poet, Richard Crashaw.

The 16th century English clergy produced vigorous party-debates, but nothing so remarkable as the 17th century profusion: the second wind of the Puritan movement, with its massive influence on the 'English revolution' of 1642–60, and its offspring (the Evangelicals, the Presbyterians, Congregationalists, Baptists and Quakers); the Arminians and their offspring, the High Church party and the Non-Jurors; the Cambridge Platonists and the Latitudinarians from the 1650s; the secular priest 'Blackloists'; the quarrels within religious Orders over 'primitive observance' and 'contemplation'. Considering all this evidence, we might well conclude that, more than any other age except perhaps the 11th and 12th centuries, the 17th century saw the English clergy at the peak of their influence over society and intellectual life.

4. 17th century Anglican views on the Ministry

But is it possible to get behind this customary, very dazzling *prima facie* impression? We can, to some extent, probe the 17th century's 'image' of the minister of religion. For Anglicans their massive literature teemed with references to the clerical profession, with arguments about its history, its *iure divino* forms, and its precise functions, and with mountains of (usually New Testament) exhortations to the clergy. But express treatises on the Ministry were surprisingly few: Perkins 'Treatise of the Vocations or Callings of Men'; George Herbert's 'A Priest to the Temple', Jeremy Taylor's 'Clerus Domini', Burnet's 'Of the Pastoral Care'. In reading these we get a strong impression of ambiguity. On the one hand to them the Ministry is the supreme divine 'gift', a terrifyingly important, exalted and responsible post: on the other hand it is thought of as something common, earthy, utilitarian, natural, a part of the professions of magistracy and teaching, a job subject like all jobs to family, social and patronage pressures. Thus to Perkins the minister is 'the mouth of God', his professional operations are all 'sacraments'. This sounds immense. But he also insists that the nature of God's plan of redemption is such that He always acts presently and directly through the Son and Holy Spirit on human souls, and the Church and its 'regiment' are only the 'signs' and 'voluntary (not physical) instruments', or occasions declaring outwardly the will of God to give grace directly to souls when the occasions are used. Thus in preaching the minister supplies a voice outwardly, and that is the normal occasion of the interior operation of the Spirit in the heart of the hearers by the act of Christ alone. Ministers are in no way the 'deputies' of an absent Christ, wielding powers committed to their discretion. But this 'Augustinianism' is only part of the reason why Perkins downgrades the ministry's power. To him the ministry is 'regiment' — preaching the Word, administering the sacraments, the use of the power of the keys in admonition, censures and excommunications. This is an almost formal, external divine instrument of correction meant for the ordinary carnal parishioner. If we object that Perkins thinks highly of the sacraments, and especially Holy Communion, as occasions of a Real Presence and conveyance of the grace or inherent righteousness of the manhood of Christ, it is clear that Perkins thinks of the sacramental ministry as somehow the confirmation of the existing, *ab aeterno* election and faith of the few, and not the ordinary redemptive force for the multitude. Anyway to him the supreme 'gift' is not this 'regiment' or ministry but the 'calling of a Prophet or teacher'. The ministry is a utilitarian, ordinary calling, on the level of shepherds, ploughmen, magistrates, schoolmasters, lawyers and physicians. (Of course we have to remember that to Perkins all society and its callings are subsumed into the redemptive plan of God: there is ultimately no merely 'natural order'.) The Prophet-teacher, or true 'divine', is no mere don or scholastic, but the heart of the pastoral office of the Church; the universities are essentially 'schools of the Prophets'. In plain language, Perkins regards the ordinary pastoral clergy as like the Levitical priesthood; true ministry is confined to the highly trained university clerk theologian. Thus vocation for the ordinary clergy is usually a plain matter of choice by parents, masters, tutors and 'the Governours of the Church'. Perkins nowhere rejects the existing oddities of the ecclesiastical benefice and patronage system. As in a system of arranged marriages, this system went with acceptance by ordinands and later growth into realisation of their vocation. He knew there were plenty of misfits, and his theological system made generous allowance for strange divine mercies.[44]

With slight differences of style and emphasis George Herbert and Jeremy Taylor presume much the same view of the clergy. To Herbert their prime function is "to reduce Man to the obedience of God", to Taylor it is "government". The great mass of the people are litigious, ignorant, quarrelsome, even hostile to the clergy, and certainly incapable of deep religion. They need from their clergy correction, admonition, "present rewards and punishments" (Herbert), and a steady drilling by catechism and services into at least the outward habits of religion. Here and there, relatively rarely, a predestinate faith and righteousness will appear. It was significant that Perkins, Herbert and Taylor had all of them a very short and slight experience of the ordinary parson's lot; they looked down from the eminence of the 'prophets and teachers', intellectuals relying on the company of those of their own degree, at home only in 'gathered congregations' of well-educated, devout people. Herbert, for instance, only spent inside three years at Bemerton. Previously he had been much concerned in the foundation of Ferrar's select, 'gathered' community at Little Gidding, and in the rebuilding (on highly intellectual, scholarly liturgical principles) of the ruined nearby church of Leighton Bromswold. It general it is hard to resist the conclusion that 17th century Anglican thought on the Ministry (Puritan or Arminian) was basically intensely traditional, and, like traditional thought, very much conditioned by the social, educational and economic realities of a preindustrial society. It was traditional that there should be a 'monastic' distinction between an elite, highly educated clergy, spiritual guides, confessors (a function much stressed by both Puritans and Arminians), writers and preachers, and the ordinary clergy dealing with the bread and butter 'regiment', religious and secular, of the rough mass of the population. It was also traditional that the 'monks' should always hope some day to 'monasticise' even the ordinary clergy, but admit that, de facto, that day was still remote in the future.[45]

5. 17th century English Catholic views on the Ministry

17th century English Catholic thought on the Ministry has to be pieced together from many scattered references: from Appellant literature, Bishop Richard Smith's 'Monita Quaedam utilia pro sacerdotibus, seminaristis et

---

[44] Ibid., pp. 747ff., A. Treatise of the Vocations or Callings of Men.
[45] HUTCHINSON, F., ed., The Works of George Herbert, London, 1941; BURNET, G., Of the Pastoral Care, 3rd ed. London, 1713, in spite of BURNET's reputation for liberalism, is almost medieval in its traditionalism: the ordinand should form himself mentally from Cicero, Horace, Seneca and The Imitation of Christ.

missionariis Angliae', Kellison's writings, the 'dictates' used by missioners, Navarre's 'Enchiridion' (long used at Douai), Augustine Baker's 'Treatise on the Mission', controversial literature on the sacrificing priesthood. In general we find much the same view of the Ministry as amongst Anglicans, in all its traditionalism. But the picture is made very sharp in outline because fierce debates between seculars and regulars, and both with educated laymen, fixed especially on the problem of the status and functions of the clergy. The battle of ideas between Catholic and Protestant, and the battles of factions within both camps appear to have been strictly civil wars: all parties accepted the traditional broad view of the clerical state and its place in society, while disagreeing violently about the relative positions of the component features of the picture. Thus the laity (unless under strong clerical influence), whether Puritan or Catholic, tended to accept that there must be a strong, patriarchal religious-secular 'regiment', in which the clergy should play a prominent part. But they stressed the traditional distinction between a learned, prophetic, 'monastic' clerical élite, and the ordinary, utilitarian, 'secular' clergy. The former might well exercise a strong guidance over the 'regiment' and the laity, simply as a religious influence, without juridical sanctions; the latter, with their canonical 'regiment', were the natural servants of the gentry. This point of vew was expressed equally by ordinary Anglican gentry, Puritan gentry (Presbyterian or Independent alike), by the Catholic gentry who memorialised Bishop Richard Smith, and by Lord Baltimore and his agent, Lewger, in battle with the Jesuits in Maryland. It was, basically, the attitude of both James II and his Whig opponents.[46] The vocal elements amongst the Catholic secular clergy, Appellant, in the Archpriest controversy, the Smith controversy, and the Blacklo 'stir', constantly insisted on real and juridical clerical control of the religious-secular 'regiment'. They wanted ordinary episcopal government, with its traditional secular legal sanctions (obtainable only under a Catholic king), to rescue them from their subjugation to control by an alliance of the Catholic gentry and the 'monastic' clergy. Yet these secular priests accepted the traditional distinction between the 'monastic' élite clergy and the rest: but they tried to maintain that this distinction did not coincide, in real life, with that between regular and secular missioners. They insisted that the religious state only provided a formal 'opportunity' for 'perfection', which was often, in reality, unused by religious, whereas the secular priesthood (and some added, the lay state) provided an informal, but more real and effective 'opportunity'. Thus, in their view, regular missioners as regulars had no automatic title to superiority (or, indeed, right to be on the mission at all); as priests they had the right, and an equal 'opportunity' for superiority over the 'regiment', with the secular priests. Only God could decide which priests, secular or regular, by predestination and grace would attain that superiority and right to rule. In any case it was assumed that only a small minority (marked out externally by higher degrees in divin-

[46] HUGHES, T., History of the Society of Jesus in North America, New York, 1907, vol. 1, pp. 370 ff.; HUGHES, P., Rome and the Counter-Reformation in England, London, 1942, pp. 250 ff.

ity) would attain the goal: the majority of clergy, secular and regular, could expect, in this evil world, to remain more or less utilitarian hacks and underlings. Catholic religious seem to have been divided on these matters. Some held that all regular missioners as regulars were automatically the élite clergy set over both secular priests and gentry. Augustine Baker disagreed. He thought the religious state did offer a unique haven of spiritual vantage, but that, in the predestination of God, that state could be attained outside the formal discipline of religion, and even outside the priesthood and the sacramental system. Indeed such true 'contemplatives' or 'monks' were the best missioners. It appears that he accepted the necessity, *propter peccata*, of 'regiment', and hence of an ordinary clergy who were not contemplatives, and so only formal, external missioners. His views owed much to his peculiar intellectual background. He had had no formal ecclesiastical or theological education, but was self-educated, particularly in late medieval and 'Devotio Moderna' spiritual literature, and in monastic history. He had left an Italian monastic novitiate before profession, was professed as a monk privately in England, and was generally at odds with his English religious superiors and absent from choir duties during his very intermittent residences in their monasteries. His voluminous writings, constantly recast, did not see publication until after his death and never had much circulation: but his personal influence, and that of his small body of 'Bakerist' disciples were important. He was an eccentric, but his thought represented a powerful strand in classical and medieval Catholic tradition, and a strand strong in the 17th century right across the denominational spectrum, in some Jesuit thought, in Mary Ward and her controversial 'English Ladies', amongst the English Capuchins (Benet Canfield and Archangel Pembroke), strongly in Anglican devotional works, and amongst the sectaries and Dissenters.[47]

6. The theory and practice of Anglican 17th century clerical training

Anglican views on the education of ordinands will have to be pieced together from many scattered sources, such as William Perkins' 'Workes', Seth Ward's 'Vindiciae Academiarum' (1654), Obadiah Walker's 'Of Education' (1673), Laud's Oxford Statutes, the series of 'Guides' or 'Directions' for undergraduates, the 16th and 17th century books in Oxbridge college libraries (with their inscriptions and *marginalia*), many *obiter dicta* of most major clerical writers of the century. Perkins stresses that the major divine gift of Prophecy (or Teaching), and the minor one of Ministry are exalted callings demanding more spiritual fitness and Bible-reading than any other calling. So he constantly warns ordinands against mere professionalism and intellectualism. They must concentrate on 'experimental divinity' and 'cases of conscience'. He is particularly wary of 'school (or questionary) divinity' and Patristics. School divinity should only be read by students after prayer to be saved from temptations. Both subjects are

[47] BAKER, A., Holy Wisdom, ed., CRESSY, S., London, 1948; WATSON, Decachordon, op. cit.

dangerous on two grounds: they are so fashionable and intellectually exciting that many students neglect experimental divinity and cases for them; school divinity is rooted in a medieval tradition making human opinion the judge of Scripture. We should therefore imagine that Perkins — like Barrow the sectary — must have wanted to remove ordinands entirely from the universities into 'academies' associated with devout 'gathered' congregations. After all Perkins himself exercised an extra-collegiate, congregational ministry to undergraduate ordinands and educated laity in Cambridge. But, on the contrary, he still favoured a university setting for the training of ordinands. He had inherited the medieval idea that 'the service of God' is necessarily a learned profession with a high technique far above the grasp of the uneducated, and requiring rare gifts of application, a special kind of intelligence and years of arduous mental drill. 'Clerk' equalled 'scholasticus'; universities were seminaries; divinity was 'the art of arts', not only the apex of learning but its governing influence throughout. The Bible taught the primacy of universities. The 'schools of the prophets' (Joshua XV: 15) were 'the city of books, or, as we say the University'; the college of the apostles was a university. Universities must be brought back to their essential function, the training of ordinands through Arts and Divinity courses supervised by tutors who were devout divines. Perkins realises that such divines will never be more than a small minority even in universities, but they must control and leaven the lump — the layboys, students reading law or medicine, ordinands never going to get beyond Arts. The prophetic ideal must be set before all and rub off to some degree on all. The Divinity course must centre firmly on Scriptural commentary, allied with 'cases'. But though 'school divinity' and Patristics must never take precedence, they have an essential place as ancillary disciplines, using St. Thomas' 'Summa' and the works of St. Augustine, St. Bernard and St. Gregory Nazianzen. He was hostile to shortened, formalised 'dictates' in 'positive divinity' and 'cases', of a kind which he knew to be fashionable amongst Catholics and spreading at the English universities. To Perkins this was not learning, and ordinands (either divines or artists) taught in that fashion would be bad spiritual guides and confessors. We get an impression that his lectures to artists (and educated lay undergraduates) in experimental divinity and cases were personal *tours de force*, shortened and simplified, but still fully representative of his complete course for divines.

After Perkins his ideal of a seminary-university appears to have remained standard orthodoxy amongst most Anglicans to 1700: it was defended by Seth Ward (1650s) and Obadiah Walker (1670s). The 'case divinity' of Sanderson, Jeremy Taylor, Beveridge and South could only have been written with such an ideal in mind. Some Anglicans despaired of its chances of fulfillment and toyed with the foundation of seminaries outside a university setting — for instance the Ecclesiastical Seminary and General College projected on a grandiose scale at Ripon in 1590-1605 and Burnet's seminary at Salisbury in the 1690s. The ideal had to be defended ever more strenuously against such defeatists and also against the 'moderns', whose vision of a declericalised university took shape in Gresham College from 1600, and in the Durham University of the 1650s. As for Perkins' ideals for the divinity curriculum for both divines and artists, it appears that the general line remained orthodoxy, while later writers acquiesced in practice in methods of execution of it which would have outraged Perkins. This was probably because Perkins was a very exceptionally gifted teacher, and his ideal one which very few dons could execute in all its purity.[48]

There is a dispute amongst historians about the effectiveness of divinity teaching at the universities down to 1642. Some are inclined to be impressed by the number of devout college tutors (for instance Meade, Preston, Holdsworth, Goffe, Duport), and the evidence of abundant extra-curricular courses, and so think the Perkins ideal worked well to 1642. Others are unimpressed, think that teaching standards were generally poor and the Arts and Divinity courses so formalised, uninspiring and traditionalistic that real life and originality in divinity only existed outside Oxford and Cambridge. Certainly the book lists in the 'Guides' and the bookshelves of colleges show a very heavy dependence on Continental textbooks. In Arts Ramist and other Protestant 'Christianised' texts gave way to Jesuit books in Logic, philosophy (Suarez), Rhetoric and Ethics. In Divinity Melancthon's and Zanchius' 'Loci Communes' and Calvin's 'Institutes' largely gave place to separate manuals for Scripture, Positive and School Divinity. The usual diet now consisted of Keckermann, Maresius or Wendelin (Protestants) with St. Thomas' 'Summa' (usually in simplified Jesuit versions) and Melchior Cano's 'Loci Communes' (Catholic). It is odd that so few English Protestant manuals of divinity (usually only Perkins and Davenant) rubbed sides on the college bookshelves with such a mass of Continental manuals. Even in 'Cases' it seems unlikely that Ames, Davenant, Sanderson and Taylor succeeded in ousting from favour the Catholic (mainly Jesuit) manuals in use. In the 1590s Perkins had already lamented increasing use at Cambridge of such Catholic manuals. In 1616 Ralph Cudworth, his editor, listed the Biblical commentaries most in use in Cambridge: almost all were Catholic. His only criticisms are objective and utilitarian: thus Alphonsus, Tostatus and Salmeron are far too verbose and tedious; on the other hand Emmanuel Sa 'the Jesuit' is altogether too brief, but Lyra, Hugh of St. Caro and Comestor are just right, and Comestor best of all, 'a good text man.' There seems to be little doubt that, at least to 1642, the universities remained islands of academic tradition, which obstinately ran in its own course in spite of government efforts to control it, and Puritan efforts to canalise it. Wooden academic formalism coexisted with lively originality, bone idleness with very hard work, paternalistic rigour with licence, idealism with hard academic practicality. Ramism failed, in spite of its intellectual appeal, because it simply did not work in the lecture-room. 'Scholasticism', never abandoned, now had a new, strong lease of life, largely because its Humanistic opponents had failed to provide a viable alternative spine to the curriculum, and 'scholasticism' was an academic discipline which could readily adopt, and exist alongside, almost any new subject or

---

[48] BUSSBY, F., The Ecclesiastical Seminary at Ripon, Journal of Ecclesiastical History, vol. 4, 1953, pp. 154–161; CLARKE, T. E. S. and FOXCROFT, H. C., Life of Gilbert Burnet, Bishop of Salisbury, Cambridge, 1907, p. 292; for Anglican pleas for seminaries see BURNET, Of the Pastoral Care, op. cit., and NELSON, R., Life of Dr. George Bull, Oxford, 1816.

The academic careers of some 17th century Anglican clergy illustrate
John Williams, later Lord Keeper and Bishop of Lincoln, went up to St.
Cambridge in 1598. His college had long been renowned for its size, the
th of its divinity and of its internal disputes. Williams remained unaffected
is, or by the contemporary peak of Perkins' evangelism. During and after
Arts course, he devoted most of his energies to extra-curricular studies in
Greek, Hebrew (with a rabbi), music and French. It was a very secular education. Good patronage then procured him a chaplaincy to the Lord Chancellor
and he was ordained. In his ample leisure in London he gravitated to a bookish,
intellectual circle in Westminster, read cosmography with a Westminster Abbey
divine, studied history with Spelman and Cotton, and read Baronius and widely in the Fathers. He had had no systematic course in divinity, experimental
or school. John Preston went up to Queens', Cambridge in 1603 with too much
money and no ideas on a career. He began the Arts course with distaste, and
dodged it for music: he contemplated leaving for the Sorbonne. Eventually he
went through with the Arts course, and then sampled all the higher courses: he
found divinity 'a kind of honest silliness'. So he began to read medicine (a
notoriously bad course in England) and spend more time on archaeology. In
1611 he was converted by a sermon by a devout tutor and decided to be an
ordinand. Embarking on the Divinity course, he soon found it distastefully arid,
and deserted the lectures to read for himself, mostly the Schoolmen, Aquinas,
Scotus and Ockham. Then he went through to divinity graduation brilliantly,
and became a celebrated tutor of ordinands, university lecturer in divinity and
college head. The width of his interests made him *persona grata* in London as
well as a very effective divinity teacher. William Cartwright was a Student of
Christ Church, Oxford who never graduated in divinity, but taught Arts, was a
famous evangelist preacher, and a brilliant academic playwright. He was a prod-
igiously hard worker. It is therefore not very surprising that, even after 1670,
when complaints about academic standards multiplied, most Anglicans persisted
in believing that, with all their obstinate faults, the universities were irreplace-
able as the main clerical seminaries.[49]

7. Developments in English Catholic clerical training

The clerical training of English Catholics in the 17th century is fairly well
documented from surviving seminary and regulars' records, from 'dictates',
from surviving books which belonged to missioners, from Richard Smith's
'Monita', from the published works of Catholic divines and from *obiter dicta* in

[49] KEARNEY, op. cit; HACKET, J., Scrinia Reserata, Oxford, 1693; CLARKE, SAMUEL, Lives of
Thirty-Two Divines, London, 1713. There are other examples of very learned clergy who
were self-taught or largely tutored outside universities: Richard Baxter (Autobiography,
London, 1931; SYLVESTER, M., ed., Reliquiae Baxterianae, London, 1696); George Bull
(Nelson, op. cit.); Edward Stillingfleet (SYKES, N., From Sheldon to Secker, Cambridge,
1959).

correspondence and controversial works. In 1610, when Robert Persons died, there were 11 English Catholic training establishments for ordinands: the colleges for seculars at Douai (staffed by secular priests but with Jesuit confessors), Rome, Valladolid, Seville and Madrid (probably staffed the same way, but with rather more Jesuit control), secular priest 'residences' at San Lucar and Lisbon; a Jesuit college at St. Omer (also a preparatory school for secular ordinands), a Jesuit novitiate and house of studies for scholastics at Louvain, and two small Benedictine novitiates and juniorates at Douai and Dieulouard (Lorraine). Moreover there were always a few English ordinands outside this system, getting ordination from the Jesuit Germanicum in Rome, in Poland, Italy or even Ireland. A good many English regulars were in training in non-English houses: Benedictines in Italian and Spanish monasteries, Franciscans, Capuchins, Minims, Augustinians, Dominicans, Carmelites and perhaps an odd Oratorian, in houses in Flanders, France and Italy; there were English Jesuits scattered from Poland to Sicily. The whole system was expanding, but its future very insecure. The English Jesuits were in process of setting up a Provincial organisation, in the teeth of opposition from many quarters: from the Jesuit Generals (who were about to discourage expansion), from the Spanish government in Flanders (moved by James I), from the university authorities at Louvain (who bitterly resented the Jesuit presence there), and from an alliance of some English secular priests (who wanted the seminaries free of Jesuit influence) with the Benedictines (largely formed from dissident, anti-Jesuit seminarist recruits). The seminaries were periodically convulsed by anti-Jesuit demonstrations. The death of Persons disturbed his whole elaborate and precarious structure of patronage arrangements. The English Benedictines only established themselves at Douai after a battle with the Jesuits there, and their superior at Dieulouard was a prominent anti-Jesuit. They found it impossible so far to persuade many English Benedictines of Italian and Spanish congregations to join the English Congregation, and they had many more ambitious projects for expansion than they had manpower and money. Their Congregation, being formed as a typical 'reformed' one, was balanced ideologically on a sharp knife-edge between 'primitive observance' contemplative influences and activists. The other English religious were still struggling, usually in vain, to win the right to establish English Provinces of their Orders and to devise means of finding and financing houses and disciplining the missioners they had in England.

In the event the fortunes of these English establishments between 1610 and 1642 were mixed but better than had been feared. The Jesuits acquired their full Provincial rights in 1623, with a novitiate moved from Louvain and its bitterness to Watten, and houses of studies at Louvain, Liège and Ghent. In 1619 the English secular priest opposition wrested full control of the English College, Douai from them. The arrangement seemed sensible. Douai was by far the largest seminary and would supply the secular mission. The Jesuits retained fair control of the other, smaller secular seminaries, but could recruit students for them from their own college at St. Omer and so expect to avoid disturbances. In effect, it was hoped, the missioners in England would henceforward be clearly divided into three compartments, Douai seculars, Jesuits and 'Ignatian seculars'

9*

together, and other regulars. The mass of the secular missioners would thus be
free of Jesuit control and organised under an Archpriest or Bishop. These hopes
of peace were not really fulfilled. The division of the seminaries and mission
contributed, along with many other causes (not least the aggressiveness of Bishop
Richard Smith) to harden and widen the cleavage between Douai seculars and
the Jesuits (and their auxiliaries). Of the smaller establishments, Madrid and
Seville became moribund, San Lucar failed to grow into a seminary; in Portugal,
Lisbon eventually became a second 'Douai' secular seminary. Thus by 1642 the
expansion of seminary places for 'Douai' secular ordinands and the shrinkage of
output of 'Ignatian' seculars from Jesuit-controlled seminaries (due to an increase in Jesuit vocations from the colleges and the loss of Lisbon, Madrid and
Seville) gave the anti-Jesuits a considerable numerical superiority amongst
secular missioners. Meanwhile the other regulars were having their own travails.
In the 1620s the English Benedictines over-extended themselves by a multiplicity
of very diverse new houses and works (at Paris, Chelles, St. Malo and La Celle
en Brie in France, and Rinteln and Lamspring in Germany). These were largely
politico-religious moves, made possible by the Catholic reform movement in
France and the Hapsburg Counter-Reformation advances in Germany. By 1642
the Benedictines had been forced to relinquish most of these acquisitions. The
survivors, St. Edmund's, Paris and Lamspring in Hanover were respectively a
Congregational house of studies for the Sorbonne and a semi-independent
Imperial abbey – the latter an embarassment in a Congregation organised without abbots. The internal struggle between contemplatives and activists had been
patched up by making Dieulouard a contemplative 'house of primitive observance'. The English Franciscans succeeded in establishing a Provincial organisation in 1623 with a house of studies at Douai. The Dominicans, after long
struggles and a string of apostasies, founded a small Province in the 1650s. The
other, smaller Orders struggled on in vain. Besides all this several 'Colleges of
Writers' came into existence. These were partly to house priest scholars engaged
in controversial writings, and partly hostels for priests studying for higher
degrees. In 1611 the anti-Jesuits set up Arras College in Paris. Under various
names (Arras, Cambray, Tournay or St. Gregory's College) and in various
premises, it lasted out the century on a very small scale. The Jesuits appear to
have had their own college of writers attached to their house of studies at Louvain in the 1620s and 1630s. During the same years Matthew Kellison, rector of
the English College, Douai formed an *ad hoc* writing and publishing group with
some of his staff.[50]

In spite of numerous crises due to the reasons sketched above and to war
conditions (the English College, Douai was very near extinction in 1610–1), the

---

[50] HUGHES, op. cit.; CHAUSSY, Y., Les Bénédictins Anglais Réfugiés en France au XVIIe
Siècle, Paris, 1967; LUNN, D. M., The Origins and Early Development of the Revived
English Benedictine Congregation, Cambridge Ph. D. thesis, 1970; CHADWICK, H., St.
Omer to Stonyhurst, London, 1962; GUILDAY, P., English Catholic Refugees on the Con-
tinent, 1558–1795, London, 1914, p. 106 n., 322–323, and TIERNEY, op. cit., vol. 4,
Appendix cclxix, on Arras College and Douai writers.

seminaries, secular and regular, seem to have profited as much as the Protestant universities and schools in England from the fashionable educational boom of the years 1610–42. Then war conditions in England in 1641–6 with the disorganisation of the English mission and economic slump played havoc with them. In 1641 Kellison's successor as rector at Douai found a huge debt and only 8 ordinands and lay boys in the house. In 1642–4 the English Jesuit Provincial had to circularise foreign Provincials to ask if they could find employment and keep for 80 of his subjects. A recovery began in 1646–8 as numbers picked up. After 1660 they remained mostly stable, but below the peak of 1620–41. There was a short-lived boom of ordinands in 1685–8.

In spite of the obvious, broad differences between this Catholic seminary (and house of study) system and the Anglican university systems, there was a considerable similarity in aims and methods. The general view on both sides was the normal setting for the training of ordinands should be a university, and that country seminaries were a *pis aller*. Persons had no illusions about university conditions throughout Europe: an increasing flood of lay students, ecclesiastical students and studies being driven into a corner, much extra-curricular teaching, student unrest, a general and violent professional suspicion of Jesuits on the part of university authorities. The Jesuits were widely suspected of trying to infiltrate into university teaching posts (so ousting secular priests), of drawing away students to attend lectures in Jesuit colleges in university towns, of sometimes getting legal university status for Jesuit colleges near established universities. Yet Persons was resolute in trying to fit the English seminaries into university settings. He thought that perhaps preparatory schools and novitiates (St. Omer and Watten) were best kept in the country, but had doubts whether he was right. Much of the teaching in such establishments had to be done by scholastics, and shortage of manpower and money made it difficult to allow them more than short intermissions in their own university studies. He thought an academically 'learned' priesthood essential for staffing schools and seminaries, for converting or controverting Protestant divines, for impressing the increasing numbers of educated laity, and as good confessors. So major seminaries must be connected with universities, though the degree and nature of the connection had to vary with circumstances. He personally thought some things were essential: a very strict house discipline, censored and directed reading, a very full programme of classes taught by dictation, memorisation of the dictates and testing of the memorisation by 'exercises'; teachers must also be 'safe'. The founders of the Benedictine, Franciscan and Dominican provinces seem to have agreed with most of this. Hence the whole developing complex of English establishments, secular and regular, by 1642–60, stood firmly in a university setting. Thus associated with the university of Douai were the English College, the Benedictine and Franciscan houses of studies and Scots and Irish seminaries. The English College, Rome had long had a papal grant of the right to award higher divinity degrees, and was associated with the Jesuit Gregorianum university. The English college, Valladolid was linked with the universities of Valladolid and Salamanca. The unsuccessful colleges at Madrid and Seville appear to have been part of Jesuit plans to found their own Arts and Divinity faculties (or even complete universities) there. The English college and Irish seminary at Lisbon were linked originally with the Jesuit university of Coimbra. The Benedictine house of studies and Arras College of Writers at Paris frequented the Sorbonne, and the English Jesuits and Irish Franciscans at Louvain the university there. The regulars generally had their novitiates and 'houses of retreat' in the country-side, but even they had university links. Novices and juniors often did their Arts courses there and were then moved for further Arts or Divinity to houses of their Province (or of foreign religious) in universities. Dieulouard, deep in the Lorraine countryside, was a 'house of retreat' to 1658, and, in principle, tried to educate its monk-students right up to the priesthood inside the confines of the house, having superiors (William Gifford and Edward Mayhew) who were very competent university clerk divines. But even before 1658 students were some-times sent to the nearby Jesuit university of Pont-à-Mousson. After 1658, when Dieulouard ceased to be a house of retreat, the more able monk-ordinands were regularly sent to the universities of Pont-à-Mousson, Douai, Paris or Trier. The even more isolated Benedictine houses in Germany also had university connec-tions: Rinteln (only an English house in 1629–33) was actually itself a papal university in miniature, staffed with graduate religious able to run Arts and Divinity faculties for German students; Lamspring ordinands frequented the universities of Trier, Douai and Paris.[51]

In all of these cases relations with the academic life of the universities was real but limited. We need to be far better informed about the inner workings and politics of European universities in the 17th century before we can interpret the numerous references to English ordinands matriculating, taking degrees or teaching in university colleges and faculties. The Anglicans had, roughly speak-ing, three grades of ordinands. The first grade (and great majority) simulta-neously read the full university Arts course and a private, extra-curricular, course (or just reading) of simple Divinity, perhaps attending college or univ-ersity lectures by divines as far as time allowed. The second grade graduated in Arts, and then either at the university before ordination, or outside it after ordination, did a similar private course. The third grade read Arts and then Divinity (even if they did not complete the Divinity course) at the university. (There was, of course, a fourth grade of those who never saw a university.) The Catholic system had two clear differences from this. Firstly, Catholic ordinands did not normally take the full university Arts courses; secondly, their private, domestic Divinity courses were a good deal more officially organised than Anglican ones. But, even when we take into account these differences and the more intensive devotional life of the average Catholic establishment, the practical workings, and effects on the students, of the two systems seem to have been very similar. On arrival in a seminary or novitiate, Catholic students were graded according to their academic background, age and ability (all of which varied considerably). Hence, since the establishments were usually small, teach-ing arrangements proved complex and difficult. Some students were badly gounded in Arts and unintelligent: if they were young enough, they usually did

---

[51] AVELING, H., The Education of 18th century English Monks, op. cit.

a domestic Arts course (of a heavily simplified kind, called 'Humanities'), skipped the full Arts course, and went straight on (as *Positivi*) to a very elementary 'gentleman's' course in Divinity for 3 years before ordination. Those of this kind who were older (for instance Thomas Thwing, who arrived at the English college, Douai in 1600 aged 27 and very ill-grounded in Grammar) often skipped both Humanities and Arts and did a 'crash' 'Positive Divinity' course in two years or even less to ordination. These domestic Positive Divinity courses seem to have consisted of a rapid run though dictated notes on Controversies, Cases of Conscience, Positive Theology and Rubrics (of the Missal, Breviary and Ritual), with retreats on entry and before ordination. 'Controversies' meant stock, short answers to Protestant objections mostly taken from Bellarmine and simplified, with exegesis of some texts of Scripture; 'Cases' were drawn from Navarrus or Toletus; 'Positive' might be a run through the Catechism of the Council of Trent; it might, more ambitiously, be Cano's 'Loci Communes' much simplified, or, less ambitiously, merely be some doctrinal prolegomena to the Controversies and Cases, with reliance on what a student could pick up from sermons in college and some directed reading. The 'crash' course for older men, and perhaps mostly for all students of this level, seems to have been taught in English. It is not easy to make out what proportion of Catholic ordinands were *Positivi* (young and older). Lewis Owen, in his 'Running Register' in 1626, wrote: 'I have known many made priests and sent into England that ... never learned the Grammar, for there are but few of them that study Logick, Philosophy or Divinity, but their only study is in Cases of Conscience'. We have to make allowances for Owen's rhetoric, and by 'Cases' here he doubtless meant the whole Positive course, which was often called 'Cases' *tout court* at Douai. It is hard to find seminary lists of classes after 1619 (when the creaming off of the best students from Douai to Valladolid and Rome finally ceased) or, indeed the size of Cases classes. At least we can be certain that the body of missioners contained a sizeable proportion no better, or only very slightly better, educated than non-graduate Anglican clergy. Panzani and other observers in the 1630s remarked that lack of education was one cause of the many laxities and irregularites occurring amongst missioners. At that period it was generally agreed that the regulars were somewhat better-educated than seculars, with the glaring exception of the 'Cassinese' and 'Spanish' (not in the English Congregation) English Benedictine missioners and the few belonging to small Orders. In 1610 a list of the Jesuit missioners by *doctrina* contained 37 *Theologi* (School Divines), 15 *Positivi*, and one *Humanista* (a temporal coadjutor). Later in the century the Benedictines had a respectable proportion of *Theologi* but a majority of *Positivi*. The *Theologi* missioners, many of whom had taught in houses of studies, generally had respectable personal libraries, and the Benedictine Northern Province, by the 1670s, had a small but impressive common library of French theology and recent editions of the Fathers, acquired through the patrimony of a monk from a wealthy family.[52]

---

[52] Douai Diaries, op. cit.; HARRIS, P., ed., Douai College Documents, 1639–1794, Catholic Record Society, vol. 63, London, 1972; FOLEY, op. cit., vol. 7/1, p. lxix.

A third grade of Catholic ordinands arrived fairly well qualified in Humanities, or even in parts of the Arts course. They generally were matriculated at the university and went through (if they stayed the course) to a baccalaureate in Arts. Since most Arts teaching in European universities was then done 'domestically' within colleges, it was generally easy to have these students taught wholly either by the seminary staff in the house (if it was recognised as a college of the university) or by such of the seminary staff as were university teachers (or others) at the Jesuit college or other religious house in the town. Thus members of the teaching staff at the English college and at St. Gregory's, Douai were not infrequently university lecturers teaching at the Anchin and Marchiennes colleges of the university. After the third grade students became bachelors, or abandoned the Arts course, they became *Theologi*, studying School Divinity for four years. As far as possible the teaching for this was done 'domestically'. The more able *Theologi* were sometimes employed part-time teaching Arts or the easier parts of Cases. The weakest third grade men sometimes were excused a year or more of the course. Moderate students completed it but were not presented for the university 'exercises' leading to the award of the baccalaureate in divinity. The ablest students took the baccalaureate, were retained to teach 'domestically', and sometimes later allowed to proceed to a doctorate. Early in the century Anglicans and Catholics had been scornful about each other's divinity degrees. But, although there is sufficient evidence of doctorates being granted, throughout the century, both in England and abroad, with suspicious ease and speed, when it came to the point neither side rejected each other's degrees outright. Indeed Anglican undergraduates and graduates often frequented European universities. From 1597 the Roman Curia tried to ensure that English Catholic students only proceeded to higher divinity degrees after 4 full years to the baccalaureate and another 4 to the doctorate. Whether due to the operation of this decree at Douai (where in fact it alone applied), or, more likely, to a lessening urgency to man the mission and an increasing demand for divines to staff English establishments, things worked better for the rest of the century. Most ordinands or priests who were capable, and desirous, of taking divinity degrees seem to have had a chance to take them, even returning from the mission for that purpose. Most divines served as teachers in seminaries or houses of studies, and a few went on to profess divinity at universities at a distance — for instance Henry Holden at the Sorbonne.

8. A comparison of the two training systems

It is not easy to decide which of the two training systems, Anglican and Catholic, produced better results. Manifestly they shared some weaknesses. Some of these (narrow academic formalism in approach, syllabuses and teaching methods, an inability to do more than drill the unacademic in forms of words and rituals, a chronic shortage of money) were parts of the common academic inheritance they shared. On both sides these particular weaknesses were, in part, alleviated by the same factors. To both the religious revival up to the 1650s brought a new energy, increasing numbers, bursaries and scholarships, new colleges. Both were affected, even if very slowly, by the increasingly liberal currents in contemporary lay society. This produced wider interests, and a distinct *penchant* for mathematics and science amongst some divines. Clerical amateurs in these fields were to be found amongst Puritan divines (for instance Archbishop Ussher and his chaplains, Lawrence Chaderton as a botanist, John Preston *in materia medica*, Samuel Ward as a geometrician), Arminians (Peter Turner as a Gresham Professor of Geometry), Godfrey Goodman the eccentric bishop of Gloucester, bishops Sprat and Seth Ward. Doubtless a few such amateurs were to be found amongst Catholic priests. A very lively and distinguished group of amateur scientists existed in the 1650s and 1660s amongst the Lancashire recusant gentry: most of them had been educated by priests at Douai or Jesuits at St. Omer. The 'new philosophy' (Cartesianism) crept in amongst clergy and dons at Oxford and Cambridge from the 1670s, and was adopted by the Cambridge Platonists, though still, even in 1700, it was unable to capture the academic ecclesiastical seats of power. We still do not know when, and to what extent, the 'new philosophy' affected English Catholic seminaries, *studia* and divines. It had certainly gained a predominance over them by the 1730s and 1740s. Amongst both Anglicans and Catholics the violent reaction of the ecclesiastical Establishment against this liberalism helped to produce clerical rebels and radicals: amongst Anglicans there were John Hales, William Chillingworth and the Latitudinarians; amongst Catholics the regulars, Thomas Preston als. Widdrington, John Barnes and Christopher Davenport, and the seculars, Blacklo, Fitton and Henry Holden.[53]

In theory the Catholic training system was undoubtedly the better of the two. It was free of the trammels of the benefice system in England and Oxbridge academic traditionalism. It was better organised. It was far closer to the wide field of international scholarship. But in practice there was probably little to choose between the two systems. The strictures of Edward Knott S.J. in the 1630s on the culture of educated Anglican clergy are probably just as true of well-educated Catholic clergy, and certainly reveal the narrowness of Knott's own education: 'their learning consists in some superficial talent for preaching, languages and elocution, without any deep knowledge of Philosophy, especially of that solid, subtile and succinct method of School-Divinity.' Jeremy Taylor criticised impartially both clergies for much the same faults of woodenness of principles combined with a facile verbal dexterity and a superficial interest in all the latest ecclesiastical controversies. The 17th century Anglican and Catholic divines shared much the same weaknesses: a cult of great erudition, acquired by over-rapid 'riding post' through too many books and keeping indexed commonplace books of quotations, while all too often falling into inaccuracies: a striking literary facility covering an inability to see through clearly to the end the consequences of points which they could throw out so easily. They were incurably

[53] HILL, C., Intellectual Origins of the English Revolution, Oxford, 1965; KEARNEY, op. cit.; WEBSTER, C., Richard Towneley, 1629–1707, and the Towneley Group, Transactions of the Historic Society of Lancashire and Cheshire, vol. 118, 1966, pp. 51–76.

combative and spent ink in defending quite indefensible positions: the absolute
superiority of Aristotle; the apostolic origin of a variety of (mutually exclusive)
forms of Church government; that the pre-Nicene Fathers taught *verbatim* the
Nicene Faith; the necessity of some absolutely certain *regula fidei*.[54] Finally it is
interesting that both Anglican and Catholic clergy fought the claims of women
to a new liberty and voice in religion. Thomas Fuller notes the leading part
played by women in the troubles of 1642–60 as one of the evils of the age.
Aubrey was probably speaking for his relatively liberal clerical friends when he
wrote that women were the chief pillars of superstition. Amongst Catholics
there were at least two spiritual battles on this issue in the course of the century:
amongst the English Benedictines over the devoted defence of 'Bakerism' by
Augustine Baker's nun friends at Cambrai, and the astonishing affair of Mary
Ward and her English 'Jesuitesses' (which provoked her superb defence of
women against traditional male denomination, and the savage response of
seculars, regulars and the Roman Curia.)[55]

9. English 17th century clerical parties

The many English clerical parties and controversies of the 17th century are
often cited as proof positive of the clergy's intellectual vigour. But this view has
lately been attacked on two grounds: that the parties were very small minorities
and most clergy solidly uninterested in real intellectual issues; and that each
major party or controversy so far examined closely and critically has proved to
be based far more on material and accidental issues than on real ideological
points. Even impressively religious or philosophical debates (like the row over
Baianism, the 'De Auxiliis' disputes, the debate on Arminianism, the Jansenist
dispute and the quarrel between 'the new philosophy' and its traditionalist opponents), it is argued, were intimately bound up with university politics, problems of academic expansion and jobs, struggles between religious Orders, struggles between rival clerical parties or between seculars and regulars to influence
sovereigns and patrons so as to procure ecclesiastical seats of power or benefices,
the defence of threatened institutions, livelihoods and power. These very material
sides to the disputes, in an age when the clergy in general felt underprivileged,
underpaid, dominated by the laity and insecure, must account for widespread
and even passionate clerical interest in the great quarrels. The wider spread of
education amongst the clergy, albeit a thin spread, enabled then to make some

[54] KNOTT, E., Charity Maintained, (no place), 1630; TAYLOR, Jeremy, Clerus Domini,
Works, vol. 14, pp. 414ff., Oxford, 1839.
[55] COLLINSON, P. The Role of Women in the English Reformation, in: Studies in Church
History, vol. 2, ed. CUMING, G., Leiden, 1968, pp. 258ff.; CHAMBERS, M. C. E., Life of
Mary Ward, London, 1882, vol. 1, pp.15ff., 375ff., and MARY WIGMORE's MS Vie de
Marie Ward (Bar Convent Archives, York); BOSSY, J., The English Catholic Comunity,
1903–25, in: SMITH, A. G. R., ed., The Reign of James VI and I, London, 1974; BAKER,
Sancta Sophia, op. cit., on Contemplation (far more frequently found in women than in
men); FULLER, op. cit., Mixt Contemplations in Better Times, 1st series, i.

sense of the abstruse and technical nature of the party arguments used. But the superficiality of clerical learning amongst the ordinary clergy and their obsession with the material interests at stake surely deprived the ecclesiastical disputes of a real intellectual force. It is also arguable that the controversies were, at root, the result of deep-seated, and apparently universal, tensions in society. These were tensions between an absolutist, 'Augustinian' rigorism and a 'devout humanist' (in some almost agnostic) reaction against it; an increasing liberalism and a very strong, fearful reaction towards paternalistic authoritarianism. These tensions appear to have existed, in varying degrees and combinations, within the household of faith. There was an internal civil war in the minds of individuals, clerical movements, religious Orders, denominations. The same tensions apparently ran like earthquake faults across denominational boundaries. This must account for a good many features of the century: agonised interior psychological conflicts; a permanent inability to decide between conflicting views in some, and in others an obsession to seek some absolute, exclusive truth as the only escape from all-devouring doubt; the many internal contradictions and tensions characteristic of 17th century clerical parties; the prevalence of conversions of many kinds. The psychological conflicts, along with the 'anxiety neuroses' bred of perfectionism and the thirst for absolute religious assurance, must help to account for the widespread vogue in all denominations for casuistry, spiritual directors, and 'instant' ways to holiness and certainty. It was an explosive age for the clergy. The Anglican Church was twice cut asunder by major schisms. The English Catholics only narrowly avoided a schism from Rome of the kind which actually happened in the United Provinces. The Dissenters were much divided. Such a violent and widespread disorder surely requires violent and general causes to account for it — a 'civil war' of tensions deep in educated society, beyond rational analysis (given as the age was to self-analysis), and a very general (if often incoherent) involvement by the ordinary clergy.

It is probably therefore not surprising that the major clerical parties defy analysis. Recent determined attempts by specialists to define 'Puritanism' have largely failed. It cannot be identified *tout court* any longer with anti-Remonstrant Calvinist doctrines of Predestination and Reprobation, or with 'moral Augustinian' or 'Jansenist' attitudes, since these doctrinal and moral attitudes were very widespread indeed up to 1642, far beyond the bounds of the group of clergy and laity then regarded by their opponents as 'Puritans'. It was the Benedictine, Augustine Baker, who wrote: 'The senses are not given to be possessed of any affection at all or fruition, but the mere simple use of them is allowed us for the good of the soul and the contentment the appetite naturally takes in them is no further to be admitted than inasmuch thereby the spirit or rational will is enabled more cheerfully to pursue its supreme good.' As the author of a recent book on early 17th century Anglican divinity has said perceptively, it is misguided to judge theologians by lifting single passages, or even the exposition of particular doctrinal points, out of the whole context of their thought. Perkins obviously accepted a fully Augustinian doctrine of Predestination and Reprobation, and 'Jansenistic' moral passages exist in profusion in his 'Workes'. But these features are very much softened and refracted by many other passages on the Incarnation, Church and Sacraments, on sanctification and the combat of flesh and spirit which are full of an 'optimism of Grace' and of deep humanity. Pretty well every writing divine of the century, Anglican Puritan, Arminian, Dissenter, Catholic expressed ideas which were equally curious mixtures of predestinarian absolutism and humanity, of moral severity and liberalism. It has been suggested that, even so, it is possible to separate out Catholics from Protestants, and, amongst Protestants, Puritans from Arminians by subtle and distinctive 'flavours' common to the divines of each group. We can add, of course, that the clerical parties can be distinguished by their differing attitudes to certain contemporary shibboleths: between Catholics and Protestants these were the Papacy, Transubstantiation, the Sacrifice of the Mass, the seven Sacraments, praying to the saints; between Puritans and Arminians they were the Bible and *adiaphora*, 'relics of Popery', *iure divino* Episcopacy. We may reasonably wonder whether either of these two suggested sets of lines of division had much real doctrinal content. Unusually discerning 17th century divines on both sides of the Anglican-Catholic divide (Perkins, Chillingworth, Davenport, John Barnes) do not seem always to have been very sure that the barrier was unsurmountable.[56]

No historian has yet attempted a very thorough-going analysis of 'Arminian' and 'High Church' theology, though it has been noted that these clerical parties were neither very united in views on policy or in doctrinal opinions. What are we to make of 'Arminians' who were 'Calvinists', or of the 'Arminian' William Chillingworth, who was a liberal, an acid critic of 'Augustinian' orthodoxy and of academic School Divinity? The Catholic Appellants and opponents of the Archpriest Blackwell were regarded by Martin Array, Blackwell's proctor, as heretics by implication, if not by outright statements. The Appellant priest William Watson, flatly lumped together the teachings of Calvin, Machiavelli and Robert Persons as equally 'turkized atheism'. (These are fair examples of the habitual tendency of 17th century clerics of all parties to make abundant use of the argument from the 'flavour' of an opponent's writings and to turn party shibboleths into absolute, metaphysically certain, principles.) What are we to make of Thomas White als. Blacklo, by far the most prolific, original and influential English Catholic divine of the century? He was variously regarded by his Catholic opponents as a heretic, a Jansenist, a Gallican, a 'Hobbist' (he was a crony of Thomas Hobbes, widely regarded by the orthodox as a Machiavellian secularist and atheist). By his very respectable Old Chapter and secular priest friends and his able theologian pupils, Fitton and Holden, he was regarded as an orthodox divine, albeit very obscure and using to the full the speculative licence allowed to School divines. Meanwhile no specialist has yet attempted the massive work of analysing the vast *corpus* of his writings and those of Fitton and Holden. By the latter years of the century 'Gallican' and 'Jansenist' were being freely applied as terms of abuse in Catholic clerical party warfare. 'Gallican' was clearly a term with a meaning, though in practice susceptible of very wide

---

[56] BAKER, Sancta Sophia, op. cit., on Mortification; NEW, J. F. W., Anglican and Puritan, the Basis of their Opposition, London, 1964.

variations and degrees in different groups and individuals. At least one Jesuit historian is now ready to consider the real possibility that there were Jesuit 'Gallicans'. It is arguable that the great majority of English non-Jesuit clergy in 1642—1700 were 'Gallican' in some sense: 'Gallican' French manuals were certainly in wide use in English seminaries and *studia* early in the 18th century. A French historian has lately suggested that 'Jansenism' as a coherent body of doctrines may be a myth and creation of other French clerical parties. Be this as it may, the English Benedictines in Paris said Mass for the Port Royal nuns up to 1661; the English Benedictine nuns of Paris were very devoted to the Port Royal community, whose earliest spiritual director had been the English Capuchin, Archange Pembroke. Jansenius had a good many English priest friends; Bishop Richard Smith was a close friend of St. Cyran. It has been pointed out that English Catholic apologists (at any rate seculars) comparatively rarely mention, or condemn, 'Jansenism'. As for the theory of the 'flavour' of doctrines, it seems noticeable that in the mid-18th century some English Jesuits and Jesuit-directed nuns and laity had all the supposed 'flavour' of 'Jansenism' while they overtly and violently equated 'Jansenism' with all that was bad and heretical, and other English clergy, generally thought to have been tinged with 'Jansenism', show traces of a liberal optimism of Grace. It is also strange that some leading English Catholic priests of the mid-19th century 'Second Spring', themselves bearing for life in their minds (as converts from Anglicanism) strong influences of their Evangelical upbringing, judged that traditional English 'recusant Catholicism' was shot through with Gallicanism and Jansenism.[57]

10. Did the economic and social status of the clergy change?

Granted therefore that the English clergy as a whole were very possibly rather more numerous, and certainly more uniformly and a little better (or perhaps just a little differently) educated in 1700 than their predecessors in 1600, were there any other changes in their state? Modern historians of the Anglicans and Dissenters are uncertain about the answer to this question. The economic position of the Anglican clergy in 1700 does not seem to have differed markedly from that of 1600. The real income of benefices and curacies seems, with inevitable periods of lagging and difficulty and variations between groups and areas of

[57] TYACKE, N. R. N., Arminianism in England in Religion and Politics, 1604—1640, Oxford D. Phil. thesis, 1968; McGRATH, P., Papists and Puritans under Elizabeth I, London, 1976, pp. 31—46, and LAMONT, W. M., Godly Rule: Politics and Religion, 1603—60, London, 1969, pp. 56—78, 136—59, for the debate on Puritanism and Arminianism with references; LAW, T. G., The Archpriest Controversy, vol. 1, p. 117 (Array), p. 220 (Watson); BRADLEY, R. I., Blacklo and the Counter-Reformation, in: CARTER, C. H., ed., From the Renaissance to the Counter-Reformation, New York, 1965, pp. 348—370; CLARK, R., Strangers and Sojourners at Port Royal, Cambridge, 1932, pp. 10—13 and chapter II; PUGH, R., Blacklo's Cabal, (no place), 1680; BLET, R., Jésuites Gallicans au XVIIe. Siècle?, Archivum Historicum Societatis Jesu, vol. 29, 1960, Rome; COGNET, A., Le Jansénisme, Paris, 1965.

the country, to have kept pace with the rising cost and standard of living. This
left in place all the long-standing inequalities between the incomes of a clerical
aristocracy of wealth and pluralities, those of a middle group of incumbents of
fairly good benefices, and those of poor incumbents and stipendiary curates
especially in outlying and depressed areas. A wide variety of small changes
during the century partly alleviated, and partly accentuated, the chances and inequalities, so that the effects seem to have cancelled each other out. These
changes were an increase in the number of lecturers, house chaplains and naval
chaplains, a more solid acceptance of clerical marriage and the rise of clerical
dynasties, the relieving of the poorer clergy of some taxation after 1609, and an
apparent slight increase in the number of noble or gentry clergy after 1660.
The Anglican clergy were thus most probably no nearer forming a homogeneous
economic group in society by 1700. The economic status of the Dissenting clergy
from 1662 cannot have seemed anything novel. Anglicans had then long been used
to a good many clergy being, in whole or part, dependent on stipends from
patrons or congregations. The Catholic English mission in 1700 had some features
of canonical organisation it had lacked in 1600. It had episcopal Vicars-Apostolic
with 'districts', archdeacons and deans. But these bishops still had few of the
powers of ordinaries. They were subject to Propaganda in Rome; they had
relatively little control over the large body of regulars on the mission; and
bishops, the superiors of the regulars and the missioners, secular and regular,
were *de facto* severely hemmed in by their strait economic dependence on gentry
patrons and congregations. The decrees of Trent had not been promulgated in
England, so missioners and people were still theoretically bound by medieval
canons which presumed a religious situation very different from that prevailing in
reality. Hence the economic status of missioners can have changed little in the
course of the century. Stipends of family chaplains probably lagged behind the
rise in the standard (if not the cost) of living, but the discomforts of this were
usually cushioned by benefits in keep and kind, payment for sermons and
supplies, Mass stipends and the missioners' private incomes. Religious either had
peculium (the Benedictines) or maintenance by their superiors in times of unemployment, sickness or need. 'Missions', which steadily increased in numbers,
especially after 1660, had incomes and allowances which depended on a host of
private arrangements. These were increasingly supplemented (at least until the
numbers of Catholic gentry declined notably towards the end of the century) by
Mass endowments or endowments for priests. A list of the 50 missioners in Lancashire in 1639 (26 seculars, 14 Jesuits, 10 Benedictines) seems to show that they fell
into three groups: family chaplains, peripatetic missioners serving several houses
of minor gentry with their tenants, and 'householders' serving more proletarian
congregations from one centre. Anglicans, Dissenters and Catholics suffered alike
greatly from strait economic dependence on the laity. The secular priest William
Watson, Augustine Baker, Bishop Richard Smith, George Herbert, Laud,
Richard Baxter and Calamy condemned the subservience it inflicted on the clergy.
All denominations made numerous efforts in the course of the century to alter the
system — for instance Bancroft's scheme of 1610 to restore tithe and glebe
universally to incumbents, unite small benefices, revive mortuaries and prevent

simony; Laud tried to recover impropriated tithes and increase church rates; the Puritans tried to increase clerical stipends at the expense of bishops and cathedral Chapters; Burnet was still trying to achieve something in the 1690s. Amongst Catholics there were the efforts of the secular priest 'Brotherhoods' to secure an equitable allotment of 'residences', Bishop Smith's plans to put pressure indirectly on patrone, the efforts of the Vicars-Apostolic after 1688 to regularise and increase mission endowments. The most drastic of all these schemes (the expropriation of bishops and Chapters) was actually carried out by the Commonwealth but reversed at the Restoration. All the other schemes foundered on the rock of lay patronage and patrons' property rights.[58]

It is also hard to see that any significant change occurred in the social standing or prestige of the clergy. Admittedly there were factors at work during the century which may have tended to increase the standing of some of them, but these seem to have been effectively offset by other forces tending to depress the clergy as a class. Amongst the Anglican clergy the favourable factors were: the great increase in the number of clerical graduates, the rise of clerical dynasties closely allied with other professions, a possible increase in the number of younger sons of gentry (and nobility after 1660) being ordained, the political alliances and affiliations of clerical parties, the authoritarian reaction against Dissenting 'enthusiasm' and schism (since the firm support of the clergy was necessary to such a reaction). On the other hand the Anglican clergy, especially after 1662, had to bear the unpopular burden of the Establishment. Because of its nature as a 'regiment', with its economic charges on the community and its legal powers of moral surveillance, this was resented by the laity by long tradition. In the course of the 16th and early 17th century the legal burden had actually been increased. The events of 1642—62 had inevitably put an end to the traditional view that the clerical Establishment was, however burdensome, obviously right and inevitable. From 1662 a very large proportion of the population (Dissenters, Papists, the poor and irreligious) openly rejected the system. It was understandable that the Dissenting leader, Richard Baxter, should see the clerical Establishment as the source of all spiritual evils. In his 'Catholick Theologie: Plain, Pure, Peaceable for Pacification of the Dogmatical Word-Warriors' (1675) he wrote: 'I need not tell any learned Man, how many even moderate Papists, much more Protestants, have thought that Constantine and other Emperors that over-exalted the Clergie poured out Poyson into the Church.' The Establishment, he thought, bred anticlericalism; it required, as its justification, an extreme clericalism which bred 'Clergie tyranny', clerical party warfare and exaggerated dogmatism. It was the core of Popery and by retaining it, Anglicans split English Protestantism and played into the hands of the Papists. But even the Bishop of Salisbury, Burnet, in his 'Of the Pastoral Care' (1692) hinted at the same conclusion obliquely: "A

---

[58] TINDAL HART, A., Clergy and Society, 1600—1800, London, 1968, chapter 4 and references merely demonstrates the absence of detailed studies of Anglican and Dissenting clerical economics after 1660; HEMPHILL, B., The Early Vicars-Apostolic of England, London, 1954; AVELING, H., Northern Catholics, op. cit., pp. 329 ff.; BURNET, G., History of His Own Times, London, 1723, vol. 1, Book 2.

Clergy-man, by his Character and Design of Life, ought to be a man separated from the Cares and Concerns of the world and dedicated to the Study and Meditation of Divine Matters." With extraordinary openness, Burnet remarked that the Catholic Counter-Reformation had manifestly succeeded where the English Reformation had failed abysmally: to cut the clergy loose from material cares and make them esteemed as men of God. He painted an unreally exaggerated picture of contemporary Catholic missioners as devoted pastors, free of ambition and legal cares.

It has recently been suggested by Hill and Kearney that all the social, economic and educational forces affecting the Anglican clergy in the course of the century ultimately made astonishingly little difference to their character as a group and their place in society. For all his snobbery and sentimentality, John Aubrey's conscious and unconscious estimate of the post-Restoration clergy was probably accurate. Like Pepys, he detested 'the cassock' as such ('Faugh: the Cassocke stinks'), and that was his main reason for refusing to consider ordination seriously even when it was the only way he could escape bankruptcy. He was conscious of the existence still, in considerable numbers, of rustic, ignorant clergy (like the father of his friend Thomas Hobbes), throwbacks to "the Clergie of Queen Elizabeth's time", with livings worth £6 or £7 a year. They were proletarians, peasants belonging to the old world of fairies and witches which Aubrey watched in its slow decline with a mixture of nostalgia and dislike. Then there were ordinary parsons, generally graduates and a cut above the clowns, but devoid of cultured or literary tastes and clearly outside the gentry and Aubrey's circle of friends. Next came real university clerks, beneficed or not. These were almost invariably bred in the tradesman (or, more rarely, professional or clerical) rank but with the luck to get 'their Rising' to more prestigious jobs by fortunate university connections and patronage, or perhaps good marriages (like John Wilkins) or dynastic clerical nepotism (like Edward Davenant). Such clergy usually owed most to their wit, literary tastes and interest in 'the mathematiques' or 'experimental philosophy'. Thus Stillingfleet's 'Origines Sacrae', his brilliant pamphlets and sermons and his wit lifted him out of a country rectory to London lectureships, pluralism and high preferment. Burnet similarly offset his obscure Scotch origins by writing, wit and running 'though some courses of chemistry' in his laboratory. Such clergy were fit company for gentry but never themselves had real gentry status. There were gentry by birth amongst the clergy, but they were relatively few. The younger sons of the gentry took freely to trade and secular professions, but in 1700 they still showed a marked reluctance to seek ordination.[59]

There were factors operating to maintain, or even increase, the prestige and status of the Catholic clergy. The growth of their system of schools abroad meant that a substantial section of the recusant gentry now had a semi-clerical

---

[59] KEARNEY, op. cit., pp. 28—33, 142—4; HILL, Economic Problems, op. cit., pp. 338 ff.; AUBREY, op. cit.; CLARKE and FOXCROFT, op. cit., p. 177.

education and hence ties of outlook with their clergy, and especially with the religious, who had 'Old Boy networks' cemented by family connections and pious confraternities. There was some small increase in the number of missioners of gentry birth, and even a few sons of peers. Throughout the century 'Court Catholicism' existed and some extra prestige accrued thereby to a few priests. Finally, by 1700 the Catholic clergy had a well-defined mission organisation and class of secular and religious superiors. But, on the other hand, there were in operation factors depressing the status of the clergy. Freedom from the burden of the Anglican Establishment did not, as Burnet imagined, create an ideal environment for missioners. The Appellants, the Jesuits, Bishop Richard Smith, the Old Chapter, the Vicars-Apostolic, the clergy Brotherhoods all, in varying ways, stood for a (in the event largely unsuccessful) clerical struggle against strait subservience to gentry patrons and congregations which was the lot of most missioners. The very proliferation of (often rival) 'clerical defence organisations' witnessed to the peculiar and acute difficulties of mission life. The wills of missioners and recusant gentry family papers witness to the fact that some missioners could achieve economic security, a happy relationship with patrons and fruitful mission work. But there is abundant other evidence of chronic insecurity, bad relations with patrons, bad treatment by scattered congregations, acute boredom and a steady crop of clerical scandals. 'The bond of education' between gentry and priests was often slight. Lay boys were commonly educated apart from ordinands, and, by the later years of the century, had a tendency to leave early for private tutorials or French Oratorian schools. After 1660 the numbers of recusant gentry sharply declined. Education by clergy, alike in English universities or Catholic schools, often inculcated a knowing distaste for clerical tutelage and ways. Particularly after 1660 the great majority of Catholic clergy were drawn from the same tradesman class as Anglican and Dissenting clergy. Many Catholic recusant gentry families never produced a priest.[60]

The Dissenting clergy, in spite of Richard Baxter's theories, most probably had similar experiences. The domestic closeness of their communities (dwindling, like those of the Catholics) by 1700, and the fact that ordinands and lay-boys were educated together in Academies, only accentuated the tensions, insecurities and humiliations of a minister's life in strait dependence on patrons or elders and trustees of congregations. The personal *charisma* of a great preacher, writer, revivalist or pastor could (for a Richard Baxter, Oliver Heywood, Richard Davies or John Bunyan) give a special 'prophetic' prestige. But in general ministers' social and economic standing depended on accidental circumstances: birth and family connections, patronage, Anglican ordination (at any rate in the early years after 1662), academic status, cure of a congregation of sufficient size and local standing, the mastership of a successful Academy (after the Toleration Act), or even a socially profitable marriage. Possession of most of these qualifications could go far to offset the acute disadvantages of exclusion

[60] AVELING, H., Northern Catholics, op. cit., pp. 329ff.

from the Anglican Establishment: lack of them by 1700 reduced many ministers to poverty, insecurity and having not even a quasi-clerical popular status.[61]

VI. Conclusion

The generally accepted view of 17th century English history is that it was 'an age of revolution', of which one important facet was the last spasmodic bid for power of medievalist clericalism, its failure and final definite collapse: by 1700, on this view, clerical claims to control the mind and morals of society were finally discredited, and the clergy reduced from 'a separate estate' to become merely 'one of many professions, much the worst remunerated.'[62] Professor G. Elton has challenged this view in general. He has suggested that society did change 'somewhat, as well in its organisation as in its attitudes', but that there only took place 'adjustments in the methods by which the inherited constitution was made to work.'[63] There is much to be said for his view, at least as far as the English clergy were concerned. As we have seen the whole body of the clergy in the course of the century had to endure, in the form of a kind of warring party dialectic, new fashions in ideas and rival clericalist idealisms. But the salient fact is that the clerical body, and society at large, were so firmly wedded to acceptance of a traditional pattern of religion and Church organisation that by 1700 the explosive forces had been assimilated and contained, and the pattern still stood in its basic outlines. 'Experimental philosophy' had certainly accentuated changes in attitudes already evident in the 16th century, but the divines of the warring clerical factions united successfully to prevent its impact destroying a traditional religious outlook. The decline of Church courts and coercive jurisdiction, evident long before the 17th century, became very overt after 1660. The power of lay patrons over clerical livings, very strong in the 16th century, increased notably. But these changes were really superficial, since neither patrons nor the bulk of the clergy showed any enduring, real intention of departing from the main traditional Church pattern meant to dominate society. The schisms in existence in 1700 were real enough, but still only weakened the hold of the pattern superficially. Their adherents were relatively few and actually declining. In many ways their witness served both positively and negatively to buttress the Establishment: positively they assisted its defence against irreligion and supported, from the outside, some of its salient features; negatively they provided it with a valuable 'roughage' and with encour-

---

[61] CRAGG, op. cit., pp. 186 ff.; WHITING, C. E., Studies in English Puritanism from the Restoration to the Revolution, 1660–88, London, 1931; CALAMY, E., The Nonconformist's Memorial, ed. PALMER, S., London, 1802.

[62] HILL, C., The Century of Revolution, 1603–1714, London, 1961, pp. 211–2, 263.

[63] ELTON, G. R., Studies in Tudor and Stuart Politics and Government, Cambridge, 1974, ii, pp. 155 ff.

agement by their obvious weaknesses. A close reading of some of the typical clerical literature of the late 17th century (for instance the cumulative Anglican-Papist controversial pamphlet – mainly by Leyburne and Stillingfleet – 'A Papist Misrepresented and Represented', 1685; Thomas Bennet's collation of Anglican attacks on Dissenters in 'An Answer to the Dissenters Pleas', 1699; or the 'Of the Pastoral Care', 1692, of the ostensibly radical Whig Gilbert Burnet) gives an overwhelming impression of *plus ça change, plus c'est même chose.*

Postscript

Since this article was completed very little has been published directly on the English clergy of the 16th and 17th centuries and the preoccupations of the authors have never quite coincided with mine.

ROSEMARY O'DAY, The English Clergy: the Emergence and Consolidation of a Profession, 1558–1642 (Leicester, 1979) deals primarily with the recruitment, career structure, preferment, patrons and life-style of the Anglican clergy. The authoress has much less to say about the Reformation ideal of the clergyman and his training or the realities of the training. The final Chapter, 'Comparisons', is very general indeed and leaves out of sight the English Catholic clergy. CLAIRE CROSS, Church and People, 1450–1660 (London, 1976) deals for the most part with the growth of lay control of the Anglican Church. P. SEAVER, The Puritan Lectureships (Stanford, 1972) deals faithfully with one small feature of Anglican clerical life; ed. F. HEAL and R. O'DAY, Church and Society in England: Henry VIII to James I (London, 1977) has important chapters by R. HOULBROOKE on the Anglican episcopate and by F. HEAL on the Anglican clergy's economic problems. R. HOULBROOKE, Church Courts and the People during the English Reformation, 1520–1570 (Oxford, 1979) is a very well-documented study of the operation of Anglican church courts in some dioceses, seeking to establish that they were relatively effective, respectable and socially useful institutions. J. BOSSY, The English Catholic Community, 1570–1850 (London, 1975) deals mainly with the community as a whole, but contains many illuminating and original comments and suggestions about the history of the Catholic clergy – a history which is still largely unwritten. He is particularly interesting on the finances of the English Jesuits. My own 'The Handle and the Axe' (London, 1977) covers the same general ground: the chapters on the English Catholic clergy embroider the themes I had already touched on in this article. My 'Elizabethan Catholic Households in Yorkshire' (to be published in Northern History, Leeds, 1980) attempts to deal incidentally with clerical devotion. My 'A History of St. Peter's, Yaxley' (Spalding, 1972) was an effort to use the unusually abundant local records of a Huntingdonshire Anglican parish to show the impact of its clergy on the religious practice and mentality of the people. C. HAIGH, Reformation and Resistance in Tudor Lancashire (Cambridge, 1975) is primarily a powerfully argued contribution to the debate about the nature and extent of regional religious differences in 16th century England. G. H. TAVARD, The Seventeenth Century Tradition: a Study in Recusant Thought (Leiden, 1978) is a study by a theologian of the place occupied by the writings of a group of 17th century English Catholic clergy in the development of Catholic thinking on the relations of Scripture and Tradition. The author contributes one small but important piece of evidence to our picture of the English clergy: the positive effects on the Catholic theologians of their running controversy with Anglicans. THOMAS F. TENTLER, Sin and Confession on the Eve of the Reformation (Princeton, 1977) should be read in conjunction with J. BOSSY's two articles, The Social History of Confession in the Age of the Reformation (Transactions of the Royal Historical Society, 5th series, 25, 1975) and Review Article, Holiness and Society, Past and Present, no. 75, May 1977. Catholic historians in France, Germany and Italy long ago laid rather sketchy foundations for a history of sacramental practice in Europe, but largely because of pressures by authority and lack of time left their materials buried deep in scores of obscure ecclesiastical periodicals. So far TENTLER and BOSSY have indicated the great importance of these materials for academic historians and suggested ways in which they may cast light on problems which concern the historians today.

Then there are four important articles which approach the history of the Catholic Counter-reformation from a sociological point of view. One is A. D. WRIGHT, The People of Catholic Europe and the People of Anglican England, The Historical Journal, 18, 1975. The other three are by J. BOSSY: The Counter-Reformation and the People of Catholic Europe (Past and Present, 47, May 1970), The Counter-reformation and the People of Catholic Ireland (Historical Studies, 8, Papers read before the Irish Conference of Historians, ed. T. D. WILLIAMS, Dublin, 1971) and Blood and Baptism: Kinship, Community and Christianity in Western Europe from the 14th to the 17th Centuries, in: Studies in Church History 10, Sanctity and Secularity, ed. D. BAKER, Oxford, 1973. None of these articles deal directly with the English clergy, but they all suggest a new and much wider and more adventurous approach to its history.

Anglican/Roman Catholic Relations, 1717–1980.
A Detection of Themes

by The Archbishop of Dublin, Most Revd. H. R. McAdoo

To the members of ARCIC
in grateful remembrance
of work done together.

Contents

Introductory Note

The period of estrangement between the Roman Catholic Church and the Churches of the Anglican Communion has lasted for more than four centuries, and during that time various efforts at very different levels of intensity and involvement have been made to probe the possibility of discussion and to institute a dialogue. The period covered here from the beginning of the eighteenth century to the present time has been perhaps the richest in such attempts, especially in the nineteenth and twentieth centuries. In consequence, the story of Anglican/Roman Catholic relations in respect of these later endeavours to seek reconciliation is very well documented. Victorian and Edwardian 'Lives' and collections of letters as well as modern biographies and studies have furnished remarkably full documentation concerning personalities, events and trends. Most recently, the study, 'Rome and Canterbury Through Four Centuries' (London 1974) by Bernard and Margaret Pawley, sets out to gather up in one comprehensive account and assessment the records of the various contacts which took place between 1530 and 1973. Thus, through modern as well as through contemporary eyes the picture has been viewed thoroughly both as a whole and in detail.

Inevitably, the pages which follow must take individual account of the different instances of such contacts over the past two hundred and fifty years. The secondary aim, however, is to avoid un-necessary reduplication of historical research already done, while the primary purpose — within the framework of fact and happening — is to detect and discern the basic themes which in each set of circumstances broke surface through the current of events. Because we are not solely recording what is past but also examining living elements and continuing factors which bear now on the Churches in their separation, there must be a constant theological assessment by means of which the themes in their historical settings are evaluated and related to the present state of dialogue between Rome and Canterbury. It is in this area that divergence began and ultimately it is in the area of themes that reconciliation must be sought. It can be sought only by a vigorous process of mutual questioning in charity and of answering in humility. It can be achieved only by the equally demanding exercise of rebuilding meanings through the fresh understanding and insight thus obtained as each Church begins to descry the outline of its own reflection in the face of the other.

This study is respectfully offered to all who are concerned with the ecumenical movement and particularly to the members of ARCIC from whom the writer has learnt so much, though the views here expressed are personal and not necessarily an expression of the Commission's standpoint on any given issue.

I. The Eighteenth Century: Archbishop Wake and the Gallican Theologians

1. 'In Religion Very Nigh?'

In 1896, with the publication of 'Apostolicae Curae'in which Leo XIII declared that Ordinations carried out according to the Anglican rite have been and are absolutely null and utterly void, Anglican/Roman Catholic relations plummeted to their nadir. The ensuing process of polarization, in which the first Vatican Council of 1870 with its declaration of papal infallibility had been a potent factor, was helped on at the day-to-day level of church-membership by the Ne Temere decree of 1908 on mixed marriages. By the nineteen twenties the process was pretty well complete in terms of stances and entrenched positions on either side, of triumphalism and of reaction against it, though it would be the worst kind of facile reporting not to stress, from the positive angle, the part played in all this by a deep concern for the truth of the faith "once for all delivered." The effects were however visible, at every level, of a theology with a strong juristic element and of a concept of revelation which was in effect largely propositional. Inevitably, such a situation revived the old polemics and created some new versions, and the separation between the two Communions appeared, in spite of the pious hopes of successive Lambeth Conferences, to be total and irremediable. The efforts of a few valiant spirits on either side, such as Mercier, Halifax and Portal, merely served to highlight the reality as most people then conceived it to be on the evidence of their own experience.

Today there is an Anglican/Roman Catholic International Commission, officially appointed by the highest authorities in both Churches. Its unanimously agreed statements on the eucharist, on ministry and on authority were allowed by Lambeth and the Vatican to be published without any alteration beyond the note stating that they were at this stage simply agreements of the Commission and not documents ratified by either or both Churches. The work of the Commission may be described as the construction of a platform from which in the future, if they judge that the Spirit is so guiding them, the Churches may make a venture of faith. What is being done is essential preliminary work to ascertain whether there is a substantial identity of faith in certain areas sufficient to warrant a forward step in spite of continuing divergences in other areas. The question then will be whether, weighed against the convergences, the divergences are such as must keep the Churches for ever from establishing, as a start and initially, some form of intercommunion. All the time the search for, and the debate about, criteria remains to the fore in the dialogue. It was there as early as 1564 in a conversation between Archbishop Matthew Parker and the French ambassador and the Bishop of Coutances, from the record of which the title of this sub-section is taken. Writing to Sir William Cecil, the Archbishop said "In fine they professed that we were in religion very nigh them. I answered that I would wish them to come nigher to us, grounding ourselves (as we do) upon the apostolical doctrine and pure time of the Primitive Church."

Today, difficulties persist on both the doctrinal level and that of day-to-day membership, as the Common Declaration of 1966 by the Pope and the Archbishop of Canterbury implied. When due allowance is made for elements of theological paranoia on either side and for the inhibiting effects of inherited stances, problems remain, and, equally important, an agreed way of handling them must also be found. To underrate the difficulties would be irresponsible, but at the same time the evidence lies all around us of a changed and changing atmosphere and of a different approach. What has happened and in what way has it been happening? How much real and deep change has come about and can we locate the areas in which this is taking place? Can we also pinpoint the areas in which, if probability be any guide, a particular kind of agreement to differ is not only an essential preliminary but also an authentic exercise of legitimate freedom within a Church united? Can an evolving process be discerned and what can be looked for in the immediate future? Is it possible to chart a realistic course towards an ultimate objective?

Light may be thrown on these questions not only by analysing what is now going on in Anglican/Roman Catholic relations but also by looking for parallels with other more tentative rapprochements during the past four centuries of estrangement. What we are proposing here is less a historical survey than a *detection of themes*, an assessment and sifting of these and the relating of them to the present doctrinal and pastoral position of both Churches.

There are those who assert that there is no fundamental change in the situation and there are those who claim to discern hopeful signs in plenty. The latter point to the words of Pope Paul VI at the canonization of the forty martyrs in

1970: "There will be no seeking to lessen the legitimate prestige and the worthy patrimony of piety and usage proper to the Anglican Church when the Roman Catholic Church — this humble 'servant of the servants of God' — is able to embrace her ever beloved sister in the one authentic Communion of the family of Christ: a communion of origin and faith, a communion of priesthood and of rule, a communion of the saints in the freedom of love of the spirit of Jesus". They acclaim the reply of the Archbishop of Canterbury in a sermon at Canterbury Cathedral in which he quoted from his Christmas letter to the Pope ". . . and you can be sure that your warmth of feeling to us Anglicans is reciprocated in anglican hearts and minds in the hope that one day there will be between us a consummated unity which conserves all that is true and good in our several traditions".[1] On the other hand, exegetes of such pronouncements ask, What does this amount to? Between the high-level pronouncements and the theological encounters, in that everyday area of membership, loyalty and inter-church relations, what substantial changes and real advances can be undeniably indicated?

Not surprisingly, at the present moment, many people's feeling about ecumenism is pendulum-like, swinging without intermediate pause from euphoria to hypochondria and back again. Is there then any real change which goes deep enough to suggest that *in saecula saeculorum* need not necessarily be written over the existing state of affairs? Perhaps then a realistic answer to the question lies more in the area of a detection of themes than in a survey of Anglican/Roman Catholic relations which vary considerably from country to country. Important and informative though such collation of facts unquestionably is for an evaluation in terms of what is actually happening, it inevitably remains nearer the surface of the totality of the situation. What lies beneath could be more significant in the long run.

Change has become so much a part of being human in the nineteen eighties that it is possible, while accepting factually all the changes in the Churches, theologically, liturgically, and in the attitude to authority and the style of its exercise, not to perceive that there is a real sense in which change is also part of being Christian. It is not that the faith was not "once for all delivered" but that, although the Gospel does not change, people change and grow into it by way of a changing self-understanding on the part of modern man and by way of his changing method of apprehending its truth. It is not simply that he must comprehend and communicate the faith in his own idiom; it is not solely that he sees the Gospel as event more than as proposition. Both of these emphases are there, but it is more than that. His own self-understanding, the way in which he sees himself, has changed and with it his understanding of his world. The effects of this, as far as the Christian Church is concerned, may be seen in almost every field from moral-ascetical theology to the theology of revelation.

Since obviously change is not peculiar to any society or generation, although the range and rate of change can and does vary enormously, it should

---

[1] Both texts quoted in: Documents on Anglican/Roman Catholic Relations (United States Catholic Conference, Washington 1972), pp. 42–44.

be one of our objectives to relate this factor to themes which may be found to recur at different stages in the history of Anglican/Roman Catholic relations, for this is not without relevance to where we are now. Changes in thinking and in theological development, as these appear in any period, bear on a particular theme, on the understanding of it then and now, and therefore on the search for agreement in truth. Could anyone claim, for example, that thinking on priesthood is the same now in the Roman Catholic Church as it was in 1896? Or, what has been the effect of modern Biblical studies on the search for a doctrinal criterion in both Churches? Do not both sets of facts, and the changing understanding of them and their setting, bear directly on themes which have been at the heart of our separation and may yet be at the centre of our reconciliation?

An attempt at a detection of themes within the time-settings of different periods could then be an instructive way of trying to discover whether and how far genuine change is occurring and what likelihood there is of further change. It would be prudent also to take account of the possibility of retrogressive as well as of creative change.

Obviously then, as one attempts to evaluate the historical movement in Anglican/Roman Catholic relations, the events, the people and the climate of their times will enter into the assessment. As one seeks to discern a pattern at this level one should also try to keep a theological exercise going. This would involve not only an identification of what was being talked about and of what, if anything, kept recurring, but also the relating of this to where we are in the nineteen eighties.

2. William Wake, Archbishop of Canterbury, and the French Theologians

The first significant but tentative steps in the direction of a rapprochement were taken in the second decade of the eighteenth century, and then only in the form of a correspondence and not by way of a conference or even of a meeting. It was a private correspondence, enveloped in a cloak-and-dagger atmosphere to the extent that the Archbishop of Canterbury would not even entrust a secretary with it and transacted it in his own hand; "I dare not trust my secretary with it."[2] In fact, events justified the caution as in the end there was an intervention by the French civil authorities.

To those who would say that it was merely an individual correspondence with dissident theologians whose Gallicanism made their views unrepresentative, there are those today (including some Roman Catholics) who would claim that Italianism has had the effect of similarly distorting the concept of the primacy from the opposite angle. Indeed, writing of the effects of the formidable Italian vote on the concept of the Roman primacy during the debates at Vatican I,

---

[2] *William Wake, Archbishop of Canterbury,* Vol. I, p. 284, by NORMAN SYKES (Cambridge 1957).

Garrett Sweeney deliberately coined the term on the analogy of Gallicanism.[3] Under the heading of Italianism, he lists from the records of the Council speeches ingredients such as "a belief in the inerrancy of the Holy See in matters of discipline", extraordinary powers associated with the office, "the rejection of the *sensus fidelium*, now recognised by Vatican II as an authentic source of infallible truth, as a *locus theologicus*", and "an almost complete insensitivity to the ecumenical mission of the Church".

Sweeney also sees the effects of contemporary secular thought on the thinking of the participants in the Council of 1870: "The rise of papolatry coincided with the growing political ascendancy of Bismarck's Prussia, and with its underlying Hegelian concept of the State as 'God walking on earth'." Events were also contributory causes for it was a time of political and national centralization.[4] The fact is that, just as at the first Vatican Council there were majority and minority opinions, so throughout the history of thinking about the Roman primacy there have been 'Gallicanists' and 'Italianists', and the story is not yet concluded as the Church of Rome strives to reconcile what was defined in 'Pastor Aeternus' with reviving oncepts such as the collegiality of bishops, coresponsibility in the Church, the importance of the local church and models for the primacy conceived in terms of love or of service or as a symbol of unity. Certainly whether there may be a way in here, as the Lutheran/Roman Catholic dialogue in the United States has recently suggested,[5] will depend as far as Anglicans are concerned on how these concepts are allowed to surface and on what form they take.

To dismiss the Gallican correspondence on the grounds that it was with Gallicanist theologians would then be beside the point. Moreover and far more important, the themes which emerged in the course of this early eighteenth-century exchange of views were not simply concerned with the Gallican and Anglican attitudes to the papal primacy but were concerned with other and fundamental questions. Among these there can be discerned the early appearance of themes which were to recur in the twentieth-century contacts between the two Communions. Historically and ecclesiastically speaking, not the least noteworthy feature is that one of the correspondents was an Archbishop of Canterbury. Furthermore, Wake's theology was classically Anglican, if the phrase may be allowed, and this is clear not only in his dealings with the French Roman

---

[3] GARRETT SWEENEY, The Primacy: the small print of Vatican I, The Clergy Review, Vol. LIX, February 1974, No. 2, p. 168.

[4] "Salvation, both in Church and State, lay in strong centralized governments, dominating unified and obedient populations. It was no mere coincidence that the definition of the Primacy came within the same twelve months which saw the proclamation of the German Empire and the unification of Italy; came shortly after the United States had asserted its unity in the Civil War; and was to be followed in a few years by Victoria's crown of Empire, and liberal England's brief excursion into Imperialism", loc. cit., pp. 106–7.

[5] See Papal Primacy/Converging Viewpoints (1974), a statement of the Lutheran/Roman Catholic Dialogue Group for the United States (published in: Origins, Vol. III, March 1974, No. 38).

Catholics but in his correspondence with Continental reformed theologians such as Turretini.

William Wake, seen in Sykes's magisterial biography, emerges as a man of courage and integrity, competent in his theologising and constructive in his ecclesiastical statesmanship. If, in certain directions, the anti-papalism of the age (and indeed of his French correspondents) together with the particular historical setting of the whole enterprise imparted a narrower range to his ecumenism, still the outreach of this towards Roman Catholics and Reformed alike places him well ahead of his times by reason of his vision of the *una sancta* and of ecumenical possibilities. No doubt this creative attitude had been strengthened for Wake, as is so often the case, by personal contacts during his residence in Paris in his younger days. The main and chief difference between the ecumenical setting of the Gallican correspondence and the contexts of later meetings was that Wake saw the detaching of the French Church from the papacy as a step towards setting up a communion of national churches or a corporate union of the two churches. The objective was partly shared by his correspondents and they saw the concept of national churches as a means of uniting the Churches of the West.[6] Wake conveys an impression of confidence and serenity as he deals with questions which so easily lend themselves to partisanship and the point-scoring of polemics. He is realistic in the practical sense and at the same time profoundly aware of the real issues. Perhaps the chief impression of the man through his correspondence is one of a pervading honesty.

The initiative came from the Frenchmen, two Gallican divines, doctors of the Sorbonne, Du Pin and Girardin, contact being established through William Beauvoir who was then chaplain to the British Ambassador in Paris. Every student of this fascinating interlude in the early history of ecumenical contacts is indebted to the masterly and detailed survey by Norman Sykes, and we shall be dependent on him for the record of the course of events.[7] If we can then undertake a theological exercise and proceed to separate in the correspondence the main themes as they arose, we can attempt an assessment and see how they relate to the Malines Conversations and to the current "serious dialogue".[8] Where, if anywhere, are there changes of content and emphasis? Have these been influenced by later theological developments and by the contemporary climate and by events such as the growth of the ecumenical movement and the holding of the second Vatican Council?

The political and ecclesiastical background to the correspondence was a fairly confused one in that the death of Louis XIV had brought about some changes in religious policy in France with which, however, England had been at war for a good part of the Sun-king's reign. Moreover, in England the Jacobite

---

[6] SYKES, I, p. 255.
[7] Loc. cit., I, chapters IV and V.
[8] See The Common Declaration (1966): ". . . they intend to inaugurate between the Roman Catholic Church and the Anglican Communion a serious dialogue which, founded on the Gospels and on the ancient common tradition, may lead to that unity in truth, for which Christ prayed."

rebellion was a very recent memory and Roman Catholic proselytism under James II had not been forgotten. This did not make for a climate favourable to such an ecclesiastical enterprise and Wake's caution in the execution of it is as understandable as his courage in undertaking it is clear. The Archbishop of Paris, Cardinal de Noailles, kept in the background, though favouring the correspondence and this drew sharp comment from Wake. It was rather like the Mercier-Davidson situation in reverse at the outset of the Malines conversations. Cardinal de Noailles' attitude was explicable in view of the tangled course of recent events in his country, involving as it did the aftermath of the Jansenist controversy (Du Pin had had to endure exile), the papal condemnation of Quesnel and the rejection of this by the Sorbonne. The regent and the civil power intervened in various ways and de Noailles' situation was delicate and his position a vacillating one although he was strong enough to appeal openly to a General Council, as did four other French bishops, against the papal bulls 'Unigenitus' and 'Pastoralis Officii'. The Archbishop of Paris published his appeal at the time when the correspondence with Wake was in its early stages and to understand the setting is to understand how the correspondence came into being and got under way so quickly. All unwittingly the trend of events had prepared for it in spite of an unfavourable politico-ecclesiastical climate. There is evidence to hand also that those who desired to reform the French Church from within at that time were consciously looking to the reformation of the English Church.[9]

It was from within this setting that Louis Du Pin, wellknown as scholar and author, wrote to William Wake in February 1717/18.[10] His objective and the method of attaining it declare themselves at once in this opening letter: "I will add one thing with your permission: that I wish most earnestly some way might be found for the English and French Churches to enter into union. We are not so entirely different from each other in most matters that we could not be mutually reconciled. And I would that all Christians might be one fold under one supreme shepherd, even the Lord Jesus Christ our Saviour. This has the chief place in my prayers, and for so good a work I would gladly lay down my life."[11]

Beauvoir, who had supplied Du Pin with a Book of Common Prayer in French, informed the Archbishop that the French theologian was actually at work on a draft-scheme for union (*one of the first such documents in modern times?*) and this was Du Pin's 'Commonitorium'. The chaplain asked for directions 'how to behave myself in this important affair' and from the start secrecy was aimed at — "None is privy to it but one doctor of the Sorbonne and myself."[12] This circle inevitably widened, at any rate on the French side of the

[9] SYKES, loc.cit., I, pp. 256–257.

[10] "The correspondence was accordingly begun by Dr. Louis Ellies Du Pin, famous for his great corpus 'Nouvelle Bibliothèque des auteurs ecclésiastiques', of which thirty-five volumes had been published between 1698 and 1711 (with further volumes to follow during the course of his negotiations with Wake) . . .", ib. I, p. 257.

[11] Ib. I, p. 258.

[12] Ib.

Channel, and the letters were shown to the Archbishop of Paris whose hesitations drew the comment from the Archbishop of Canterbury to Beauvoir that
little could be hoped for from the negotiations and that matters would have to be
put on another footing if results were expected: "My task is pretty hard, and I
scarce know how to manage myself in this matter. To go any further than I have
done, even as a divine only of the Church of England, may meet with censure.
And as Archbishop of Canterbury I cannot treat with those gentlemen. I do
not think my character at all inferior to that of an Archbishop of Paris; on the
contrary, without lessening the authority and dignity of the Church of England,
I must say it is in some respects superior. If the Cardinal were in earnest for
such a union, it would not be below him to treat with me himself about it. I
should then have a sufficient ground to consult with my brethren, and to ask His
Majesty's leave to correspond with him concerning it . . . and it would be very
odd for me to have an authoritative commission to treat with those who have no
manner of authority to treat with me."[13]

This is parallel to the similar insistence nearly two centuries later of another
Archbishop of Canterbury, Randall Davidson, on the need for authority on
both sides to be seen to be involved as the Malines conversations of 1921–26
began to take shape. Nevertheless, it in no way reflects the general tone or
matches the usual substance of most of the Gallican correspondence, for Wake's
vision of unity closely resembled that of his correspondent and he wrote to Du
Pin: "I pray God to prosper all your charitable and pious attempts for the peace
and unity of his church, which, as no one can have more at heart than myself, so
I esteem it the most fortunate work of my life, if I can any way contribute to the
promotion of it."[14]

3. The Course of Events

In as brief a sketch-outline then as possible, the pattern of the correspondence unfolded, the contents of the letters being richer than the events were exciting, save that there was a civil intervention when rumour circulated publicly
about the interchange of views and resulted in crowds of Parisians frequenting
the Anglican services. The cloak-and-dagger atmosphere hovered over events to
the end as Wake's last letter to Du Pin was sent by the Governor of Minorca to
make sure of its delivery and later Le Courayer was censured by ecclesiastical
authority and felt obliged to take refuge in England.

Wake's first letter, his reply to Du Pin, was in the nature of a position
paper on the Anglican stand-point and dealt with the role of fundamentals and
of the creeds, the threefold ministry and episcopal succession in Anglicanism,
stress being laid on the Anglican appeal to Scripture and the Primitive Church.
In a covering note to Beauvoir he sketched some principles of union which look
like a brief pre-view of the Bonn Agreement of 1931 between Anglicans and Old

[13] Ib. I, p. 266.
[14] Ib. I, p. 264.

Catholics, and underlined the need both for secrecy and for developing the contacts. Du Pin replied that he was engaged on completing his plan of union and at this juncture he was joined by Girardin who had just addressed the Sorbonne on the Gallican-Anglican project of union and had emphasized the importance of distinguishing fundamentals and non-essentials. To this Wake replied that he considered the point to be of the first importance for any such project.[15] Cardinal de Noailles appears to have been shown the correspondence at this stage and to have approved it, though Archbishop Wake did not think that he would publicly identify himself with the project. Beauvoir acted for both sides of the correspondence in a sort of commentator's capacity, relating glosses and observations to and from both parties. He kept the Archbishop abreast of the progress of Du Pin's 'Commonitorium', or union-project, and this was finally sent to Wake by its author for his response and comment.

It is clear from Wake's correspondence with Beauvoir that at this time the problem of reactions by church and state authorities and of their attitudes was making its impact felt in that Wake was conscious of an unevenness in the dialogue. In brief, he looked for a commitment from Cardinal de Noailles equivalent to his own and for some form of authoritative commission on both sides. In all the circumstances of the times, this would call for a political as well as an ecclesiastical involvement and Wake was not optimistic either about the Cardinal or the Regent: "But till the time comes that the state will enter into such a work, all the rest is mere speculation."[16] He also feared, not without justification, that he was putting his own official position at risk in England and it says much for his commitment to the quest for unity that, although he received no satisfaction on this score, he continued the correspondence, giving to it so much personal labour that he had to ask that the French theologians should write one at a time or be content with one answer to both.[17]

Wake was critical of certain matters in the 'Commonitorium', particularly the implication that Roman Catholic teaching could be regarded as a standard of assay for Anglican doctrine. The primate insisted to Beauvoir, "the Church of England is free, is orthodox; she has a plenary authority within herself. She has no need to recur to other churches to direct her what to believe or what to do; nor will we otherwise than in a brotherly way and with a full equality of right and power, ever consent to have any treaty with that of France. And therefore if they mean to deal with us, they must lay down this for the foundation, that we are to deal with one another upon equal terms."[18]

---

[15] Dr. Patrick Piers de Girardin sent a copy of his oration to the Sorbonne. The oration was designed as a preparative for Du Pin's treatise on union and he apologised to Beauvoir for certain harsh expressions in it which were really intended to get him a hearing: "Like other negotiations for ecclesiastical union this Gallican-Anglican overture suffered from the need of each party to have regard to the susceptibilities of its fellow-churchmen, unenthusiastic not to say worse." Sykes, I, p. 261.

[16] Ib. I, p. 265.

[17] Ib. I, p. 275–276.

[18] Ib. I, p. 266.

The exchange of letters went on, Wake commenting on Du Pin's 'Commonitorium' and on the six points raised by Girardin as a preliminary to union.[19] The doctors of the Sorbonne considered that Wake's reply contained the basis for an agreement. As the correspondence developed, themes emerged and at the same time things began to happen and this is reflected in the letters of both parties. At this stage, Girardin hoped that the *procureur-général* might favour the project of union and the turn of events seemed to point in the same direction. Sykes notes "Moreover the action of Rome in issuing a quasi-excommunication of the appellants by the bull *Pastoralis officii* of 28th August seemed to have helped the theologians considerably by rallying to their support De Noailles and the political leaders. The Cardinal-Archbishop of Paris was moved openly to associate himself with the appeal to a future General Council."[20]

Rumours were being spread in France about the correspondence, while Wake affirmed that "nobody here ever saw one of my letters"[21] and he expressed his consciousness of his own isolation in the affair. There followed shortly an intervention by the French civil authority and Du Pin's correspondence was seized. A contributory factor here seems to have been the attendance of crowds at Anglican worship in Paris, interest having been aroused by the circulation of rumours about Church union. The authorities took fright, people were arrested at some Anglican services, and information began to reach Rome. Wake, on his side, withheld further letters for the time being: "Yet still I do not like to have my letters exposed in such a manner, though satisfied there is nothing to be excepted against; and I think I shall be kind to the doctors themselves to suspend, at least for a while, my farther troubling them."[22] In the meantime he prepared the way for letting it be known at home that the correspondence had been taking place.

Sykes's comment duly marks the radical change wrought by events in the situation: "The negotiation was therefore at an end. But the correspondence continued."[23] Death was to make a still more serious inroad for when Du Pin died on June 6 1719 his passing from the scene had much the same effect on the correspondence as Cardinal Mercier's death was to have two centuries later on the Malines Conversations. Wake was grieved at the loss, as Randall Davidson was to be at Mercier's death, for in both cases trust and friendship had grown up. Du Pin's last letter to the Archbishop agreed that "the hierarchical succession" had been continued in the Church of England and "provided that we agree in doctrines" there appeared to be no serious obstacle to union. He never received Wake's reply agreeing with Du Pin's statement of the position, and in which, after referring to the success of the civil authorities and the opponents of union, the Primate consoled his correspondent with words which he was never to read: "May it suffice to have designed something in so great a task; and

---

[19] Ib. I, p. 268.
[20] Ib. I, p. 269.
[21] Ib. I, p. 277.
[22] Ib. I, p. 291.
[23] Ib. I, p. 292.

perhaps to have cast some seeds in the ground which at length will bear manifold fruit. Meanwhile let us (for this none can deny us), embrace each other as
brethren and members of the same mystical body."[24]

Those who down the years have worked for the unity in truth of separated
Christians and who have laboured to build bridges over which they themselves
were not destined to cross, will recognise an authentic and familiar note across
the intervening centuries.

During the next ten years, Du Pin's colleague Girardin kept in contact with
Wake by letter and visited England. Wake also received a letter in 1720 from a
new figure who now came briefly on the stage, the Abbé Quinot, to which the
Primate replied, both correspondents finding themselves in accord on the important question of fundamentals and non-essentials. No further letters between
them survive and, as Sykes points out, Quinot's main interest lay in the area of
Anglican orders in which the chief protagonist on the French side was to be
Pierre le Courayer whose first letter to Wake in 1721 marked a new development and a fresh direction in the correspondence. Quinot died in the following
year and one may fairly say that what remained was now an exchange of theological views carrying with it no undertones of a negotiation.

Le Courayer's correspondence with Wake was a very full one and his two
books, the 'Dissertation sur la Validité des Ordinations des Anglais et la Succession des Evêques de l'Église Anglicane' (1723) and the 'Défense de la Dissertation' (1726, a reply to Le Quien), were well known and important, but Le
Courayer was censured by twenty-two French bishops despite the fact that he
had the support of Cardinal de Noailles.[25] He found himself constrained to seek
refuge in England where he had some powerful friends, and when he died he
was buried in the cloister of Westminster Abbey. Perhaps history may yet come
to record this as a proleptic gesture. Girardin alone remained, courageously
carrying on, thus amply disproving Beauvoir's poor opinion of him, and maintaining to the end his correspondence with the Archbishop.

4. 'Saving on both sides the Faith and Verity of the Catholic Church'

What concept of unity informed the thinking of Wake and the French
theologians? In the long term it differed little from that sought concord on
questions of faith and order which the ecumenical movement of modern times
and the various reunion schemes hold as their objective. In the short term, the
difference for both parties lay in the realm of strategy, in a union of independent
national churches, and in this area the State could not be ignored as having a
significant role because of the Church and State relations obtaining in both
countries. Something of both these aspects of the matter and also of the basic
agreement in principle of the correspondents, is apparent in Wake's preliminary
comment to Du Pin on the latter's 'Commonitorium': "At the moment I will

[24] Ib. I, p. 293–295.
[25] Ib. I, pp. 295, 362.

make no further answer to your 'Commonitorium'; in which as many things are
welcome, so this point principally, that in your opinion we are not so far
removed from each other, but that, if the inauguration of a fraternal union
should be deliberated by public authority, a way might easily be found to
establish peace between us, saving on both sides the faith and verity of the
catholic church."[26]

Between the poles of the long and the short term objectives, between the
faith and verity of the catholic church on the one hand and the mechanics of
union, involving public and ecclesiastical authority on the other, lay the enduring heart of the matter — themes, or what today we call the search for substantial agreement. To that quest Wake and Du Pin gave themselves generously,
the French theologian sharing the conviction of his English counterpart. Du Pin
had written to Wake about his desire for union and in an almost identical phrase
had voiced that conviction; "We are not so entirely different from each other in
most matters that we could not be mutually reconciled."[27]

5. Primary Linked Themes: Fundamentals and the Nature of Agreement

For Wake, Du Pin and Girardin this was the essential and realistic starting-
point implying as it did not only the will to unity and the belief in the real
possibility of unity but also the necessary acknowledgment of the existence of a
legitimate diversity within a reconciled and reconciling Church. Something of
this was quickly to make itself felt two and a half centuries later in the deliberations of the Joint Preparatory Anglican/Roman Catholic Commission.[28] *It could
yet be the hinge on which all turns*, and it will be remembered that the Agreed
Statements of the International Commission claimed that while therein both
Anglicans and Roman Catholics would "recognize their faith" what was offered
was a substantial agreement. This differs from full agreement and it is of the
greatest moment for the ecclesial, the theological and the pastoral angles to
pause and attempt a clarification here. Factually, the link-up with Wake and the
Gallicans in this connection will make itself clear. More important however, the
immediate relevance to the current dialogue between the Churches will also
become evident. For here is a theme with which others are intertwined and the
importance of which has only been heightened by time, event and theological
development. Straight away, therefore, we find ourselves facing what may well
be characterised as a cardinal issue, a hinge-factor, in the total situation of
separated Christians.

---

[26] Ib. I, p. 272.

[27] Ib. I, p. 258.

[28] See the papers delivered to the JPARC Commission by Cardinal J. C. M. WILLEBRANDS,
'To what extent can or should there be diversity in a United Church? — Freedom and
Authority' and by Bishop J. R. H. MOORMAN and Professor HOWARD E. ROOT, 'Unity
and Comprehensiveness', in: Anglican/Roman Catholic Dialogue (Oxford 1974, ed. ALAN
C. CLARK and COLIN DAVEY), pp. 60—83.

In a letter to Beauvoir, Archbishop Wake observed: "To frame a common confession of faith, or liturgy, or discipline for both churches is a project never to be accomplished. But to settle each so that the other shall declare it to be a sound part of the catholic church and communicate with one another as such: this may easily be done without much difficulty by them abroad, and I make no doubt but the best and wisest of our church would be ready to give all due encouragement to it."[29] If one abstracts this (which looks, as we have said, like a pre-view of the Anglican/Old Catholic Bonn Agreement of 1931) from the setting of the times, a principle clearly declares itself. It was amplified by Wake in a letter written in 1719 to the reformed theologian Turrettini: ". . . the peace of Christendom can no way be restored but by separating the *fundamental articles* of our religion (in which almost all churches do agree) from others, *which in their several natures though not strictly fundamental, may yet be of more, or less, moment to us in the way of our salvation*; and if possible, to dispose men to think that *the first being absolutely provided for, and the others which are nearest to them, as much secured as conveniently can de done*, communion should not be broken for the rest, but a prudent liberty be granted to Christians to enjoy their own opinions, without censuring or condemning any that differ from them."[30]

Consideration of Wake's very carefully weighed wording here uncovers a principle which is at least partially reflected in Vatican II's 'Decree on Ecumenism' (11), an important passage which requires closer examination: "When comparing doctrines, they (i.e. Roman Catholic ecumenists) should remember that in Catholic teaching there exists an order or 'hierarchy' of truths, since they vary in relationship to the foundation of the Christian faith." Nor was the point missed by the Joint Preparatory Anglican/Roman Catholic Commission as this primary question worked its way up through the discussions during the course of their work in 1967. The 'Malta Report', having referred to areas of basic agreement and also to agreement "that doctrinal comprehensiveness must have its limits", posed clearly as matter for dialogue the possible convergence "between the Anglican distinction of fundamentals from non-fundamentals and the distinction implied by the Vatican Council's references to a 'hierarchy of truths' (Decree on Ecumenism, 11), the difference between 'revealed truths' and 'the manner in which they are formulated' (Pastoral Constitution of the Church in the Modern World, 62) and diversities in theological tradition being often 'complementary rather than conflicting' (Decree on Ecumenism, 17)."

At this stage, we are simply drawing attention to a theme, or rather to two inter-locking themes. The immediate aim is to set out the themes which arose in the eighteenth-century correspondence and to signalise those which have re-emerged later in different conditions and often with changed shades of emphasis.

The themes of fundamentals and of the limits of comprehensiveness broke surface early in the Gallican correspondence and, as we have suggested, the equally vital theme which flowed out of the consideration of these two is that of

[29] Ib. I, p. 260.
[30] Ib. I, p. 253. Italics not in original.

the nature of agreement and of the degree or kind of agreement necessary for communion in faith and truth, "saving on both sides the faith and verity of the catholic church." Is the present Anglican/Roman Catholic International Commission correct then in contending that the only and the right starting-point is substantial agreement? Certainly this is the line along which Wake and the Gallicans found themselves moving. Bearing in mind the earlier contact but more particularly relating our thinking to the situation as it now obtains between the two Churches, it looks as if an essential clarification-exercise is needed here.

In the first place, we should ask whether full agreement is possible, and whether in fact there are instances of it. Again, it appears that an honest answer in the affirmative to this question will at the same time point directly and also by implication to substantial agreement as the only possible and authentic instrument for achieving reconciliation. Full agreement is a real if strictly limited concept, and instances of it exist in the present dialogue. Yet by reason of the very depth both of revealed truth and of the richness of experience in apprehending, interpreting and proclaiming it, full agreement in all respects is "a project never to be accomplished", and that for good reasons of theology and not for bad reasons of a hopeless endeavour.

The 'Malta Report' (7) lays it on the line that examples of such full agreement exist between the two Communions: "We recommend that the second stage in our growing together begin with an official and explicit affirmation of mutual recognition from the highest authorities of each Communion. It would acknowledge that both Communions are at one in the faith that the Church is founded upon the revelation of God the Father, made known to us in the Person and work of Jesus Christ, who is present through the Holy Spirit in the Scriptures and his Church, and is the only Mediator between God and Man, the ultimate Authority for all our doctrine. Each accepts the basic truths set forth in the ecumenical Creeds and the common tradition of the ancient Church, although neither Communion is tied to a positive acceptance of all the beliefs and devotional practices of the other."

Significantly, the document, in asserting that there are fundamental areas of full agreement, moves almost at once into an assertion that this kind of agreement should not be looked for at all levels. In this it mirrors certain features of the Gallican correspondence and of the Bonn Agreement between Anglicans and Old Catholics. Similarly, the 'Report' thankfully records not only this "common faith", but also "our common baptism in the one Church of God; our sharing of the Holy Scriptures, of the Apostles' and Nicene Creeds, the Chalcedonian definition, and the teaching of the Fathers; our common Christian inheritance for many centuries with its living traditions of liturgy, theology, spirituality, Church order, and mission." (3).

There is, therefore, together with an area of full agreement, an even larger area of shared inheritance deriving from baptism, and the 'Malta Report', significantly again, goes on to emphasise that "divergences since the sixteenth century have arisen not so much from the substance of this inheritance as from our separate ways of receiving it" (4). The paragraphs which then follow home directly on the questions of full and of substantial agreement and of their relationship in the strategy of reconciliation. There is agreement on the given-ness of revealed truth in Scripture and also on the historical conditioning of the dogmatic definitions in which it can be and has been formulated. There is agreement, furthermore, that while doctrinal comprehensiveness must have limits, this diversity can be creative and in itself desirable (5). The impact on this of the fundamentals/non-fundamentals concept, of the "hierarchy of truths" and of theological plurality, is then brought forward as matter for future dialogue (6). Here, once again, we are at the nub of a central theme. It is worth stressing that the 'Malta Report', the official first-fruits of the first official Anglican/Roman Catholic contact for fifty years, has things to say which, *mutatis mutandis*, Wake, Du Pin and Girardin were saying two hundred and fifty years earlier.

The second question, then, to be posed concerns the nature of the agreement which is to be sought. Full agreement in certain areas is established as a right and essential objective, and does in fact exist. Without it there could be no admissible basis for authentic *koinonia*. This is very different, however, from positing full agreement as a blanket-concept, covering all or most levels of the Church's *kerygma*, mission, faith, practice and life. Such a concept of full agreement would be real only on the assumption that the "faith once for all deliver-ed" can be once for all and totally expressed dogmatically in euclidean defini-tions. It would also have to assume that theology's chief function was that of commentator on definitions rather than that of searching into the living truth which the definitions seek to express, and of helping the people of God to make it their truth in the varying situations of their own setting and living. Divided Christians then will have to seek, as well as a full agreement on fundamentals, a certain pluralism of doctrine and practice within the Body which lives through a Life not its own and which lives to proclaim the Gospel. So it is of the first importance to understand that here, at this living centre, the concept of fundamentals contains, delimits, and gives direction to the concept of comprehensiv-eness. Here, the concept of a hierarchy of truths comes alive and becomes creative of unity within the legitimate diversity of a Church reconciled.[31] There

---

[31] Cp. "The polyvalence of comprehensiveness thus obliges the Roman Catholic side on the one hand to become more open to a healthy pluralism, admitting that such does not necessarily destroy the unity of the faith and life, and, on the other hand obliges it to recognise that the time has undoubtedly come to state in the clearest terms that diversity does exist in its own camp – a fact that calls for a clarification of the doctrinal position in regard to its own tradition", J. M. R. TILLARD, O.P., a member of ARCIC, in: One in Christ, Vol. VIII, 1972, No. 3, p. 255 ('Anglican-Roman Catholic Dialogue').
Cp. also another comment by the same writer: "True enough, this substantial agreement has to be sought in the midst of a variety of doctrinal emphases, divergent theologies, dissimilar practices and especially basic differences of attitude. On one side there is the preoccupation with the need to respect the incomprehensibility of the mystery and to pre-serve it unsullied from too much rational definition. On the other, there is the endeavour to flood with light all that it is possible to discern in it. For all that we are surely close to one another. What we must now discuss is whether, granted the legitimacy of a doctrinal pluralism, a substantial agreement of this kind is sufficient for us to be able to say that the question of the Eucharist no longer constitutes an obstacle to our *communion*." (From a

is in fact no other instrument for reconciliation save that of substantial agreement. Has it been clearly and adequately recognised how this has coloured the
approach of the International Commision and the methodology of its Agreed
Statements?

We have uncovered a complex of themes in the Gallican exchange of letters
and they rank high in the tabulation of the themes which persist in the current
dialogue. If event and theological development have added some hopeful clar-
ifications here in our own day, the last word may be allowed to the eighteenth-
century correspondents, for they recognised a difficulty still with us, that of
defining fundamentals. Commenting on a passage in Girardin's Sorbonne oration which accepted the differentiation between fundamentals and non-essentials, Wake wrote:

"You have remembered rightly and wisely that in treating of articles of
evangelical doctrine, fundamentals should be carefully distinguished from non-
essentials and matters of greater moment from things of lesser weight; lest by a
promiscuous treatment of these issues any occasion should be given to the in-
cautious of deceiving themselves, as if the chief point of all religion turned on
those things concerning which good men may either err themselves or differ
from each other without peril. Neither ought the peace of the church to be
entirely broken for articles of this nature. *It is indeed a work of greater difficulty, not to say danger, to distinguish the essential articles of doctrine from the
rest, in such wise that nothing in them is either superfluous or lacking; that
nothing essential to salvation is omitted, nor anything non-essential included in
the number of essentials.* Certainly so far as concerns the peace of the church, I
know of nothing which will enable it better to be realised than that when these
matters have been accurately distinguished, all those everywhere should be recognised as truly catholic brethren, amongst whom there is agreement in the
necessary and fundamental articles of Christian doctrine, even though differing
from each other in matters of lesser importance; which not only the history of
the church testifies, but also the holy scriptures themselves indicate with sufficient clarity, to have been done by the apostles of old themselves, and their
successors."[32]

Thus were the themes linked and regarded as constituting a priority, and
the extracts from Wake may be compared with a passage from a sermon by
Cardinal Willebrands.[33] Speaking at Great St. Mary's, Cambridge, in 1970, he
commented on the idea of the hierarchy of truths and said:

"The importance of this idea has not escaped the theological world, but
what is meant by the phrase is no less important. It does not mean any part of
Revelation is less true than another, nor does it deny that we have to accept with

paper, 'Roman Catholics and Anglicans: The Eucharist', prepared for ARCIC and published
    in Nouvelle Revue Théologique, 1971, Tome 93, No. 6, and in One in Christ, Vol. IX,
    1972—1973, No. 2).
[32] Ib. I, pp. 262—263. Italics not in original.
[33] Cp. also the extract from WAKE already quoted.

the same act of faith all revealed truths. However, besides the formal aspect of revealed truths we have to consider also their content. In this respect religious truth is more important in proportion to its relationship to the foundation, or we may also say, to the Centre of Christian faith. In the explanation of this phrase given by the responsible conciliar commission, it was said: 'Truths upon which all Christians agree as well as truths in which they differ, should rather be weighed than counted.'"[34]

6. Further Themes in the Correspondence

Inevitably in the exchange of views between Wake and the French theologians the consideration of further themes flowed from those already discussed. Here, these can only be briefly itemised with an indication of how the correspondents handled them. Three such sets of themes can be selected and they have continued to be live issues in the dialogue down to the present time: the nature of the Church, papal primacy and eucharist and ministry.

Ecumenists today confront the cluster of questions: Who are the Church? What constitutes an authentic Church? Where is the true Church? Helped forward somewhat by the famous 'subsistit' of Vatican II, they must produce candid answers capable of being theologically substantiated.[35] For many, the answer may well appear to be that there is a fragmented presence of the true Church,[36] and the relevance to this of the question of degrees of communion will be clear.

As to what constituted the Church, Wake and Du Pin found little matter for disagreement. The latter concurred with the first paragraph of the Anglican Article 19[37] and commented "The definition of the church which is contained in Article 19 does not depart from the truth; but there should be added "under legitimate pastors", for the church is established on the bishops, priests, ministers and faithful laity, and is governed by its pastors. This is not denied by the Anglicans".[38] In fact, the whole history of Anglicanism, the Book of Common Prayer and the Ordinal, not to mention a literally huge Anglican literature on the subject in the seventeenth century, confirmed this and demonstrated

---

[34] Documents on Anglican/Roman Catholic Relations (United States Catholic Conference, Washington 1972), pp. 36—37.

[35] See the Dogmatic Constitution on the Church (8), The Documents of Vatican II (ed. WALTER M. ABBOTT S.J.), pp. 22—23: "This is the unique Church of Christ which in the Creed we avow as one, holy, catholic and apostolic . . . This Church, constituted and organized in the world as a society, subsists in the Catholic Church . . .".

[36] See THOMAS MARSH, The Definition of the Church (The Furrow, March 1971).

[37] In effect, Article 19 sees as elements constitutive of the Church those elements referred to in Acts 2: 41—42, baptism, eucharist, worship, the apostolic faith and the common life: "The visible Church of Christ is a congregation of faithful men, in the which the pure Word of God is preached, and the Sacraments be duly administered according to Christ's ordinance in all those things that of necessity are requisite to the same."

[38] SYKES, I, pp. 305—306.

Anglican adherence to episcopacy and to the threefold ministry. The position taken in the 'Commonitorium' on the indefectibility of the Church and on General Councils is not radically different from the Anglican approach and from the Thirty-nine Articles.[39]

On apostolic doctrine as a constitutive element of the Church, Du Pin's view of the supremacy of Scripture and of the confirmatory and interpretative role of tradition is indistinguishable from the Anglican position. He agreed with Article 6 that "Holy Scripture containeth all things necessary to salvation", provided that tradition were not excluded "which does not set forth new articles of faith, but confirms and illustrates those things which are contained in the sacred writings, and defends them with new securities against those who think otherwise; so that new things are not affirmed but old things from time to time newly expressed."[40] There is awareness on both sides throughout the correspondence of the markedly ecclesial context of the Anglican appeal to antiquity — an integral part of the Anglican ethos[41] — Wake informing Du Pin that the Church of England was content to abide by the results of a comparison between itself and the Primitive Church.[42] This appeal to Scripture and to the faith and practice of the early and undivided Church was regarded by Anglicans as integral to the establishment of ecclesial authenticity — "let that be accounted the true Church, whose Faith and Doctrine is most conformable and agreeable to the Primitive." So wrote William Payne, giving expression to a total Anglican conviction and methodology.[43] For Wake, the constant link-up here was with the theme of fundamentals and its rôle in restoring unity. Thus he stressed, in a letter to Quinot, the rôle of the credal summaries of fundamentals, "These sufficed to define the catholic faith in the first five centuries of the Church."[44] He wrote elsewhere, "And I am much mistaken if they must not at last come to the creeds of the four first General Councils, if ever they mean to restore peace to the Church."[45]

But what of primacy, and the Roman primacy in particular, in relation to the Church? Was it essential to the true being of the Church, an integral element in authentic ecclesiality, a mandatory guarantee of catholicity, or was it an optional extra? This was the crunch question for Anglicans and Gallicans,

---

[39] SYKES, I, p. 306.

[40] SYKES, I, p. 304.

[41] Cp. The Spirit of Anglicanism (London and New York 1965), H. R. McADOO, Chapters IX and X.

[42] SYKES, I, p. 259 and cp. WAKE to Du Pin: "From this you will see how much we on our part ascribe to ecclesiastical antiquity and how far removed we are from those to whom the innovations of the last two centuries count for more than the venerable authority of the preceding fifteen hundred years. Certainly I would make bold to claim that, whatever other Churches adhere firmly to the Vincentian rule, the Church of England is preeminent amongst them; nor will ever repudiate anything which has been believed everywhere, always and by everyone," loc. cit., p. 282.

[43] WILLIAM PAYNE (1650—1696), quoted in: Anglicanism (London, 1935), ed. MORE and CROSS, p. 141.

[44] SYKES, I, p. 297 and cp. p. 259.

[45] Loc. cit., p. 264.

approaching it from different theological backgrounds and from a totally different historical inheritance and experience. Wake had no doubt that "the subject of the pope's authority [is] the first thing to be settled in order to an union." Here is a theme which since Wake's time, because of the decree of the first Vatican Council in 1870, has become even more difficult for Anglicans and Orthodox and which continues to be twined around the roots of ecclesial separation. How did Wake and the Gallicans handle it?

The general attitude of traditional Anglicanism to which Wake was heir was one of unyielding opposition on theological and historical grounds to contemporary concepts of papal supremacy, of temporal and spiritual jurisdiction, and to such expressions of the notion of papal infallibility as were then current. From Jewel's 'Apology' (1562) onwards this is the case.[46] Theologically, the grounds of opposition were broadly that there was no Scriptural basis for the claims which could not therefore be *de fide* or essential to the being of a true Church. Historically, it was held that the claims could not be substantiated from antiquity, the Fathers, and the teaching and practice of the Early Church. Throughout, this attitude was part and parcel of the overall appeal to Scripture, to antiquity and to the Vincentian Canon, which was and remained an essential part of Anglican theological method.[47]

---

[46] E. g. JOHN COSIN denied that the Pope "is the vicar general of Christ or that he hath an universal jurisdiction over all Christians that shall be saved" (Works, ed. L.A.C.T., Vol. II, p. 332); so did FRANCIS WHITE (Reply to Fisher, p. 157); and ISAAC BARROW (A Treatise of the Pope's Supremacy, Works [ed. 1859], Vol. VIII, pp. 269—271 etc.); THOMAS JACKSON's writings show many examples and he states the problem as it appears to Anglicans, "Whether by Divine testimony it can be proved that St. Peter had such an universal, infallible, absolute authority as these men attribute unto the pope; whether by like infallible testimony it can be proved the popes from time to time, without exception, were Peter's undoubted successors, heirs apparent to all the preeminences or prerogatives he enjoyed; whether either the sovereignty or universality of their authority, (supposed probable in itself or to themselves) or particular injunctions derived from it, can be so fully notified to all Christians, as they need not question whether, in yielding obedience to decrees of like consequences as were the former, they do not grievously disobey God's word" (Works, 1844 ed. Vol. II, p. 233). JACKSON also deals with infallibility, as does GEORGE HICKES (The Spirit of Enthusiasm Exorcized, 1680, p. 37) and ROBERT SANDERSON, (Works, ed. L.A.C.T., Vol. II, 246—248, and Vol. IV, 63). HENRY DODWELL also analyses the concept (Account of the Fundamental Principle, 1688, p. xii.). JEREMY TAYLOR's 'Dissuasive' (1664) is an example throughout of the method, the appeal to Scripture and antiquity, and handles theologically and historically the question of papal supremacy from the angle of the collegiality of all bishops as "successors of the apostles", (Chapter I, Section X). LAUD and BRAMHALL take similar views of the general question and RICHARD FIELD's great book 'Of the Church' (ed. 1628) furnishes a classic example of a detailed and scholarly examination of the whole question theologically and historically in which he claims that the Anglican position is similar to that of antiquity on the universal jurisdiction, the supremacy and the infallibility of the pope (Book V, Chaps. 31—45).
There can be little doubt that a full and detailed survey would confirm the conclusion indicated by this selection which spans more than a century from Jewel to the time of Wake.

[47] A typical example of this approach to the question is JOHN BRAMHALL's 'Schism Guarded' (1658) in the prefatory epistle of which is set out both the method and its application to

It is a position shared by Wake and to which the Gallicans were far from averse, but when we come to the question of a simple Roman primacy, we find instances of a flexibility which arise from the writers' knowledge of Church history and from the fact that there is no inbuilt resistance in Anglicanism to the concept of primacy *per se*. It is noticeable that Wake, like other well-known Anglicans such as Field, Bramhall, Cosin and Laud, could conceive of a primacy of order or dignity within a strongly collegial setting.[48] It is important to compare with this a modern Anglican statement on 'Episcopacy, Collegiality, Papacy' from the report of Section III at the Lambeth Conference of 1968, given in full at the end of this essay.[49] From this it will be seen that the Anglican Communion today shares Wake's views about primacy having its essential context in collegiality; recognizes the growing emphasis on this in the Roman Communion since Vatican II; experiences difficulty in fitting the teaching of Vatican I on infallibility and imediate jurisdiction into this framework — "We are unable to accept this teaching as it is commonly understood today"[50] — and accepts that an ongoing process of clarification and commentary is needed.

Archbishop Wake was prepared to go so far as to allow a primacy of order: "we may all agree, without troubling ourselves with the reason, to allow him a primacy of order in the episcopal college."[51] He was ready to concur with Du Pin that such a primacy of honour had been known in antiquity: "The honour which you ascribe to the Roman pontiff, I consider to differ little from that which our wiser theologians voluntarily have conceded."[52] For him, such a primacy could be acknowledged if the details could be worked out at a real General Council in which Anglicans and others could take part. Wake firmly repudiated any papal jurisdiction over other churches by right of office and constantly emphasized collegiality.[53] For him, and the phrase is his own, the chair of Peter is preserved in all catholic churches.[54]

the problem, "whether the Bishop of Rome ought by divine right to have the external regiment of the English Church".

[48] For an assessment of examples, see Appendix A, pp. 273—277 below.

[49] See Appendix B, pp. 277—278 below.

[50] Loc. cit. Appendix B.   [51] SYKES, I, p. 285.

[52] Ib. pp. 281—282. Du PIN had written "We acknowledge his primacy, that is that he holds the first place amongst bishops, as the whole of antiquity and the Greeks also (although separated from the Roman Church) confess. But this primacy does not give him a superior order amongst bishops; he is still their fellow-bishop (coepiscopus), though first among bishops" (ib. p. 280).

[53] WAKE noted "If Christ has committed to him any power over other bishops, let the proofs be produced, let the claim be demonstrated, and we do not refuse to yield to it. If any prerogative were granted to the bishop of the imperial city by the Councils of the Church (although with the fall of the empire that prerogative also might justly be held to have ceased), so far as I am concerned, provided that the rights of kingdoms are always safeguarded together with the liberties of their churches and the dignity of the bishops, and provided that agreement is reached on other matters, he may enjoy this kind of primacy". But, added WAKE, it is not acceptable "that he should dominate other churches; that he should claim for himself alone and not as a common gift, that episcopate which Christ bequeathed in part to each several bishop to be held in common." (SYKES, I, p. 271).

[54] Loc. cit., p. 274.

The Gallican theologians expressed similar views.[55] On the question of jurisdiction, Du Pin, adverting to the denial of it in the Anglican Article 37, observed that "if this is understood of temporal jurisdiction it is certain; if also of immediate spiritual jurisdiction, it is likewise true. But it cannot be denied that the Bishop of Rome, whose primacy the English do not contest (at least the more moderate of them), by virtue of his primacy has this right, to watch that the right faith is everywhere kept and the canons observed . . . This is the sole jurisdiction we ascribe to the Roman Pontiff."[56]

This is a more theological assessment, ascribing as it does to the papal primacy the rôle, later to be questioned by many on historical and theological grounds, of custodian of 'the right faith'. Since that time, what Du Pin denied was affirmed by Vatican I's decree, 'Pastor Aeternus', which declared not only papal infallibility but the ordinary and immediate jurisdiction of the Pope over the whole Church. Admittedly, the decree insists that this *potestas ordinaria et immediata, vere episcopalis* of the Roman primacy aims not at eliminating but at strengthening the *potestas ordinaria* of the local bishop. Yet the whole edifice is based on the assumptions challenged from before Wake's time to the present. The question then remains an urgent one as to whether an ecclesiology exists within which can be accommodated two different historical experiences of what it means to be the Church.[57]

Were Wake and his French correspondents saying, from within their own setting, anything which differs essentially from the recent reflections of Karl Rahner S.J.?[58] Rahner insists that, since the theologians have done or are doing their part with some measure of progress, "the initiative in this question must pass from the theologians to the office-holders."[59] In his view, the current ecumenical procedure should now be reversed, and in the light of agreements already reached by the theologians the goal of achieving full unity of faith should be seen henceforth as a consequence of institutional unification.[60] Wake, Du

---

[55] Loc. cit., pp. 280, 285–286.

[56] Ib. p. 309.

[57] On the one hand, there is the Roman Catholic experience of the Church with a primacy which has developed more and more and includes the concept of papal infallibility; on the other hand, there is the experience of the Church by those who have found that catholicity does not depend on the existence of such a primacy, apart altogether from the critique of the arguments used to undergird the concept. Compare a comment by John Coventry S.J., an observer at the Lambeth Conference of 1968: "A deeper experience needs to be recounted – more theological, more ecclesial. It is a remarkable experience for a Catholic priest to live for a month with virtually all the bishops of a world-wide Communion that has no central government, and to discover in a personal way, what is already obvious as a fact of history, that the Anglican Communion is nonetheless in a very true sense a Church." (Lambeth 1968, One in Christ, Vol. V, No. 1. 1969).

[58] KARL RAHNER, The Shape of the Church to Come (1972, English edition, London 1974, from which the references are taken).

[59] Loc. cit., p. 107.

[60] Ib. pp. 104–105: "Hitherto . . . we have tried to tackle the question of union from the theological and confessional aspect and regarded institutional unification purely as a consequence of this settlement of controversial issues. Would it not perhaps be possible to

Pin and Girardin would have concurred and could be expected to see recognisable features in Rahner's suggestion that the "Petrine ministry" could be introduced into such an institutional unity, Roman Catholics maintaining their view of the papal office, while other Christians who cannot accept Vatican I and its doctrinal consequences might admit what he calls "a certain function for the Petrine ministry."[61] A similar suggestion has been put forward by the American Lutheran George A. Lindbeck who linked it specifically with Vatican II's concept of a hierarchy of truths.[62]

What is involved here is not the easy way (which leads nowhere in particular) of agreement to differ but the theologically respectable notion of a parallel between the hierarchy of truths and the fundamentals/accessories distinction so insisted on by Wake and Du Pin. It is indeed a basic and liberating theme.

But something more important still underlies this whole area, namely, the task of developing an ecclesiology of sister-churches. What precisely did the allocution of 25th October 1970, in St. Peter's Rome, mean when it referred to the Anglican Church as an "ever beloved sister"? Is it the language of ecclesiastical hyperbole or merely a courtesy of inter-Church diplomacy, or was the Pope giving theological content and explication to the words through the phrase which followed: "There will be no seeking to lessen the legitimate prestige and the worthy patrimony of piety and usage proper to the Anglican Church when the Roman Catholic Church – this humble 'Servant of the servants of God' – is able to embrace her ever beloved sister in the one authentic Communion of the family of Christ: a communion of origin and of faith, a communion of priesthood and of rule, a communion of the saints in the freedom of love of the spirit of Jesus."[63]

proceed in the opposite direction? Could we not consider full unity of faith and theology as a consequence of institutional unification, particularly since the latter need not mean institutional uniformity based on dogma as hitherto envisaged by the Code of Canon Law?"

[61] Ib. pp. 105–106.

[62] GEORGE A. LINDBECK, The Future of Roman Catholic Theology (1969, English edition, London 1970, from which the following quotation is taken, p. 107): "This immediately raises the question of whether the Roman Catholic Church might conceivably at some future time rate the papal and Marian dogmas which are peculiar to it so low in the hierarchy of truths, so remote from the central Christological dogmas, that it could ask other churches simply not to deny them or to accept them as legitimate theological opinions rather than as dogmas which must be affirmed. Is it possible that this might someday be considered a sufficient doctrinal consensus for the re-establishment of full communion? The Roman Catholics would in addition doubtless insist on arrangements for governing and preserving the unity of the Church which would include the 'practical' primacy of the Petrine see at least in the sense of a final court of appeal . . . But it is at least an open question whether they are dogmatically committed to insisting that the non-Latin churches of the East accept this primacy as part of revealed truth, as de jure divino, in the sense implied by Vatican I."

[63] Documents on Anglican/Roman Catholic Relations (United States Catholic Conference, Washington, 1972), pp. 42–43.

Whatever the hermeneutics of the passage, the last sentence points clearly to two elements integral to the development of the theme of sister-Churches – a fuller and deeper understanding and examination of the concept of degrees of communion and the notion of "substantial agreement" in faith. Wake and the Gallicans in their correspondences were reaching after both ideas; so was the Malta Report of 1968 and it will be remembered that Vatican II permitted a limited *communicatio in sacris* between the Roman Catholic Church and the Eastern Orthodox Churches which do not accept primacy as expressed in the papal terms, or papal infallibility.[64]

Of recent years, there has been between Orthodoxy and Rome a developing vocabulary of communion. The letter 'Anno ineunte' of Pope Paul VI to the patriarch Athenagoras I (25th July 1967) made use of the term "sister-churches" and explained its content. In 1971, the Pope declared that "between our Church and the venerable Orthodox Churches there already exists an almost total, though it be not a perfect, communion." The following year, the Pope affirmed "We are in almost complete communion with the Orthodox Churches . . ."[65] If, bearing in mind the "special place" accorded to the Anglican Communion,[66] this developing concept of sister-Churches is linked with the terms of the allocution of 1970, can there be discerned across the ideas of degrees of communion and of substantial agreement, a possibility of movement? The 'Decree on Eastern Catholic Churches' (24–29) explains that a "valid priesthood" and "valid sacraments" are the basis for the limited intercommunion already referred to, and this leads naturally into the final theme selected from the correspondence of Wake and the French theologians.

Eucharist and Ministry are the two subjects on which so far the Anglican/Roman Catholic International Commission has achieved substantial agreement.[67] The handling of these themes in the Gallican correspondence reveals elements anticipatory of modern theological insights. This serves to reinforce our conviction that by constantly relating the earlier treatment of themes to the current discussions, we are engaged, not in an antiquarian exercise, but in dialogue with

---

[64] The comment of the Orthodox commentator, SCHMEMANN (The Documents of Vatican II, ed. WALTER M. ABBOTT, [New York 1967], pp. 387–388) that the Decree misinterprets the Eastern institution of patriarchates serves to emphasise further the relevance of this permission to the current dialogue, since the Orthodox do not grant a personal jurisdiction to the office of Patriarch who "is always a *primus inter pares*". But compare J. MEYENDORFF: « L'ecclésiologie orthodoxe exclut l'idée qu'une Église locale puisse posséder une jurisdiction universelle, mais elle n'exclut aucunement celle d'un centre, où se manifesterait, d'une façon permanente, la conciliarité de l'Église. » (Istina, 1975, Orient et Occident, p. 46).

[65] For Orthodox and Roman Catholic analysis of 'Églises-sœurs: Implications ecclésiologiques du Tomos Agapis', see 'Istina' (1975, No. 1 Janvier–Mars) and cp. 'La Théologie et le Rapprochement entre les Églises Catholiques et Orthodoxe', by P. DUPREY (Mélanges Y. Congar, Théologie, le service théologique dans l'église [Paris 1974]).

[66] By Vatican II's 'Decree on Ecumenism' (13).

[67] An Agreed Statement on Eucharistic Doctrine (London 1972): Ministry and Ordination: A Statement on the Doctrine of the Ministry (London 1973); generally referred to as the Windsor and the Canterbury statements respectively.

the living Church and with a continuous living tradition taking on occasion divergent forms but springing from the one source. All that space permits is the tabulation of certain features and, as will be further noted in Sections III and IV, they afford interesting points of comparison and of contrast with the handling of the same themes at Malines and by the present International Commission.

For example, as in the present dialogue but in contrast to the nineteenth-century approach, the eighteenth-century correspondents put doctrinal agreement — "substantial agreement" in faith — *before* questions of Orders. Having studied the question of the episcopal succession in England, Du Pin wrote to Wake: "From this it is clear that the hierarchical succession has been continued amongst you, nor is there anything to hinder the Church of England from being numbered amongst the catholic churches, provided that we agree in doctrines."[68] Obviously, they would find difficulty in this respect as they confronted, for example, the formulations of the Anglican Article 28, of the Fourth Lateran Council and of the Council of Trent. What is remarkable, in view of the method to be adopted centuries later in the Windsor and Canterbury Statements, is the readiness of both parties to go behind formulations to the reality which the definitions tried to encapsulate. Du Pin was willing, for instance, to forego the use of the word transubstantiation, so long as "there is agreement concerning the thing" by which he meant that "the bread and wine are truly and really changed into the body and blood of Christ, and are truly and really received by those who receive the consecrated bread and wine, although this oral reception is ineffective unless accompanied by faith and holiness in the recipient."[69] It is worthy of note that Wake, in a letter to Beauvoir, was ready to make a parallel concession: "The surest way will be to begin as well and go as far as we can in settling a friendly correspondence with one another; which on their side is very easy, there being nothing in our offices in any degree contrary to their own principles; and would they purge out of theirs what is contrary to ours, we might join in the public service with them: and yet leave one another in the free liberty of believing transubstantiation or not, so long as we did not require anything to be done by either in pursuance of that opinion. The Lutherans do this very thing . . . and we never enquire whether they believe consubstantiation . . ."[70]

For both sides, there is an evident attempt here to concentrate on the reality of the eucharist, rather than on the 'how' of the presence. This should be compared with the 'Windsor Statement' (1): "An important stage in progress towards organic unity is a substantial consensus on the purpose and meaning of the eucharist. Our intention has been to seek a deeper understanding of the reality of the eucharist which is consonant with biblical teaching and with the tradition of our common inheritance, and to express in this document the

---

[68] SYKES, I, p. 293.
[68] Ib. p. 308.
[70] Ib. p. 292. Liturgical revision in both Churches has since removed the difficulties referred to in the first part of WAKE's comment.

consensus we have reached."[71] (The same principle is enunciated as the working method for the 'Canterbury Statement').

If it be so, as is asserted in the 'Windsor Statement'(footnote 1 to para. 6), that for contemporary Roman Catholic theology the doctrine of transubstantiation affirms the fact of the presence and of a mysterious change in the inner reality of the elements and is not taken as providing the only and essential explanation of the 'how', then modern theology has succeeded in narrowing the gap which Wake and Du Pin sought to close through a similar insight in respect of this vital theme. A short comparison between Du Pin's thinking and traditional Anglican teaching and a relating of this to the 'Windsor Statement' (Appendix C) convinces that neither then nor now was the insight unfounded or the gain illusory.

Again, as he writes of sacrifice and the concept of memorial Du Pin's comment on the Anglican Article 31 provides a striking parallel with the modern agreement, and, like the 'Windsor Statement', he begins with the uniqueness and perfection of Christ's sacrifice: "We acknowledge as one and perfect the sacrifice of the cross by which Christ fulfilled and abolished all sacrifices; nor do we call the oblation of the host an unbloody sacrifice in any other sense than because in it there is a memorial of this sacrifice and the offering of it is continued by the several members of the church who offer together with the priest."[72] From the angle of recurring themes and their treatment, a comparison between this and the 'Windsor Statement' (5) is very interesting not alone in respect of the emphasis on the memorial concept but in the reference to the continued offering of the memorial by the *whole* Church.[73]

This matter was taken up by Le Courayer who looked towards a reunion of the two Churches and who defended Anglican orders, the English Ordinal and, specifically, the relation of sacrifice in the eucharist to the priesthood, which leads directly to the theme of ministry. His full-length treatment of Anglican Orders produced controversy and linked him in correspondence with Wake. He had pointed out that priesthood did not depend on the formula about offering sacrifice since this was not a feature of any ordinal before the eleventh century. Furthermore, Le Courayer cited numerous seventeenth-century Anglican theologians to show that they held there to be a sacrifice both repre-

---

[71] A similar emphasis is to be found in two other modern eucharistic agreements, that of the Roman Catholic and Reformed Group of Les Dombes (1972) and that of the American Lutheran/Roman Catholic discussions (1967). All three documents, together with the eucharistic statement of the Faith and Order Commission of the World Council of Churches are grouped together in 'Modern Eucharistic Agreement' (London 1973) with foreword by ALAN C. CLARK and introduction by H. R. McADOO.

[72] SYKES, I, p. 308.

[73] An Agreed Statement on Eucharistic Doctrine (1972): "Christ instituted the eucharist as a memorial (*anamnesis*) of the totality of God's reconciling action in him. In the eucharistic prayer the church continues to make a perpetual memorial of Christ's death, and his members, united with God and one another, give thanks for all his mercies, entreat the benefits of his passion on behalf of the whole Church, participate in these benefits and enter the movement of his self-offering." (5).

sentative and commemorative in the eucharist, and that this was in accordance with patristic thinking.

Wake devoted a great deal of time, not only later with Le Courayer but also at the beginning of his correspondence with Du Pin, to underlining the unbroken episcopal succession in Anglicanism and the Church's firm adherence to the three-fold ministry. He summarised the position to Du Pin: "If you look at the government of our Church, we both preserve — and believe [it] ought to be preserved for ever — that ancient and clearly apostolic system, which has obtained from the first foundation of Christianity in these islands. We possess not only the names, but also the functions and grades of bishops, priests and deacons in every respect as we had in times past. We rightly claim for ourselves an uninterrupted succession of these; and we are prepared to prove this clearly to anyone denying it, from the public and authentic records which still remain with us."[74]

In the event, Wake was to set forth these proofs in great detail to Girardin and then to Le Courayer to whom he passed on much historical and theological material.[75] Thus, the theme of Anglican Orders moved into the forefront of the correspondence, unencumbered by the events which were to follow in 1896, and the reaction to Wake's exposition on the part of his correspondents is all that requires noting at this stage, save to remark that the Archbishop had made it clear to some of his Continental Reformed correspondents that he regarded an "orderly episcopacy" as essential to any reunion.[76]

In his 'Commonitorium', Du Pin had set out his opinion on Anglican Orders and his suggested procedure is one which has been canvassed by some contemporaries today: "I should be unwilling for the ordinations either of English bishops, priests or deacons to be pronounced invalid; though perhaps some may be so; but there is nothing to prevent the Gallican Church from approving them, just as the Council of Nicaea ratified the ordinations (be it said without offence) of the Meletians and Novatians. If therefore a union is achieved, all the bishops, priests, deacons and beneficed ministers of the English communion shall be continued in their orders, functions, ministries and benefices, either of right or by concession of the Church."[77]

Le Courayer, who went into the whole question more deeply and who set it in its true and full context, was more positive and decisive, perhaps because he had the advantage of the material supplied by Wake, and his judgment was wholly favourable. Here one ought in fairness to comment that for Wake (and it remains an Anglican attitude) the implication he thought to discern in the 'Commonitorium', that the Anglican position in faith and order needed to be 'rectified' by the criterion of the Roman Catholic Church, was quite unaccept-

---

[74] Sykes I, pp. 258—259.
[75] Ib. pp. 316—317, and C.V., passim, on 'The Validity of Anglican Orders'. See also: L'Union des Églises Gallicane et Anglicane (Paris 1928) by E. Préclin, which deals specifically with Le Courayer and Wake.
[76] Ib. pp. 300—301.
[77] Ib. pp. 308—309.

able.[78] He held by a different criterion, that of Scripture and the Vincentian canon. In this, he had the support of Le Courayer who observed that to make the Roman Church, which he regarded as "the first among the Churches", the equivalent of the Universal Church was to confuse completely distinct concepts.[79]

7. The Question of Results

As far as results go, of outward and visible signs there were none. Sykes's assessment of the reasons why there was no practical issue of the correspondence and negotiation is just.[80] The conditions of success were lacking particularly because of the Church-State situation obtaining at the time in France. Moreover, those of Gallican sympathies were unquestionably a minority in the French Church. It is fair to say too, and Wake's letters confirm this, that opposition to the project within the Church of England would not have been negligible.[81] Furthermore, one could add to the factors adduced by Sykes the fact that this whole area of Anglican/Roman Catholic relations was crusted over with a thick ice-cap consisting not only of ecclesiastical and political antipathies but of layers of folklore. In addition to the genuine theological differences and the authentic historical heritage on eigher side, there existed a folklore of religious and of national hostility in both countries. Given this, and the existing political and ecclesiastical tensions of the time both in England and France, the openness and candour of the correspondence has possibly not been fully appreciated considering all the circumstances in which it took place.

As a personal view, it would seem that the major achievement and the lasting benefit of the Gallican correspondence was just this, that it succeeded in demonstrating clearly that the differences between the two Communions could be abstracted from the setting of polemics and antagonism, that they could be discussed freely and charitably and above all theologically. Even more than this, the correspondence indicated that they could be reduced with honesty to manageable proportions and that a way through them could be visualised by both sides. Controversy could and did become dialogue and that two and a half centuries ago. Why was this gain allowed to slip back and to disappear again beneath the surface until the nineteen twenties and later? The answer must be sought in the lack of concern for and will towards unity on the part of the authorities in both Communions.

Again as a personal view, one might hazard the opinion that as well as the genuine differences intellectually formulated and the folklorist element which was a felt thing rather than something thought through, another factor in the eighteenth-century relations between the Churches has to be taken into account. That factor is the marked difference in the dogmatic and theological setting as

[78] Cp. ib. p. 312.
[79] Ib. p. 358.
[80] Ib. I, pp. 298–302.
[81] Ib. I, pp. 299–300.

compared with that of later times. For there is a real sense in which the *theological* situation of Wake and the Gallicans was paradoxically a more open one
than that of their successors in that the Roman Catholic dogmas of 1854, 1870
and 1950, still lay in the future. Neither was the juristic emphasis as strong as it
was to become later. It is not without significance that to the participants in the
Gallican correspondence a broad convergence appeared not too difficult of
achievement. It may well be that the factor just mentioned is one of the chief
reasons for this and that it has bearing on an essential difference of situation as
between the eighteenth-century correspondents and the twentieth-century conversationalists.

Viewed in retrospect the basic weakness of the earlier rapprochement lay in
the fact that it was and remained mainly and chiefly a correspondence. It never
had the chance of spilling over into the workshop of a wider and more representative group. In the nature of things and by reason of the times this could
hardly have happened. Constrained by circumstances, it was forced into a
mould essentially élitist, limited and faintly academic. Nevertheless those who
took part in it touched unerringly and with discernment on much of the matter
and substance which later conversations, made more complex by the doctrinal
and situational factors already alluded to, found it equally necessary to discuss.
The method and range of priorities of Wake, Du Pin, de Girardin and Le Courayer can stand the test of time's comparison. Wake's conviction remains as a
challenge and a call: "Neither do I think that we ought faintheartedly to despair
of an union of this kind, nor shamefully to cease from pursuing it. Often God
unseals the paths undiscerned by our eyes. Let us faithfully discharge what
belongs to our part and leave the issue to him."[82]

II. Meeting at Madeira: Viscount Halifax and the Abbé Portal

1. Personalities and Backgrounds

One hundred and fifty years after Wake's death, the chance meeting at
Madeira in 1890 of an English layman, Viscount Halifax, President of the
English Church Union, and a French Lazarist priest, Etienne Fernand Portal,
was to reopen the volume and eventually to liberate the themes into the wider
field of an actual inter-Church contact at Malines years later. Even then it was
still to remain a largely Anglo-French enterprise and would not acquire an international complexion until after the second Vatican Council.

"That accidental meeting" wrote Halifax "was the beginning of an intimacy
which has given me a friend such as few men possess."[1] It was the beginning of
the road to Malines when, thirty years on, Halifax who would then be eighty-

[82] SYKES I, p. 283.
[1] HALIFAX, Leo XIII and Anglican Orders (London 1912), p. 9.

two had begun to think and say that his life was over.[2] But Madeira was for both an illumination and a reorientation, an experience in which the friends mutually educated one another and enlarged and deepened their understanding of where both Churches stood and of the problems and task which lay ahead. For them, writes Régis Ladous, "Madeira was not simply a Sinai, but a university."[3] "Never shall I forget" wrote Portal to Halifax "that first walk we took together," and the letters of both correspondents frequently hark back to that walk along the *caminho novo* which Portal clearly regarded as symbolic of the new way they discovered together. Those walks, recalled by Halifax in another letter, gave them their first intuitions of what they might be called to do and were consciously looked back to by both in after years as a shared experience at a deep level of understanding and vocation.

Both as a Frenchman and as a Roman Catholic, Portal moved against a background in which many forces had been at work to build up a rich and sometimes contradictory inheritance. Since the days of the Gallican correspondence the revolution had toppled the monolith of the French Church and destroyed its position of total and privileged monopoly. "In the eighteenth century" writes Vidler "religion had become an uninspired moralism like Latitudinarism in England, and in France there had been no counterpart to the evangelical revival."[4] Moreover, the great inequalities in clerical life and status meant that some of the rank and file of the clergy were not at the beginning ill-disposed to the ideals of the Revolution as then set out. It took the Reign of Terror and the deliberate policy of dechristianization to reveal the true features of the régime. The events which followed the convening of the States-General in 1789 and preceded the bloody phase of the revolution had also shown that Gallicanism was far from dead. The clergy threw in their lot with the Third Estate and the Assembly turned to overhaul the ecclesiastical system: "All were interested in the reform of the Church. It is significant that it occurred to no one to turn to the pope for guidance or direction, so firm was the hold of the Gallican tradition."[5] The Civil Constitution of the clergy was a fairly radical document, putting into practice some of the old Gallican principles. Although it kept clear of doctrinal issues it allowed to the papacy only a primacy of honour. Yet, in fact, the constitution succeeded in dividing the French Church in two and it was left to Napoleon to heal the rift. His conviction was that the only solution to France's problems lay in a centralised government and a settlement with the papacy. The resulting compromise was the concordat of 1801, which in effect sought to maintain Gallican liberties by ultramontane methods. The ecclesiastical history of France and indeed of Italy during the years leading up to the meeting of Portal and Halifax is a tangled story.

---

[2] J. G. LOCKHART, Viscount Halifax (London 1935–1936), Vol. II (1885–1934), p. 265.

[3] RÉGIS LADOUS, L'Abbé Portal et La Campagne Anglo-Romaine 1890–1912 (Lyon 1973), pp. 53–57.

[4] A. R. VIDLER, The Church in an Age of Revolution (London 1961), p. 12.

[5] VIDLER, ib. p. 15.

What bears chiefly on the background of Portal and the inheritance which he brought to his meeting with Halifax is, of course, the effects of the protracted conflict between Gallicanism and Ultramontanism in his own country. C. S. Phillips has stressed the importance of recognising the difference between the ultramontanism of 1830 and that of 1870 if a true perspective of what was happening in the French Church over that period is to be otained. What separated the two forms was the condemnation of modern ideas and the authoritarian approach associated with the new ultramontanism of Veuillot and his friends, and this drove the earlier upholders of the theory such as Montalembert and Dupanloup into opposition over against the later ultramontanism. For Veuillot the Pope was the apex of the human pyramid and the ultimate authority whose decision was final because he was the infallible organ of divine truth. Liberty and freedom of thought must then be resisted by the Church since they were the source of all ills.[6] The older Ultramontanes on the other hand had stood for the vital principle (central also to Keble's Assize sermon and to the whole Tractarian movement in the Church of England for which the sermon was reckoned the starting-point) that the Church was a spiritual and universal society. It was therefore in their view not subject to State interference and accordingly they had insisted that "the cause of the Pope was the cause of spiritual freedom."[7] This almost total reversal of meaning is important: a school of thought founded to preserve the independence of the spiritual against the temporal power became a school which set the spiritual power in one form above not only governments but councils and bishops. This is what Archbishop Sibour of Paris meant when in 1853 he wrote to the Comte de Montalembert (a fellow-ultramontane of the earlier type) that "the new ultramontanes have rushed to extremes in both directions, and in reckless exaggeration of the principle of authority have argued *à outrance* against all liberties — those of the State and those of the Church alike." Montalambert replied, agreeing that ultramontanism had been then a school of liberty which "defended the rights of the Holy See, of justice and liberty, against the Gallicanism of the lawyers and *universitaires* . . . The attempt is now made to turn it into a school of slavery — and with only too much success."[8]

Ten years later there was a Congress — at Malines, of all places. Montalembert was the chief attraction at the gathering and he and his friends supported a progressive Catholicism and a Church, free and pursuing its mission in reliance on the truth of its nature, calling and gospel, in a comity of nations come to maturity. Catholicism and liberty in a new democratic society was the theme and as a result Montalembert was condemned by the Pope in a private letter. It was in the following year, 1864, that the Roman Catholic Church declared its public hostility to all the ideas associated with Malines in the Encyclical 'Quanta Cura' to which was appended a 'Syllabus Errorum' condemning "among a number of things that every Christian at least is bound to reprobate, not a few of the principles which the great majority of civilized mankind have come

---

[6] Cp. C. S. PHILLIPS, The Church in France 1848—1907 (London 1936), pp. 12—14.
[7] Ib. p. 9.
[8] Ib. p. 1.

to regard as axiomatic."[9] The Vatican Council of 1870 marked the culminating success of the steady progress of ultramontanism and to understand in part its triumph, even in France where Gallicanism had been so persistent, it is necessary to relate it to the trend of events during the pontificate of Pius IX, at the outset of which he had been regarded by many as a liberal (Metternich had said "I had foreseen everything except a liberal Pope"). The conflict about the pope's temporal power, soon to be abolished, and the rise of Italian nationalism and the events of 1848 which drove the Pope into exile, set the seal on all this and helped to forge the shape of his subsequent attitude to European liberalism. His alignment of the Roman Catholic Church with the forces in Europe which were blind to the emergence of a totally different style and substance of life and politics tied in with the activities of the ultramontane group at work in France where the struggle between them and the liberal Catholics was perhaps most acute. The effect of the 'Syllabus', rapturously welcomed by the ultramontanes, was to perplex many loyal members of the Church and to provide much ammunition for French anti-clericalism. Pius IX was however not accidentally but deliberately committed to advancing ultramontanism and his personal charm, as Vidler has pointed out, built up the *mystique* of veneration for the Pope which "is such a striking feature of modern Roman Catholicism" but which hardly existed before his reign. This was to be fostered in France by Veuillot and in England by Manning and Ward so that for the ultramontane press it became a test of true membership. In this sense, the Vatican Council of 1870 was the climax of a movement.[10]

The bearing of all this on the themes emerging in Anglican/Roman Catholic rapprochement is evident in that the thrust was persistently towards inflexibility and towards the citadel mentality over against the modern world and Churches not in communion with Rome. This was part of Portal's inheritance, but the re-moulding achieved by ultramontanism affected both its intellectual formation and its inner substance. Not only had the old French diocesan liturgical uses been gradually replaced by the Roman rite, mainly through the influence of Guéranger, by 1875, but "the old-fashioned French piety – the piety of Saint-Sulpice – with its grave, restrained flavour," (more akin to that of the English), had been obliged to give way to a different type "imported from beyond the Alps."[11]

Moreover, Portal's background as a Frenchman and a Roman Catholic included yet another element and one which continued active down to the time of the Madeira meeting and on to the turn of the century. The modernist movement began in France, encouraged by Leo XIII's support of critical and biblical historic studies even if his encyclical of 1893, 'Providentissimus Deus', declaring the complete inerrancy of the Bible, soon put a limit to the work which his earlier policy had appeared to promote. The anti-modernist oath, the decree 'Lamentabili' and the encyclical 'Pascendi', were still around the corner of the

---

[9] Ib. p. 122.
[10] VIDLER, loc. cit., pp. 153–154.
[11] PHILLIPS, loc. cit., pp. 20–21.

new century, but Loisy was teaching in Paris in the year when Portal and Halifax established their lasting friendship. Victor Emmanuel had been King of Italy for six years when Portal was born at Hérault near the foot of the Cévennes, the son of a shoemaker and at the other end of the social scale from the man who was to value him above all others. While Halifax knew a great deal about the background of Portal and of his Church and its claims and position, Portal knew little or nothing about the English background of his friend and less about the Church of England: "Halifax eut tout à faire, et Portal tout à accepter."[12]

On the surface, the contrast between the two friends could hardly have been more extreme. Their birth, background and intellectual formation, their ecclesiastical inheritance and allegiance, were totally dissimilar.

The life-style of Halifax was that of the English country gentry of his time, elaborate, ordered and paternalist. But if Halifax was quite out of sympathy with democracy as he understood it,[13] there was at the centre of this life-style an active social conscience and a committed Christian faith for he and others like him were the heirs of Victorian serious-mindedness, dedication and responsibility. If Régis Ladous could describe him as a Stuart cavalier disguised as a nineteenth-century viscount, the same author noted that Portal's friend felt himself born to serve the less fortunate just because *noblesse oblige*. Halifax fell under the spell of the Tractarian movement as a young man at Oxford and it is significant that his first meeting with Pusey came about when they were both helping in a hospital to look after the victims of a cholera epidemic. The friendship thus established was a close one, as was Halifax's association with Liddon, the leader of the second generation of Tractarians. He also maintained an exasperated and often mutually exasperating friendship with Charles Gore, one of the new generation of Tractarians, who was to become an outstanding figure in the Church of England down to the nineteen thirties and who would later join Halifax on the road to Malines. The centre of the life at Hickleton, Halifax's country house, was the chapel with its daily eucharist. It was this daily pattern, the greater part in truth, which lay behind his constant involvement in ecclesiastical affairs and his presidency of the English Church Union. It created the individuality which he brought to his zeal for unity and it gave depth to his utter conviction of the catholicity of the Church of England. One who knew this pattern at first hand wrote: "However early I went to the chapel . . . there was always kneeling in the front row of seats . . . and almost invisible, the venerable figure of Lord Halifax . . . Perhaps there was the light of a pocket torch if he was using a book . . . there was an intensity about him and the sense of entire recollection . . . he received Holy Communion with deep devotion, and, returning to his prayerdesk, knelt and again remained quite still. And so he did remain for a long long time."[14]

As well as assisting at the daily eucharist it was his custom to say Matins and Evensong daily. It was all of a piece with the deep and ordered sacramental

---

[12] LADOUS, loc. cit., p. 57.
[13] Cp. LOCKHART, loc. cit., II, p. 95.
[14] LOCKHART, II, p. 358.

and liturgical piety of the Church of England which had bred him and which reached one of its finest flowerings in the seventeenth century — just as his doctrine of the Church and of Ministry was at one with the theology of that same period, sometimes called the golden age of Anglicanism.

This hidden motivating aspect of Halifax's personality has to be set over against the readiness to enter the lists and the single-minded pursuit of aims. Neither should the history of the contentious years be allowed to obscure the picture of a bright spirit whose humour and sincerity made such an impression on contemporaries. One of his friends wrote, "To be with him is like breathing a pure mountain air of which one cannot imbibe enough, and which strengthens one for weary months with other people."[15]

At the time of the Madeira meeting, religion in England was in some respects outwardly at its zenith and the Church of England, having gone through some traumatic experiences, was at its most dynamic for a long time. There was much building of churches and schools and much evidence of positive and active concern for the underprivileged. At the same time there was a strong missionary thrust so that the Church of England during the whole of the nineteenth century was in the process of becoming the Anglican Communion. The year 1867 had seen the first Lambeth Conference, a preliminary step of corporate self-realisation in mission, concern and ecumenical vocation. From the Lambeth Conference of 1888 onwards, the central position of the Anglican Communion in ecumenical development became more marked and the Archbishop of Canterbury increasingly came to carry a unique ecumenical responsibility.[16] If one result of this fresh dynamic was the Church's rediscovery at many levels of its true nature, proclamation and mission, a less fortunate outcome was the hardening of party spirit in the Church of England and this bore heavily at times on the enterprise of Halifax and Portal, as did the earlier promulgation of the Roman Catholic dogmas of 1854 and 1870. To bear in mind the nature of their respective religious and ecclesiastical inheritances is to understand and evaluate the extent of the contribution made by the two friends.

2. Emerging Themes

There is no doubt that, initially, what Portal hoped for from the meeting was the conversion of Lord Halifax to Roman Catholicism.[17] What happened was the conversion of Portal to a newly-found goal and objective, a true *caminho novo*.

The study of Portal's papers has enabled Régis Ladous to evaluate afresh Portal's place in the overall history of Anglican/Roman Catholic relations and in particular to understand the rôle played by Anglicanism in the evolution of his

---

[15] LOCKHART, I, pp. 155–156.

[16] See H. R. T. BRANDRETH in: History of the Ecumenical Movement, quoted in: DEWI MORGAN, The Bishops Come to Lambeth (1967), p. 141.

[17] LADOUS, loc. cit., pp. 58–60.

ideas.[18] These papers together with those of the Abbé Hemmer and the Halifax
papers, now brought together after half a century, form a coherent whole and
permit a deeper understanding both of the men and of the movement up to
1912. Throughout the interplay of personalities and events it will become clear
that one theme would come to have special significance. Its emergence is bound
up with the mutually educative nature of the friendship between Halifax and
Portal, but before it solidified into a goal and principle of action, another theme
had to make itself known to them both.

The primary theme, new to Portal and requiring a complete change of outlook for him, was that of *union by convergence*. Hitherto he had shared the
common view of nineteenth-century Roman Catholic reunionists that reunion
meant the 'return' to Rome of the separated brethren. Madeira gave him a new
vision, but first he had to see and understand and make his own another theme,
that of the ecumenical vocation: "Towards the end of that year, Portal accepted
his vocation and was converted."[19] Writing to Halifax in the following year
Portal said, "You have changed my centre of gravity."[20] To promote and
advance in his own Church the theme of unity by means of convergence and
reform became Portal's life-work. The story, with all its substantial setbacks and
transitory successes, is an essential preliminary to Malines, but Malines itself
was only a further stage. The search for convergence, begun in the Gallican correspondence and taken up as guiding principle by the friends at Madeira, would
be carried a step forward in the nineteen sixties and seventies by linking it with
the idea of substantial agreement. To highlight the theme was possibly the major
contribution of Portal and the influence on his thinking of his contact with
Anglicanism is seen as a measurable and important element in what began at
Madeira. Ladous' final conclusion is: *«Au fond, c'est moins l'influence de Portal
sur les rapports anglo-romains que l'influence de l'anglicanisme sur Portal, et, à
travers lui, sur le catholicisme 'progressiste' du début du siècle, qui est la plus
lourde de conséquences. La condamnation des Ordres anglicans fut un épisode.
La conversion de l'Eglise catholique romaine à un idéal de convergence et de
réforme permanente est un phénomène capital de longue durée, dont il est encore
difficile de mesurer les conséquences, ne serait-ce que sur les rapports de Rome et
de Cantorbéry. Ainsi, Portal aura eu d'autant plus d'influence sur l'évolution de
l'œcuménisme anglo-romain qu'il en aura eu d'abord au sein de l'Eglise de
Rome. Missionaire, le lazariste l'aura été davantage chez les catholiques qu'en
terre anglicane.»*[21]

With the benefit of hindsight, it is a just estimate to say that, if the major
contribution of the Madeira meeting and the life-long friendship which followed
was to centralize and throw into relief the theme of unity by convergence, the
most unfortunate outcome of Halifax's and Portal's activities was to create a
situation which permitted a premature and one-sided showdown on Anglican

---

[18] LADOUS, loc. cit., p. xii.
[19] Ib. p. 60.
[20] Ib. p. 63.
[21] Loc. cit., p. 481.

Orders. It was unfortunate because the stated intention of the two protagonists was to use the question simply to open up the way to joint conference and dialogue which, as their letters show, they regarded as the essential first step. In the event this step was not taken until thirty years later at Malines.

It was unfortunate also for the dialogue — and Archbishop Benson of Canterbury perceived this — in that it put the cart before the horse, theologically speaking. Ministry and Orders should not have been the first subject chosen, but events and the strategy of other people forced the issue with results which were nearly disastrous for Anglican/Roman Catholic relations. It was unfortunate furthermore in that the time was wrong because of the kind of theology which was then in the ascendant in the Roman Catholic Church and because of the hypersensitive state of relations between the two Churches in Victorian England. The complex record of events reveals at times an all too human story and some of the actors in the drama emerge in a better light than others. Nor is it, as the controversialists on both sides tried to present the story, a simple question of the conflict of light and darkness, but rather of opposing and often mistaken sincerities. So while we may well judge some of those sincerities as being less informed than others and their upholders less than meticulous in respect of means and ends, there remains a rather frightening picture of the damage that good sincere men can do and that can be produced by misunderstandings which were there in plenty on both sides as Halifax and Portal travelled their *caminho novo*. The friendship grew at the deepest level as the years of success and of defeat went by and not the least interesting aspect of the relationship is a certain reversal of rôles. At Madeira, Portal was Halifax's pupil, but thereafter he became in many ways the senior partner, the activist, the missionary of ecumenism who moved to a tempo more urgent than that of his contemporaries.

3. The Course of Events from 1890

Only a condensed analysis of the events leading up to 1896 is possible here, nor is anything more elaborate necessary because the reunion campaign and the parts played by individuals have been fully covered not alone in Halifax's own book, 'Leo XIII and Anglican Orders' (1912), but in numerous ecclesiastical biographies. To mention but a few, books such as J. G. Lockhart's 'Viscount Halifax', A. C. Benson's 'The Life of Edward White Benson', J. C. Snead-Cox's 'Life of Cardinal Vaughan', Shane Leslie's 'Cardinal Gasquet, a Memoir', and E. S. Purcell's 'Life of Cardinal Manning', provide adequate documentation. The correspondence recorded in such 'Lives' and Gasquet's often criticised 'Leaves from my Diary', with all the interpersonal chemistry, the ecclesiastical controversy and the strategic moves which they record and evaluate, forms a complex and fascinating account of how events built up, not without some unedifying episodes, to a *dénouement* which had all the appearance of being terminal as far as Anglican/Roman Catholic relations were concerned. Yet through it all Halifax and Portal moved, their vision of what might be remaining basically unspoilt and their resolution unbroken. Something of this comes through, making the picture more three-dimensional, in the modern works of Régis Ladous and of John Jay Hughes, as a result of the melding of the recently discovered Portal and Hemmer papers with those of Halifax and Gasquet.[22]

Between the Madeira meeting of 1890 and the manoeuvrings which preceded 'Apostolicae Curae' in 1896, themes and events became intertwined. As in the case of the Gallican contacts, movement was again due to individuals who refused to be overwhelmed by the situation as the majority read it and who were bent upon persuading their contemporaries to face a different and potentially more creative set of facts. Halifax went to Madeira for the sake of what the climate could do for the health of his son Charles. Portal too had been sent there for his health's sake by his superior general and to help look after a small institution run by the Sisters of Charity. From that chance meeting there emerged for them both the outlines of a common task to be undertaken. Portal had first of all to divest himself of the concept of "reunion by submission", in which he was helped by Halifax's firm rejection of the suggestion that he should join the Roman Catholic Church. It meant, further, a concentrated effort on the Frenchman's part to understand another Church and its history and to enter into an appreciation of its ecclesial life and theological position. After several months, Portal had made his own the goal of unity by convergence and had come to adopt the standpoint that "although divided, we are essentially one."[23] His concept of reunion became corporate and ecclesial just as his theological approach began to take account of the significance for unity conversations of the Anglican insistence on the principle of which the Vincentian canon was a classic instance. Thus a theme heavily accented by Wake reappears in a changed setting and in different circumstances but Portal's views on the papacy remained unaltered and were the official views of his Church at that time. Lockhart's personality assessment is just and constitutes a fundamental comment on all that was to follow: "Like Halifax, he had a mind which minimised practical difficulties by comparison with ultimate ends, a characteristic which was the strength, as well as the weakness, of both men."[24]

The relationship reshaped itself in that Portal soon became the organiser and director and when Halifax was dilatory about writing articles to advance the cause, Portal saw the need for a second meeting, this time at the seminary in Cahors, to revitalise their aims and to plan for action.[25] Both regarded the reunion of Rome and Canterbury as *the distant aim* — "a work for the next century" as Halifax put it[26] — but Portal saw as the *immediate objective* a campaign

---

[22] LADOUS, loc. cit.; JOHN JAY HUGHES, Absolutely Null and Utterly Void (London—Sydney 1968).

[23] Cp. his 'Journal' for 2nd August 1894.

[24] Loc. cit. II, p. 42.

[25] LADOUS, loc. cit., p. 72; « Ce fut comme une seconde naissance de l'entreprise œcumenique. »

[26] In a letter to Portal, 6 May 1894 (LADOUS, ib. p. 73) and see also: Leo XIII and Anglican Orders, p. 385: "No one, certainly neither the Abbé Portal nor myself, supposed that such a reunion was an immediate possibility."

to spread information and to overcome the prejudices rooted in ignorance of one another's traditions. He also hoped to win over Leo XIII to the project. Matters then hung fire for a while and in the interval Portal discovered the problem of Anglican Orders and the fact that for Anglicans it was a non-problem.[27] The question of Orders thus suggested to Portal a fresh short-term objective and a method of moving into action.

With the benefit of hindsight, a case can be made for maintaining that the reunion campaign went wrong at the start by a too early introduction of the theme of Orders. Yet two points should be noted: it went wrong because of the way in which the theme and the events were managed by those who did not favour the project and not because of Portal's intention. His intention and that of Halifax was to treat the question of Orders as a means of promoting inter-Church discussion leading on to an Anglican/Roman Catholic Conference which would set up a formal dialogue aimed at corporate reunion. Halifax made this clear and also made clear the complete absence of any doubt about their Orders on the part of Anglicans in his speech to the English Church Union in 1896: "It is, then, as a means to this end, the reunion of Christendom, not because we have any doubt as to the Orders of the English Church, or require a recognition from Rome to add to our complete assurance of their perfect validity, that the question has been brought forward in France, and is now being discussed in Rome."[28] Wake himself had not laid it on the line more unequivocally.

Theologically speaking, Portal also made the mistake in his approach to the theme of Orders of regarding it as « une question de fait et non de foi »,[29] and the different handling of the theme in the contemporary dialogue is significant.[30] But in terms of the immediate aim of arousing widespread interest in both countries, Portal's strategy of jumping in at the deep end had a gratifying success at first. 'Les Ordinations Anglicanes' by F. Dalbus was published in 'La Science Catholique' in 1893 and as a brochure in the following year and quickly produced the desired results and the reunion campaign got under way.[31] 'Fernand Dalbus' was a pseudonym covering the identity of Portal and, as is now

---

[27] Archbishop BENSON's comment was a typical Anglican reaction. He honoured Portal for admitting the facts but since Anglicans had no doubts as to their Orders there was no more reason to be grateful "for seeing the facts, than I should be grateful to him for acknowledging the Copernican or Newtonian systems." (ARTHUR C. BENSON, The Life of Edward White Benson, Vol. II [London 1899], p. 592).

[28] Leo XIII and Anglican Orders, p. 293.

[29] Cp. LADOUS, loc. cit., p. 80; HUGHES, loc. cit., p. 35.

[30] See Ministry and Ordination (1973), the Canterbury Statement of the Anglican/Roman Catholic International Commission.

[31] It ran to two editions in six months and LOCKHART comments, "The hunt was now fairly up on both sides of the Channel. Cardinal Bourret, Bishop of Rodez and Vabres, wrote to Portal criticising such of his conclusions as favoured the Orders, and Dr. Wordsworth, Bishop of Salisbury, such as disputed them; and both The Guardian in London and the Univers in Paris opened their columns to a learned but lively controversy". Loc. cit., II, p. 46.

known from their papers, that of the Anglican theologian F. W. Puller. The long friendship thus begun introduced Portal to an exponent of that solidly patristic and theologically confident Anglicanism which was in direct line of descent from the seventeenth-century theologians. Dalbus refuted the arguments for the insufficiency of the Anglican rite, showing the apostolic succession to have been preserved, and then, with what Lockhart calls "a slightly disingenuous line of argument"[32] disallows the validity of Anglican Orders on grounds which he knew would be refuted by all scholars — the absence of the *porrectio instrumentorum*. The fact that this ceremony was a medieval addition to the rite and unknown in the Eastern Churches was duly pointed out by Duchesne and Portal's case for Anglican Orders was made, as he had planned. He also sought the support of the press and succeeded in enlisting the active interest of the editors of 'Le Monde' and of 'L'Univers', thus providing the campaign with a public forum. Furthermore, the general ecclesiastical atmosphere just then was favourable to ecumenical activity, not least because of Leo XIII's avowed concern for Christian unity and his friendly overtures to the Orthodox during the Congress at Jerusalem. An Anglican/Roman Catholic rapprochement appeared to fit into this scene since it had not yet become clear that two completely contradictory concepts of unity lay hidden in the fog of an illusory sense of well-being — unity by corporate 'return' and unity by convergence. Thus Portal's campaign met with some initial success and in July of the same year, 1894, he paid his first visit to England as the guest of Lord Halifax.[33]

4. Visits in England

Now the stage suddenly becomes crowded with those who would play rôles of varying importance in the events leading up to 1896. As he began to familiarise himself with the Church of England, Portal was taken to see the historian of the papacy, Mandell Creighton, then Bishop of Peterborough, and he and Halifax visited Maclagan, the Archbishop of York. With a theologian's precision, Creighton replied to Portal's question as to whether the primacy of the bishop of Rome was a difficulty for Anglicans: « une certaine primauté », said Creighton, might be acceptable.[34] The Archbishop of York warmly received Halifax and Portal and said, "Let us hope and trust that we are at the beginning of something really great in the interests of the Church."[35] Moved by this interview, the friends next waited upon the Primate of All England. The Archbishop of Canterbury received them with reserve and "made it plain to them beforehand that they were not to regard themselves as emissaries."[36] While he expressed the

---

[32] Loc. cit., II, p. 46.

[33] Hughes says "August", loc. cit., p. 49.

[34] Ladous, loc. cit. p. 121 and cp. Lockhart, II, p. 48. Creighton had been a major contributor to the 'History of the Papacy during the Period of the Reformation' (London 1882, 1894), Vols. I, II,. pp. xxiii, 453, and XX, 555, III, IV, pp. xvi, 307 and XII, 314.

[35] Lockhart, ib. and cp. Hughes, loc. cit., pp. 50—51.

[36] Lockhart, ib. p. 50.

hope with personal kindness that the contact would continue it was clear that for the Archbishop all this was something quite different from an official approach.[37] Years later Portal was to attribute responsibility for the way things developed to Leo XIII and to the Archbishop.[38] In fact, Portal and the Pope misunderstood each other's intentions, as was to become clear later, because they had different concepts of unity. Nor did Portal perceive how the Archbishop's attitude was coloured by his determination that there should be no shadow of a suggestion that Anglicans were seeking recognition from Rome.[39]

In the meantime, owing to a letter going astray, Portal received too late an invitation to luncheon with Cardinal Vaughan at Westminster. Halifax was there, and Canon Moyes who, with Gasquet and Merry del Val, would soon be playing major parts in the events culminating in 'Apostolicae Curae'. This mishap did nothing to allay the Cardinal's suspicious of the French visitor who had been making a round of Anglican calls although it can hardly have affected the outcome since Vaughan was temperamentally and from his own standpoint totally opposed to any such project. Completely devoted to his Church, intolerant of opposition, partisan and theologically rigid, devout and exclusivist, inheritor of the old tradition of an oppressed English minority and a vigorous controversialist, Vaughan manifested a certain duality which contemporaries observed. His friend, Wilfrid Ward, saw in him "a curious combination of romantic ideals with intensely unromantic details."[40] Halifax described him to Portal as "an admirable Christian" and also "a true inquisitor".[41] The Cardinal's career and his anti-unionist activities over the next two years illustrate the assessment of Ladous: « S'il était romantique de sensibilité et idéal, il devenait implacable et n'hésitait devant aucun moyen quand il passait à l'application pratique.»[42] Vaughan understood only submission – a term he used – and individual conversion, and saw the reunion movement in terms of a threat to the Roman Catholic Church in England; "Such was the man on whose stubborn and unyielding opposition the soaring hopes of Halifax and Portal were to suffer shipwreck."[43] If in temperament, breeding and background, Vaughan and Halifax

---

[37] PORTAL's comment as they left was "We are far from York" (HUGHES, loc. cit. p. 54) and HALIFAX noted the different tone of the two meetings though he felt that "It did very well".

[38] « Au Vatican et à Cantorbéry, on manque de décision et de grandeur d'âme », LADOUS, loc. cit. p. 151.

[39] HUGHES, loc. cit., p. 53.

[40] HUGHES, loc. cit., p. 41.

[41] LADOUS, loc. cit., p. 143.

[42] Ib. p. 143.

[43] HUGHES, loc. cit. p. 45 and cp. p. 201 in which is quoted HALIFAX's severe judgment on the Cardinal and the Archbishop: "I say it with regret: the whole of Cardinal Vaughan's conduct, as I think the correspondence makes sufficiently clear, was unworthy of him; and it is no less painful to have to admit that what is true of Cardinal Vaughan is true in its degree of Archbishop Benson ... On Cardinal Vaughan's shoulders rests the chief responsibility for the failure of all that was attempted, but a share of that responsibility must also rest on the shoulders of Archbishop Benson." (Leo XIII and Anglican Orders, p. 386). In an earlier judgment, HALIFAX wrote that perhaps he did Benson an injustice in that "men's minds were not ready for it."

had more than a little in common, they were poles apart in theology and in their understanding of the Church. Lord Halifax, with what has been called his transparent honesty, kept the Cardinal fully informed of his hopes and plans and those of Portal. But "Vaughan did not hesitate" writes Hughes "to use the information thus supplied to him to frustrate what Halifax was trying to accomplish. Both in private and in public he consistently misrepresented the motives of Halifax and Portal."[44] He organised a campaign against the validity of Anglican Orders in the 'Tablet' and the 'Month' and wrote a personal letter to the 'Times' denying that the Roman See could ever accept the ordinations. Anglican feeling was not unnaturally aroused and Vaughan's interventions antagonised the Archbishop of Canterbury at a delicate and quite unexpected stage of development in the Halifax-Portal endeavours to make the Church leaders at least consider the possibility of contact and dialogue.

5. Visitors to the Vatican

What next took place was — from the point of view of the two campaigners for unity — that the impossible happened. Portal was told by Cardinal Rampolla, the papal secretary of State, that Leo XIII wished him to come to Rome. It seemed to Halifax, who had hurried over to Paris, and to Portal, that their objective, the beginning of official dialogue was all but attained. Portal even felt that he should now disappear from the scene so that authority could take over.[45] In fact, their hopes were destined to decline as opposition increased and misunderstandings grew. Chief among the latter was the inability of the other side either to understand or to accept what was for Portal and Halifax the master-theme, that of unity by convergence.

Rampolla received Portal cordially, advised him and listened to his report on the situation and on his English visit: "Evidently" said the Cardinal "something should be done, but what?"[46] Portal decided to suggest at the next interview the move which he and Halifax had envisaged, that the Pope should write privately to the two English Archbishops. Leo XIII received Portal on September 12th with the words "I should very much like to speak with you about the Anglican Church."[47] Portal repeated the account he had given to Rampolla and suggested a letter to the Archbishops of Canterbury and York, seeking their co-operation in the work for unity and inviting them to join in setting up inter-Church conferences. The subject would be Anglican Orders regarded as a convenient introduction to the real differences. The Pope agreed to

---

[44] HUGHES, loc. cit., p. 38 and LADOUS, loc. cit., pp. 142–147.

[45] LADOUS, loc. cit., p. 136.

[46] For an account of this interview see PORTAL's letters and journals quoted by LADOUS, pp. 131–136; HALIFAX's 'Leo XIII and Anglican Orders' and also LOCKHART, pp. 52–54 and HUGHES, pp. 54–60.

[47] The Pope also congratulated PORTAL on his 'Les Ordinations Anglicanes' which he had been reading (Leo XIII etc., p. 122).

write the letter: "I shall write that letter . . . if only reunion with the Anglicans were possible . . . then I could sing my *Nunc Dimittis*."

All now seemed set for movement to the extent that Rampolla requested Portal to draft such a letter and even discussed with him a possible location for the reunion conferences, prophetically suggesting Belgium as being midway between Canterbury and Rome. It seemed too good to be true, and so in fact it was.[48] Three days later Rampolla had to tell Portal that the Pope would not after all write the letter in case of an Anglican refusal and because he wished to go more deeply into the matter. Rampolla was to write the letter to Portal, to be shown to Halifax and then, if the archbishops responded, the way would be open for the direct approach.[49] The letter itself, if general in tone and substance, was noteworthy by reason of its acceptance of a mixed conference which assumed that reunion would be by joint study and seeking for convergence.

In the event, however, the change of plan proved most unfortunate. When Halifax and Portal brought it to the Archbishop of Canterbury, the latter made it clear that the letter left the Pope uninvolved and therefore refused the suggestion that he should reply to it and thus become unilaterally involved. The Archbishop agreed that the letter was friendly but maintained that it was negatived by Cardinal Vaughan's recent attack on the Church of England at Preston. The most he would say was that he too would further consider the matter. The public hostility of Vaughan who was deeply disturbed at the prospect of the Pope writing to the Anglican archbishops (he had been kept informed by Halifax) was thus a major factor from the start, and his visit to the Vatican in the following January (1895) would consolidate the opposition. Even the Archbishop of York, who had worked hard and unsuccessfully to obtain from the Archbishop of Canterbury a suitable letter for Halifax, was obliged to confess to the latter that Cardinal Vaughan had postponed any hope of reunion to an indefinite future.[50] It was at this point that the initiative really passed to the anti-unionists and the ecumenical horizon, fleetingly glimpsed, was shortly to contract to vanishing point by reducing the project for Anglican/Roman Catholic dialogue to the proportions of a domestic decision by one Church about the Orders of another.

Contacts between the protagonists moved on as did other events which at the time seemed hopeful. Lacey and Denny's defence of Anglican Orders 'De Hierarchia Anglicana' appeared in 1895 and the Abbé Duchesne, at the Pope's request, had drawn up a memorandum favourable to the Orders, a conclusion reinforced by Gasparri.[51] Meanwhile, at a more popular level, Portal was working to arouse interest in France, encouraged by his superior in spite of Vaughan's demand for sanctions against him. He set about founding an association to promote unity by convergence and also created the first ecumenical

---

[48] « *Le miracle était énorme, trop énorme. L'histoire et les institutions ne pouvaient pas se faire oublier plus longtemps* », LADOUS, loc. cit. p. 137.

[49] For the text of the letter, see Leo XIII and Anglican Orders, pp. 153 ff.

[50] Leo XIII and Anglican Orders, p. 166.

[51] Cp. LOCKHART, loc. cit., p. 59.

review 'La Revue Anglo-Romaine'. For this latter project he had to obtain
permission from the Archbishop of Paris who tied it and the association to the
mother house of Portal's Order in Paris. In this way, Portal's free-lance position
was exchanged for one which was increasingly vulnerable.[52] In fact, the time
would shortly come when Portal would be summoned before the Archbishop of
Paris to be "informed that the *Revue* had fallen under the Pope's displeasure."
Halifax was to say bluntly that this sort of thing justified everything that was
usually said of Rome.[53] In the meantime the review earned the strong disapproval of Cardinal Vaughan.[54]

The Cardinal had already been received by the Pope (January 1895) and had
found Leo XIII in an ecumenical frame of mind as a result of interviews with
Rampolla and Portal. He proceeded to adjust the Pope's perspective by presenting his own picture of the English religious situation and by casting serious
doubts on Portal's loyalty and judgment.[55] When Vaughan informed the Pope
of the unanimous Anglican rejection of papal authority, Leo XIII's comment
"*Ma questa é una questione di dottrina*" served only to show how completely
the Pope and Portal had failed to get through to one another. The Cardinal
suggested that, instead of writing to the English Archbishops, it would be altogether better to write an encyclical on the Church and her Head.[56] Having thus
succeeded in heading off moves towards *rapprochement*, Cardinal Vaughan at
once set Dom Francis Gasquet to work. This English scholar whose inaccuracy,
not to say worse, has been much criticised, shared to the full Vaughan's attitude
on the reunion movement and he quickly became a central figure in events.[57] By
March of the same year Gasquet's researches convinced the Pope, who spoke of
this to Vaughan, of the invalidity of Anglican Orders. The fact that a personal
judgment, based for the time being on one man's studies, had been made at this
stage bears directly on the setting up in the following year of a papal
commission of inquiry and inevitably raises questions as to its nature and functions.[58]

---

[52] LADOUS, loc. cit., p. 203.

[53] LOCKHART, loc. cit., pp. 77—78.

[54] "The Cardinal does not love the *Revue* et all — he clearly detests it" wrote HALIFAX to
Portal, LOCKHART, loc. cit., p. 67.

[55] "The Cardinal proceeded to give Leo XIII a seriously misleading account of Portal's activities," HUGHES, loc. cit., p. 69 and cp. LOCKHART, loc. cit., p. 61.

[56] LADOUS, loc. cit., pp. 169—176; LOCKHART, loc. cit., pp. 60—61.

[57] « *Intelligent, tenace, sans scrupule, persuadé que la plus grande gloire de Dieu et du Cardinal Vaughan justifiait tous les moyens, Gasquet arriva à Rome le 31 Janvier 1895,* » LA-
DOUS, loc. cit., p. 174. Cp. HUGHES, loc. cit., pp. 72—73; "But not even Bishop could
prevent Gasquet from filling his books with innumerable errors and misstatements. Gasquet's habitual inaccuracy, and even more his refusal even to correct his errors or to take
any notice either of criticism or of any other work inspired by his own, caused him, after
two decades of scholarly succees, to become generally discredited even before his death in
1929. Gasquet played a leading rôle in the condemnation of Anglican Orders, and his standards of accuracy will be dealt with in detail in the course of our narrative."

[58] For the evidence and for the original notes for GASQUET's 'Leaves from My Diary', see
HUGHES, loc. cit., pp. 72—85.

Another visitor now arrived at the Vatican. Lord Halifax was received by Leo XIII apparently a few days after the Pope had formed his judgment on Anglican Orders. On the surface of things, Halifax and Portal (who joined him in Rome) seemed to have much to hope for when Halifax at a cordial meeting with the Pope and Cardinal Rampolla presented his memorandum and dossier. But in fact, the other group of English visitors headed by Cardinal Vaughan had already turned the stream of events in a different direction.[59] April would see, not a letter from the Pope to the Anglicans, but the papal letter 'Ad Anglos', drafted by Vaughan and Gasquet before Halifax's visit. It was published on 20th April after certain changes in the draft had been discussed with the Pope's English language secretary, Mgr. Merry del Val, who from this point onwards became a prime mover in the events leading up to the condemnation of Anglican Orders.

6. From 'Ad Anglos' to 'Apostolicae Curae'

'Ad Anglos' was couched in general terms, appealing for prayers for unity but making no suggestions about dialogue or conferences. Although it was addressed to the English people it made no mention whatever of the Church of England, and the Archbishop of Canterbury commented unfavourably on this while noting the friendly tone of the letter. The genesis of the document and the circumstances of its origin not being understood and known by the general public, it was on the whole well received. Even Portal believed that it signalized the beginnings of *rapprochement*, and he may be forgiven because of the circumstances since during the previous summer (in June) Rampolla had encouraged him to continue with this "important question".[60] As a result, he had left Cahors for Paris and concerned himself with the Association and with the 'Revue'.[61] As far as the public was concerned, 'Ad Anglos' paradoxically gave a temporary fillip to the movement for unity and succeeded in generating a surprising optimism, being favourably received even by Low Church opinion in England.[62]

In England, the point-counterpoint movement continued. Halifax addressed the English Church Union in June giving an account of his and Portal's endeavours and the opposition encountered and making a plea to Anglicans to respond to the Pope's desire for unity as expressed in 'Ad Anglos'. Vaughan, who knew more about 'Ad Anglos' and Leo XIII's thinking, made an intransigent reply at the Bristol meeting of the Catholic Truth Society in September. The following month, the Church Congress met at Norwich and

---

[59] "Though something like a very dignified tug-of-war was taking place between the two parties of English visitors, their mutual relations continued to be most amicable", LOCK-HART, loc. cit., p. 63.

[60] LADOUS, op. cit., p. 192.

[61] Cp. LOCKHART, op. cit., p. 67.

[62] Cp. LADOUS, loc. cit., p. 240.

Halifax set out with clarity some classical Anglican views on papal primacy, quoting Bramhall and Thorndike.[63]

Norwich was important in that the theme of convergence, quite unacceptable to Halifax's opponents, now surfaced publicly. It was important also in that it gave an opportunity for a quasi-official Anglican reaction to the papal letter. The chief speaker was Maclagan, Archbishop of York, who openly responded to 'Ad Anglos' by advocating a movement of convergence. With what must have taken courage at the time he invited his listeners to consider a primacy which, with the Church's freedoms duly safeguarded, might potentially be a centre of unity. Differentiating between the Roman primacy as understood in the sixth century and in the nineteenth, he suggested that "a return to the earlier conception is not beyond the bounds of hope."[64] Thus, two themes among others, those of primacy and of convergence, run through the Gallican correspondence, the nineteenth-century controversy, on to the Malines Conversations and to the present.

In France, there was a simultaneous and hopeful awakening of interest fostered by the Association and the review and due in no small part to a successful Paris conference at which Halifax had been the main attraction. This state of partial euphoria continued right up to the summer of 1896, even to the extent of evoking a favourable intervention by no less a public figure than Mr. Gladstone in May of that year when 'Apostolicae Curae' was but four months away.[65] The intervention resulted in the matter being transformed from an inter-Church concern into a question of general public interest and it was treated as such in the English and continental press. It also served to increase public optimism at a time when the ecclesiastical opposition was hardening and the ground was being prepared for the destruction of the reunion movement and the condemnation of Anglican Orders.[66] Hughes notes that "A crucial rôle was played by the half-English, half-Spanish, Mgr. Raphael Merry del Val, then thirty years old and a

---

[63] HUGHES, loc. cit., p. 96 and cp. Appendix A, pp. 273–277 below.

[64] Leo XIII and Anglican Orders, p. 230.

[65] BERNARD and MARGARET PAWLEY write (Rome and Canterbury through Four Centuries: a study of the Relations between the Church of Rome and the Anglican Churches, 1530–1973 [London 1974], p. 248): "In May 1896 Gladstone produced a paper giving his personal reflections on the subject. 'It is to the last degree improbable [he wrote] that a ruler of known wisdom would put in motion the machinery of the Curia for the purpose of widening the breach . . . If the investigations of the Curia did not lead to a favourable result, wisdom and charity would in any case correct them at such a point as to prevent their becoming an occasion and a means of embittering religious controversy.' Gladstone little knew the zeal and determination of Vaughan and his chief assistant, Dom Aidan (later Cardinal) Gasquet in the opposite direction . . . the success of their persuasion was soon to be visible."

One may comment that while GLADSTONE was mistaken about the Pope he had fairly gauged Vaughan's opposition, as may be seen from his comment in a letter to Halifax, dated in the same month (20th May): "My belief is that Cardinal Vaughan and his band will omit no opportunity and will not greatly scruple any means of defeating the Pope in his present purpose." (Leo XIII and Anglican Orders, p. 305).

[66] Cp. LADOUS, op. cit., pp. 269–273.

special protégé and favourite of the eighty-five-year old Pope, Leo XIII, who saw Merry del Val daily and placed special trust in his opinion, especially in regard to English affairs. A number of letters written by Merry del Val and preserved amongst the Gasquet Papers at Downside Abbey show the invaluable assistance he was able to render to Cardinal Vaughan."[67] For Halifax, he was "an influence altogether hostile to our action"[68] and he spearheaded Vaughan's and Gasquet's moves by contesting at every point the efforts of the more well-disposed Cardinal Rampolla. In fact, this contest had continued throughout the month of July in the previous year,[69] and most significantly, one of the subjects was "the real basis of reunion", as Merry del Val wrote to Vaughan. Rampolla fought a strong rear-guard action but in the end the Pope was won over and Merry del Val was able to write in August to Gasquet that he thought all would be well.[70] A commission would be appointed on Anglican Orders and by September Cardinal Vaughan had set up his own committee to prepare the case against the Orders. The secretary of the papal commission would be Merry del Val himself who strongly disapproved not only of the unity campaign but of Portal and his activities. In fact, he had described the latter's views as heretical and during the summer of 1895 had sought to have the 'Revue' suppressed,[71] and Portal had been duly cautioned.

To return to 1896, there then appeared on June 30th the encyclical 'Satis Cognitum'. In itself a colourless document expounding contemporary Roman Catholic teaching on the papacy but underlining also the rights of the episcopate as successors of the apostles, two sets of circumstances gave it importance. Ecclesiologically speaking, and from the angle of the development of events, its significance lay in the fact that by implication − since its subject was the unity of the Church − it rejected unity by convergence. Throughout, the thread which guides through the events is the theme which formulated itself during the Madeira meeting.

As to the attendant circumstances, the encyclical appeared at a time when illusory expectations still prevailed that there might be some sort of follow-up to 'Ad Anglos' and to Mr. Gladstone's comment on the possibility of inter-Church conferences. Accordingly in some quarters there was an attempt to make the best of the encyclical's positive features, notably on the part of the Archbishop of York. This tendency however was largely cancelled out by the manner of the encyclical's publication in England, only selected passages prefaced by a letter from Cardinal Vaughan dismissing all thought of Anglican/Roman Catholic conferences, being published in the 'Times': "In Halifax's opinion, he gave to

---

[67] Loc. cit., p. 97.
[68] Leo XIII and Anglican Orders, p. 273.
[69] LADOUS, op. cit., pp. 270−272: «*Pendant trois semaines, Léon XIII fut littéralement assiégé par Merry del Val et par Rampolla, qui, chaque matin, apportaient au Pape des informations et des avis parfaitement contradictoires au sujet de l'Angleterre.*»
[70] «*Je pense que nous sommes sûrs maintenant d'obtenir par n'importe quel moyen que la question soit complètement réglée quand elle viendra sur le tapis.*» LADOUS, 273.
[71] HUGHES, loc. cit., p. 103.

the excerpts a colouring which was not borne by the encyclical as a whole. In this he was abetted by a leading article in the same issue of the *Times*."[72] Halifax reacted sharply with an open letter to Vaughan, and, at long last, the deduction began to be made that if the Cardinal declared corporate reunion to be impossible this was because the Vatican thought so too. The press also veered round and sympathised with Halifax — and with Gladstone.[73]

Privately, Halifax was deeply discouraged and wrote to Portal "The Cardinal has certainly brought off his *coup*, and the Pope has aided him well . . . for the moment, it is all up with us here and there is nothing more to be done."[74] His friend was more tenacious and proposed that Halifax should call a meeting in London. This took place on July 13th and Portal spoke on the subject of the encyclical, receiving an ovation. While he never mentioned the English Cardinal, simply interpreting 'Satis cognitum' in a different sense, there is no doubt that Portal knew what he was doing by committing himself publicly to the cause of corporate reunion.[75] On his return to Paris two days later he found himself forbidden to concern himself further with Anglican affairs. On the 17th, he was informed through a letter from Cardinal Perraud to Cardinal Richard of Paris that the 'Revue' might even be put on the Index since it was too much "in the hands of Lord Halifax and Anglicans who wish to conduct affairs as equals rather than simply submitting (et non s'humilier simplement)."[76] The word 'humiliation' was altogether too much for Halifax who replied to Portal "If that must be the last word, there is not a single one of my countrymen who would not be ready to hang anyone who should talk to him of Rome and of union with her." Neither Wake nor Benson could have reacted with more toughness. Ecumenism and convergence seemed at a discount and worse was to follow.

The papal commission set up in March 1896 to inquire into Anglican Orders was in session in the meantime. Though the records of its meetings were not published and information has been pieced together from various sources, the outcome is history and contemporary accounts and modern studies supplement each other.[77] In brief outline, the president of the commission was Cardinal Mazzella and the three English representatives, nominated by Cardinal Vaughan, were Gasquet, Moyes and Fleming who were known to regard the Orders as invalid. The Spaniard de Llavaneras, reckoned by some commentators

---

[72] LOCKHART, II, p. 75.

[73] LADOUS, loc. cit., p. 342.

[74] LOCKHART, II, p. 76.

[75] He had written beforehand to his friend Levé, "What I shall say over there will be a reply" and to Halifax, "What I shall say can be published from the housetops; but circumstances will give to my words a character which will invest them with importance", LOCKHART II, p. 76 and LADOUS, p. 347.

[76] LOCKHART, II, p. 77 and LADOUS, p. 350.

[77] See in particular J. J. HUGHES, Absolutely Null and Utterly Void (London–Sidney 1968), IDEM, Stewards of the Lord (London–Sidney 1970), and RÉGIS LADOUS, L'Abbé Portal et la Campagne Anglo-Romaine 1890–1912 (Lyon 1973).

as neutral and by others as sharing the English Roman Catholic view,[78] was one of the two members added to the commission. The other was Fr. Scannell who was hurriedly appointed "after the Pope had asked Vaughan to send to Rome an English theologian who would represent a point of view different from that of the three men he had already nominated."[79] De Llavaneras seems to have been included by way of a counter-balance, and, in the event (according to Merry del Val's recollection) he voted for invalidity.[80] Of the remaining members of the commission, Gasparri favoured a verdict of probable validity and Duchesne and de Augustinis (with Scannell) held Anglican Orders to be valid. The president and the secretary, Merry del Val, were in accord with Cardinal Vaughan's views. The theologians on the commission were then amongst those who were favourable and Gasparri and Duchesne felt the need for the help of Anglican specialists and asked for it. As a result, T. A. Lacey and F. W. Puller went to Rome to make themselves available. At the same time they made it clear that they went as private experts and in no sense as Anglican representatives and still less as seeking recognition of Anglican Orders.[81] Lacey's 'A Roman Diary' (London, 1910) has left a record of their doings and impressions, and of their intention and purpose as just outlined.[82] In fact, the use made of them was minimal and, as Hughes observes, "the Anglican case was never properly or fairly presented."[83]

"The Commission took only a few months to deliberate on what had been discussed for three centuries", wrote Bernard and Margaret Pawley.[84] But even at that, if Ladous' arithmetic is correct the commission was in session for only about twenty-seven hours.[85] From contemporary correspondence of interested parties, it is clear that there were strong disagreements and difficulties, but the only available source for knowing details of the outcome is a letter from Merry del Val to Moyes. Relying on his memory, the votes against the Orders numbered four, half the Commission. In favour of the Orders were either three for validity and one for probable validity or, in Merry del Val's recollection, two for each viewpoint, though Fleming's memory contradicts this.[86] The com-

---

[78] B. and M. Pawley, loc. cit., p. 250 and Ladous, loc. cit., p. 304.

[79] Hughes, loc. cit., p. 115.

[80] « De plus, pour rétablir l'équilibre, le Pape nomma un nouveau membre hostile aux ordres anglicans: pour faire bonne mesure, on choisit un capucin espagnol, consulteur du Saint-Office, le Padre Calasanzio de Llavaneras, qui demandait très sincèrement s'il fallait une autorisation du gouvernement pour célébrer la messe en Angleterre », Ladous, loc. cit., p. 296.

[81] Portal described his friend Puller as "an intransigent Anglican". Lacey was, of course, the co-author of 'De Hierarchia Anglicana' and a Latinist so distinguished that Leo XIII was said to have wished that he had someone who could write Latin with comparable skill.

[82] Loc. cit., pp. 8–9.

[83] Hughes, loc. cit., p. 119.

[84] Loc. cit., p. 250. On the sessions and method of working of the Commission, see Ladous, loc. cit., pp. 305–316.

[85] Ladous, pp. 314–315.

[86] Ladous, op. cit., p. 316.

mission of inquiry found itself expected to conclude abruptly — «*les principaux problèmes n'avaient été qu'effleurés*» — and to make its report on this basis for transmission to a commission of cardinals.[87] Hughes analyses the subject-content of the eleven meetings so far as is known from various sources and comments "There is no evidence that the question of intention, which has figured so prominently in polemical works against the Orders, and which was to be one of the grounds of condemnation, had played more than an incidental rôle in the discussions."[88] Such was the work of the commission which dealt an all but mortal blow to Anglican/Roman Catholic relations. The commission of cardinals, meeting for two and a half hours under the procedure known as Feria V, the Pope presiding, confirmed that the Holy Office had previously decided the question and that the commission of inquiry's conclusions supported this — the recollection is Gasquet's, confirmed by Merry del Val.[89]

It remained but to draft the Bull, a task entrusted to Merry del Val who was assisted by Tarozzi and Gasquet. It was dated 13th September 1896 and promulgated five days later.

If the Gallican conversations had had no visible results, the final outcome of the Madeira meeting was disastrous. It turned a rift into a rupture: "One of the worst features of the situation was the exultation of Cardinal Vaughan and the organs of Roman Catholic publicity in England. Shortly before the publication of the Bull the *Tablet* had said that 'the status of the Anglican Church is that of a sect in manifest heresy and schism and as such as hateful as the contradictions of Korah, Dathan and Abiram.'"[90]

It meant the destruction of the reunion movement, and the contrast between two sets of sincere men, hopelessly at variance, is illustrated by the "happy and exciting dinner" in Gasquet's house and the sad exchange of letters between the Madeira friends throughout which still sounded the note "the thing is as certain as ever."[91]

Portal's fortunes varied thereafter: rehabilitated in 1897 and condemned again in 1908, he and Halifax continued and deepened their friendship. "I owe you all of what has been best in my life" he wrote to Halifax in 1911 and writing again on the appearance of his friend's book, he said "Your book brings to a close the succession of events begun by my brochure. It is an ending. Let us hope that it is only the end of a first stage."[92]

A second stage would come about when, a quarter of a century later, the two friends would travel the road to Malines together.

---

[87] LADOUS, op.cit., pp. 314—315, 324—326.

[88] HUGHES, loc.cit., pp. 159—160. He agrees with Ladous as to the total time spent at work by the Commission. The latter words more strongly a comment on intention: «*Et l'on a aucune preuve, aucun signe que la question fondamentale de l'intention, sur laquelle se fonde en grande partie la Bulle Apostolicae Curae, ait été seulement abordée au cours des débats*», loc.cit., p. 315.

[89] LADOUS, loc.cit., pp. 324—326; HUGHES, loc.cit., pp. 185—191.

[90] B. and M. PAWLEY, loc.cit., pp. 251—252.

[91] Ib. pp. 252—253, and HUGHES, loc.cit., p. 199.

[92] LADOUS, loc.cit., pp. 469—477.

III. Themes at Malines: The Malines Conversations 1921–1925

Malines marked a new stage in that it became a conference and was therefore an advance in Anglican/Roman Catholic relations. Even if the advance was soon stopped short und no formula of concord or agreed statement on doctrine or polity emerged, it established a measure of formal contact in charity and gave an opportunity to the major themes to surface in the context not of polemic but of dialogue. This may well be the chief significance of the Conversations at Malines that this interchange of views took place at a time when rigidity and fixed stances prevailed in theology and ecclesiology. Of course, the Malines meetings were held in a general climate which was slowly but surely undergoing radical change, the passage from a Christianity of culture to a Christianity of choice, but the effects of this were not yet universally realised or experienced and its impact on the relative positions of the conversationalists was marginal. Indeed this profound change may have been largely unperceived as far as the participants were concerned since they themselves were living within the beginnings of the transition. Ecumenically and theologically speaking, there were no collaborating external factors such as a meeting of Pope and Archbishop and a second Vatican Council to help towards a *rapprochement*. But there *was* the Appeal to all Christian People by the sixth Lambeth Conference of 1920, and, indirectly, this was what sparked off the Conversations at Malines.

1. Contact is Made

The accepted account of the genesis of the dialogue is true as far as it goes. The publication in 1927, in English and French, of the report by the Anglican members to the Archbishop of Canterbury together with an account of the meetings and a Roman Catholic memorandum, had this to say about the origin of the Conversations: "In the Autumn of 1921 Lord Halifax paid a visit to His Eminence Cardinal Mercier at Malines, and asked him if he would be disposed to receive some of his friends, members of the Anglican Communion, who like himself were anxious to labour for a *rapprochement* of the Anglican Church to the Roman Catholic Church.

The moment, he said, was favourable, since the Anglican Bishops, united to the number of two hundred and fifty at Lambeth Palace, had expressed in a very explicit and exact way their eager wish for the realisation of a visible catholic reunion of Christendom.

The Cardinal gladly assented to the request of Lord Halifax and of the Abbé Portal who came with him." (There follows a quotation from the Lambeth Appeal to All Christian People, IV, concerning "the goal of a reunited Catholic Church").[1] The account then notes "It was in the hope expressed in

---

[1] The Conversations at Malines, 1921–1925 (Oxford, 1927), pp. 7, 8.

these words that two of Lord Halifax's Anglican friends assented to his proposal that they should accompany him to Malines." These friends were Armitage Robinson, Dean of Wells, and W. H. Frere, Superior of the Community of the Resurrection.

In 1930, Lord Halifax edited the original documents, because of "the attempts to discredit the Malines Conversations", and in order to make the material available which "will enable everybody to judge for themselves of the nature of the Conversations". He added that an additional motive for publication was to do justice to the Abbé Portal's work and to Cardinal Mercier's intentions.[2] The agreed account of the origin of the dialogue which ascribes it to the initiative of the Madeira friends and to the impact of the Lambeth Appeal is thus correct. But Bernard and Margaret Pawley have produced new evidence from the Malines Archives which shows not only Mercier's intentions but his commitment to the cause of unity before the approach was made and prior to his receiving the Lambeth Appeal. In a letter of 21st December 1920 to Pope Benedict XV, the Cardinal in fact suggested an inter-church meeting of theologians at Malines and the same Archives contain three other corroborative pieces of evidence.[3] Evidently the principals on both sides had been independently moving in the same direction. The contact was then made but initial difficulties had to be resolved before what began as a personal enterprise could acquire a degree of official backing.

2. The Pattern of Events

A summary record of what took place between 1921 and 1925 will serve to place the themes in their setting of the events which were fully described ten years later in four books appearing within a year of one another. These were G. K. A. Bell's 'Randall Davidson, Archbishop of Canterbury' (1935), G. L. Prestige's 'The Life of Charles Gore' (1935), Walter Frere's 'Recollections of Malines' (1935) and J. G. Lockhart's 'Charles Lindley Viscount Halifax' (1936). The happenings which led up to the Malines conversations and the story of the meetings, unlike the complicated tangle of events and personalities of the earlier reunion movement, constitute a comparatively simple record. While the fact that the talks actually took place was of primary importance, it quickly became clear

---

[2] Preface to The Conversations at Malines 1921–1925, Original Documents, edited by Lord HALIFAX (London 1930). These two books with similar titles must not be confused. See LOCKHART's comment (Viscount Halifax, 1936, II, p. 339): "In 1930, with a magnificent disregard of the Law of Copyright and in face of the objections of his old companions, who held to their promise and were especially insistent on the confidential nature of Dom Lambert Beauduin's contribution, he published the papers." Both Van Roey and Kidd objected, as did GORE a copy of whose paper on 'Unity with Diversity' HALIFAX had not been able to procure, but HALIFAX went ahead and wrote to 'The Times' that he had destroyed "the conspiracy of silence which certain people in authoritative quarters had set up against the Conversations".

[3] B. and M. PAWLEY, loc. cit., p. 281–283.

that what was talked about would be of equal importance. One must therefore qualify the view that "it was because it happened, and moreover was allowed to happen, that the dialogue is of such significance: what was discussed is of secondary importance."[4] In fact, the constant insistence by Archbishop Davidson on the doctrinal issues as being pre-eminent both in his letters to Cardinal Mercier and in the memoranda which he drew up shows clearly that this aspect had for him the highest priority.

Halifax's visit to Cardinal Mercier, to whom the Archbishop had sent a copy of the Lambeth Appeal, has been already mentioned. The Archbishop received a letter from Halifax informing him of his plans and intentions and asking for a letter of formal introduction to the Cardinal. Halifax and Portal brought this letter to Mercier who, on asking why the Roman Catholic authorities in England had not been approached, was informed that their disposition was against it.

The Archbishop of Canterbury, for his part, could not but admit Lord Halifax's contention that the Lambeth Appeal could be taken to cover an Anglican/Roman Catholic dialogue. His letter was, however, extremely cautious and stressed that Halifax did not go "in any sense as an ambassador or formal representative of the Church of England . . . Anything he says therefore would be an expression of his personal opinion rather than an authoritative statement of the position or the endeavours of the Church of England in its corporate capacity."[5]

Davidson did not regard Halifax as being truly representative and thus, at the very beginning, the question of the status of the talks and of the nature of the authorisation to be given to those involved came up, just as it had for Archbishops Wake and Benson. In this case, however, the conversations did succeed in achieving a degree of official approval on both sides without which Davidson would have refused to lend his support.[6] The first meeting in any event was exploratory and had no official backing, though the Archbishop was kept privately informed both by the Cardinal and by the Anglicans.[7] It was in fact set up on the private initiative of Halifax and the Cardinal and the participants were invited by them on their own responsibility. Thus, Armitage Robinson, Dean of Wells, W. H. Frere, Superior of the Community of the Resurrection, Mgr. Van Roey, Vicar-General of Malines and E. F. Portal, assembled with the two principals at Malines for the first conversation, 6th–8th December, 1921. "Are we not at the point where we were in 1894?" wrote Halifax to Portal.

At once, familiar themes fundamental to the consideration of Anglican/ Roman Catholic relations made their re-appearance; the nature of the Church and the Sacraments (in a memorandum by Lord Halifax) and the question of the

---

[4] Ib. p. 284.

[5] G. K. A. Bell, Randall Davidson, Archbishop of Canterbury, 3rd. edition (London 1952), p. 1255.

[6] Cp. B. and M. Pawley, loc. cit., p. 284.

[7] G. L. Prestige, The Life of Charles Gore, a great Englishman (London–Toronto 1935), p. 479; Bell, loc. cit., p. 1255.

difference between fundamental and non-fundamental dogmas. For the moment, we may simply locate these themes and others within the sequence of events.

At this juncture, the death of Benedict XV was followed by the election of Mercier's friend, Cardinal Ratti, as Pius XI, in February 1922. Mercier was anxious to recommend to the new Pope the private conversations with Anglicans approved by his predecessor, who had said «*Je ne vois que du bien à ces réunions.*»[8] In September, the Cardinal told Halifax that the Vatican approved the continuation of the conversations, and this at once brought to a head the question of official recognition and authorisation.[9] The suggestion was made that the English Archbishops might informally nominate delegates to a second round of talks and that they might also suggest an outline for discussion.[10] Archbishop Davidson was ready to cooperate but he was adamant that a parallel Vatican authorisation was essential. Writing to Halifax (30th October 1922) he insisted that "unless there be an authoritsation on the part of the Vatican corresponding to that which is given from Lambeth" there could be no formal dialogue. The credentials of both sides must be equally authoritative and even then such emissaries could not bind the Church at large — "They would go to confer and to make suggestions — nothing more."[11] Bell's own part in arranging agreement on the delicate business of authorization (he was then the Archbishop's chaplain) may be gathered, not from his own book, but from Pawleys' survey which also mentions the comment of Fr. Leslie Walker, an English Jesuit, to Mercier. This was to the effect that, in the conversations, the Anglicans must be brought to see "that the faith-basis must be ours not theirs."[12] Bishop Gore's paper later on at Malines would reject this arrogant type of claim completely. Convergence as a theme had still not caught on amongst Roman Catholics.

On the 25th November 1922, Cardinal Mercier received authority from Rome through Cardinal Gasparri, the Papal Secretary of State, saying that the Pope «*autorise Votre Eminence à dire aux Anglicans que le Saint-Siège approuve et encourage vos conversations, et prie de son coeur le bon Dieu de les bénir.*» Prestige emphasises that the words "Saint-Siège" are significant as indicating that the approval was not merely personal.[13] Halifax, with that unquenchable optimism which carried him throught the greatest disappointments, wrote to Portal "We have reached the goal we had set before our eyes thirty years ago."

The Archbishop of Canterbury, replying to Cardinal Mercier on 2nd February 1923 noted the significant phrase, and in the event it was important because neither of the principals had heard the last of this aspect of the conversations at Malines. From this time onwards the Cardinal and the Archbishop

---

[8] B. and M. PAWLEY, loc. cit., p. 285—286.

[9] BELL, loc. cit., p. 1256—1257; PAWLEY, loc. cit., p. 287.

[10] PRESTIGE, loc. cit., p. 479.

[11] BELL, pp. 1257—1258.

[12] B. and M. PAWLEY, pp. 286—287.

[13] PRESTIGE, p. 479; for the text of MERCIER's letter to the Pope and of GASPARRI's letter to Mercier, see LOCKHART, II, pp. 282—283.

corresponded directly with each other and it is particularly noticeable that again and again Davidson kept bringing the whole matter back to the theological themes on which he insisted that everything depended. At this stage, Halifax saw the English Cardinal Bourne and found him sympathetic, but Portal registered the contrary impression and also believed "that the conflict of rival influences would soon begin at Rome."[14]

The second conversation (14th–15th March 1923), if not official in the full sense, had nevertheless a quasi-official status and the Archbishop clearly indicated a line to the Anglican representatives: "Don't detract from the importance of the XXXIX Articles. Don't budge an inch as to the necessity of carrying the East with us in ultimate Reunion steps. Bear constantly in mind that in any admission made as to what Roman leadership or 'primacy' (?) may mean, we have to make it quite clear too that which it must not mean – i.e. some of the very things which the Cardinal's Pastoral claims for it."[15] In fact, the second conversation never got down to themes, and after the meeting the participants were firmly recalled to the doctrinal issues by the Archbishop in letters to the Cardinal and to the Dean of Wells. Cardinal Mercier's lengthy reply in the same vein helped to ensure that the meetings henceforth concentrated on the dogmatic and ecclesiastical themes which lay at the root of separation.[16]

The second conversation dealt with the way in which the two Churches might be brought into union, supposing the doctrinal difference could be resolved. This was to put the cart before the horse with a vengeance and the meetings concentrated on the relationship of the Archbishop of Canterbury to the Holy See; on the position of the Roman Catholic hierarchy in England and on the retention of characteristic Anglican rites and customs, recognising the central position of the Papal See. The suggestion was made that the Archbishop and the Anglican metropolitans should receive the *pallium*.[17] Both sides drew up statements, each signing their own and attesting the correctness of the other by their signatures. The difference between the signing and the attesting was not made clear to the Archbishop who was alarmed by the three Anglican names attached to the French statement. This was not surprising since the French document clearly did not reflect union by convergence and actually used the phrase « *l'entrée en masse dans le giron de l'Église Romaine serait ainsi facilitée.* »[18] Accordingly, the Archbishop wrote to the Dean of Wells, directing that his letter "must be kept inseparably with the other papers, as recording his own view of the situation."[19] The letter is important because of its insistence on the priority of doctrine, and high on the list of themes was "the position, the jurisdiction and the powers of the Papal See. The deep significance of that matter

---

[14] BELL, p. 1260 and cp. PRESTIGE, p. 480.
[15] BELL, pp. 1260–1261.
[16] For the text of these letters of 19th and 24th March 1923, see BELL, pp. 1265–1273.
[17] BELL, pp. 1262–1263; B. and M. PAWLEY, pp. 288–289.
[18] Both the Statements are in 'The conversations at Malines 1921–1925', ed. Lord HALIFAX (see n. 2 above).
[19] BELL, p. 1265.

may very easily be slurred over in common talk by admitting as an historical and practical matter of so-called general knowledge the 'primacy' of the Bishop of Rome. In certain senses this is an indisputable historical fact. But as used by Roman Catholics his primacy means a great deal more . . .". The letter refers also to eucharistic and Marian doctrines and Davidson concluded in terms which set out his position clearly: *"Subject to what I have said as to the attainment of agreement on the large doctrinal questions, I am ready to say that the sugges-*tions which the two Memoranda contain are well calculated to furnish the basis for future discussion and conference."[20]

The Archbishop was further confirmed in his criticisms by a letter from Bishop Charles Gore complaining about "the concessiveness" of the Anglicans at Malines and it was altogether to the benefit of the Conversations, theologically and representatively, that Gore quickly suffered the fate of all who make critical suggestions and was appointed as an additional Anglican member at the third Conversation. Lord Halifax did not like the Archbishop's letter to Armitage Robinson, but, in truth, he had missed the real point since the Archbishop was not only being Anglican but wise and realistic. In fact, Mercier's reaction was similar. Davidson wrote to him and the Cardinal replied and the letters bear ample testimony to the conviction of both that the themes and the doctrinal issues must first be dealt with in conference and that the papacy and its position must "be candidly faced before further progress can be made."[21] So wrote the Archbishop to the Cardinal, adding that the ambiguity of the term primacy was part of the basic problem.[22] The points raised and the Cardinal's lengthy reply require to be noted not least because of Mercier's comments on the nature of papal authority in its relation to the authority of the bishop, a subject under discussion in the contemporary dialogue.[23] The Archbishop replied, again at length, on May 15th and he still desired to get to grips with "the underlying questions of a fundamental character" before any "outward arrangements suggested in the signed paper" can be usefully discussed.[24] In a letter to the Archbishop, Halifax suggested that Mercier was keener on reunion than Davidson was. Here, Lord Halifax again missed the point which was that any unity conversations which did not come to some agreed conclusion as to what diversity was consistent with unity in faith could not hope to succeed, and the Archbishop knew this. He also did not perceive that Mercier did not fully grasp what

[20] BELL, pp. 1265–1267.

[21] For the text of both letters (24th March and 11th April 1923) see BELL, pp. 1267–1273.

[22] "The ambiguity of the term 'primacy' is well known to us all. It has an historic meaning which can be accepted without difficulty. If, however, it is understood as implying that the Pope holds *jure divino*, the unique and solemn position of sole Vicar of Christ on earth, from whom as Vicar of Christ must come directly or indirectly the right to minister validly within the Church, there ought to be no delay in discussing that implication and expounding its essential bearings . . . such a doctrine of papal authority is not one to which the adherence of the Church of England could be obtained", BELL, p. 1268.

[23] For text of letter, BELL, pp. 1268–1273. The letter is really a commentary on this aspect of 'Pastor Aeternus'.

[24] For text of this letter, BELL, pp. 1273–1276.

was the problem for Anglicans, even though Portal had said of the Cardinal to his friend, *«Au fond, il ne comprend pas votre position.»* Frere registered the same impression: "The largeness of his heart embraced us all, but his head did not seem to take in our position."[25]

Bell notes in connection with the third conversation that "There was some talk of obtaining another Anglican, representing a moderate or evangelical point of view, but it came to nothing."[26] Does this modestly conceal Bell himself? His biographer, Ronald Jasper, writes "such was his influence behind the scenes in the Anglican-Roman Catholic conversations at Malines, that, when the extension of the Anglican membership was under consideration, the Archbishop seriously considered adding his name to the delegation."[27]

In the event, Bishop Gore and B. J. Kidd, Warden of Keble College, Oxford, were appointed and Mgr. P. Battifol and Fr. Hippolyte Hemmer were added on the Roman Catholic side. Before the meeting, the Archbishop drew up yet another memorandum insisting on the necessity of facing the fundamental themes on the doctrinal level. He instanced "The position and authority of Holy Scripture, the meaning and authority of Tradition, the existence or non-existence of a Supreme Authority upon earth, a Vicariate of Christ, and what it means as regards both doctrine and administration: then further, the introduction of such dogmas as that of the Immaculate Conception, or again, and in another field, the definite teaching of the Church of Rome as to Transubstantiation and the attendant or consequent doctrines and usages . . ."[28] He also saw the Anglican delegation at Lambeth before they went to Malines for the Third Conversation, 7th–8th November 1923, where, following on the Primate's repeated insistence, Petrine primacy and Papal authority constituted the subject matter. Position papers were read and it became clear that the Anglican Church "could not accept the phrase 'universal jurisdiction' as applied either to St. Peter personally or to the Roman Church."[29] Gore even rejected "general superintendence", preferring "spiritual responsibility" – to Halifax's annoyance, though the other Anglicans felt that Gore's points were of the essence of the matter.

The question of publicity then arose as it was felt that the Church at large must be informed of the conversations. The Archbishop of Canterbury decided to issue a Christmas letter to the Anglican Metropolitans on the effects to date of the Lambeth Appeal, devoting some space to Malines. He even accepted some suggestions for revision from the Cardinal and from Halifax. The Archbishop's letter, describing the conversations as being at an "elementary stage", stressed once more the importance of doctrine for Anglicans,[30] but inevitably its publica-

---

[25] WALTER FRERE, Recollections of Malines, p. 50.

[26] BELL, p. 1278.

[27] RONALD C. JASPER, George Bell, Bishop of Chichester (London 1967), p. 31.

[28] BELL, pp. 1278–1279.

[29] PRESTIGE, loc. cit., p. 482.

[30] The Archbishop wrote: "It seemed to me to be fair to the Roman Catholic members of the Malines Conference, now augmented by the addition of Monsignor Battifol and the Abbé Hemmer, that the firmness and coherence, as we believe, of our Anglican doctrine and system should be unmistakably set forward", BELL, p. 1283.

tion produced controversy and the Archbishop and the Cardinal were criticised by both conservatives and extremists from within their own Churches. In Convocation, Davidson defended his position and asserted that "there have been no negotiations whatever. We are not at present within sight of anything of the kind." Mercier, opposing English Roman Catholics who adhered to the old Vaughan line of 'return' and 'conversion', also insisted that "our discussions were thus in no sense 'negotiations'. To negotiate, it is necessary to hold a mandate, and neither on one side nor on the other were we invested with a mandate." He stated bluntly however that he was "acting in agreement with the supreme Authority, blessed and encouraged by it." Davidson, refuting any suggestion that the Anglican participants were representatives, nevertheless also asserted that they took part "with my full encouragement".[31] The Cardinal obtained confirmation of his existing authority from Gasparri: "Officially Rome neither approved nor disapproved, but confidentially it had both approved and encouraged, and would maintain this attitude."[32] This hedging by the Vatican as to the exact status of the conversations and the differing views of Roman Catholic leaders about it are discussed with reference to various letters on the subject in B. and M. Pawley's account.[33]

For domestic reasons, chiefly the Prayer Book controversy, the Archbishop believed that the next meeting should be postponed, a view opposed by the Cardinal and by Lord Halifax. By now, both men were two old saints in a hurry, constrained by the love of Christ and ardent for the unity of the 'Christifideles', their hearts ruling their heads. The Cardinal had not a year to live and though Halifax would soldier on until 1934, to be buried on the eight anniversary of Mercier's death, both felt an urgency not experienced by the Archbishop whose head ruled his heart in matters theological. Mercier wrote to his English friend on 6th March 1925, "In proportion as the Sovereign Pontiff, and the Cardinal Secretary of State at the Vatican, affirm with increasing distinctness their confidence in our humble efforts, and thus indirectly disavow certain oppositions of the English Roman Catholics, it would seem as if on our side the nearer hopes of re-union seemed likely to be realized, the more sensitive the good Archbishop of Canterbury seems to grow as to his responsibility to his own people, and to desire to put off, rather than to hasten, the definite bringing together of both sides."[34] But the Cardinal failed to notice that while the Archbishop had courageously and publicly shown his hand, the Pope, as Bell remarked, "never emerged from the background."[35]

The fourth conversation, which was in effect to be the last, took place 19th—206h May 1925 with the same participants on both sides. Thematically, it was the most substantial of the meetings and the subjects examined closely resemble some of the subjects treated by the Joint Preparatory Anglican/Roman

[31] BELL, pp. 1285—1287.
[32] PRESTIGE, p. 485.
[33] Loc. cit., pp. 291—293.
[34] BELL, p. 1289; B. and M. PAWLEY, p. 293.
[35] Ib. p. 1280.

Catholic Commission over forty years later. A clear disagreement was registered by the Anglican members with the official Roman Catholic views on the Episcopate and the Papacy from the theological and historical aspects as set forth in papers by Van Roey and Hemmer. They would not accept the "definition of the *jus divinum* of the Papacy."[36] The surprise of the meeting was a paper read by the Cardinal but written by a canonist, Dom Lambert Beauduin on 'L'Église Anglicane unie non absorbée.' In effect a proposal for a rather more than Uniat status, the memorandum "may well prove" in Bell's phrase "to be not the least enduring result of Malines."[37]

The fundamental themes of the basis of faith and of unity with diversity surfaced strongly once more, as they were to do again in the work of the two modern commissions. It became clear, as it had done in the Gallican correspondence, that for Anglicans the basis of faith could only be the credal faith of the Councils, liberty being allowed in what was not *de fide*. Gore put this insistence on the Scriptural criterion and on the Vincentian canon as strongly as Wake had done. In his paper 'On Unity with Diversity' (to which Battifol wrote a reply) Gore posed the root difficulty as Anglicans see it: *"The at present insuperable obstacle to such reunion, in either case, is the demand for submission, as to de fide dogmas, to certain doctrines, which, as claiming to be part of the essential faith, seem to us to conflict with history and with truth."* This remains an unresolved difficulty to the present time, tied in as it is with the concept of papal infallibility. When Gore continued that this kind of dogmatic process freed the teaching authority of the Church "from all those restrictions of universal agreement and unvarying tradition and scriptural authority – which in our judgment make the fact of faith rational",[38] his words still evoke a clear echo in the contemporary Anglican/Roman Catholic dialogue. The deposit of faith, the *hapax*, and the definition of Vincent of Lérins, remain living concepts vital to the authentic Gospel proclamation for Anglicans, and the efforts of 'Dei Verbum' to marry two really divergent views of the relation of Scripture, tradition and the *magisterium* have not satisfied them.

At home in England, the Jesuit Fr. Woodlock was on the warpath, in Lockhart's phrase, and Halifax corresponded with him in vigorous terms. Significantly, he summed up the whole difference between Woodlock and himself by saying that he believed in corporate reunion and the Jesuit did not.[39] The concept of convergence had to fight for existence right down to and past the second Vatican Council. Cardinal Mercier's reproof to Fr. Woodlock was not published.

In fact, this turned out to be the last of the conversations, a fifth meeting being held on October 25th 1926 simply as a tidying-up operation and in order to draw up a Report. It met under the shadow of a double loss. The warmhearted and gallant Mercier died on January 23rd 1926, and two days before his

[36] LOCKHART, II, p. 315.
[37] BELL, p. 1291.
[38] BELL, pp. 1291–1293, PRESTIGE, pp. 487–488, B. and M. PAWLEY, p. 294.
[39] LOCKHART, II, pp. 320–321.

death sent a loving letter to Lambeth − «'*Ut unum sint*', *c'est le vœu suprême du Christ, le vœu du Souverain Pontife; c'est le mien, c'est le vôtre. Puisse-t-il se réaliser dans sa plénitude.*»[40] Halifax had gone to Malines to take his own farewell of the dying Cardinal. On June 19th of the same year he lost that dearest of friends, his fellow-forerunner, the Abbé Portal. Without these two, the mainspring of the endeavour was broken. The English Cardinal Bourne made the unhappy choice of Easter Day in the following year to mount an attack at York on the Church of England, and the resultant controversy was not productive of an atmosphere suitable for discussing the results of the Malines Conversations. There was the usual sensitivity on both sides about publishing the Report but on January 19th 1928, Portal's second anniversary, it was at last published for the Church at large.

The changing climate as the thirties approached, not without triumphalist overtones, produced a Roman Catholic closure of the Conversations, though in fairness it is not certain that the Archbishop of Canterbury could have been convinced that they should continue: "On January 6th, 1928, Pope Pius XI, who had on March 24, 1924, expressed to the Sacred Consistory his satisfaction and gratitude for these very conferences, launched his Encyclical, *Mortalium Animos*, in which he repeated the doctrine of the Papal Supremacy in unmistakeable terms, and condemned many Churches and many movements towards unity. The *Osservatore Romano* (quoted in *The Times*, January 21st, 1928) definitely announced that the Conversations were to cease."[41]

So once again, a door was closed and Anglican/Roman Catholic accord, a will-o'-the-wisp for many and a Holy Grail for some, seemed as elusive as ever. Perhaps Lockhart's judgment is as far as one can go in assessment − "Neither Church was at that time ready for more than a beginning."[42] Must this however remain the permanent alibi of the office-holder and of the institutionalist?

3. Comments on the Themes

A survey of themes from Wake to Malines shows a marked recurrence of the same doctrinal problems, admittedly with different shades of emphasis due to variations in the theological and ecclesiastical thinking and situation of the times. For example, the themes of papacy and of Mariology were greatly sharpened in their divisive effects by the nineteenth-century dogmas, and perhaps the only nineteenth-century newcomers among the themes running through Anglican/Roman Catholic relations were that of unity by convergence and the theme of the ecumenical vocation. How hard they have had to struggle for a foothold in the twentieth-century scene the record of events shows.

---

[40] BELL, p. 1299.
[41] BELL, p. 1302.
[42] Loc. cit. II, p. 341: PORTAL had written to Halifax at the outset of the Malines Conversations. "As you said, we are beginning again" (LOCKHART, II, p. 271). Only death could quench the indomitable efforts for unity of the Madeira companions.

Some brief notes on the themes as they were handled in the Malines Conversations may serve to measure the extent to which certain of the doctrinal problems remain intractable without some radical changes in the theology and ecclesiology surrounding them. Lockhart's five chapters devoted to the five Conversations constitute much the most detailed examination of how matters were discussed at Malines.[43] Greatly assisted by the Malines papers sent to him by Lord Halifax a few weeks before the latter's death, Lockhart's theological evaluation of the Conversations is valuable as is his reconstruction, from various sources, of incident and event. The purpose of this section, however, is not to give a résumé of what is set out in detail by Lockhart. Rather is it to take various points from the papers discussed at Malines and briefly to relate them to the present position in respect of the same themes. The chief sources here are then the papers delivered at Malines and the records of the meetings.[44] *Unity by convergence*, though it was not specifically discussed under that heading, managed to come through in at least two significant forms during the Conversations. Explicitly, it was formulated as an objective by Frere during the first meeting even if as a principle it was imperfectly grasped by the Cardinal who nevertheless during the fourth conversation brought forward a proposal consistent with it.[45] This was contained in the unscheduled paper read by the Cardinal and written by Dom Lambert Beauduin on 'L'Église Anglicane Unie non absorbée.' This may be termed the 'Uniat theme' and it so far agrees with the concept of unity by convergence that it has been revived recently by at least one member of the International Commission although the idea has not so far formally been included in ARCIC's published work.[46] But, as pointed out earlier, Beauduin's was a rather more than Uniat concept taking full account of the historical specifics: the paper builds on the fact that, effectively, the Archbishop of Canterbury in pre-reformation times enjoyed a virtually patriarchial status. To restore this patriarchate in the context of an Anglican Church retaining its liturgy, customs and canon law, but in communion with the Roman See, and to do so on the basis of Leo XIII's encyclical 'Praeclara' (20. June 1894) and of the Constitution 'Orientalium dignitas' (30 November 1894), which provided a modern Eastern analogy – this was Beauduin's proposal. Bell may have been right in judging it the most durable result of Malines, but then, as now, all depended on what was meant by, and claimed for, the Roman primacy.[47] If the theme of unity by converg-

---

[43] LOCKHART, II, Chapters XVIII–XXII, pp. 265–343.

[44] For these see The Conversations at Malines 1921–1925 (London 1927) and The Conversations at Malines 1921–1925, original Documents, edited by Lord HALIFAX (London 1930).

[45] FRERE said, « *Nous ne demandons pas de revenir sur les chemins parcourus dans le passé, mais que chaque Église ou Communion tende a l'unité par une marche en avant convergente* », The Conversations at Malines (1930), p. 22. Of Mercier, LOCKHART wrote "He never visualised reunion, as most Anglicans would visualise it, in the form of an honourable agreement between two Churches of commensurable standing; to him it was more the reconciliation of a body of schismatics with the Catholic Church," loc. cit., II, p. 305.

[46] Bishop C. BUTLER, The Tablet (14th November 1970), pp. 1098–1099.

[47] Cp. LOCKHART, II, p. 316; The Conversations at Malines (1930), pp. 254–255.

14*

ence has achieved the position of being implicit in the modern dialogue as compared with that of Malines, a similar advance can hardly be claimed in respect of
the theme of primacy which without question was the major subject at the
Belgian meetings.

Unity by convergence linked in with another theme which also worked its
way up at Malines and which, in a sense, is the same theme from a different
angle, that of *sufficient agreement*. It is a theme which has escaped the notice of
the earlier commentators on Malines perhaps because it seemed either so obvious
or so chimerical, but it was there and it is more noteworthy today because it is
part of the methodology and chosen strategy of ARCIC which seeks to build a
substantial agreement concerning, for example, eucharist and ministry, upon a
full agreement concerning the centre of the faith. This was spelt out in the Malta
Report of the Joint Preparatory Commission but it is worthy of remark that
those who met at Malines were alive to the importance of the theme. Halifax's
memorandum, at the outset of the conversations, proposed that they should
begin by trying to uncover the areas of their agreement and he at once linked
this with a further connecting theme which would loom large at Malines, the
theme of *unity with diversity*.[48] In fact, the conversationalists at their first meeting saw the establishing of the existence of this sufficient agreement as the
necessary justification for holding and continuing the conversations: « *Le but
immédiat de ces réunions serait de constater par le témoignage des personnes
présentes qu'il existe entre les deux Églises un accord suffisant pour justifier les
présentes réunions et aussi pour avoir peut-être, plus tard, d'autres réunions avec
l'agrément de nos autorités respectives.* »[49] In the document drawn up by the
Anglicans at the fourth Conversation, the phrase 'substantial agreement' is
actually used in reference to the passage in the French Report dealing with the
sacraments.[50] This report, being the memorandum drawn up by the Roman
Catholic members, is of great interest in that it deliberately chooses as its key-
note the policy of giving "a summary embodying those points of doctrine
wherein the Anglicans had agreed with them upon certain common statements."[51] This is very significant, and, from the point of view of detecting the
themes in Anglican/Roman Catholic relations, it is worthy of remark that the
form of the memorandum bears some remarkable resemblances to that of the
Malta Report of 1969. Since the compilers of the latter were not as a group
consciously aware of the earlier report and since their own document grew solely

---

[48] Cp. LOCKHART, II, p. 272.

[49] The Conversations at Malines (1930), p. 10.

[50] "As regards other dogmatic points, incuding those that were handled briefly in the First
   Conversation, and, in particular, the doctrine of the Sacraments, we say no more here
   because they are sufficiently treated in the French Report with which we are in substantial
   agreement, and also because there is an opening for further discussion which, we think,
   would be profitable, and would lead not only to a better understanding but also to a greater
   measure of general agreement upon the matters in question", The Conversations at Malines
   (1927), p. 44. This further discussion would not be resumed until 1968.

[51] The Conversations at Malines (1927), p. 73.

out of the experience and work of the Joint Preparatory Commission, the fact is noteworthy and indeed carries its own warning.

The French Report summarises "the points stated and discussed at the Malines Conferences upon which there was evident agreement."[52] Admitting the obstacles to unity, it lists the agreement of both Communions in the belief that Christ founded one single true Church and that all must labour to maintain its unity; that this unity is not merely external but involves "a Faith held by all"; that this faith is contained in certain articles of general obligation. While there may be difficulty in establishing the full range of inter-Church agreement, there is "undoubted agreement in the doctrine defined by the first Oecumenical Councils" and "this agreement extends equally to the Articles of the three Creeds." Both agree as to the "prominent place" of Holy Scripture among the means of determining religious truth, though they differ as to the place accorded to tradition.

Dealing with some other matters, such as the place of the Thirty-nine Articles and the possibility of reconciling them with the Council of Trent, the Report passes on to the sacraments and gives a striking list of points on which "an agreement is reached without much difficulty" (See Appendix D). The question of Orders was regarded as being given a new context by the Lambeth Appeal of 1920 though the idea of mutual commissioning was not mentioned for whatever reason. Today, the same question is seen as acquiring a new and more hopeful context since modern Roman Catholic thinking on priesthood since Vatican II differs significantly at many points from that of 1896.

The Report continues "With regard to the special position of the Pope in the Church, the divergences in belief and opinion are more serious and more difficult to reconcile." This theme which held the front of the stage at Malines requires further comment, but the French memorandum holds that to the agreement about a "primacy of honour", there might be added a "primacy of responsibility". The compilers felt that divergence was inevitable but not so radical "as to prevent the question being taken up on a future occasion."

The last brief section of the Report refers to the Uniat Eastern Churches as a possible model for Anglican/Roman Catholic relations, but stresses that such a suggestion was made by the Malines conversationalists without any official sanction. Two sentences stand out as descriptive of the ethos and of the objective of the Malines Conversations: "Dogmatic truths, for the most part, occupied the attention of both Roman Catholic and Anglicans at Malines" and "in proportion as mutual understanding and doctrinal agreement advance, it will become possible to arrange a satisfactory adjustment of disciplinary rules, however delicate a matter that may seem at present."

The other theme, linked with all this by Halifax at the start and by the subsequent development of the dialogue, was that of *unity with diversity*. Here we have not only an old acquaintance from the pages of the Gallican correspondence, but also the familiar interconnected concepts of fundamental/non-fundamental and *de fide* together with the question of *criteria*, still vital today as are

---

[52] The Conversations af Malines (1927), pp. 72–94, for text of the French Report.

the others. And there was not available even such help as can be afforded by the idea of a hierarchy of truths enunciated in the Decree on Ecumenism of Vatican II. At the very first meeting "attention was at once focused on the principle of diversity within the unity of the Catholic Church" and there was immediate discussion of the doctrinal criterion — Holy Scripture as the ultimate standard of faith, and the Roman Catholics desired to add "in accordance with the tradition of the Church".[53] Thus the three linked themes of unity with diversity, of the criterion as establishing what are fundamentals and as setting the legitimate limits of diversity in faith, all emerged together and, in one form or another, were never absent for long from the talks. They reappeared once more during the work of the Joint Preparatory Commission, and the Malta Report asks whether there are parallels between aspects of the concept of hierarchy of truths and the Anglican differentiation between fundamental and non-fundamentals. At Malines, it was the theme which occasioned the warmest debate, particularly between Gore and Battifol, for Gore's paper brought the question to a clear issue. Lockhart notes this as "What was *de fide*? What was at most pious opinion? What was fundamental?"[54] and Gore asked of Rome to consider demanding from the Anglicans and the Easterns no more articles of faith than those which "fall under the Vincentian Canon."[55] This he saw as the only basis for a reconciliation, as Jeremy Taylor, long before, had outlined as the accepted Anglican position in his 'The Liberty of Prophesying' (1647), and Gore too insisted that this must be considered as a permanent element in the position of Anglicans — "the demand for the distinction (between fundamentals and non-fundamentals) will go on."[56] It was also suggested by one of the Anglicans that they should be free not to give adherence to dogmas defined since the separation and in the formulation of which the Anglican Communion had taken no part.

At the outset of the first session, Lord Halifax in his memorandum had stated that "the fundamental question which has to be decided in any discussion or conference held to promote the reunion of Christendom is, *what constitutes the Church?*"[57] In his own exposition of an answer, Halifax's definition of the Church is not very different from the conclusions in the Venice working papers of the International Commission.[58] But for the conversationalists at Malines an inevitable progression followed on from the discussion as to what constituted a true and authentic Church to the discussion of whether a papal primacy, however defined, was of the essence of such a Church or was simply an optional extra. This theme of a Roman primacy occupied by comparison with the others a major part of the time at the Malines gatherings, and it cannot be said that

---

[53] The Conversations at Malines (1927), pp. 10—13, and cp. The Conversations at Malines (1930), pp. 15, 18. « Les anglicans demandent a quel criterium les catholiques discernent les vérités de foi definie de celles qui ne le sont pas. »

[54] LOCKHART, II, p. 317.

[55] Ib.

[56] The Conversations at Malines (1927), pp. 38, 40.

[57] The Conversations at Malines (1930), pp. 71—78.

[58] These were published in 'Theology' and in the 'Clergy Review'.

much progress was made beyond a necessary clarification of understanding on both sides. The French Report was more optimistic on this subject than Gore would allow to have been the case or than the Archbishop of Canterbury would grant in his two letters to the Cardinal assessing the results of the conversations.[59] In fact, before long, Halifax "had come round to the Archbishop's view that the primacy of the Roman See was the fundamental question which must have priority."[60] At Malines, Dr. Kidd had rejected Mgr. Van Roey's claim that the papal supremacy is part of the divine constitution of the Church. The approach in the papers on various aspects of the Papal primacy which were delivered by both sides is of the theologico-historical type. Van Roey put the official Roman position quite clearly and rather rigidly and Kidd responded in the same way "It is, however, one thing to accommodate ourselves to an order or constitution of the Church which, in the course of history, has actually arisen. It is quite another to affirm that this constitution was divinely intended. To make that affirmation seems to us to be going beyond the evidence."[61]

Anglicans could accept the Roman primacy as a simple matter of fact, and as something which developed in the course of history. Some might even consider it reasonable to regard it as a providential development in history, but all this was very different from the claim to a *jus divinum* for the papacy which the Anglicans could not accept as essential to the being of a true Church.[62] Armitage Robinson observed that "it was right to make it plain that they could not admit the 'universal jurisdiction' claimed either for St. Peter individually or for the Roman church, but only a spiritual leadership and a general solicitude for the well-being of the Church as a whole."[63] In their view, the evidence all pointed the other way and this was the tenor of the Dean of Wells' paper on 'The position of St. Peter in the Primitive Church: A summary of the New Testament evidence'.[64] The argument from 'The Petrine Texts as Employed to A.D. 461', (in a paper by B. H. Kidd)[65] fared no better nor was there much help in Mgr. Battifol's comment in his paper 'Le Siège de Rome et Saint Pierre'[66] that « *Ce catholicisme antique diffère du catholicisme évolué qui est le nôtre: qui le contesterait? Ce n'est pas le lieu de discuter cette évolution.* »[67] For in fact this was *exactly* the place to discuss the matter since the whole Anglican position at Malines was that this evolved Catholicism was being treated as the norm and the ecclesiastical criterion by which to determine what is and is not 'Church'. Frere

---

[59] BELL, pp. 1294–1298.

[60] LOCKHART, II, p. 287 and cp. p. 300: PORTAL to Halifax "our next conference must succeed in convincing Gore that an understanding in regard to the Primacy is not impossible . . .".

[61] The Conversations at Malines (1930), p. 182.

[62] LOCKHART, II, pp. 315.

[63] The Conversations at Malines (1927), p. 34.

[64] The Conversations at Malines (1930), Annexe V.

[65] Ib. Annexe VII.

[66] Ib. Annexe VIII.

[67] Ib. p. 149.

wrote afterwards "My own impression at the time was that our biblical arguments had not been really faced."[68]

Kidd affirmed the indefectibility of the Church but considered that the
dogmas of 1854 and 1870 were instances of adding on to the faith rather than
necessary and true deductions from it.[69] The Anglican rejection of the assertion
that the supremacy and jurisdiction were among the elements constitutive of the
Church in its full truth and authenticity remains unaltered from the days of the
earlier Anglican/Roman Catholic contacts. The "primacy of honour" seemed a
possibility at Malines as it had appeared to Wake and the Anglican theologians
before him, but since Wake's time the assertion of the *potestas ordinaria et immediata* by Vatican I had complicated the issue further and Kidd's question as to
whether there were two such heads in each local church is still being asked and
studied today.[70] With Kidd, modern ecumenists are saying "we should like
further elucidation of the point."[71] The Anglicans at Malines did not hold the
papal primacy to be necessarily a centre of unity but they considered that it
could fulfil such a rôle, with certain significant qualifications: "We wish for
unity, and, if the necessary preliminary conditions had been duly met, we
should not shrink from the idea of a Papacy acting as a centre of unity, but in so
saying, we have in view not the Papacy such as it exists in theory and practice
among Roman Catholics at the present time, but a concept of unity such as may
emerge in the future."[72]

This reserved statement should be compared with the passsage from Lambeth 1968 and with the Lutheran/Roman Catholic statement of 1974, both of
which have been already mentioned. Thus, certain limited advances in the matter
of primacy may be noted, but they are very slight indeed when one remembers
that more than two centuries had elapsed since the time of the Gallican correspondence. Furthermore, Malines did not really see the primacy in the context
of collegiality as the earlier theologians had done, possibly because 1870 was
casting a long shadow at the time. Halifax, who had some prophetic insights in
matters theological, had said to the Cardinal « *qu'il faudrait se rendre compte de
l'objection qu'on pourrait faire aux remarques de Son Eminence sur la nécessité
d'un chef. Il semblerait à beaucoup qu'on oublie que c'est par l'Esprit Saint que
l'unité de l'Église est maintenue.* »[73] The Anglican conviction that what Christ
promised to His Church was not infallibility but an infallible Guide, the Spirit,
breaks through here and remains a permanent element in the total outline.
Strangely enough, at no point did the Malines Conversations touch on the purpose of authority and what was the reason for its existence in the Church.

---

[68] Recollections of Malines, p. 43.
[69] The Conversations at Malines (1930), pp. 184–185.
[70] Ib. p. 183.
[71] Ib. p. 184.
[72] The Conversations at Malines (1927), p. 14.
[73] The Conversations at Malines (1930), p. 20. Another such insight at Malines was his comment on the approximate and incomplete nature of all theological statements by reason of
which allowance could legitimately be made for divergences on important matters (LOCK-
HART, II, p. 272).

Davidson's letters to Mercier (1st August and 9th December 1925) have a certain clinical quality in their assessment of the themes and how these fared at Malines. The conversations were "fruitful of good" and created an improved atmosphere all round, but "I dare not in honesty adopt the phrase suggested by Your Eminence that we have made 'progress in agreement'."[74] Surveying the various questions, he was not conscious of much real movement under the headings which he itemised,[75] and perhaps he touched on a reality of the situation when he wrote "The difference betwen Your Eminence's view and my own, where it exists, may be not so much a difference of faith or charity in dealing with the same problem, as a difference in our conception of what the problem is and what its solution involves."[76]

IV. 'A Document Full of Hope': The Work of the Joint Preparatory Anglican/Roman Catholic Commission

Such was Cardinal Willebrands' description of the report of the Joint Preparatory Anglican/Roman Catholic Commission when, in a sermon at great St. Mary's Church, Cambridge, in 1970, he spoke of the report made by that body to the Pope and to the Archbishop of Canterbury: "It (i.e. the spiritual elevation and the geniality of the visit by the Archbishop to the Pope) continues to shine through the earnest purpose of the report which the Joint Preparatory Roman Catholic/Anglican Commission made – a document full of hope, on which a letter of the revered Cardinal Bea set the mark of Roman Catholic approval, while the resolutions of the Lambeth Conference showed how much it mirrored the aspirations of the Anglican episcopate."[1]

1. Visits before and after the Council

But before the Cardinal (himself a member of the Commission and later head of the Vatican Secretariat for promoting Christian Unity and now Primate of Holland) could so characterize the first-fruits of contemporary Anglican and Roman Catholic co-operation, other things had to happen. These were the events which made it possible to call into being, with full and open authorization on both sides, a commission with the same aim as the Malines conversations but with a different ethos. If one were to attempt to pin down that difference in a phrase, one might say that while Malines was a conference, the Preparatory

---

[74] BELL, p. 1294.
[75] Ib. pp. 1294–1295.
[76] Ib. p. 1296.
[1] Documents on Anglican/Roman Catholic Relations (United States Catholic Conference, Washington 1972), p. 35.

Commission was a dialogue, thus indicating a further progression from the individual exchange of ideas with a view to unity which characterized the Gallican correspondence. In this respect, JPARC was the visible expression of the intention of the 'Common Declaration' of 1966 in which the Pope and the Archbishop proposed to inaugurate between the two Churches "a serious dialogue."[2] Behind this in turn lay the liberating influence of the second Vatican Council, but prior to the Council in order of time and sequence was the visit in December 1960 of the 99th Archbishop of Canterbury to Pope John XXIII which broke the ice of centuries. That the operation was hedged around with difficulties is clear from Archbishop Geoffrey Fisher's own account of the meeting in which he referred to the Pope overruling Tardini's attempt to prevent his meeting with Cardinal Bea. Tardini, the Secretary of State, had insisted on certain conditions for the visit which amply explain the Archbishop's reference to "the icy wastes of the Vatican curia."[3] The story of the visit, with the Archbishop personal recollections, is told by William Purcell in his biography 'Fisher of Lambeth.' The record shows how the two principals, the Pope and the Archbishop, quietly disengaged themselves from the tangles created by Vatican officialdom, ranging from the 'secret' meeting at the British Minister's office to the 'astonishing conditions' (the phrase is Fisher's) laid down by the Secretary of State.[4] There was a sustained attempt to play down the meeting (even to the extent of forbidding photographs) and the 'Osservatore Romano' described it as *"una semplice visita di cortesia."* Cardinal Willebrands, in his Cambridge sermon, reversed this evaluation and put the meeting in its true context: "For the first time since the Reformation the Archbishop of Canterbury met the Pope. This fraternal encounter in historical perspective so much more than a mere gesture of courtesy, was a stroke of vision pointing firmly towards the future."[5]

---

[2] They intend "to inaugurate between the Roman Catholic Church and the Anglican Communion a serious dialogue which, founded on the Gospels and on the ancient common traditions, may lead to that unity in truth for which Christ prayed." (Common Declaration of March 24, 1966).

[3] Fisher of Lambeth (London 1969) by WILLIAM PURCELL, p. 284 and cp. p. 281 where the Archbishop recalls "Then I found that Tardini, the Secretary of State, had laid down certain conditions, because Scarlett told me what they were. They were astonishing conditions to be greeted with: (1) There should be no official photograph of me with the Pope. To make sure of this, Tardini had sent away the official photographer on a fortnight's holiday. So that was off. It had never occurred to me that there would or would not be official photographs; but he, Tardini, obviously thought it was important; (2) It was stated that I should not see Cardinal Bea, the Head of the department recently set up by the Pope to foster relations with other Churches. This sounded a preposterous thing, but there it was; (3) There was to be no kind of press release after my meeting with the Pope. That was a little odd, as I had already drafted one; (4) The Minister was not to invite to meet me at meals at his house any of the Vatican officials. Nevertheless, the press communiqué I had written and revised was taken to Tardini. He said it would not do, and it was brought back and I wrote a third, and gave this to the Minister, asking him to see it through Tardini, if possible."

[4] PURCELL, loc. cit., pp. 280—288.

[5] Documents on Anglican/Roman Catholic Relations, p. 34.

One incident in the visit requires comment since it underlines the slowness with which the central theme of convergence won acceptance. Referring to the Pope, the Archbishop wrote ". . . at one point he said: 'I should like to read to you a passage from an address that I recently gave.' He read, in English, a passage which included a reference to 'the time when our separated brethren should return to the Mother Church.' I at once said: 'Your Holiness, not *return.*' He looked puzzled and said, 'Not return? Why not?' I said: 'None of us can go backwards. We are each now running on parallel courses; we are looking until, in God's good time, our two courses approximate and meet.' He said, after a moment's pause, 'You are right.' . . . This sudden check took him by surprise, but he adapted himself to it at once. This was a notable thing at his age and bore fruit."[6] The visit was indeed "a stroke of vision" and doubtless contributed to the "special place" which the Decree on Ecumenism accorded to the Anglican Communion, a move appreciated by Anglicans however much they would subject its particular phrasing to historical and theological criticism.[7]

The second Vatican Council was in some sense an unfinished agenda, which may be all to the good for the future of ecumenism. During its sessions from 1962 to 1965, some of the themes which loom large in Anglican/Roman Catholic relations fared better than others. Among the latter, the primacy, jurisdiction and infallibility of the Bishop of Rome remained a virtually unaltered blockage, modified somewhat perhaps by the fresh stress on collegiality and by the growth of the concept of co-responsibility in the Church. Ecclesiology as a theme, however, received distinct help from the famous 'subsistit', from the strong emphasis on the common baptismal inheritance and from the clear recognition of degrees of ecclesial reality in the separated Churches of the West and of the effectiveness of their means of grace. The permission also for limited *communicatio in sacris* between the Church of Rome and the Orthodox Churches which reject the papal claims opened up a fresh avenue of approach to the basic question, Who are the Church? In the same way, a shift in the concept of priesthood from the emphasis on the cultic man and on sacerdotal 'powers' created the possibility of *rapprochement* between Anglican and Roman Catholic understanding of priesthood and ministry. The Council's view of Scripture, tradition and the magisterium, while not approximating to the Anglican view *in toto*, nevertheless laid the ghost of a two-tier source of revelation, so greatly divisive in the past. One of the most valuable contributions of Vatican II was the concept of the hierarchy of truths which may yet prove to be, ecumenically speaking, one of the most creative factors emerging from the debates of the council. One could continue the tabulation, but not least in beneficial effect was the spirit which emerged from the Council producing, as far as non-Roman Christendom was concerned, an opening Church instead of a closed Church. Theological rigidities were being softened and the effects would be far-reaching. Pope John's opening speech to the Council on October 11th, 1962, struck this

---

[6] PURCELL, loc. cit., p. 283.

[7] "Among those in which some Catholic traditions and institutions continue to exist, the Anglican Communion occupies a special place", Decree on Ecumenism, 13.

note among others when, referring to the fact that the guardianship of the deposit of faith did not imply a concern only with antiquity, he said: "The substance of the ancient doctrine of the deposit of faith is one thing, and the way in which it is presented is another." Also another note was struck — and this too evoked response from other Churches — when in the apostolic constitution of December 25th 1961, convoking the Council, the Pope twice referred to "Churches separated from Rome" in the context of the "rebuilding of the visible unity of all Christians." The presence of observers at the Council from the other Churches visibly marked this changing atmosphere.

Hard on the heels of the second Vatican Council, solemnly closed on December 8th, 1965, came the visit, from 22nd–24th March 1966, of the 100th Archbishop of Canterbury to Pope Paul VI. From that meeting stems the setting up of the Joint Preparatory Anglican/Roman Catholic Commission, the possibility of which had earlier been mentioned when the Anglican observers at the Council were received by the Pope in the month prior to its ending.[8] The meeting of Pope Paul and Archbishop Michael Ramsey was in sharp contrast with that of their predecessors a few short years before. Not only was there full publicity, a service and joint blessing at St. Paul's-without-the-Walls, the gift of a ring by the Pope to the Archbishop, and a discussion between them with a specific objective in view — but there was a Common Declaration on 24th March 1966 setting out their hopes and intentions. Cardinal Willebrands said of the visit, "Has there ever been a meeting at Rome so official and so solemn in character which in so limited a space of time gave rise to events of such great importance? I remember that in preparing for this meeting the Pope wished that a very special protocol be worked out which would characterize the event as the visit of one Church to another and not just as a meeting of Heads in a consecrated spot."[9]

"The visit of one Church to another" — surely this is a phrase marking a stage onward from the unhappy nineteenth century and one which is creative for the future. Certainly, at their meeting the Archbishop spoke of the "formidable difficulties of doctrine" and "the difficult practical matters" as he voiced his hope for dialogue in patience and charity, but the movement was steadily forward and things could hardly ever be quite the same again. The Pope's reply indeed stressed "the historical value of this hour" which could inaugurate a new relationship between Rome and Canterbury.[10] On this, their Common Declaratijon set a seal indicating as it did not only a procedure but a spirit, that of "respect, esteem and fraternal love." Such an inter-Church document marked a completely new departure for the Roman Catholic Church and it was under such distinguished and hopeful auspices that the Commission was set up, arising directly as it did from the Declaration itself: "They affirm their desire that all those Christians who belong to these two Communions may be animated by

---

[8] Anglican/Roman Catholic Dialogue: The work of the Preparatory Commission (Oxford 1974), by ALAN C. CLARK and COLIN DAVEY, p. 5.

[9] Unitas 19, 1967, 8–17, 74.

[10] CLARK and DAVEY, loc. cit., p. 6.

these same sentiments of respect, esteem and fraternal love; and in order to help these develop to the full, they intend to inaugurate between the Roman Catholic Church and the Anglican Communion a serious dialogue which, founded on the Gospels and on the ancient common traditions, may lead to that unity in truth, for which Christ prayed."

The last sentence provided at once the charter and the methodology of the future Commission.

2. The Setting up of the Joint Preparatory Anglican/Roman Catholic Commission and its Work

After preliminary discussions, including a visit by Bishop (now Cardinal) Willebrands to the Archbishop of Canterbury and a meeting of representatives at the Vatican Secretariat for Unity, the names were chosen and released to the press on 4th November 1966.[11] The first meeting was arranged for 9th–13th January 1967 at the Villa Cagnola, Gazzada, in North Italy, and it is worth noting that the Commission completed its work and went out of existence almost exactly a year later, holding its final meeting at Mount St. Joseph, Mosta, in Malta from 30th December 1967 to 3rd January 1968. In between, it met at Huntercombe Manor, Buckinghamshire, in England from 30th August to 4th September 1967.

The recently published account of the work of JPARC by Alan C. Clark and Colin Davey, listing the papers given at each meeting, commenting on some of the discussions which followed and describing the process by which the final report came to be written, conveys admirably an accurate impression of how the Commission functioned.[12] The selection of papers enables the reader to appre-

---

[11] Anglican Delegates: The Bishop of Ripon (the Rt.Rev. J. R. H. Moorman), the Rev. Canon James Atkinson, the Rev. Canon Eric Kemp, the Rev. Professor Howard Root, the Bishop of Llandaff (the Rt.Rev. W. G. H. Simon), the Rev. Dr. Massey H. Shepherd, Jnr., the Rev. Professor Eugene R. Fairweather, the Bishop of Colombo (the Rt.Rev. C. H. W. de Soysa), the Bishop of Pretoria (the Rt.Rev. E. G. Knapp-Fisher); Secretaries, the Rev. Canon John Findlow, the Rev. Canon John R. Satterthwaite.
Roman Catholic Delegates: The Rt.Rev. Charles H. Helmsing, Bishop of Kansas City-St. Joseph, the Rt.Rev. William Gomes, Titular Bishop of Porlais, Auxiliary to the Archbishop of Bombay, the Rt.Rev. Langton D. Fox, the Rev. Louis Bouyer, the Rev. George Tavard, the Rev. Charles Davis, the Rev. John Keating, the Rev. Adrian Hastings, the Rt. Rev. Mgr. J. G. M. Willebrands, Titular Bishop of Mauriana; Secretary: The Very Rev. Canon W. A. Purdy.
The Rev. Charles Davis was replaced by the Rev. Michael Richards and four new members joined the Commission at Huntercombe: two Anglicans, the Rev. Professor Albert T. Mollegen of Virginia Theological Seminary, a liberal Evangelical from the Episcopal Church of the U.S.A., and the Rt.Rev. H. R. McAdoo, Bishop of Ossory, Ferns and Leighlin, of the Church of Ireland; and two Roman Catholics, the Rt.Rev. Christopher Butler, OSB., formerly Abbot of Downside and now an auxiliary Bishop of Westminster, and Fr. Camillus Hay, OFM., from Australia.
[12] CLARK and DAVEY, loc.cit., see pp. 5–25.

ciate something of the momentum and progression of thought by which JPARC
reached the structure for its report, that of a concept of unity by stages. To do
more than summarise such a recently published record of events would be otiose
and all that is required is to indicate in outline Clark and Davey's picture of the
Commission at work and to add some brief comments.

At Gazzada, the Bishop of Ripon (J. R. H. Moorman) and the Bishop of
Kansas City-St. Joseph (C. H. Helmsing) were appointed Co-chairmen, and the
Commission commenced its work by the discussion of two subjects, 'Why is
dialogue now possible?' (papers by Bishop Moorman and Bishop Willebrands)
and 'Where should dialogue begin?' (papers by Professor Fairweather and Fr.
Richards).[13] The paper by Fr. Richards provoked a discussion on the shape of
the Commission's work and as a result a sub-committee drew up a programme
of seven papers for the next meeting. These would concentrate on 'the Word of
God' and 'the Church': "By starting with these fundamental points of faith,
rather than their instruments — Scripture and Tradition — it was hoped that a
sufficient basis of agreement could be built from which to set out to tackle the
more problematic and divisive issues."[14] This approach is interesting in that it is
paralleled by the methodology adopted in the two published statements of the
International Commission. Thus, while all the familiar themes would emerge in
the course of the Commission's work, a freshness of approach and method in
handling them appeared from the first. At Gazzada certain practical proposals
were made in respect of meetings between bishops and other clergy of both
Churches, common study groups, university and seminary collaboration, joint
use of buildings and the need for common liturgical texts. The question of
mixed marriages was considered sufficiently urgent for the members to recommend the setting up of a special Commission to deal with the problem as being
one of the "matters of practical difficulty" referred to in the Common Declaration.[15] Most of these proposals appeared in the final report.

The second meeting at Huntercombe was designed to "draw up a programme and establish priorities in the theological dialogue, as well as
considering matters of practical ecclesiastical cooperation". The Commission
was seeking both to define the major issues and to formulate a way forward
which could provide both the content and shape of its report. It resorted again
to the services of a sub-committee, chaired by Bishop Butler, which was asked
to put its proposals at the end of the meeting. The Commission then turned to
the papers and in the debate which followed nearly all the major themes were
handled or received mention; papacy, collegiality, Scripture and tradition,
ministry, the local Church and the universal Church, fundamentals and secondary truths, diversity and unity, together with recurring references to the
problem of authority. The papers were 'What is the Word?' (Father Tavard),

---

[13] Two of these papers are included in their volume by CLARK and DAVEY: 'Why is Anglican/
Roman Catholic Dialogue possible today?' by Bishop J. G. M. WILLEBRANDS (pp. 26—36)
and 'Where should Dialogue begin?' by Professor EUGENE R. FAIRWEATHER (pp. 37—59).
[14] CLARK and DAVEY, loc. cit., p. 12.
[15] Ib., p. 13.

'How is the Word received by man?' (Canon Atkinson), 'How does the Church proclaim the Word?' (Father Richards), 'What should be the minimum structure and essential life of the local Church?' (Canon Kemp), 'How do local Churches form the unity of the Universal Church?' (Father Bouyer), 'To what extent can or should there be diversity in a United Church? – Freedom and Authority' (papers by Bishop Willebrands and by Bishop Moorman and Professor Root). The last two papers are printed in Clark and Davey's book and they give prominence to that theme of diversity in unity to which Gore had attributed such importance at Malines. Both papers were and are important in the over-arching context of communion, partial communion and intercommunion. They bore also on the theme which was steadily emerging, that of unity by stages, which was formulated as part of its recommendations by the sub-committee under the chairmanship of Bishop Butler. It was suggested that "the proposed document should begin with a general introduction underlining the present unprecedented situation of a world convergence towards Christian unity and the need for unprecedented, but theologically justified, steps to be taken to meet it. It would consider the feasibility of an officially authorised progress towards unity by stages. It would suggest that 'neither side should require from the other, as a condition of very much greater unity, a positive acceptance as of faith of every article in one's own creed.' Conditions of intercommunion might then be spelt out."[16] This was the genesis of the 'Malta Report' and the Commission directed that Bishop Butler and Bishop McAdoo with the assistance of Fr. Richards and Professor Root, should draft a document for consideration by the next meeting. Canon Findlow and Canon Purdy were also requested to consider how the question of Anglican Orders should be handled.

At the third and final meeting in Malta, Bishop Butler and Bishop McAdoo presented a short document jointly drafted, together with papers by each entitled 'Unity: An Approach by Stages' to provide the background to their draft document.[17] Canons Findlow and Purdy recommended that the matter of Anglican Orders should be taken "in the context of the doctrine of the Church, sacraments, and ministry" and, with the documents referred to, this "formed the basis of the discussion and work at Malta."[18] The 'Malta Report' requires individual comment in the light of the themes running through the history of Anglican/Roman Catholic relations, but the Report in itself was a first-ever. The Press Release noted "We believe that in the perspective of post-Reformation history this report stands out, as containing the first formal joint statement ever made of the faith we rejoice to share."

This is what made it "a document full of hope" and it is in the manner of its composition, in its general approach and in its methodology, that it marks a clear stage onwards from Malines. Before making specific comments on the report, however, a few unrelated but relevant extracts from notes of the Commission's meetings may serve to illustrate the main pre-occupation of this essay,

---

[16] Ib. p. 21.
[17] Both papers are printed in CLARK and DAVEY, pp. 84–100, and 101–106.
[18] Ib. p. 23.

the themes and how they fared, whether developing or crystallising as they found themselves in different ecclesiastical and theological climates over two and a half centuries.

If, at Gazzada, the members felt that by reason alone of the fact that they were meeting with full official authorization, they were in a fresh and potentially quite different atmosphere and that they were part of a new dynamic, — at Huntercombe they saw the difficulties in a clear light. Looking back, Huntercombe was pivotal for JPARC. At one stage, there may have been a tendency to slip into trenches dug long ago, but it was resisted and the result was frequently that old themes received new handling. For instance, when an Anglican asked what concept of papacy would be acceptable to us all in a United Church — one not tied in with infallibility and universal jurisdiction — a Roman Catholic replied that Roman Catholics had come through many changes in this area and would need dialogue with other Christians so that, living together, we can find what we should all become. In another intervention, another Roman Catholic member, pointing out that dogmas on primacy, infallibility and mariology, "divide us from the Anglicans", stated that these matters also separated Rome from Orthodoxy with which limited *communicatio in sacris* was permitted. Why not then, at meetings such as this, ask permission for sacramental intercommunion?

The work of the Commission was characterised by both constructiveness and candour and, with the benefit of hindsight, it is striking to recall how some of its debates anticipated not simply the subject matter of ARCIC deliberations (this would hardly be surprising since the themes shaped the debate) but subsequent lines of approach. Members will recall the recurrence in different forms of the problems of the doctrinal criterion: How does the Church say what the Word of God is? What *is* the deposit of faith? (One may compare Wake on the difficulty of defining fundamentals). What is the relationship of ultimate authority in the Church to Scripture, to the *sensus fidei* of the whole body of the faithful? With this was linked the question of fundamentals/secondary truths and the concept of a "hierarchy of truths". One speaker asked, Why cannot we agree on fundamentals and not insist on each other accepting all developments of doctrine? Bishop Willebrands' paper should be carefully noted here in which are examined, within the context of the freedom-authority tension, the legitimate limits of diversity within the life of a United Church.[19] In fact, almost all the themes emerged during the Huntercombe meeting and it was the Commission's task to sort them and to decide on priorities within the framework of a report which would be conceived in terms of unity by stages. Thus ministry and Anglican Orders were discussed, with suggestions for a solution ranging from a mutual laying on of hands to an acceptance of the Anglican position. One speaker drew attention to the nineteenth-century result of taking the question of Orders in isolation, and noted that if other matters were agreed upon, a way could be found of dealing with the question — the real problem was the basis of faith. Various speakers underlined the importance of not mapping out precisely

---

[19] CLARK and DAVEY, loc. cit., pp. 60—73.

the various stages but rather of allowing the relationship to grow. Moving to one stage might not necessarily carry with it a commitment to the next stage, but the one should develop gradually from the other. In connection with inter-communion, a good deal was said on degrees of communion and the terms appropriate to define these. The Bonn Agreement between Anglicans and Old Catholics, the meeting between the Pope and the Patriarch Athenagoras and the doctrinal implications of it, and the status of Uniat Churches (a Roman Catholic speaker commented that previously they were only 'rites' but at the Council, Roman Catholics discovered they were Churches) – all these linked up with diversity within the unity and with the fundamentals/secondary truths theme. A discussion of the concept of sister-Churches revealed two very distinct Roman Catholic emphases in answer to the question whether Roman Catholics could speak of Anglicans as 'sister-Churches'. For one, a question mark remained, for reasons not defined; for the other, sister-Churches were "those other Churches in which we can see the mystical Body of Christ." Mixed marriages again came up within the context of the whole discussion, subserved by the other themes, concerning, Who are the Church? Where is the authentic Church? A member quoted from a high Roman Catholic source to the effect that ecumenism comes to a standstill before the canonical description of mixed marriages. The ecclesial implications of this were what concerned the Commission just as much as the effects on inter-Church relationships. The Malta Report faithfully reflects the range of the Commission's concerns and the order of its priorities.

3. The 'Malta Report'

There is a sense in which the 'Malta Report' represents the belated triumph of Halifax and Portal, in that its shape is created and its content to a large extent moulded by the concept of unity by stages which represents in another form their *caminho novo*, the theme of unity through convergence. This becomes clear from the underlying structure of the first seven paragraphs, in which the governing thought is "our recent growth towards greater unity and mutual understanding" from the already existing measure of unity through baptism (1). A similar phrase towards the end of the report, "the present growing together of our two communions" (19), serves to enclose the findings and recommendations of the Commission within this framework of convergence seen in terms of unity by stages.

The report builds not only on "our common baptism", but on "our common faith", and on "our sharing of the holy Scriptures, of the Apostles' and Nicene Creed, the Chalcedonian definition, and the teaching of the Fathers; our common Christian inheritance for many centuries with its living traditions of liturgy, theology, spirituality, Church order, and mission" (3). This is seen as the firm and extensive base upon which to rebuild Anglican/Roman Catholic relations.

Very significantly, the next paragraph (4) introduced the fact of divergence by way of contrast with that quest for growing convergence which the report visualises as the joint task of the two Communions. And, equally significantly, it states that such "divergences since the sixteenth century have arisen not so much from the substance of this inheritance as from our separate ways of receiving it" (4). This is a key-thought for interpreting the 'Malta Report' which sees the objective as substituting a convergent process for the divergences of the past four centuries, but all the time on the solid basis of an acknowledged and shared inheritance of faith. The report by no means plays down the extent or the depth of these divergences, coming as they do "from our understanding of the manner in which the Church should keep and teach the faith." It urges further study to ascertain what differences are real and "which are merely apparent" (4). This, in fact, has been the work of ARCIC, plotted in general outline by the 'Malta Report' (21—23). Still working from the centre of a common inheritance, and weighing both convergences and divergences, the report goes on to emphasise "the growing agreement of theologians in our two Communions" on the fact that dogmatic definitions are subject to historical conditioning in their formulation (5). Behind this sentence lies the ecumenically thwarting problem of the meaning of irreformability of doctrinal formulae. The report claims positively that within limits diversity has true creative value. The Commission suggested that, as things now stand between the two Churches in respect of this whole important area, there might be a way in through "the following possible convergences of lines of thought: first, between the traditional Anglican distinction of internal and external communion and the distinction drawn by the Vatican Council between full and partial communion; secondly, between the Anglican distinction of fundamentals from non-fundamentals and the distinction implied by the Vatican Council's references to a 'Hierarchy of truths' (Decree on Ecumenism, 11), to the difference between 'revealed truths' and 'the manner in wich they are formulated' (Pastoral Constitution on The Church in the Modern World, 62), and to diversities in theological tradition being often 'complementary, rather than conflicting' (Decree on Ecumenism, 17) (6)."

Whether these analogies referred to can be established as close or not, the help which Vatican II has given is to provide what was not there before as between the two Churches, namely, an accepted doctrinal perspective for the assessing of convergence and divergence. The "hierarchy of truths" does not furnish an instant ecumenical solution nor is it intended to be a ready-reckoner showing that some truths are more equal than others. Its practical value for the situation of the separated Churches is the assertion that truths "vary in their relation to the foundation of the Christian faith" (Decree on Ecumenism, 11). This may indeed be compared with the Anglican differentiation between fundamental truths ("their relation to the foundation") and truths which are not fundamental. This opens up the whole question, for a United Church, of the nature and extent of the agreement in faith necessary for union. Granted full agreement in the central areas of Christian belief, outlined in the 'Malta Report' (3) and (7), what other areas require agreement? Will substantial agreement in some (e.g. Eucharist and Ministry) and liberty in others be sufficient? "Each accepts the basic truths set forth in the ecumenical Creeds and the common tradition of the ancient Church, although neither Communion is tied to a positive acceptance of all the beliefs and devotional practices of the other" – so goes the Report (7), echoing a phrase from the Bonn Agreement. One recalls too in this connection that Archbishop Pangrazio, who put the concept of the hierarchy of truths into circulation at the Council, regarded the touchstone here as relation to the centre, to Christ himself.[20]

The Commission then went on to "recommend that the second stage in our growing together begin with an official and explicit affirmation of mutual recognition from the highest authorities of each Communion" (7). The basis of this recognition would be the fundamental acknowledgment "that both Communions are at one in the faith that the Church is founded upon the revelation of God the Father, made known to us in the Person and work of Jesus Christ, who is present through the Holy Spirit in the Scriptures and his Church, and is the only Mediator between God and Man, the ultimate Authority for all her doctrine."

The following section of the Report (8–16) makes a number of practical recommendations, many of which have been increasingly implemented since the Commission closed its last session at Mount St. Joseph, Mosta, overlooking St. Paul's Bay. Common liturgical texts are now in use and shared worship on occasions is now normal in many lands and here and there shared churches mark an advance. There have been, however, only slight improvements in the matter of mixed marriages which remains a constant irritant in relationships between the Churches. Co-operation in many fields of endeavour and the changing climate which makes this possible have to be set over against the hard-line attitudes, both clerical and lay, which persist at all levels, if in varying degree, in some countries.

The final section of the Report (17–24) opens with a disclaimer: "We cannot envisage in detail what may be the issues and demands of the final stage in our quest for the full, organic unity of our two Communions" (17). It closes with words quoted in the Common Declaration, "Forgetting those things which are behind, and reaching forth unto those things which are before, I press towards the mark for the prize of the high calling of God in Christ Jesus". In between, it sorts the themes and recommends a Permanent Commission to undertake the urgent task of examining and reporting on them. These themes are assessed in relation to a time-table similar to that of Halifax and Portal, for "the fulfilment of our aim is far from imminent". But another factor, not present in the 1890's, bears on the situation and is part of it: "In these circumstances the question of accepting some measure of sacramental intercommunion apart from full visible unity is being raised on every side. In the minds of many Christians no issue is today more urgent" (18). Aware that the *christifideles* may out-strip the theologians and the authorities by simply ignoring them, the Commission insists on taking a responsible attitude aimed at movement on a Church-to-Church rather than on an individualistic basis. Intercommunion requires "both a true sharing in faith and the mutual recognition of ministry" (19) and the

---

[20] Council Speeches of Vatican II (London 1964), ed. CONGAR, KÜNG and O'HANLON, pp. 124–126.

report stresses that ministry is part of ecclesiology and that 'sufficient agreement' (the wording significantly anticipates ARCIC's theological method) on
priesthood is also an essential preliminary to approaching the question of
Anglican Orders. It is important to stress, for the sake of the record, that such
phrases as are used in (19) in this connection tend to reflect an official Roman
Catholic view, not necessarily shared by all Roman Catholics, while for
Anglican members of JPARC this was a non-problem as they had no shadow of
doubt concerning the complete validity of Anglican Orders by any historical or
theological standard of assay. This theme of Church, Ministry and intercommunion is then, as the Commission handled it, one linked theme and this is
different from and theologically preferable to the way in which these themes
tended in the earlier contacts to be handled separately. JPARC pinpointed this
area of themes as a priority for the Permanent Commission, the setting up of
which it proposed to its authorities in the Report (21–22).

With the same type of approach, peculiar to itself and marking the
theological individuality of the Commission, the Report gathers the familiar
themes of "the indefectibility of the Church, and its teaching authority, the
Petrine primacy, infallibility and Mariological definitions" (20) into another
inter-related group, under the heading of "the nature of authority with particular
reference to its bearing on the interpretation of the historic faith to which both
our Communions are committed." This was fresh thinking on old themes and it
has been followed up and developed by ARCIC in its current work since the
vital questions are, What is authority for? and, What is its function in respect of
maintaining the Church in the truth?

Accordingly, the 'Malta Report' advocates a changed style for evaluating
the themes in relation to the present separation of the two Communions. It will
be seen in the next section how, and to what extent, the International Commission adopted this stance or altered it. Finally, the report recommended "joint
study of moral theology" (23) since in that area some of the most striking differences are to be found together with a remarkable convergence of method as the
work of writers such as Häring, Fuchs, Curran, McDonagh and many others
bring Roman Catholic moral theology close to the classical Anglican moral
theology which never allowed the subject to fall into the hands of the canonists
and which kept insisting that moral-ascetical theology was one science, not two
subjects.

The 'Malta Report' was signed on 2nd January 1968 and forwarded to the
appointing authorities. In November of the same year it was leaked to the
press and was widely printed and discussed. Official reaction was favourable, as
may be seen from the letter (10th June 1968) of Cardinal Bea, head of the
Secretariat for Promoting Christian Unity, to the Archbishop of Canterbury,
and from the resolutions of the Lambeth Conference of 1968, the members of
which had received the 'Malta Report'.[21] Both bodies approved the setting up of
a Permanent Joint Commission. The members of the new Commission, fewer in

---

[21] For the Text of Cardinal Bea's letter and for the resolutions and report of Section III of
    the Lambeth Conferences, see CLARK and DAVEY, loc. cit., pp. 116–122.

number than the Preparatory Commission, were appointed in 1969, eight out of the eighteen members of the Permanent Commission having belonged to JPARC. One of the first actions of the new Commission was to change its name to the Anglican/Roman Catholic International Commission, as the implications in the word 'Permanent' of talking until the Parousia were not liked.

A postscript at York (1969) and at Malines (1971)

There were twelve official Roman Catholic observers at the Lambeth Conference of 1968, five of whom had been members of the Preparatory Commission,[22] and a sixth representative was the nephew of Cardinal Mercier's secretary.[23] Bishop J. G. M. Willebrands addressed the Conference and brought the greetings of the Roman Catholic Church. Halifax and Mercier and Portal would have been gratified but not satisfied, for that was an essential part of the charism with which they were each so richly endowed. All three had the gift of pressing forward and at the same time never losing sight of the ultimate objective no matter how hard the going was on the way.

At the Lambeth Conference, the Roman Catholic observers gave to some of us a small photograph of Cardinal Mercier, on the reverse side of which was written:

"Ut Unum Sint . . . . .

In happy remembrance of the saintly men who initiated the move towards unity between the Anglican and Roman Catholic Churches

Désiré Joseph Cardinal *Mercier*
and
Charles Lindley 2nd Viscount *Halifax*

Malines Conversations
(1921 – 26)

To those who will carry on . . . . .

From the R. C. Observers at the Lambeth Conference
1968

. . . . . Soul knit to soul in a common unity of thought . . .
(Philip. 2, 1–4)."

On Sunday, 27th April, 1969, Cardinal Suenens, Archbishop of Malines and Primate of Belgium, visited York Minster and preached on the work of

---

[22] Bishop Christopher Butler, Bishop J. G. M. Willebrands, Bishop William Z. Gomes, Canon W. Purdy, Father Herbert Ryan S.J.
[23] Canon Josef A. Dessain.

Lord Halifax and Cardinal Mercier: "They started the first ecumenical dialogue for many, many years. At first sight, it seemed an impossible task. But difficult is what you can do at once; impossible is what needs a bit more time. The silence of five centuries was broken that day at Malines." Afterwards, the Cardinal and the Archbishop of York jointly unveiled and blessed a plaque in the Choir Sanctuary. The inscription reads "In Thanksgiving to God and in Memory of the Friendship of Désiré Joseph Cardinal Mercier (1851–1926) and Charles Lindley 2nd Viscount Halifax (1839–1934) and of those who worked with them in the cause of unity between the Roman Catholic and Anglican churches in the Malines Conversations, 1921–1926." Inset in the chalice used was the episcopal ring given by the dying Cardinal to Halifax as a token and symbol of hope.

Two years later, on May 14th–17th 1971, the then Archbishop of York, Dr. Coggan, paid a return visit to Malines as the guest of Cardinal Suenens. The Archbishop attended a concelebration in English in the Mercier Chapel of the Cathedral, the Cardinal being the principal celebrant. In the course of the programme for the visit, the Archbishop lectured at Louvain on 'The Bible and Unity' and during the discussion put a question about the stage reached in the relationship: "Is the Holy Spirit leading us to make a break-through with inter-communion? Is it the case that we are held up on other points because we have not taken this step, without which they will remain insoluble?"

V. 'A Serious Dialogue': The Work of the Anglican/Roman Catholic International Commission

1. Preliminaries

Because dialogue is an on-going process, the words taken from the Common Declaration are used above to describe not simply the work of JPARC which lasted for a year but chiefly the work of ARCIC which continues, and for which the Report of the earlier Commission was the essential *point de départ*. Among the necessary preliminaries to the setting up of the Commission and the announcement of its membership, was an informal meeting on 10th May 1969, held in Dublin, to prepare an outline of work and to settle the arrangements for the first meeting. Much of this was tentative and designed to help the Commission to do what ultimately nobody else could do for it, to find its true identity and function. At that meeting were present for the Anglican Communion, the Bishop of Ossory (Bishop McAdoo), Professor H. E. Root and Canon John Satterthwaite, of the Church of England Council for Foreign Relations (now bishop of Fulham and Gibraltar). From the Roman Catholic Church there were the Auxiliary Bishop of Westminster (Bishop Butler), Father J. Hamer O.P. and Canon W. Purdy, both of the Vatican Secretariat for Christian Unity. The Archbishop of Canterbury had expressed to the Bishop of

Ossory his hopes for the Commission,[1] that it should not only get down to an examination of the common faith held by the two Churches and to their differences, but that, for some time, it should also fill the rôle of a catalyst. He agreed that sub-commissions should work on authority, on intercommunion and on moral theology, and that the work of the sub-commission on mixed marriages should be encouraged as a pressing matter. He gave permission for the passing on of these points to the Dublin meeting at which it became clear, as a result of Father Hamer's remarks, that the views of the Vatican Secretariat for Unity were similar. It was soon evident that the meeting was in agreement about the Commission encouraging regional dialogue as well as its own specific theological task and that it should help in promoting the implementation of the Malta Report, particularly those items contained in paragraphs 8, 9, 13–16, and 22. It was accordingly decided that the first meeting of the new Commission would take place from 9th–15th January 1970 and that Canons Purdy and Satterthwaite should prepare a factual survey of what progress had been made in inter-Church relations since the Malta Report had been produced. This was to be circulated for the first meeting at Windsor and it was further decided to consider four subjects, in papers to be written in advance by joint pairs from both Churches, a method inherited from JPARC but not later continued in the procedure of ARCIC. Tentative proposals as to the authors were made and with one change these were in the event the writers who were to produce the first papers for the Commission. It was also agreed to inquire whether both authorities would approve an Observer being requested from the World Council of Churches.

The names of the members were published in the press on 11th October 1969 and were as follows:

Anglicans: Bishop J. R. H. Moorman of Ripon; Bishop E. G. Knapp-Fisher of Pretoria, S. Africa; Bishop Co-adjutor (afterwards Archbishop) F. R. Arnott of Melbourne, Australia; Bishop H. R. McAdoo of Ossory, Ireland; Professor Henry Chadwick (later Dean of Christ Church, Oxford), Regius Professor of Theology at the University of Oxford; Rev. J. Charley, Vice-rector of the London College of Divinity; Dr. J. Kelly, Rector of St. Edmund Hall, Oxford; Professor H. E. Root, Professor of Theology at the University of Southampton, and Professor A. A. Vogel (later Bishop of West Missouri), Professor of Theological Dogma, Nashotah House, U.S.A. Dr. Kelly had unfortunately to resign owing to other commitments and his place was taken at the second meeting by Professor Eugene Fairweather, Keble Professor of Divinity, Trinity College, Toronto, Canada.

---

[1] In a conversation at Lambeth, 29th April 1969. The Archbishop's constant care for the Commission, his concern for its work and his visits to some of its meetings were a real source of encouragement to the members who were deeply grateful for his support. His successor visited the Commission (at Oxford in 1975) and spoke to the members and his interest and advice were likewise warmly appreciated as has been the assistance of Cardinal Willebrands who has also visited Commission meetings and given his counsel as well as his backing to its work.

Roman Catholics: Bishop Christopher Butler, Auxiliary Bishop of Westminster; Bishop Alan C. Clark, Auxiliary Bishop of Northampton (now Bishop of East Anglia); Father Barnabas Ahern, Professor of Sacred Scripture, Rome; Father Herbert Ryan S. J., Professor of Religious Studies, Loyola University, Los Angeles, U.S.A.; Dr. J. J. Scarisbrick, Professor of History, University of Warwick; Father Georges Tavard A. A., Professor of Theology, Methodist Theological School, Delaware, U.S.A.; Father J. M. R. Tillard O. P., Professor of Dogmatic Theology in the Dominican Faculty of Theology, Ottawa and in Brussels; Father Pierre Duprey W. F., Under Secretary, Vatican Secretariat for Promoting Christian Unity. The two Co-chairmen, Bishops Clark and McAdoo, were nominated by the appointing authorities and the Secretaries to the Commission were Mgr. W. A. Purdy of the Vatican Secretary and the Rev. Colin Davey of the Church of England Council for Foreign Relations, later succeeded by the Rev. Christopher Hill, from the same Council. Before the first meeting took place the World Council of Churches accepted the invitation and appointed as its Observer the Rev. Dr. Günther Gassmann, Research Professor at the Centre d'Etudes Oecuméniques, Strasbourg.

2. The First Meeting at Windsor (Windsor I)

The Commission assembled[2] for its first meeting at St. George's House, Windsor Castle, Windsor, from 9th—15th January, 1970. The themes, with something of their fresh grouping as suggested by the work of JPARC already apparent, may be seen from the titles of the papers circulated beforehand and discussed during the twelve sessions of the meeting: 'Fundamentals of the Faith held in Common' (The Bishop of Pretoria and Fr. Edmund Hill O.P.); 'The Church, Intercommunion and the Ministry' (Professor A. Vogel) together with a second paper of the same title in French by Fr. J. M. R. Tillard O.P.; two papers on 'Authority — Its Nature, Exercise and Implications' (Bishop Butler and the Dean of Christ Church, Oxford); a joint paper by Canon W. Purdy and Professor H. E. Root on 'Growing Together — an assessment of the opportunities for collaboration between the two Churches'; a report of progress in Anglican/Roman Catholic relations since the presentation of the 'Malta Report', compiled by Canon J. Satterthwaite and Canon W. Purdy.[3]

From the beginning, there was an atmosphere of friendship which soon grew into a genuine fellowship and this made frank and open discussion both

---

[2] The Rev. Dr. Kelly having resigned, the Anglicans begged leave to suggest to their authorities that a representative from Canada would be welcomed. Fr. P. Duprey was absent through illness and his place was supplied by Fr. Stransky, from the Secretariat at Rome. Fr. Edmund Hill O.P. was present as a consultant jointly presenting a paper with the Bishop of Pretoria.

[3] ARCIC agreed that papers tabled before the Commission could be published if the authors agree and provided that the papers are described as questions which are being studied by the Commission. This is to avoid the papers being regarded as agreed pronouncements of the Commission.

natural and profitable. As these important papers, seminal for ARCIC's future programme, were debated certain key-areas were identified. The themes of 'The Church and Authority', 'The Ministry' and 'The Eucharist' were handed over to three groups who, after two days intensive work, reported to the plenary session in three outlines which were then amended by the Commission. By this time ARCIC's future programme had in fact declared itself and what came to be its future method of working was also emerging. The three themes were allotted to three sub-commissions, based in the United Kingdom, the United States and South Africa respectively, who would work on material for drafts on the subjects to be circulated to the Commission within six months as a preparation for the second meeting of ARCIC in September of the same year.[4] It was also decided to move on to consider paragraph 23 of the Malta Report and to have four papers on two aspects of moral theology at the next meeting. The subjects would be converging trends in moral theology generally and the relationship between men and women, particularly married life and family planning. Consultants could be used on all subjects and invited to the meeting at which their particular contribution was being discussed. This decision has been sparingly but very profitably utilised over the total spread of the Commission's meetings.

Rather than proceeding by the method of providing a full commentary on the contents of the papers, it may prove more serviceable to an understanding of the developing momentum of the Commission's work, to stress aspects of them which show how, in these papers and at this first session, the main outlines of the task became clear almost from the start. This is also consistent with an overall thematic presentation of the subject. "Where will they decide to start?" asked an article in the 'Times' (7 January 1970), "The range of possibilities is immense." The article went on to suggest that Anglican Orders and 'Apostolicae Curae' constituted an obvious crux and the only question was at what point ARCIC would decide to involve itself in the complexities of the problem. In the event, as has been noted, a different strategy evolved, that of beginning on four fronts at once. This would shortly be reduced and each subject would be taken separately thereafter but the Commission's work had first to find its own logic and sequence. These began slowly to build themselves up as the members considered and discussed the papers. That on fundamentals posited an explicit holding in common of the fundamentals of the Creeds and went on, in the context of the Malta Report, to choose four topics in this area to discover the extent of agreement and divergence. These subjects were Revelation and Faith, Scripture and Tradition, Church and Authority, Dogmatic Definitions and Comprehensiveness. On the first theme, the paper registered complete substantial agreement and on the second, a measure of agreement but also real continuing

---

[4] The 'Church and Authority' subcommission was to be based in the U.K., Dr. Chadwick and Bishop Butler being convenors. The 'Ministry' group, based in the U.S.A., would have Professor Vogel and Fr. Tavard as convenors, working with Bishop Arnott (Australia) and a group there. The sub-commission on 'The Eucharist' would be based in S. Africa, the Bishop of Pretoria being convenor working with the existing South African ARC and the Rev. J. Charley and Father Tillard acting as correspondent members.

differences while some disagreements were held to be more apparent than real. Vatican II was seen as leaving open the relationship between Scripture and Tradition but as removing Anglican suspicions about a two-source theory of revelation. The third theme inevitably produced divergence on infallibility/indefectibility and the teaching authority of the Church, or rather on the exercise of this and the nature of the criteria adopted. Under the fourth heading the authors found differences as to distinguishing between fundamental truths and those upon which some degree of latitude in understanding is allowable. The question as to what developments can claim to be in accord with Scriptural truths and so be required to be accepted as *de fide* raised the problem which Gore prophetically saw at Malines as not only central but continuing.

The second paper served a similar purpose of gathering and sorting themes in a new context, but also with a fresh approach. Its basis was the assertion that a full treatment of the eucharist involves a complete ecclesiology and a full ecclesiology necessarily involves a doctrine of the ministry. Thus in Bishop Vogel's paper as in that of Bishop Knapp-Fisher and Fr. Hill, not only were the main themes grouped and put in the perspective of where the Churches are now, but the subject-matter and the sequence and style of its treatment by ARCIC during the following years took shape at an early stage. The paper looked at Church, intercommunion and ministry in the context, first, of the human condition: if man is constituted as a person through body, word and community, his life has a 'eucharistic' significance, since men receive the Body of Christ, the Word of God within the living community. Among the matters raised in this paper were some which pointed on to the work which would issue in ARCIC's two published statements. For instance, in addition to the baptismal faith what explicit agreement about the eucharist is necessary before sharing a specific eucharistic celebration? How *much* unity should there be before eucharistic participation? Or again, it was forecast that the most problematic dimensions of the Church (for Anglican/Roman Catholic relations) would be those of authority and ministry. In the latter connection, ministry was firmly located in the community of faith, and the understanding of the role and nature of the ordained ministry and its relation to the royal priesthood, should be developed in this context. These points, and many others, manifestly look ahead to the Windsor and Canterbury Statements, and behind them lies the basic question, constantly recurring in Anglican/Roman Catholic dialogue, Who are the Church? This theme was picked up again in the second meeting at Venice, as may be seen in the published Venice working-papers, just as the fundamental/secondary truths theme and the question as to what determined a doctrine as being *de fide*, raised in the paper on fundamentals, re-emerged in the further discussions of the Commission.

Dean Chadwick's paper on the nature, exercise and implications of authority also anticipated something of the debate which would evolve in the later stages of the work. Authority was first considered in general terms: its need for sanctions; its relation to loyalty and conscience and to rationality rather than to the mere imperative; the need for it to be seen as a service to society. It appeared in three forms, the traditional, the functional and the charismatic. Within the history of the Christian Community, the same problems can be discerned in regard to authority and to its function and media. What then are the chances for a restatement of religious authority in the modern western world? What are the fundamental differences inherited by both Churches from the past and which still influence them? While Anglicans and Roman Catholics were not divided on the principle of authority, differences of emphasis could be important. In fact, an important discernible difference lies in what may be conceived as the prime function of Christian authority, the preservation of the Church from error. The infallibility/indefectibility debate at once becomes relevant here and includes the authority of papacy, of conciliar decrees, of Scripture and of 'the teaching Church'.

The paper on 'Growing Together' by Canon Purdy and Professor Root was valuable and practical in that it sought to outline the scope of opportunities for collaboration outside the specifically theological field. The approach was parallel to the search for "reconciling answers" in theology (Malta Report, 17) and served to keep the members aware of the unsatisfactory existing situation "on the ground", and of the fact that ideally the Commission should function on two levels. When all these matters were put through the sieve of discussion in sub-commissions and in plenary sessions, the shape of the task and a way of handling it began to assume clearer outlines. This development of the Commission's programme and *modus operandi* was not however something inevitable nor was it a steadily-moving and uninterrupted process. There were trough periods in most meetings, and checks, hesitations and false starts as well as daunting obstacles. The pattern had to be hammered out and in all the meetings the degree of progress achieved had to be striven for continually. It should be said that this process took place against a general background of the desire to say positive things, to look at differences in the light of the objective to be reached rather than in a Reformation-Counter Reformation context, and to establish realistically why the two Churches are not in communion now and how the barriers to this can be reduced.

Running through the discussions at Windsor were certain matters which tended to recur in different areas and to be linked with one another. For example, the themes of fundamentals and the faith-basis linked up with that of authority, and both together evoked a general inquiry as to, Who are the Church? If communion with the Roman See is claimed in any way as constitutive of authentic ecclesiality, what about the limited *communicatio in sacris* now promoted with the Orthodox, whose faith-basis is not the same as that of the Roman Church? How then to restore comunion with Anglicans? What would be necessary for this? The whole area of the basis of faith and of ministry at once dovetailed with the problem of what constitutes the Church. Basically, the Anglicans stressed that the fundamentals are in the Creeds (though this was not unsupported from the Roman Catholic side), that the criterion is Scripture, and that consonance with Scripture legitimises 'development'. The Roman Catholics tended to ask, what authority (pointing to papal infallibility) decides whether a doctrine is Scriptural or not or whether a doctrine is a legitimate development or not. Anglicans held that the fundamentals were self-evident and that, as the

Articles stress, the Church has authority to decide controversies. They thought in terms of the faith "once for all delivered" which allowed for development in theological interpretations but not in terms of the faith. Was the dogma of the Assumption (apparently the only infallible pronouncement by Authority) a legitimate Scriptural development or an addition to the fundamentals? Some Roman Catholics regarded it as a fundamental while for others it was an explication. Clearly, since the Church is constituted in time and space by continuity of doctrine, life and succession, the theme of fundamentals and the basis of faith merges with that of ecclesiology and ministry. This in turn demands a doctrine of the Church which is not tied up with canonical verification but which builds on a re-appraisal of 'subsistit', of where the Church is, and of the reality of the ministry of the Word and Sacraments outside the Roman Catholic Church. The Decree on Ecumenism has pointers in this connection, and there were reflections of this in the various discussions. A Roman Catholic suggested that the Spirit, the Eucharist and the Pope constituted the Roman Catholic Church, and asked what happens when there is a Church with the Spirit and the Eucharist working under episcopal oversight. Does this not make for partial communion with Anglicans? The question was asked, what is the basic structure which enables a Church to recognize itself in the ministrations of another? This focused the spotlight clearly on eucharist and ministry and the resulting consensus, equally positive from both sides, was on the necessity for an agreement first on eucharistic faith and teaching. Given such agreement, how then can communion be restored? If organic unity is the ultimate goal, then with what lesser goal can the Churches be temporarily satisfied? Partial communion and Uniat status were both referred to and it was generally felt that preliminary agreement on the Church and on the Ministry was required. This raised the questions of validity, of the effect of new thinking on ministry and priesthood in Roman Catholic circles, and of Anglican Orders. While this latter was a non-problem for Anglicans, they were ready to help reassure their brethren in the spirit of the Lambeth Appeal to All Christian People (1920) in a way consistent with their conviction of the complete juridical validity of their Orders. Here there was an interesting reaction which cut across denominational lines. Many favoured a reconciliation service which would commission priests in each other's respective communions. The view was freely expressed that some sort of official recognition or act of concrete verification was needed. Suggestions included a formal declaration, a reconciliation service or some arrangement for conditional reordination. It is of interest that the latter was turned down by several Roman Catholics speakers.

It was along these lines that the Commission reached its decision to do additional work on the Church and Authority, the Ministry and the Eucharist. In a sense, ARCIC was reaching the conclusions already set out by JPARC, but, as a new or partly new group, it had to find its identity and establish conclusions for itself. And, of course, it did more, since it took the first steps in implementing the 'Malta Report''s recommendations and in so doing began to evolve a methodology of its own.

3. The Second Meeting at Venice

The second meeting of the Commission took place in Venice from 21st–28th September, 1970. The members were housed in the Istituto Ciliotta and the plenary sessions were held in the Fondazione Giorgio Cini on the island of San Giorgo Maggiore, a centre used for a wide range of conferences and the setting for the meeting of Paul VI and the Patriarch Athenagoras. The Commission's main business was to carry further the programme begun at Windsor in the preceding January, upon which the sub-commissions had been at work in England, the U.S.A. and South Africa during the intervening period. In addition, it had to consider four papers on moral theology, following the recommendations of the Malta Report. The nature and extent of the material and the necessity for handling it in depth meant that a considerable part of the time available had to be given over to sub-commissions whose draft findings were then discussed in detail by the full Commission. It became clear at Venice that the programme was over-loaded and that in future ARCIC would be obliged to concentrate on one subject at a meeting and endeavour to produce an agreed statement on that subject. This became the existing pattern of work save that in practice it was found that each of the agreed statements took a longer preparatory period. As a result of discussing the papers and draft submissions of the three groups, it was decided that the eucharist would be the main topic of research and that this investigation should be conducted under three headings by three sub-commissions working during the intervening period and presenting their findings with a view to a statement for publication by the Commission after its meeting in September 1971. A group based in England would take the subject, 'The Notion of Sacrifice in the Eucharist in Anglican and Roman Catholic Theology.'[5] The second subject, 'The Real Presence in Anglican and Roman Catholic Theology' would be handled by a group in Canada and the U.S.A.[6] The South African Anglican/Roman Catholic Commission, with the Bishop of Pretoria as convenor, would work on 'An Examination in Depth of our Various Eucharistic Rites.'

The Commission unanimously requested permission from the respective authorities to publish material, such as the three draft reports referred to and the papers on moral theology. It would make clear that all such material was of the nature of working papers and not agreements ratified either by the Commission or by the Churches. The purpose would be to assist in carrying out ARCIC's task of promoting interest and guiding dialogue throughout the Church. This permission was given and the Venice Working Papers were published.[7] The Isola San Giorgio has been described as "an isle of hope" and it was in a spirit of sober hope that the members of the Commission left Venice after a week of searching debate in which the next stage of the programme had been evolved.

---

[5] Convenors: Fr. Yarnold and Dr. J. Halliburton (Consultant). Other members, Bishop Butler, Dean Chadwick, Professor Root and the Rev. J. Charley.

[6] Bishop Vogel, Fr. Ryan, Fr. Tavard and Fr. Ahern.

[7] See Theology, Vol. LXXIV, February 1971, No. 608, and The Clergy Review of the same month.

At the beginning of the second session of the Commission the members had already been provided with a group of eight short papers, by different writers, on the Church and Authority. These had been got together by the sub-commission on the subject and by the Rev. Dr. R. J. Halliburton of St. Stephen's House, Oxford, who has subsequently attended meetings as an Anglican consultant. The Rev. Fr. Herbert J. Ryan S.J. had also produced a paper on 'Ministry in a Divided Church'. This preliminary work in these essays helped to bring the work into focus, indicating as it did that theological movement could be discerned in the field of infallibility/indefectibility and that a line of approach to Anglican Orders for Roman Catholics could be for them to show that there is a genuine development of Roman Catholic doctrine in respect of some of the concepts underlying 'Apostolicae Curae'. This would suggest that a new situation exists between the two Churches requiring a change of practice to fit in with the doctrinal development. The Church as *koinonia* also became a major element in the discussion.

Something of these three sets of ideas was reflected in the Venice Working Papers. That on 'The Church and Authority' and 'The Church and Ministry' both referred to the problem of papal office and primacy, the former dealing also with developments in teaching on the *koinonia* while the latter referred to the relation of a development of doctrine to the theological assumptions underlying 'Apostolicae Curae'. Important also was the statement in 'The Church and Authority' that there are three elements constitutive of a Church, the profession of the apostolic faith, the use of the sacraments, and the oversight of a fully accepted ministry. Also, the same paper noted that the truths necessary to communion between the Churches 'are those which directly relate to the Incarnation and Redemption as recorded in the Scriptures.' All this marked a certain advance and laid the ground for more solid achievement later. The third paper, that on 'The Church and Eucharist', saw this as an area in which there was the possibility of convergence and the Commission chose the subject as the chief material for its meeting in September 1971.

Four papers were presented on moral theology and these were written by three specialists, Professor Gordon Dunstan (Anglican), Mgr. Delhaye, Dean of the Faculty of Theology, Louvain (Roman Catholic) and Fr. Maurice O'Leary (Roman Catholic), all of whom attended the meeting. The subjects were 'The Making, Commending and Enforcement of Moral Judgments within the Church' and 'The Relation of Men and Women'. The papers covered the sources of moral knowledge as visualised by both Churches and questions of sexuality, marriage and divorce. These papers performed an important service by demonstrating many convergences and fewer divergences. Anglicans were made aware that many Roman Catholic theologians were shifting from a moral theology based on natural and canonical law to one founded on scriptural teaching as its basis. This revealed a very similar structure to that of traditional Anglican moral theology. Instances of convergence were, – the basing of moral theology on Scripture and the kerygma; the merging of what used to be called ascetic theoloy with what used to be known as moral theology, with the consequent emphasis on 'the new life'; the emphases on the normative rôle of charity and on response and responsibility; the imitation of Christ and incorporation in Him; the frequent use of the category of the disciple rather than that of the penitent. The nature of marital breakdown and the need for seeing this in the context of the whole marriage relationship pointed in the same direction and the nature of marriage as contract, as sacrament or as covenant was discussed with its direct bearing on indissolubility.

Divergence was felt to exist in that Anglicans stress the process of moral reasoning as opposed to what seemed to them to be morals by decree. It was considered that there was a need for an investigation of the nature and rôle of the magisterium in this field, and of the inter-relation of conscience, freedom and authority. It proved impossible, owing to pressure of work, for the Commission to draw up considered views on these important questions to which it hopes to return.

If one impression more than another requires to be noted, it was that at the second meeting a general realisation made itself felt that there lay ahead a process of patient seeking for convergence and of honest recognition of divergent stand-points. The process of joint investigation had also become firmly established.

4. The Third Meeting at Windsor (Windsor II): an Agreed Statement on
   Eucharistic Doctrine

Once again, St. George's House, Windsor Castle, was chosen as the location for the third meeting, September 1st–8th, 1971. Before this took place, however, and following up a suggestion made at Venice by the sub-commission on the eucharist, some members of that group assembled from 12th–16th April 1971 at the invitation of Bishop Clark at Poringland, Norwich.[8] The object of this intermediate encounter was to develop the Venice Draft Document on the eucharist. The Poringland meeting resulted in a Further Statement which, in the event, proved of great value at Windsor II, much of it being incorporated in the Commission's final statement. Reactions to this paper were sought and received from members of the Commission prior to its meeting in September and these, together with other papers and material provided by the three sub-commissions appointed at Venice, constituted the documentation from which the Commission would work at Windsor. Also in accord with suggestions made at Venice, the co-chairmen and secretaries met at Lambeth in the office of the Church of England's Council for Foreign Relations on June 10th to draft the programme for the September meeting. It was decided that the Bishop of Ossory should give a Chairman's address on the subject of partial communion, with special reference to paragraphs 6 and 7 of the 'Malta Report', and that the Commission should be invited to relate the deliberations of the sub-commissions

---

[8] Bishop Clark, Fr. Barnabas Ahern, Fr. Jean Tillard, Fr. Pierre Duprey, The Rev. Julian Charley and Dr E. R. Hardy representing Dr. A. Vogel who was shortly to be consecrated Bishop of Western Missouri.

to this subject in the light of the last two years' work. The Bishop of Elmham was to deliver a Chairman's summing-up at the end of the Conference. The intention was to keep the themes within an over-all perspective of the quest for unity by an officially-appointed Commission rather than to allow a theological society atmosphere to develop. To the same end, Fr. Eugene Schallert S.J., Director of the San Francisco Socio-Religious Institute, would be invited to attend as a consultant for a discussion of the possibility of a sociological survey being carried out to provide information on the present state of local Anglican/ Roman Catholic relations. The Bishop of Ripon was to be invited to deliver a paper on the requirements for practical communion and how it might work out in practice, Professor Root and Canon Purdy being asked to lead the discussion.

When it assembled on September 1st, ARCIC had before its members not only the material just referred to, but a collection of ten papers from the sub-commission on the eucharistic sacrifice, the secretaries of which were Fr. E. J. Yarnold S.J. and the Rev. Dr. R. J. Halliburton.[9] In addition, Professor E. R. Fairweather had provided notes on 'The Presence of Christ in the Eucharist' and Fr. J. M. R. Tillard O.P. had written a paper on 'The Presence of the Body and Blood of the Lord'. These played a considerable part in the debates and conclusions of the Commission. An examination and comparison of the Anglican and Roman Catholic eucharistic rites was presented by the South Africa sub-commission. A paper on 'Growing together' by Canon Purdy was followed by a contribution from Fr. E. J. Schallert on the techniques of socio-religious research as these might be utilised in the furtherance of the Commission's task.

In the course of the third session much concentrated work was done by sub-commissions, by the plenary meetings and by drafters, the final outcome of which was the first published document of the Commission, 'An Agreed Statement on Eucharistic Doctrine' (Windsor 1971). Since then, the statement has been very widely circulated and debated, received much approval and some criticism in both Churches, but being generally welcomed as a serious contribution and necessary step. It, and its companion statement 'Ministry and Ordination' (Canterbury 1973), while not being agreements ratified by either Church, have each the status of a consensus from a body officially appointed by the authorities of both Churches. "These authorities", to quote the note appended to the Canterbury Statement, "have allowed the Statement to be published so that it may be discussed by other theologians". Such joint statements have become a new and welcome feature of the last decade and are essential to movement and progress in the search for an end to separation.

The text of the agreed statement on the eucharist being readily available, all that is required is a note on what may be regarded as its approach and methodology. This becomes clear from the first paragraph: "Our intention has been to seek a deeper understanding of the reality of the eucharist which is consonant

---

[9] In addition to Dr. Gassmann, W.C.C. Observer, the meeting was also attended by the Secretary-General of the Anglican Consultative Council, the Rt.Rev. John Howe, the Director of the Anglican Centre in Rome, the Rev. Dr. H. R. Smythe, and Fr. Eugene Schallert.

with biblical teaching and with the tradition of our common inheritance, and to express in this document the consensus we have reached", and from the last paragraph (12): "We have seen it as our task to find a way of advancing together beyond the doctrinal disagreements of the past". The statement has a dynamic rather than a static approach, concentrating on the reality of the eucharist, its purpose and meaning, and on what it effects within the *koinonia*. It does not seek, as in the past, to define how the eucharist effects its purpose. It seeks to go behind later controversy to Scripture, to the biblical realism and to that earlier approach reflected in the words of John of Damascus: "If you inquire as to the method, how this comes to be, it is enough for you to hear that it is by means of the Holy Ghost." As Richard Hooker wrote "Shall I wish that men would give themselves more to meditate with silence what we have by the Sacrament, and less to dispute of the manner how?"[10] and "what we have by the Sacrament" is a controlling factor in the statement's methodology.[11] In what it has to say on 'sacramental presence' and 'sacrifice', the Agreed Statement opens up further a new way forward beyond past disagreements. The Commission's findings were described by Bishop B. C. Butler as "likely to be historic steps on the road of mutual understanding between the two Churches."[12] The document should thus be read as a whole in the light of its own expressed intention to move forward by a different method. More detailed theological comments on the content of the statement have been published by members of the Commission[13] but one theme, visible at earlier stages of Anglican/Roman Catholic encounter, is contained in the methodology of the Commission and is an essential component of it, that of substantial agreement. Its importance for establishing convergence is second to none, and it receives unequivocal endorsement as a working principle in the statement (12): "We believe that we have reached substantial agreement on the doctrine of the eucharist." The hinge of the method of the Agreed Statement is a combination of this with the concept of the reality of the eucharist, and this is clearly set out in the opening paragraph(1): "An important stage in progress towards organic unity is a substantial consensus on the purpose and meaning of the eucharist."[14] This theological method may well turn out to be a most productive aspect of the work of the International Commission.

The Windsor Statement taken together with the Lutheran/Roman Catholic Statement, the Les Dombes Agreement between Roman/Catholics and Protestants, and the W.C.C. document 'The Eucharist in Ecumenical Thought', of all of which the ARCIC statement is independent, nevertheless provide a remarkable

[10] Ecclesiastical Polity, V, lxvii, 3.

[11] E. g. para. 1–4, 6.

[12] The Tablet, 8 January 1972.

[13] Agreement on the Eucharist (Roman Catholic Ecumenical Commission, 1972) by ALAN C. CLARK; Modern Eucharistic Agreement (S.P.C.K., London 1973), introduction by H. R. MCADOO and foreword by ALAN C. CLARK; The Anglican-Roman Catholic Agreement on the Eucharist (Grove Booklet No., 1, 1971) by JULIAN W. CHARLEY.

[14] On the implications of the term 'substantial agreement' see 'Anglican-Roman Catholic Dialogue' (One in Christ, Vol. VIII, 1972, No. 3) by a member of the Commission, Fr. J. M. R. TILLARD O.P.

range of modern consensus as a survey of the texts shows.[15] The latest revision of the W.C.C. document (at the Faith and Order Commission's meeting in Accra, 1974) adds further to the impression of consensus, particularly in paragraph 34: "The way in which the elements of bread and wine are treated requires special attention, the act of Christ, being the gift of his body and his blood (that is, himself), the given reality symbolized in the bread and wine is his body and his blood. It is in virtue of the creative word of Christ and by the power of the Holy Spirit that the bread and wine are made sacraments, and thus, 'participation in the body and blood of Christ' (1 Cor. 10:16). Henceforth, in the deepest sense, by an external sign, they are given reality and remain so in view of their consumption. That which is given as the body and blood of Christ remains given as his body and blood; it must be treated as such."[16] This clearly owes much to the Les Dombes Agreement (19) published between the Louvain (1971) revision of the W.C.C. document and the Accra revision (1974).

The Commission's Statement was thus evolved in the context of the question of the degrees of communion and the requirements for such stages or degrees, as analysed, for example, in the Bishop of Ripon's paper on the second morning of the third meeting. The same overall question in accordance with the Malta Report's recommendation (22) was the background to the next stage in the Commission's efforts which it was decided would be an attempt to produce an agreed statement on Ministry. With this in view, the Commission distributed preparatory work as follows: the sub-commission in the U.K. would take the subject 'Ministry in the New Testament', while a Canadian group would work on 'Sacerdotium'. The U.S.A. group would write on 'Bishops and Priests' and the South African sub-commission would study the problem of orders in the context of ministry and of the obstacles to intercommunion, including the question of validity.

The date of the next meeting would be September 1972 and an interim meeting, for those who could attend, would take place in May 1972 at Woodstock College, New York, Fr. Ryan being the Convenor. The aim of this meeting would be to take the Venice paper on Ministry, together with preparatory material from the sub-commissions, and to produce a draft as a possible basis for the full Commission's work in the following September.

5. The Fourth Meeting at Gazzada

For its fourth assembly, the Commission met at the Villa Cagnola, Gazzada, North Italy, the scene of the first meeting of the Joint Preparatory Commission. The sessions lasted from August 30th—September 7th, 1972. Before the

---

[15] See Modern Eucharistic Agreement (London, 1973) for such a comparison.
[16] This revision is published, together with the revision of the W.C.C. statements on baptism and ministry, in 'One Baptism, One Eucharist', and 'A Mutually Recognized Ministry' (Geneva, 1975), Faith and Order Paper No. 73. Compare also paras. 14 and 15 of the revised W.C.C. agreement with reference to "the real presence".

main meeting a small group of members had gathered at Woodstock College, New York, from 23rd–26th May.[17] What it succeeded in doing was to provide a suggested programme of work and agenda for Gazzada. This was done by a sifting of the extensive body of papers,[18] already in hand for the fourth meeting, and by the individual members of the group submitting schemas for the treatment of the subject of ministry. Out of this process there evolved a proposed outline for Gazzada under the headings (1) Church as Eucharistic Community (2) Priesthood and Ministry in the New Testament (3) Historical understanding of the function of ministers. To which was added for 1973, (4) The three-fold order of Ministry and (5) Some Implications. Each item was spelt out in detail and points of agreement and divergence between the two Churches were noted. The complete document was circulated to all members with a covering letter from the Co-chairmen, suggesting that both the Roman Catholic and Reformed traditions, by over-emphasising certain aspects of priesthood, had produced inadequate interpretations which required to be reconciled in the light of a richer notion of ministry more consonant with New Testament teaching. It was further suggested that at the fourth meeting there should be an attempt to re-assess this central idea, to see that it has become an umbrella-term covering two distinct ideas, i. e. *sacerdotium* and *ministerium, hierateuma* and *diakonia*, and to identify the presence or absence of these 'functions' in Christ, in the Church and in the ordained ministry.

[17] Bishop Clark, Bishop McAdoo, Bishop Vogel, Fr. Tillard, Fr. Tavard, Prof. Fairweather, Mr. Charley and Fr. John Reid S.J.

[18] Among the material to hand at Woodstock and for Gazzada were: Report of 'The New Testament Teaching on Ministry' from the Oxford Sub-Commission: Supporting documents; 'Ministry and Order: A Catholic Position Paper' (R. MURRAY S.J.), 'Forms and Developments of Ministry in the First Century' (B. AHERN, C.P.), Summary by Bishop Clark of Congar's 'Quelques Problèmes Touchant les Ministères', 'Note on the Idea of Participation in the Priesthood of Christ' (J. L. HOULDEN), 'The Spirit and Institution' (R. PELLY), 'Bridging Statement from Eucharist to Ministry' (T. CORBISHLEY), 'Apostolic Succession' (J. CHARLEY), 'Ordination and Laying-on-of-Hands' (J. HALLIBURTON). The above were circulated from England while from Canada and the U.S.A. came 'La qualité "sacerdotale" du Ministère Chrétien' (J. M. R. TILLARD), 'The Minister of the Eucharist (W. J. WOLF), 'The Function of the Minister in the Eucharistic Celebration: An Ecumenical Approach' (GEORGE A. TAVARD), 'Authority and Ministry – in Theory and Practice: An Anglican View' (MAX M. THOMAS), 'Present Roman Catholic Theology of the Ministry: an overview' (WALTER J. BURGHARDT), 'The Official View of Episcopacy in the Episcopal Church in the U.S.A.' (W. J. WOLF), 'Some Notes towards the Definition of the Office of Bishop in the Church of God' (H. R. SMYTHE), 'Apostolicity and Ministry' (REGINALD H. FULLER), 'Summary of Paper on Apostolic Succession' (CRAWFORD MILLER), 'The Reformation Issues' (CLEMENT TIERNEY), 'Anglican-Roman Catholic Relations in the U.S.A.: a Pastoral Approach to Unity' (THOMAS A. FRASER), 'The Recognition of Ministry' (GEORGE A. TAVARD), 'Priesthood and Anglican Orders' (JEROME SMITH), 'Lutherans and Catholics in Dialogue IV: Eucharist and Ministry' (Report of Lutheran/Roman Catholic Dialogue in the U.S.A.). The South African sub-commission sent its paper 'Ministry' and the W.C.C./R.C. Study 'Catholicity and Apostolicity' (published in 'One in Christ') was also circulated.

16*

When the Commission gathered at Gazzada, the members were therefore in possession of a large number of papers consisting of material commissioned by ARCIC and support documents provided from different sources. Among the former was a paper 'La qualité sacerdotale du Ministère Chrétien' by Fr. J. M. R. Tillard O.P. Later published as a booklet in English 'What priesthood has the Ministry?', with a foreword by an Anglican member of the Commission, the Rev. Julian Charley, this paper[19] proved influential in the work at Gazzada and at the fifth meeting, as did also a paper on 'The Recognition of Ministry' by Fr. George Tavard. Under the first three of the Woodstock headings work was at once allotted to three sub-commissions reporting to the plenary sessions. As this process went on it became evident that the main thrust was in the direction of sub-commission (2) which had as its subject priesthood and ministry in the New Testament, although valuable insights were coming through in the other areas particularly that of apostolicity.[20] This resulted in a revision of the Woodstock working-plan. The natural drift of discussion led to a decision to concentrate on producing some provisional work on ministry in the New Testament and material was also produced on apostolicity and the historical aspect. Some of this material and a good deal of the thinking embodied in it found its way into the final statement. After close analysis in plenary session of the work thus evolved the conclusion was to establish a working plan, allotting to groups centred in England, Canada/U.S.A. and South Africa, the following subjects for study: (1) *Apostolic Succession*; its relation to the apostolicity of Christ, of the Apostles and of the Church (2) *Priesthood*; in relation to Christ and the Church, in relation to the eucharist, in relation to forgiveness of sins and in relation to other functions of the ordained ministry, special reference being made to a note on apostolicity provided by sub-commission (1). (3) *Ordination*; do we agree on the purpose of ordination and, if so, what is it? How can we be sure that this purpose is effected? What part is played by community and continuity of faith, action on behalf of a Church, tactile succession and sufficient form? What light is thrown on the functions of bishops, priests and deacons by our pontificals and ordinals?

The procedure decided upon was that each group would endeavour to send in an agreed conclusion on its area of investigation before the end of May 1973. The Commission then apointed seven of its number to meet at Poringland from 11th—15th June 1973 with the task of drawing up, in the light of these written conclusions, a draft statement on Ministry, (if such an agreement seemed possible) for submission to ARCIC in the following September.

The working pattern of the Commission, dictated largely by the spread of its membership over four continents, may seem clumsy on paper. In fact, it possesses advantages in that the procedure makes for deliberation and careful work. It can also involve all the members of the Commission by inviting them

---

[19] Grove Booklet No. 13 (Bramcote, Notts., 1973). The paper also appeared in the 'Nouvelle Revue Théologique' and in 'One in Christ' (April 1973). It was translated into English by Canon W. A. PURDY.

[20] The Woodstock meeting had seen this as a subject for the following year.

to undertake specific tasks and the wide-spread provenance of the membership incidentally ensures contact with an extended range of theological activities and developments in many countries. The working pattern also established conclusively the need for such a widely separated group to have before it a document, if only for demolition purposes, when it met. Without this, progress would become almost impossible.

In the course of the plenary discussions at Gazzada many matters received attention. For example, these included, Do the members of the Church share in the priesthood of Christ or in its effects? *Who* were apostles? Are there two levels of apostolicity, namely, a quality of the Church and signs and criteria of this? The importance of the local Church in the context of apostolic succession was emphasised and the comment was made that the recent Anglican-Methodist Ordinal and its preface contained almost all that was essential for a doctrine of ministry. Once again, stress was laid on the theological and practical importance of the concept of substantial agreement. It seemed to some that at Gazzada there was not a confrontation on ministry between two Churches, but a confrontation between two or more theologies of ministry which cut across denominational lines. Gazzada was a time of hard and far-ranging work; a process of digesting the important papers provided; a process of subjecting argumentation to close scrutiny and to frank and intensive criticism. It was an essential workshop in which as work proceeded — and though this was not always easily discernible — the shape of a future document on ministry was already in the mould.

6. The Fifth Meeting at Canterbury: an Agreed Statement on Ministry and Ordination

The Anglican/Roman Catholic International Commission held its fifth meeting at St. Augustine's College, Canterbury from August 28th—September 6th 1973. The preliminary meeting aranged at Gazzada by the Commission took place at Poringland from 11th—15th June and was attended by eight members.[21]

What Gazzada had achieved was to establish a distinction between Christ's unique priesthood, the 'royal priesthood' of the people of God, and the rôle and function of ministers within and for the whole Church. This proved significant for the form and content of the statement on Ministry as did the emphasis on the apostolicity of the whole Church.

At the Commission's request, the proceedings at Poringland and Canterbury were summarised by the Rev. Colin Davey. This summary was printed as an Appendix to the Statement in order to give some indication, not only of the Commission's method and procedure, but also of the stages by which the conclusions were reached. For convenience, the section of the Appendix relating to the work is included as an account of both meetings: "At the

---

[21] Bishop Clark, Bishop McAdoo, Bishop Butler, Bishop Moorman, Fr. Tillard, Fr. Duprey, Mr. Charley and Mr. Davey.

end of the Gazzada meeting a provisional structure for a document on Ministry was agreed. Its three main sections were: Apostolic Succession, Priesthood, and Ordination. Subcommissions in Oxford, North America and Southern Africa were asked to write a draft for each of these, which would be circulated to all members of the Commission for comment. It was arranged that a Sub-committee would meet at Poringland, Norwich, from 11 to 15 June 1973 to take the draft sections and comments and from them to complete a draft document on the Ministry from which the Commission would begin its work at its next full meeting."

In preparation for the Poringland meeting Bishop Clark and Bishop Mc-Adoo each produced a paper incorporating the material received from the subcommissions and portions of 'The Ordained Ministry in Ecumenical Perspective' by the World Council of Churches Faith and Order Commission, the French Roman Catholic-Reformed 'Groupe des Dombes' Statement on the Minstry entitled 'Pour une réconciliation des ministères', and 'Lutherans and Catholics in Dialogue IV'. Members of the subcommittee had also been supplied with a paper by Fr. George Tavard, 'A Theological Approach to Ministerial Authority', Bishop Butler's recent articles on the ministry in 'The Tablet', Bishop Clark's summary in English of an article by Fr. Louis Bouyer, 'Ministère Ecclésiastique et Succession Apostolique', and a passage on the office of bishops from the new 'Directorium de Pastorali Ministerio Episcoporum'.

At Poringland it was agreed to start not from the pattern: Christ, the Church, and the ministry, but from where we are: two churches in which there are ministries and, within these, ordained ministry; to speak next of our rôle as ministers and then to give the theological and New Testament justification for this. Discussion focused on the function of *episcope* (oversight) and the rôle of the ordained minister "as a unifying figure, as coordinator, as judge, as director, as leader who serves". Ordination as a sacramental act was also debated and emphasis laid on 2 Cor. 3:5–6, where St. Paul writes that "our sufficiency is from God" – a reminder of "the mystery of ministry", and that our faith is "in the power and authority of Christ in the Spirit in and through the minister". The Poringland draft document included sections on 'Ministries in the life of the Church', 'The Co-ordinating Ministry', 'Vocation to the Special Ministry', and 'The Special Minister and the reconciling work of Christ'. This last section spoke of the president of the eucharist, ordination in the apostolic succession, and the way priestly terms came to be used of the minister.

The Poringland document was sent to all members of the International Commission for comment and criticism. In preparation for the full meeting at Canterbury from 28 August to 6 September 1973 they also received copies of the Report of the Joint Lutheran-Roman Catholic Study Commission on 'The Gospel and the Church', the third section of which is on 'The Gospel and the office of the Ministry in the Church'; the Report of the Joint Commission between the Roman Catholic Church and the World Methodist Council 1967–1970, section 6 of which is on Ministry; the Six Propositions with which the Roman Catholic International Theological Commission concluded their October 1970 report on 'The Priestly Ministry'; and the document on 'The

Ministerial Priesthood' issued by the Second General Assembly of the Roman Catholic Synod of Bishops in 1971.

The Poringland document was the starting-point for the discussions at Canterbury which began by considering what could be added to or subtracted from it. The Commission then agreed a draft outline for what was planned to be a biblically and historically informed document on the ministry which used and applied the material completed at Gazzada and Poringland.

The Outline contained an Introduction, followed by sections on Ministries in the Life of the Church (including reference to the New Testament and early Church situation), Ordained Ministry (*episcope*, New Testament images descriptive of the ordained ministry, vocation to holiness, word and sacrament, priesthood and priestly language), Ordination (its unrepeatability, ordination in the apostolic succession), and a Conclusion indicating the import of this agreement in doctrine on the question of the reconciliation of our respective ministries.

This outline was filled out by three drafters, and their draft was then scrutinized, debated, and revised by the full Commission. Out of this process the International Commission's Agreed Statement on the Doctrine of the Ministry emerged. Its conclusion emphasises that "agreement on the nature of Ministry is prior to the consideration of the mutual recognition of ministries." It recognizes "that we have not yet broached the wide-ranging problems of authority which may arise in any discussion of Ministry, nor the question of primacy." It considers however "that our consensus . . . offers a positive contribution to the reconciliation of our churches and of their ministries."[22]

The Agreed Statement on 'Ministry and Ordination' was widely welcomed by many, including the Secretary of the Methodist Conference and the Joint Secretaries of the United Reformed Church (in a letter to the 'Times' of 19th December 1973). They commended "the return to the New Testament" and found themselves "in substantial agreement with the understanding of the doctrine of the ministry there expressed." There were criticisms of course from conservatives on both sides and there were those who wished that there had been more thrust towards recognition of actual ministries, but on the whole it was recognised that the Commission was concerned with establishing more and more common ground between the Churches as an essential preliminary. This approach was clearly stated in paragraph 17: "We are fully aware of the issues raised by the judgment of the Roman Catholic Church on Anglican Orders. The development of the thinking in our two Communions regarding the nature of the Church and of the Ordained Ministry, as represented in our Statement, has, we consider, put these issues in a new context. Agreement on the nature of Ministry is prior to the consideration of the mutual recognition of ministries. What we have to say represents the consensus of the Commission on essential matters where it considers that doctrine admits no divergence."

[22] Ministry and Ordination: A Statement on the Doctrine of the Ministry Agreed by the Anglican-Roman Catholic International Commission, Canterbury 1973 (London 1973), pp. 17–20.

The methodology of the Statement is the same as that on the Eucharist, namely, to express an understanding of the fact of Ministry "which is consonant with biblical teaching and with the traditions of our common inheritance" (Canterbury Statement [1]) and to achieve a substantial agreement: "We consider that our consensus, on questions where agreement is indispensable for unity, offers a positive contribution to the reconciliation of our Churches and of their ministries." (17). Such substantial agreement allows for "differences of emphasis within our two traditions, yet we believe that in what we have said here both Anglican and Roman Catholic will recognise their own faith" (Preface).

Detailed evaluations of the Agreed Statement have been published by individual members of the Commission covering most aspects of its structure and content.[23] Perhaps, therefore, but one matter bearing on Anglican/Roman Catholic relations requires re-emphasising. The final paragraph, pointing out that agreement about the nature of ministry is an indispensable prelude to the mutual recognition of ministries, draws attention to the development of thinking on the subject in the Churches and asserts that this development is represented in the Agreed Statement. In other words, if it can be shown that the presuppositions of 'Apostolicae Curae' are no longer those of the Roman Catholic Church today then, in fact and to quote the Canterbury Statement, the issues are indeed "put in a new context". The view, commonly held in 1896, that the essence of priesthood is the emphasis on a sacrificing priesthood, that *sacerdotium* means sacrificing priesthood and is the equivalent of ministry, never had support from the ordinals and ordination forms which did not mention sacerdotal powers,[24] and it differs from patristic theologies of priesthood. That there has been development (towards the earlier view) since then, can be seen from a study of Vatican II's 'Decree on the Ministry and Life of Priests' (described in an introduction as enlarging 'our vision of the priesthood: no longer is the focus almost exclusively on the priest as the "cult man"').[25] In the Agreed Statement, as a commentator put it, there is a "developed theology" and "it is not so much that new ideas are introduced; rather, traditional ideas are related to a new balance."[26] A similar developed theology may be seen in the Synod of Bishops' 'The Ministerial Priesthood' (1971), especially, for example, I (4): "Among the various charisms and services, the priestly ministry of the New Testament, which continues Christ's function as mediator, and which in essence and not merely in degree is distinct from the common priesthood of all the faithful (cp. L G 10) alone perpetuates the essential work of the Apostles: by

[23] E. g. The Canterbury Statement, With an Introduction and Commentary (Catholic Information Office, 1973) by ALAN C. CLARK; 'Modern Ecumenical Documents on the Ministry (London 1975)', Foreword by ALAN C. CLARK and Introduction by H. R. McADOO; Agreement on the Doctrine of Ministry' (Grove Booklet No. 22, 1973) by JULIAN W. CHARLEY; A Step Forward: the Canterbury Agreement on Ministry (Lumen Vitae, Vol. XXIX, 1974, No. 2) by J. M. R. TILLARD O.P.

[24] Cp. Stewards of the Lord (London 1970), by JOHN JAY HUGHES, pp. 23—25.

[25] The Documents of Vatican II (1967 ed. WALTER M. ABBOT S.J.), pp. 526—527.

[26] The Month (January 1974), p. 436.

effectively proclaiming the Gospel, by gathering together and leading the community, by remitting sins, and especially by celebrating the Eucharist, it makes Christ, the head of the community, present in the exercise of his work of redeeming mankind and glorifying God perfectly."[27] Similarly, the report of the Roman Catholic International Theological Commission on 'The Priestly Ministry', dated 10th October 1970, ends with six propositions which testify to this development of thinking about priesthood.[28] That this development represented in the Agreed Statement is a convergent one is clear from a comparison of the documents mentioned with the 'Reply of the English Archbishops' (1897) and with, for example, the section on priesthood in the report on 'Renewal in Ministry' to the Lambeth Conference of 1968.[29] It may well be that by its rigorous process of seeking for common ground and agreement at the level of faith, within which there can be both unity and diversity, the Anglican/Roman Catholic Commission is doing a service and making a contribution which will be creative in the future.

7. The Agreed Statement on Authority in the Church (Venice 1976)

A diary of the development of the work on the theme of Authority

The origins of the Venice Statement on 'Authority in the Church' (1976) are to be traced far back in the meetings and discussions of the Commission. Although "the question of authority, its nature, exercise, and implications" constituted the final part of the Commission's briefing as set out in the 'Malta Report' (22), it was inevitable that aspects of this theme would constantly make themselves felt throughout the dialogue.

This will be clear from the following account of the course of the Anglican/Roman Catholic Commission's discussion on authority. It has been compiled by the Reverend Christopher Hill of the Archbishop of Canterbury's Counsellors on Foreign Relations, who is also the Commission's Anglican Secretary and to whom I am indebted for the use of the material compiled as an *aide-mémoire*:

At the first meeting of the Anglican/Roman Catholic International Commission at Windsor in the January of 1970 a decision was taken to divide the Commission for part of the time into three groups, one of them concentrating on the question of 'Church and Authority' while the other two groups dealt with 'Church and Ministry' and 'Church and Eucharist.'

Papers providing a basis for an exploration of agreements and differences on the question of authority were provided by Bishop Christopher Butler, OSB,

---

[27] Published by the Vatican Polyglot Press 1971.
[28] Published in Editions du Cerf (Paris 1971).
[29] The Lambeth Conference 1968: Resolutions and Reports (London and New York 1968), pp. 100–102.

Bishop Knapp-Fisher and Dean Henry Chadwick. (These papers had been commissioned at an informal meeting in Dublin during May 1969 prior to the final
formation of the Commission itself.) Bishop Butler concentrated on the
question of the location and quality of 'official' authority in the Church
(presupposing its existence alongside that of expertise and charisma). In the
Roman Catholic view there were occasions when the formulations of ecumenical
councils or popes might not be discarded as false, Nicea's 'consubstantial' being
an example. Though such a decision was *non ex consensu*, it was nevertheless the
articulation of the mind of the whole Church. Bishop Knapp-Fisher (with a
Roman Catholic consultant, Fr. Edmund Hill, OP) examined the question of
'Fundamentals.' Areas of agreement and disagreement were explored in relation
to the problems of: 'Revelation and Faith,' 'Scripture and Tradition,' 'Church
and Authority' and finally 'Dogmatic Definitions and Comprehensiveness.'
Dean Chadwick set the specific question of Christian authority in the wider
context of the current debate on authority in general and (following Max
Weber) he discerned patriarchal, functional and charismatic categories. An
antithesis between evidence and authority as the ground of belief was eschewed
both in the general and more specifically Christian discussion. Nevertheless
there were differing emphases between Anglican and Roman Catholic exercises
of authority; a preference for a diffuse 'indefectibility' on the one hand, and a
unitative organ of 'infallibility' on the other.

After discussion in the sub-commission a draft schema on 'Church and
Authority' was presented to the full Commission. Significantly this schema was
divided into two major sections: 'Church as Koinonia' and 'Koinonia and
Authority.' All three sub-commissions were asked to prepare fuller drafts in
preparation for the next meeting of the Commission in Venice during the
September of the same year.

Bishop Butler and Dean Chadwick were responsible for convening the
'Church and Authority' sub-commission which was to be based in the United
Kingdom. It was agreed that all the sub-commissions might co-opt help from
outside the Commission itself and, acting as Secretary, Dr. John Halliburton
encouraged a number of theologians to contribute short papers on the themes of
the Windsor draft. These included a re-examination of the concept of
infallibility by Fr. Edward Yarnold, SJ.

At Venice where the Commission's Second Meeting took place, the
Windsor schema on 'Church and Authority' was discussed at length, elaborated
and amended. The resulting Venice paper on 'Church and Authority' spoke
jointly of the Church as the People of God, a community, entrusted with the
task of preserving and witnessing to the doctrine and fellowship of the apostles.
The local churches shared the same word and sacraments and were constituted a
single universal family. The chief bond of unity, both local and universal, was
the apostolic ministry of oversight. Apostolic faith, sacraments, and ministry
were thus deemed to be constitutive of the Church. Authority was to be located
in the tradition of the Christian community of which the Scriptures were the
supreme document. Creeds and councils required both consonance with Scripture and reception by the Church. Ecumenical councils could not be reversed.

Bishops were the normal teachers in the Church and their president endowed with a special dignity.

There then followed two views of the *koinonia* and of authority in the Church. On the Roman Catholic side it was noted that Vatican II implied that perfect communion was preserved in communion with Rome. The episcopate exercised its responsibility in collegial fashion, either collectively, or through its president. When it did so in a decision formulating the once for all revelation it was endowed with the charisma called 'infallibility.' On the Anglican side there was no claim to be the unique embodiment of the Church. Anglicans shared with Roman Catholics the same fundamental doctrines, papal authority excepted. A Roman primacy of service was acceptable but the decrees of Vatican I and the application of the petrine texts to the bishops of Rome were not. Indefectibility was preferred to infallibility, the Church being granted continual correction, safeguarded from final departure from the truth by the Spirit. The proposed text of the Lambeth Conference of 1968 was quoted to the effect that it was fitting that the bishop of Rome should preside over the whole College of Bishops. Hesitations remained over the pragmatic exercise of papal authority but the papal office could be not only a sign of unity but a guarantee of diversity.

The sub-commission spoke with one voice again to note the primacy of Scripture as a possible basis of a hierarchy of truths. Even differences in the interpretation of papal authority might not necessarily be a barrier to communion as an interim stage towards union.

The decision was taken at Venice that it would be in the interest of Anglican/Roman Catholic relations to publish all three sub-commission drafts, in order to show the stage the Commission's work had reached and to invite comments and criticism. After the agreement of the respective authorities, this was done simultaneously in 'Theology,' the 'Clergy Review' and 'One in Christ,' during February 1971.

It was also decided that the pattern of the Commission's future work would be to take one of the three subjects at a time, beginning with 'Church and Eucharist.' After preparatory work by individuals, a sub-commission in the United Kingdom and National Commissions in South Africa and North America, the Third Meeting of the Commission at Windsor, in September 1971, completed 'An Agreed Statement on Eucharistic Doctrine.' This was published in the December of that year. At the conclusion of the Windsor meeting, plans were made for continuing the Commission's work on 'Church and Ministry.' Papers were commissioned and sub-commissions convened in North America and the United Kingdom. The Fourth Meeting of the Commission took place at Gazzada near Milan in August–September 1972. At Gazzada the shape of the existing work was reviewed. United Kingdom, North American and South Afrcan groups were charged with the preparation of material, and a further sub-commission was asked to meet in the United Kingdom to complete a draft document from this material in preparation for the next full meeting of the Commission at Canterbury, August–September 1973. It was at Canterbury that the Statement on Ministry and Ordination was completed and published in December of the same year.

While a full discussion of the question of 'Church and Authority' had been postponed since the Venice meeting of 1970, the issues raised by it were never very far away from the surface in the discussions on the doctrine of the Eucharist and Ministry. Furthermore the methodology of the Commission had been established, a methodology which began by an examination of the present faith of the two traditions. The Commission had also learnt more of the value of the theological concepts of *koinonia* and *episcope*. These would be invaluable tools in the unravelling of the most difficult of the problems dividing the two traditions: papal primacy and infallibility.

In the following year (1974) no less than 30 papers and memoranda were circulated, from individuals, sub-commissions and national commissions, as background material in preparation for the assault on 'Church and Authority.' The English Anglican/Roman Catholic Commission offered a paper on 'Infallibility and Indefectibility'; the former seen as an aspect of the latter. The South African Anglican/Roman Catholic Commission prepared material on the 'Authority of the Bible' and the 'Redemptive Authority of Christ.' An Oxford sub-commission convened by Dr. Halliburton and Fr. Yarnold, SJ, submitted work on 'Ecclesiology in the light of Vatican II.' The Church was seen as a "mystery" as fully present in its local manifestation as in the assembly of local churches in communions. Though the bishop of a local church could not act without reference to other local churches, this did not mean that the unity of local churches implied a uniformity of devotion, liturgy or theology.

Individual papers, by no means prepared exclusively by members of the Commission, covered a further wide area. This included the treatment of Scripture and ecumenical councils in Anglican thought, the dogmatic decrees on Revelation ('Dei Verbi') and the Church ('Lumen Gentium') of the Second Vatican Council and Magisterium in the Early Church, schism, the Petrine texts, and *koinonia* as a basis of ecclesiology.

Amongst individual papers those by Fr. Herbert Ryan, SJ and Fr. Jean Tillard, OP were of particular significance. Fr. Ryan had been asked at Canterbury to write on the dogmatic decree on the Church ('Pastor Eternus') of the First Vatican Council's ascription of an "ordinary, truly episcopal and immediate power of jurisdiction" to the pope. This was then re-interpreted as essentially affirming that the question of a primacy of jurisdiction was to be answered in terms of the example of Peter. A final speculation was added as to how this might be embodied in a re-united Church, the model of "compulsory arbitration" being suggested as valuable. Fr. Tillard's paper was concerned with the *sensus fidelium*, which was not to be understood simply in terms of popular faith or devotion, nor reduced to conceptual categories. It was rather to be understood as the Word received and lived in the Church. The Magisterium was not exempt from participation in this process; its function, through 'osmosis,' was to serve the purpose of the Word by drawing out the objective content of the insights of the People of God.

The Commission also received the March 1974 Joint Statement of the United States Lutheran-Catholic Dialogue 'Papal Primacy and the Universal Church.' This spoke of the possibility, in a united Church, of the recognition of a "Petrine function" of the bishop of Rome in relation to the unity of the whole Church.

The sixth meeting of the Commission took place at Rocco di Papa, Grottaferrata, near Rome, during August–September 1974. The Commission divided itself into three sub-commissions. The first sub-commission, under the chairmanship of Fr. Yarnold, was to deal with 'New Testament and Authority:' the second, under Bishop Vogel, 'Ecclesiology and *Koinonia*;' the third under Dean Chadwick, 'Infallibility and Indefectibility.' At the end of the meeting, and after the cross-fertilization of comments in full session, the sub-commission produced three (incomplete) working papers.

The first sub-commission began with an extended preface defining the nature of authority. It then went on the speak of Christian authority in terms of the absolute claim of God upon man, instancing this from the Old Testament, but more particularly the perfect example of God's call and man's response in Jesus Christ. Though his obedience and exaltation, Christ had been made Lord of the Church. The Spirit was seen as giving particular gifts for the building up of the Church and the discernment to recognise them. From the beginning it was also the Church's responsibility to discern the mind of Christ, fidelity to whom required obedience to the apostolic tradition and the necessity of its identification in the written records which became the New Testament. Scripture was therefore recognised as both authoritative and normative. Its contemporary interpretation was the continuing responsibility of the whole community through the interaction of teachers, those in pastoral authority and the *sensus fidelium*.

The second sub-commission began with the assertion that the Holy Spirit constituted the *koinonia*, equipped the community for mission and safeguarded its faithfulness to the truth. Authentic Christian life disclosed the authoritative claim of Christ on man. Particular authority was given by the Spirit through ordination for the building up of the Body of Christ. The bishop's pastoral authority entailed the power of intervention for the sake of the community; however, all ministerial authority was to be exercised in mutual responsibility and interdependence. Even so the perception of the mind of Christ did not pertain exclusively to the ordained ministry, but rather to an interaction of all the members of the Church. There was a discernment of the insights of the whole community on the part of the ordained ministry and a response to, and assessment of, this discernment by the community.

The third sub-commission gave their working paper subtitles, beginning with 'Permanence in the Truth.' There was recognition that the Church was constantly called to penitence and reform under the Word but that the Spirit ensured that the Church would never cease to be the sign of salvation. There had been and might be, situations where the Church's chief pastors, in interaction with the whole community, were obliged to give definitive answers to decisive questions. Such definitive answers required the gift of discernment, as did their reception. There followed a treatment of 'Unity and Diversity' which repeated the Venice suggestion that the papal office might not only be a sign of the former but also a guarantee of the latter. Then came the sub-commission's historical reflection on 'The Roman Primacy.' The Gnostic crisis led to a Catholic stress on the testimony of the apostolic sees; among them a special position was occupied by the Church of Rome through its relation to the apostles Peter and Paul. In later centuries the principal basis of the primacy was this recognition of Rome as the 'apostolic see' *par excellence*. The further development of the primacy based upon the claim of the Roman bishops to be the successors of the apostle Peter, on the basis of the Petrine texts, was subsequently rejected by the churches of the Reformation. Anglicans were asked what was the maximum exercise and interpretation of the Roman primacy they would find acceptable and Roman Catholics the minimum. The fundamental question was that of the basis of any common recognition of the Roman primacy. The Anglicans suggested as an answer a view of the primacy as arising *divina providencia*. There followed a note on the difficulties concerning papal primacy and infallibility as Anglicans saw them which ended by asking whether a primacy *de jure divino* was sufficiently high in the "hierarchy of truths" to prevent unity. Complementary to this were two Roman Catholic questions addressed to Anglicans. The first asked whether there was an authority in the Church which, in order to ensure permanence in the truth, could take binding decisions. The second asked for reaction to the statement that the supreme authority in the Church resided in the episcopal college, and could exercise its authority either collectively or through its president.

After discussion on the work of the three sub-commissions it was decided that four further papers were required. Bishop Knapp-Fisher agreed to ask the South African Anglican/Roman Catholic Commission to prepare material on authority in the New Testament, Fr. Tillard agreed to investigate primacy, Dean Chadwick infallibility, and Fr. Duprey to ask Professor G. Alberigo (of the University of Bologna) to submit a study on the theology of jurisdiction. It was also agreed to hold an informal meeting at the turn of the year to reflect upon existing material, and to revise and consolidate the work of Grottaferrata (in particular the working papers of the first and second sub-commissions which possessed a continuity of style and methodology with the two previous Agreed Statements). The Commission further agreed to hold a formal sub-commission meeting, in conjunction with the steering committee, in June of the following year to continue the work begun at Grottaferrata. It was felt that a serious treatment of the local church and its bishop was essential if the question of councils, primacy and infallibility was to be seen in perspective. This interim meeting would, hopefully, be able to offer the full Commission a composite and extended draft dealing with the question of authority up to, but not including, the question of primacy and infallibility, thus leaving the next meeting of the full Commission to grasp this nettle.

In the December of 1974 the informal meeting to consolidate the material of the previous autumn duly took place at the home of Bishop Alan Clark at Poringland, Norwich. There thus emerged a document of four paragraphs incorporating the major insights and concerns of subcommission one of the Grottaferrata meeting (but excluding its prefatory definition of authority). The Poringland draft spoke of the Lordship of Christ, the authority of Scripture, the authority of the ordained ministry and the inadequacy of all human authority. These themes will be recognised as those of paras. 1, 2, 5 and 7 of the present document and the actual text of the Poringland draft is indeed substantially to be found in all but paragraph 5.

In the following June the more formal sub-commission/steering committee met in London to attempt a continuation of the extant material. The work of the South African ARC on 'Authority in the New Testament' had been circulated by this time, as had a memorandum on 'The Nature and Exercise of Authority in the Church: Notes on the implications of Anglican formularies and theology' by Bishop Henry McAdoo. At this St. Katharine's meeting (the group met at the Royal Foundation of St. Katharine, London,) the Poringland draft was taken as a beginning. Nevertheless important paragraphs on the authority of the Christian community vis à vis the world, the authority within the Church of holiness and special gifts, and of the *sensus fidelium* were interpolated and the Poringland paragraph on the authority of the ordained ministry replaced. (The paragraph on holiness and special gifts was entirely new but the remainder of this material owed not a little to the draft of the second sub-commission at Grottaferrata.) Finally the logic of the document was taken further by the addition of two paragraphs concerning the *koinonia* among local churches (reflecting the work of the Oxford sub-commission of 1974) and its expression in councils and collegiality. Paragraphs 3, 4, 5, 8 and 9 of Venice have their origin at this meeting, by the end of which there was a draft of nine paragraphs substantially identical to those finally accepted as Venice 1–9. During the course of this meeting too the outline and shape and logic of the treatment of authority eventually seen at Venice began to emerge with some degree of clarity. This pattern is now seen in a more developed form in the section and paragraph headings in the Venice Statement.

The Commission met in full at Oxford during August–September 1975 with the St. Katharine's draft before it, and the papers requested at Grottaferrata. Professor Alberigo's study of jurisdiction made the point that the term was far from univocal; its origin was to be found in the pastoral and sacramental realm. Fr. Tillard contributed a stimulating paper entitled "The Horizon of the 'Primacy' of the Bishop of Rome." The First Vatican Council's clear teaching that the "truly episcopal" jurisdiction of the pope in no way conflicted with the jurisdiction of the local bishop was seen as having fundamental significance. There was an equivocation in the use of the term *potestas ordinaria*. An understanding of primacy had to begin with the local rather than universal Church, For the ministry of the local bishop to be authentically Catholic, both in relation to his own Church and the universal Church, communion with the *centrum unitatis* was necessary. Thus the unique episcopal function of the *prôtos* of the episcopal college was to guarantee the catholicity of all the local churches. Dean Chadwick's memorandum 'Truth and Authority' delineated truth in terms of the salvation of man in Christ. The organs of authority were primarily the Scriptures, the creeds, the liturgy, the ministry, and the common consensus of all believers. The functioning of authority in the early church was to be seen in synodical and conciliar activity, culminating in general councils duly received by

the church and the great sees of apostolic foundation, pre-eminently Rome.
(The petrine texts were however never universally accepted as the basis of this
primacy.) A consequence of the modern definition of infallibility might well be
the diminution of "ordinary magisterium." The Anglican tradition agreed with
Rome that the Church could not err fundamentally, but thought of indefectibility rather than infallibility, and of a multiple authority. Infallibility needed to
be disentangled and demythologised; it affirmed the objective character of divine
truth and a gift enabling the bishop of Rome, under certain strict conditions, to
speak in such a way as not to formulate positive truth in a way would be permanently disastrous.

The Commission scrutinised the St. Katharine's document but refrained
from a detailed revision, as it was not yet complete. There was also considerable
discussion of the major papers on primacy and infallibility. It was resolved that
the Commission should work in two groups: one under the chairmanship of
Bishop McAdoo to pursue the question of infallibility with the theme 'Truth';
the other under the chairmanship of Bishop Clark to do the same for primacy
with the theme 'Unity'. The 'Unity' sub-commission was asked to continue the
line of thinking of the St. Katharine's draft, though its membership was not co-
terminous with that group.

The 'Unity' sub-commission added three paragraphs to the St. Katharine's
draft. These dealt with the emergence of primacy as a particular form of *episcope,*
the responsibility of the primate and the context of the particular primacy of
Rome, and the historical pre-eminence of the see of Rome and its ancient and
modern theological interpretation. This material is substantially identified with
Venice paragraphs 10, 11 and 12.

The 'Truth' sub-commission envisaged their material as following that of
the eventual work of the 'Unity' group which was itself to continue the St.
Katharine's draft. After reference to the full Commission at various stages, a
'Truth' document of twelve paragraphs emerged. It was declared that the
Church would endure and have the continual duty of guarding and proclaiming
the saving truth of Christ. In formulating the Church's faith, the Scriptures and
their summary in the creeds were basic, together with the testimony of prayer
and worship, preaching, councils and the consensus of the faithful. The Church
had the task of interpreting the Gospel in contemporary terms and looking back
through the tradition to the witness to Christ in the Scriptures. Such renewal
and reformation was itself historically dated, and yet the Church had so committed itself to some formulations that they had become an integral part of its
faith. This did not imply, however, that churches would be free from error. The
formation of the canon of the New Testament indicated the Church's awareness
of its ability to make permanent judgements, the test of which was reception.
Anglicans and Roman Catholics had used different language to designate
irrevocable positions: 'fundamentals' and '*de fide*' doctrines. In spite of the
wider field of the latter, there was deep agreement and much in common. The
"hierarchy of truths" indicated that some '*de fide*' doctrines were closer to the
christological centre of the faith than others, and further theological investigation was required here in relation to the Marian dogmas and papal authority.

Before the separation of East and West the bishop of Rome was seen as bearing a special responsibility in the universal Church in regard to the ratification of general councils. But in a disunited Church this role, which implied a power of judgement, in abnormal circumstances even without a council, was not clearly seen. The Roman Catholic Church taught that such an exercise of authority was legitimate in view of his headship of the episcopal college, but only in the light of the *sensus fidelium*, in consultation with brother bishops, and in conformity to Scripture. It was not a matter of personal inspiration but protection from error by the Holy Spirit. Anglicans still had grave difficulties concerning such an exercise of authority but the affirmation of the objective character of divine truth was a common reality. The work of the sub-commission was much indebted to Dean Chadwick's paper. This material was later re-worked but forms the basis of Venice 15 and 16.

At the conclusion of the Oxford meeting it was felt that both sub-commissions had reached the very brink of the problem of primacy and infallibility. As well as detailed discussion of the drafts, there was an extended debate on the work for the coming year, both sub-commissions having offered schemas for further work. Two areas needed further clarification: Anglican ecclesiology and papal primacy, and the significance of such a primacy as an object of faith. Professor Eugene Fairweather accepted a Canadian responsibility for the former question and Fr. Tavard the latter. It was decided that the three documents before the Commission (the St. Katharine's, 'Unity', and 'Truth' drafts) should be examined with a view to their being put together as a composite whole. The 'Unity' draft followed logically from the St. Katharine's draft in any case, but the style and method of the 'Truth' draft differed significantly from both. A suggestion of an informal meeting similar to the one held the previous year, was accepted. Also, following the pattern of the previous year, it was decided to hold a larger and more formal sub-commission meeting, in conjunction with the steering committee, in the early summer. It was hoped that this gathering could take the Commission over the brink by continuing the work of the two Oxford sub-commissions and offer its next plenary meeting a complete draft on authority.

During February 1976 a small group met (at Poringland again) to attempt the first of the tasks requested at the Oxford meeting: the welding of the "Truth" material on to the St. Katharine's/'Unity' document. To achieve homogeneity of style it was felt right to continue the logic of the St. Katharine's/'Unity' material, but to do so in the light of the 'Truth' document and to incorporate the latter's insights. (A member of the 'Truth' sub-commission was included in the group at Poringland.) The result was a continuation of six paragraphs, which described the exercise of authority in matters of faith in the *koinonia* of the churches. The continuation first emphasised the general point of the centrality of *koinonia* in truth. There followed two paragraphs leading on from this to an understanding of tradition as 'memory' and the prophetic interpretation of the unchanging truth in comtemporary terms. Here there was a direct dependence on themes (and to a lesser degree the actual text) of the earlier 'Truth' draft. Next came a statement of the consequential commitment of the Church to decisions of permanent value and again 'Truth' themes and material

17 Rome and the Anglicans

were incorporated. The logic then led to the particular historical responsibility of the bishop of Rome in this process, both in the endorsement of councils and in personal intervention. Finally there was a treatment of the safeguards of truth in the interaction of the *sensus fidelium* and the bishops (in respect of their responsibility for discernment) which gave ecumenical councils a unique quality and authority. The work of the Poringland sub-commission can now be substantially seen in Venice paragraphs 13, 15, 16, 17. Though there was a paragraph corresponding to Venice 18, this was later to be almost completely re-drafted.

The sub-commission/steering committee met at Hengrave Hall, Bury St. Edmunds, during the following June with the intention of attempting to draft provisional material which would complete the Poringland document. First of all, however, there was some revision of the extant material in the light of comment and criticism from other members of the Commission and in particular Bishop McAdoo, Bishop Vogel and Fr. Tavard. Three new paragraphs were then added concerning primatial authority, its collegial context and its interaction with conciliar authority. Material from these paragraphs can be seen as Venice 20, 21 and 22. Finally a concluding paragraph was drafted, spelling out the implications of the whole schema, which ran coherently from what is now Venice 1–22 though major revision was indeed still to take place.

The Venice meeting of August/September 1976 was finally to produce the Agreed Statement 'Authority in the Church'. Papers were received from Dr. Eric Jay through the Canadian Anglican/Roman Catholic Commission and from Fr. Tavard. Dr. Jay's paper outlined historical Anglican (theoretical) acceptancy of a Roman Primacy. Fr. Tavard's paper argued against regarding Primacy and Infallibility as objects of faith. The Hengrave draft was, however, the principal basis of the Commission's discussions. It was decided to concentrate on the newer material which had been less worked over by the whole Commission, that is to say the material which now stands as Venice paragraphs 13–23.

There was considerable re-drafting. A sub-commission re-introduced certain themes from the Oxford 'Truth' Sub-Commission, resulting in a fuller treatment of 'The expression of truth', 'The communication of truth' and 'Conciliar authority' (paras. 14, 15 and 16) and the Hengrave order was somewhat re-arranged. Venice paragraph 14 represents inserted Oxford material which had no place in the Hengrave draft at all. The Hengrave darft was also seen to be inadequate in its treament of the 'indefectibility' of the Church and of Ecumenical Councils and the present paragraphs 18 and 19 represent a major re-writing of the earlier material. Another sub-commission worked on this material in no less than three re-drafts of the Hengrave material all of which was scrutinized and criticised by the full Commission as work proceeded. In constructing the present Venice paragraph 18 two particular concerns were stressed: the danger of obscuring the ordinary authority of the Church by concentration on extra-ordinary situations; the Spirit's maintenance of the Church in the truth, in spite of acknowledged error in official teaching, through the interaction of bishops and people. A Hengrave footnote on the Anglican understanding of a balanced authority was also moved to this point. The Hengrave material was then considerably expanded into a separate paragraph now seen as 19, and to which another footnote was added. Like other parts of this text this paragraph was intended to be read as a whole. The Commission wanted to avoid two extremes: that an ecumenical definition had no authority subsequent to reception; and that, on the contrary, a Council owed nothing to reception. The Commission did not define the nature of an ecumenical Council, but made clear that the unique authority it spoke of could only be ascribed to those councils designated ecumenical.

A further sub-commission re-wrote the Hengrave material on 'The exercise of primatial authority', 'Primatial authority and diversity' and 'The balance of authority' now seen as 20, 21 and 22. Although the Hengrave draft had a conclusion this was not substantially taken up by yet another sub-commission which drafted the material now seen as Venice paragraph 23 'Universal primacy' and the subsequent paragraphs 24—26. Paragraph 23 was thought to sum up carefully the drift of the whole Agreed Statement. Paragraph 24 was introduced to give some recognition to the traditional emotive problems the Roman Primacy gave rise to for Anglicans. It also indicates reasons for thinking the problems less serious than has been thought previously. Paragraph 25 says something of the method of the Commission and the final paragraph asks for a positive assessment of the three Agreed Statements and a consequent moving to the next stage towards unity. At the same time as the theological drafting two editors worked through the text of the whole Agreed Statement with a view to the eradication of verbal and grammatical infelicities and the achievement of a homogenity of style. The Statement was unanimously agreed and the texts of the Co-Chairmen's Preface approved.

It was recognised that in ARCIC's Final Report something more would have to be said about the problems raised in paragraph 24, and that at that stage the Commission would try to elaborate those aspects of the Statement which proved to be less clear or less adequate than was originally thought. It is hoped that this Final Report will be completed by 1981.

(Conclusion of the Rev. C. J. Hill's *aide-mémoire* [cf. above pp. 243—253])

Following the publication of the Venice Statement on 'Authority in the Church' (1976), two events happened, both of which had bearing on the relations between the two Communions and on the work of the International Commission.

The 'Common Declaration' (1977) of Pope Paul VI and Archbishop Donald Coggan of Canterbury

The first of these was the meeting between Pope Paul VI and the Archbishop of Canterbury in the Vatican on April 28th, 1977. In the course of his greeting to the Archbishop and his party, the Pope said: "The history of relations between the Catholic Church and the Anglican Communion has been

17*

marked by the staunch witness of such men as Charles Brent, Lord Halifax, William Temple and George Bell among the Anglicans; and Abbé Portal, Dom Lambert Beauduin, Cardinal Mercier and Cardinal Bea among the Catholics. The pace of this movement has quickened marvellously in recent years, so that these words of hope 'The Anglican Church united not absorbed' are no longer a mere dream.''[30] These words, clinched by the use of the title of Beauduin's paper at Malines a half century before, seemed to sum up the not inconsiderable change in the climate since that time.

In his reply, the Archbishop referred to this growing warmth in Anglican/ Roman Catholic relations demonstrated by the visits of Archbishop Fisher to Pope John XXIII and of his own predecessor, Archbishop Ramsey in 1966, from which the impetus for the serious dialogue had chiefly derived. The Archbishop specifically mentioned the three Agreed Statements and the work of the Commission, and he invited Pope Paul to send observers to the Lambeth Conference of 1978.

After protracted and private discussions, the Pope and the Archbishop signed on the next day their 'Common Declaration'.

Those who see a *detection of themes* as the most important element in the evaluation of relationships which span a couple of centuries, will find it significant that certain themes re-emerge in this latest document. Among them is that of convergence which, as we have seen, had to fight its way into theological respectability but now appears to have received the accolade of a Pope and a Primate (Common Declaration, 3). Furthermore, there is the emphasis on the common trinitarian faith, the common baptism, the sharing in the Scriptures, Creeds, and Chalcedonian definition, together with the common inheritance in patristics and spirituality (2). Significantly again, this is simply lifted from the 'Malta Report' (3), just as the use of the term "serious dialogue" refers back to the 'Common Declaration' of 1966. Mixed marriages appear once more, and still as an obstacle (6) and this is disappointing since this blockage (which in its acute and juristic aspect is of twentieth-century origin) could be removed more easily than any other. Reference is also made to the fact that "serious obstacles remain both of the past and recent origin." (9). The last words are taken to mean that the ordination of women to the priesthood in some Anglican Provinces has introduced a new hold-up in possible movement towards unity. The debate on this goes on, with both sides receiving support within the Anglican Communion, and the matter was the subject of an irenic resolution (21) at the Lambeth Conference of 1978. While disagreement stopped short of division it is clear that the matter will not just go away, even for the Roman Catholic Church. The respectful presentation of the case by Sister Theresa Kane during the visit of Pope John Paul II to the United States in 1979 was only the tip of this particular iceberg in the American situation. No doubt, such visits on such a scale do not allow for the possibility of real dialogue with the result that, while America heard the Pope, the Pope did not really have the opportunity of hearing America.

---

[30] All quotations referring to this visit are from 'Pilgrim for Unity' (C.T.S. and S.P.C.K., London 1977), unless otherwise noted.

The 'Common Declaration' of 1977 made specific mention of the work of ARCIC and took a small but real step forward when, referring to the Windsor, Canterbury and Venice Statements, it said: "We now recommend that the work it has begun be pursued, through the procedures appropriate to our respective Communions, so that both of them may be led along the path towards unity.

The moment will shortly come when the respective Authorities must evaluate the conclusions." (4).

This process has been going on in the responses received by the Commission from many Roman Catholic episcopal conferences. These have been generally favourable though numerous matters for comment and criticism have been raised. Anglican General Synods around the world have likewise considered the statements and while criticising various points have all concluded that the documents are consonant with the faith of the Church and constitute ground for a closer inter-Church relationship. The Lambeth Conference endorsed this standpoint in 1978. Nevertheless, response on a global scale on behalf on both Communions is the necessary next step and one which may not be long delayed.

Finally, the 'Common Declaration' (9) raised the matter of intercommunion, having pointed out that our Christian witness to the world is hindered by the fact that "between us communion remains imperfect" though our divisions "do not close all roads we may travel together." Noting that there is a desire for a closer relationship on the part of many, the Declaration looks ahead to a time of movement: "Many in both Communions are asking themselves whether they have a common faith sufficient to be translated into communion of life, worship and mission. Only the communions themselves through their pastoral authorities can give that answer."

The question was put to the Churches by the Archbishop of Canterbury when, during the visit to Rome, he preached at the American church, St. Paul's-within-the-Walls, and asked "Has not the time now arrived when we have reached such a measure of agreement on so many of the fundamentals of the Gospel that a relationship of shared communion can be encouraged by the leadership of both our Churches?"

That question and the shape of an answer to it are the real agenda for the separated Churches as we enter the eighties of the twentieth century.

The Lambeth Conference of 1978

The second event which had its bearing on Anglican/Roman Catholic relations and on the work of ARCIC was of course the eleventh Lambeth Conference held at Canterbury in 1978. Resolutions 33 and 34 dealt specifically with the Anglican-Roman Catholic International Commission and with Anglican-Roman Catholic marriages respectively.[31] Resolution 33 deserves quotation in full because, having commended ARCIC's work to the active consideration of

---

[31] The Report of the Lambeth Conference 1978 (CIO Publishing, London 1978), pp. 49–51.

the whole Communion and having invited the Commission to provide "further explication of the Agreed Statements in consideration of responses received by them," it avers that:

a) in them "we can recognise the faith of our Church," and
b) that they provide a basis for a changed inter-Church relationship, and
c) recalls the Malta Report's concept of unity by stages.

The Resolution reads as follows:

"The Conference:
1. welcomes the work of the Anglican-Roman Catholic International Commission which was set up jointly by the Lambeth Conference of 1968 and by the Vatican Secretariat for Promoting Christian Unity;
2. recognizes in the three Agreed Statements of this Commission a solid achievement, one in which we can recognize the faith of our Church, and hopes that they will provide a basis for sacramental sharing between our two Communions if and when the finished Statements are approved by the respective authorities of our Communions;
3. invites ARCIC to provide further explication of the Agreed Statements in consideration of responses received by them;
4. commends to the appropriate authorities in each Communion further consideration of the implications of the Agreed Statements in the light of the report of the Joint Preparatory Commission (the Malta Report received by the Lambeth Conference 1968 – see p. 134 of its report), with a view to bringing about a closer charing between our two Communions in life, worship and mission;
5. asks the Secretary General of the Anglican Consultative Council to bring this resolution to the attention of the various synods of the Anglican Communion for discussion and action;
6. asks that in any continuing Commision, the Church of the South and the East be adequately represented."

The other Resolution, No. 34, welcomes the report of the Anglican/Roman Catholic Commission on 'The Theology of Marriage and its Application to Mixed marriages' (1975). It commented on the measure of agreement achieved and it endorsed two recommendations of the Commission designed to improve the existing unsatisfactory state of affairs. The Conference commented also on the variations of practice in different regions. The Anglican Chairman of the Commission, Archbishop Simms of Armagh, proposed the resolution, but the Conference desired its strengthening and added the final paragraph: "The problems associated with marriage between members of our two Communions continue to hinder inter-Church relations and progress towards unity. While we recognize that there has been an improved situation in some places as a result of the *Motu Proprio*, the general principles underlying the Roman Catholic position are unacceptable to Anglicans. Equality of conscience as between partners in respect of all aspects of their marriage (and in particular with regard to the baptism and religious upbringing of children) is something to be affirmed both for its own sake and for the sake of an improved relationship between the Churches."

During the Conference there occurred the death of Pope Paul VI who, with Archbishop Michael Ramsey, had inaugurated the serious dialogue. The Roman Catholic observers were invited to celebrate a Requiem in the plenary hall at which two of the lessons were read by Bishop Howe and Archbishop Simms of Armagh. The invitation and full attendance of members evoked a warm response of gratitude from the observers. The Bishop of London represented the Archbishop of Canterbury at the funeral in Rome.

His successor, John Paul I, as Patriarch of Venice, had acted as host to the Commission during one of its meetings, and on the occasion of another visit of the Commission was the guest of the members, and he took an active interest in ARCIC's work. At his funeral, coming with tragic suddenness so soon after his installation, the Bishop of London was present as personal representative of the Archbishop of Canterbury who also invited the Anglican Co-Chairman of ARCIC, Archbishop McAdoo of Dublin, to represent the world-wide Anglican Communion. The Pope's successor, Pope John Paul II, during his visit to Ireland in 1979, met the leaders of the other Christian Churches in Dublin. Quoting from his address to the members of the Secretariat for Promoting Christian Unity in the previous November, he assured those present in the course of his address: "Let no one ever doubt the commitment of the Catholic Church and of the Apostolic See of Rome to the pursuit of the unity of Christians."

The same year saw the retirement of Archbishop Donald Coggan of Canterbury, who had indeed been a "pilgrim for unity," and the arrival of his successor, Archbishop Robert Runcie, whose work for Christian unity has been in the sphere of Anglican-Orthodox relations, as the 102nd Archbishop of Canterbury.

The publication of 'Elucidations' (Salisbury 1979)

In June 1979, true to its undertaking to provide its correspondents with a provisional reply to criticisms of 'Eucharistic Doctrine' and 'Ministry and Ordination', ARCIC published Elucidations (SPCK and CTS, London 1979). Thus, the request of the Lambeth Conference, embodied in Resolution 33, was met in part and a similar response to criticisms of 'Authority in the Church' is projected. It is worth noting that the Preface states that "These *Elucidations,* agreed at Salisbury in January 1979, express the unanimous view of the Commission on the intention and meaning of the documents. The former should therefore be taken in conjunction with the two Agreed Statements as expressing the mind of the Commission on these two fundamental questions." In view of the criticism sometimes voiced about ARCIC's agreed statements that the documents are deliberately ambiguous in order to cover divergent interpretations this prefatory sentence has its own value and importance (Elucidations [4]). The document is therefore both a companion to Windsor (1971) and Canterbury (1973) and a further explication of both.

Amongst the matters dealt with are the meaning of substantial agreement (2), anamnesis and sacrifice (5), Christ's presence in the Eucharist (6), gift and reception (7), reservation (8), priesthood (12), the sacramentality of ordination (13) and the ordination of women (15). The clarification embodied in these paragraphs should go a long way to allaying legitimate fears on either side by spelling out, in reference to queries, the meaning of the statements at various points. For example, the use of the term *anamnesis* is justified by its scriptural origin (1 Cor. 11:24—5, Luke 22:19), its early patristic use (Justin Martyr) and its continuous appearance thereafter in the eucharistic prayers of East and West down to the present time (Eucharistic Prayer I in the Roman Missal; The Book of Common Prayer (1662) and the Anglican Series 3, and cp. its use by the Council of Trent and the Anglican Catechism). The Commission's comment was to the effect that "the traditional understanding of sacramental reality, in which the once-for-all event of salvation becomes effective in the present through the action of the Holy Spirit, is well expressed by the word *anamnesis*. We accept this use of the word which seems to do full justice to the semitic background. Furthermore, it enables us to affirm a strong conviction of sacramental realism and to reject mere symbolism. However, the selection of this word by the Commission does not mean that our common eucharistic faith may not be expressed in other terms." (5).

Again, in response to those who are anxious lest the word may conceal the theory of a repeated immolation or refer also to an eternal sacrifice in heaven (3), the document, after itemising the Christian use of the word 'Sacrifice', concludes that "there is therefore one historical, unrepeatable sacrifice offered once for all by Christ and accepted once for all by the Father. In the celebration of the memorial, Christ in the Holy Spirit unites his people with himself in a sacramental way so that the Church enters into the movement of his self-offering. In consequence, even though the Church is active in this celebration, this adds nothing to the efficacy of Christ's sacrifice upon the Cross, because the action is itself the fruit of this sacrifice." (5). Further examples of this valuable process of elucidating the meaning of the 'Agreed Statement' may be briefly noted. There is the comment on Windsor's phrase that the bread and wine become the body and blood of Christ (Eucharistic Doctrine, 10). The relevant section in 'Elucidations' (6) contains the following comment "*Becoming* does not here imply material change. Nor does liturgical use of the word imply that the bread and wine become Christ's body and blood in such a way that in the eucharistic celebration his presence is limited to the consecrated elements. It does not imply that Christ becomes present in the eucharist in the same manner that he was present in his earthly life. It does not imply that this *becoming* follows the physical laws of this world. What is here affirmed is a sacramental presence in which God uses realities of this world to convey the realities of the new creation: bread for this life becomes the bread of eternal life." Again, there is in (7) the assertion that the meaning of the eucharist is impoverished by an exclusive emphasis either on the presence in the elements or on the reception by faith: "In the past acute difficulties have arisen when one or other of these emphases has become almost exclusive. In the opinion of the Commission neither emphasis is incompatible with eucharistic faith, provided that the complementary movement emphasised by the other position is not denied. Eucharistic doctrine must hold together these two movements since in the eucharist, the sacrament of the New

Covenant, Christ gives himself to his people so that they may receive him through faith."

Similarly, the commentary on the Canterbury statement on 'Ministry and Ordination' (1973) takes up a number of points raised by the Commission's correspondents on such matters as the place of the priesthood of the whole people of God in the document, the sacramentality of ordination, ministerial origins and the analogical application of the word 'priesthood' to the people of God and to the ordained ministry: "There are two distinct realities which relate, each in its own way, to the high priesthood of Christ, the unique priesthood of the new covenant, which is their source and model." These considerations should be borne in mind throughout para. 13, and in particular they indicate the significance of the statement that the ordained ministry "is not an extension of the common Christian priesthood but belongs to another realm of the gifts of the Spirit."

In view of suggestions by some concerning this quotation from 'Canterbury' (13) it is important for perspective to recall that precisely the same thing was said in the Les Dombes agreement between Roman Catholics and Protestants (1973): "Ordination, the sign of a difference of charisma between the pastoral ministry and the priesthood of the baptised, far from separating ministers from God's people and making them a clerical caste, identifies them more fully with the life of the Church." Likewise in the Lutheran/Roman Catholic statement (1970) the same view is echoed. It is "a special order of Ministry" in the Church and "has a special role within the ministry of the people of God" as distinct from·the general ministry.[32]

On the difficulty raised by the ordination of women, 'Elucidations' (15), notes that where this has taken place "the bishops concerned believe that their action implies no departure from the traditional doctrine of the ordained ministry (as expounded, for instance, in the Agreed Statement.)" The Commission recognises that this has created an obstacle for the Roman Catholic Church, and confines itself to saying that "the principles upon which its doctrinal agreement rests are not affected by such ordinations; for it was concerned with the origin and nature of the ordained ministry and not with the question who can or cannot be ordained."

As we recall that the overall context of the 'Agreed statements' is the 'Malta Report', the final paragraph of 'Elucidations' needs to be quoted in full showing as it does the objective of the work of the Commission: "In answer to the questions concerning the Agreed Statements for the mutual recognition of ministry, the Commission has affirmed that a consensus has been reached that places the questions in a new context (cf. Ministry and Ordination, para. 17). It believes that our agreement on the essentials of eucharistic faith with regard to the sacramental presence of Christ and the sacrificial dimension of the eucharist, and on the nature and purpose of priesthood, ordination and apostolic succession, is the new context in which the questions should now be discussed.

---

[32] For references see Modern Ecumenical Documents on the Ministry (ed. H. R. McAdoo, London 1975), p. 13.

This calls for a reappraisal of the verdict on Anglican Orders in 'Apostolic Curae' (1896).

"Mutual recognition presupposes acceptance of the apostolicity of each other's ministry. The Commission believes that its Agreements have demonstrated a consensus in faith on eucharist and ministry which has brought closer the possibility of such acceptance. It hopes that its own conviction will be shared by the members of both our Communions; but mutual recognition can only be achieved by the decision of our authorities. It has been our mandate to offer them the basis upon which they may make this decision."

Quietly but firmly, as the work begins to draw towards its term, the Commission appointed by both Communions is putting it up to the people who are the Church, to their pastoral authorities and their institutional procedures, and asking that the twentieth century should see dialogue actually leading to movement.

An analysis of the thrust of the Venice Statement and an evaluation of the difficulties

Accordingly, it is with the knowledge of ARCIC's preparatory work on authority in mind, and against the background of the events referred to, linked as they are both with the Commission's work and with the relationship between the two Churches, that we attempt to evaluate briefly the thrust of the Venice Statement. We preface this by recalling that the subject of authority exercised the minds of the bishops at the Lambeth Conference of 1978. The Archbishop of Canterbury spoke on the subject and his remarks are printed *in toto* in the Conference Report.[33] Reminding the bishops that as long ago as 1897 the then Bishop of Albany wrote to Davidson on the subject to the effect that the forthcoming Lambeth Conference would be unlikely to support "anything in the nature of a Canterbury *Patriarchate*," the bishop believed that many wished to see "some central tribunal of reference for disputes on doctrinal or even disciplinary questions." His Grace then went on to dismiss in succession the concepts of authority centred in the person of the Archbishop of Canterbury, or centred in the Lambeth Conference, or in the Anglican Consultative Council, or in a Doctrinal Commission. Clearly the Archbishop was aware of a growing feeling that the Anglican tradition that bishops are the guardians of the faith be re-emphasised within the context of synodical government, and indeed be referred explicitly to this (see also Resolutions 12 and 13). He then proposed that the Primates of the Anglican Communion should meet on a regular basis, maintaining a close contact with the Anglican Consultative Council. Along these lines, "without a rigidity which would be foreign to our tradition, we should move towards a maturity in the exercise of authority." Resolution 11 of the Conference concurs and concluded that "The Conference advises member Churches not to take action regarding issues which are of concern to the whole Anglican Communion without consultation with a Lambeth Conference or with the epis-

[33] The Report of the Lambeth Conference 1978, pp. 122–124.

copate through the Primates Committee, and requests the Primates to initiate a study of the nature of authority within the Anglican Communion." The first such meeting of Anglican Primates took place at Ely in England in the following year, in November 1979.

It is clear that the catalyst here was the ordination of women in certain Anglican provinces and it is equally clear that here again we see the emergence of one the themes which this study has detected in the history of Anglican/ Roman Catholic relations. It was also one of the themes assigned to the work of the new Commission by the Malta Report and it constitutes the subject matter of ARCIC's Venice Statement on 'Authority in the Church' (1976).

A detailed analysis of the text of the statement would be out of place here and also unnecessary in view of the many reactions which have appeared. Among these one may note in particular the 'Response by the Church of England' which has the authority of the Faith and Order Advisory Group of the Board for Mission and Unity and 'Truth and Authority', a commentary by two members of the Commission, Dr. E. J. Yarnold, S.J., and Dr. Henry Chadwick.[34] It would be more useful and more in keeping with the design of uncovering the recurrence of certain themes throughout the history of relations between the two Communions to distinguish some major elements in and aspects of the document.

(a) To begin with, the Venice Statement decisively locates the whole matter firmly within the context of the Malta Report. Underlining the process of mutual education which would result from a closer association between the two Churches particularly in the areas of primacy and of the synodical tradition, the Preface takes the 'Malta Report' as its starting point and asserts: "We are convinced, therefore, that our degree of agreement, which argues for greater communion between our Churches, can make a profound contribution to the witness of Christianity in our contemporary society." Thus we see clearly reflected one of the master-themes of the Malta Report and, significantly, this is explicitly expounded in the final paragraph (26) of the Venice Statement: "The Malta Report of 1968 envisaged the coming together of the Roman Catholic Church and the Churches of the Anglican Communion in terms of 'unity by stages.' . . . Accordingly, we submit our Statements to our respective authorities to consider whether or not they are judged to express on these central subjects a unity at the level of faith which not only justifies but requires action to bring about a closer sharing between our two communions in life, worship and mission." Here, with the end of the Commission's allotted task in sight, the context and the immediate objective of ARCIC's work as the members see it are set out with plainness and urgency.

b) A second comment on the Venice statement is that it endeavours to meet the terms of its Malta brief by examining the nature, exercise and implications of authority in the Church (see The Malta Report, 22).

---

[34] The former, presented to the English General Synod in 1979, is published by the Church Information Office, Great Smith Street, London, and the latter by S.P.C.K. and C.T.S. London (1977).

The subject matter is authority *in the Church* which means that authority is seen both as a service to the people of God and as an aspect of authentic ecclesiality. Christian authority is not an end in itself. Built into it is a system of checks designed to prevent it from overbalancing into authoritarianism. These checks turn out to be components of the working model of Christian authority as it was understood, for example, in the Church of the Fathers, and in the multiple concept of authority which is part of the Anglican ethos and was set out in detail in the reports of the Lambeth Conferences of 1948 and 1968.[35] What are involved here are criteria — the Scriptures, creeds, *consensus fidelium*, the tradition. What then is the purpose of authority within the life of the pilgrim Church? Put simply, the answer is that the object of the authority process is to maintain the Church in the truth of the Gospel.

Process is surely the right word, since what is going on is a continuous inter-action between the guidance of the Spirit, who leads into all truth, and the human authorities in the Church as these constantly attempt to mediate the ultimate Christian authority, the Lordship of Christ, through the Church's teaching and life, proclamation and witness: "All authority has been given to me in heaven and on earth. Go therefore and make disciples of all nations." (Matt. 28:19—20). This comes through clearly and concisely in the Venice Statement (2) and its implications are followed up particularly in (4)—(7) and further in (13)—(23). So, in the course of the document the purpose of authority in the Church, its nature and the methods of its functioning are examined and the problems created for separated Churches by different emphases and instrumentalities are faced.

c) A third comment on the content and structure of the Venice Statement is that what we are ultimately talking about is the Spirit's abiding in the Church.

The Spirit's abiding in the Church has two aspects, or two areas of effect, the leading of the community of faith into the truth of the Gospel and maintaining it in that truth, and secondly, the inspiring and informing of the community of faith so that the members are called to the life of faith, helped to maintain the characteristics of this life, and strengthened therein by the Spirit through the Word and Sacraments and all uncovenanted as well as covenanted gifts of the Spirit. Belief and behaviour are inseparable in the truth of the Gospel and so this is the total area in which the effects of the Spirit's abiding in the Church are felt: "As he taught you, then, dwell in him." (1 John 2:27). This dual aspect comes through clearly in the Venice Statement (3)—(7).

What the Statement is saying is that, in the final analysis, the authority which the Church exercises in formulating the truths of the faith is none other than the Spirit's authority in leading the community of faith into the truth and evoking man's response to the truth of the Gospel: "It has seemed good to the Holy spirit and to us." (Acts 15:28). The Spirit uses human instruments and instrumentalities, and the Venice Statement deals with these in detail, including the question of infallibility. In this connection Anglicans would agree with Fr.

---

[35] See The Lambeth Conference 1948 (London 1948), pp. 65—66 and The Lambeth Conference 1968, p. 82.

Georges Tavard's comment: "What is then left of the notion of infallibility can be scarcely more than trust in the Spirit's protection and guidance of the Church's faith and of the organs which formulate this faith. The Spirit may be said to be infallible in that he infallibly reaches his goals, and we trust him to guide the Church."[36] This would seem to them to be a description of the Church's indefectibility which they recognise as a Scriptural concept.

The general rubric then which covers the Venice Statement's thinking on authority is that fundamentally what we are talking about is the Spirit's authority leading the apostolic community to recognise and to proclaim the Gospel (2). Into this process fit both authority's instruments and authority's instrumentalities. The latter are the human agencies or organs within the community of faith – episope, primacy, conciliarity, papacy and the claims made for it. The former are the theological tools used by the community to establish that the faith proclaimed is authentic, "the faith once for all delivered." These are the criteria of Scripture, the tradition, reason and reception by the faithful. All of this, within the context of the Spirit's abiding in the Church, constitutes the subject-matter of the Venice Statement.

In the first place, VS (2) makes the overall position clear with its opening phrase: "Through the gift of the Spirit the apostolic community came to recognise in the words and deeds of Jesus the saving activities of God and their mission to proclaim to all men the good news of salvation." The transmission of the Gospel is "assisted by the Holy Spirit" (ib.) and the documents recording the life and words of Jesus are normative for faith and convey the authority of the Word of God. Furthermore, "entrusted with these documents, the Christian community is *enabled by the Holy Spirit* to live out the Gospel and so to be led into all truth." (ib.) The two areas of the Spirit's work, that of authentic faith and authentic life are thus the one sphere of the Spirit's abiding in the Church. At the same time, the unbreakable link between this and the use of the Scriptural criterion from the human side of the community's assessment of its faith and life is asserted. In (3) this is further developed, and the Spirit of the risen Lord is seen as indwelling the Church, safeguarding its faithfulness and equipping it for mission in and to human society. It is "by sharing in the life of the Spirit" (4) that the members of the apostolic community find the means of being faithful to the Christian revelation and the grace which enables response. "Special gifts for the benefit of the Church" are from the Holy Spirit and among them is the *episcope* of the ordained ministry (5). The following paragraphs (6) and (7) depict the community's life in terms of a "continuing process of discernment and response" in which the Holy Spirit is continuously at work keeping the community in the faith and evoking and enabling the authentic life of faith in its members. This ceaseless work of the Spirit abiding in the Church in the basis for the conviction that the Church cannot ultimately cease to be itself, to be Christian: "It is by such means as these that the Holy Spirit keeps the Church under the lordship of Christ, who, taking full account of human weakness, has promised never to abandon his people." (7). Coupled with this assertion that the Church cannot

---

[36] Is the Papacy an Object of Faith? (One in Christ, Vol. XIII, 1977, No. 3, p. 228).

"fail" because of the promise, is a statement of *ecclesia semper reformanda* because of the inadequacies of the human organs of authority in the Church.

The Venice Statement then goes on, in (15) and (16) to reiterate the Scriptural criterion as being that with which all the Councils of the Church must be consonant as they state the faith. This is enlarged upon in the same paragraph where the importance of establishing criteria, of the subject matter of definitions and of the process of reception as these, together with the response of the faithful, are seen in terms of a gradual process "through the Spirit's continuing guidance of the whole Church." In (18) the document returns to this, emphasising how, in order to prevent "distortion of the Gospel," the Church appeals to Scripture and to antiquity (the creeds, councils and writings of the early Church,) and refers to episcopal responsibility "for promoting truth and discerning error," noting that "the interaction of bishops and people in its exercise is a safeguard of Christian life and fidelity." A footnote draws attention to the exposition of this appeal to Scripture and the primitive Church – part of the Anglican ethos – by successive Lambeth Conferences in 1948 and 1968. The same paragraph stresses that neither bishops nor people are invariably protected from errors and it concludes by explaining what is meant by the Church's indefectibility: "Yet, in Christian hope, we are confident that such failures cannot destroy the Church's ability to proclaim the Gospel and to show forth the Christian life; for we believe that Christ will not desert his Church and that the Holy Spirit will lead it into all truth. That is why the Church, in spite of its failures, can be described as indefectible."

The authority of councils, primates and a universal primate obviously concentrate in a specific and partly controversial area this whole question of authority in the Church. It is therefore noteworthy that in its section on conciliar and primatial authority (19–23), the Venice Statement reminds the reader that

a) the Church's judgmental process in matters of faith is "through the Holy Spirit," and
b) that the guidance of the Spirit in matters of the truths of faith is inseparable from the use of the criteria on the part of the human organs and authorities in the Church.

In view of the criticism made in some quarters that the Commission had asserted the inerrancy of Councils (which for Anglicans would contradict Article XXI) it is important to note what the Venice Statement actually does say – not least because Anglican General Synods around the world have affirmed the Statement to be consonant with the faith of the Church. In VS (19) it is stated that the Holy Spirit guides the Church to accept as protected from error only those judgements of General Councils which "do not add to the truth" and which are "consonant with Scripture", which are "faithful to Scripture and consistent with tradition" and which furthermore are "decisions on fundamental matters of faith" or "which formulate the central truths of salvation."

This is very far from being a blanket assertion that General Councils cannot err – we know that as a matter of history the Councils of Ariminum and

Seleucia erred. The Anglican Article XII differs from VS (19) only in emphasis while in content both documents are saying that, through and by the Holy Spirit, Councils are controlled in their judgements on fundamental matters of faith by the criterion of Holy Scripture (which *per se* cannot lead the Church into error.) Thus Article XXI says that General Councils "may err, and sometimes have erred, even in things pertaining unto God. *Wherefore things ordained by them as necessary to salvation have neither strength nor authority, unless it may be declared that they be taken out of Holy Scripture.*"

Is is illuminating in respect of this quest for convergence in this theme to note the closeness of standpoint as revealed not only in the Venice Statement and in the Thirty-Nine Articles but in the writings of Archbishop Laud in his 'Conference' with Fisher. Laud represents a typical Anglican statement in the manner in which he relates conciliar judgements to the Spirit's guidance and to the Scriptural criterion in the context of the indefectibility of the Church. His contention is that "there is no power in the Council, no assistance to it, but what is in and to the Church."

This parallels our thinking to-day and the way in which Laud develops it reproduces for his time what we are now saying about the relation of the Spirit's abiding in the Church to the maintenance of the Church in that truth which it is its mission to proclaim and live.

A General Council, writes Laud, is a "representing body," or as we would say, a representative body; "therefore the acts, laws and decrees of the representative, be it ecclesiastical or civil, are binding in their strength; but they are not so certain, and free from error, as is that wisdom which resides in the whole." Nothing "less than the assistance of the Holy Ghost" can secure a Council against error. Laud explains how there is a limitation contained in this and he notes "that the assistance of the Holy Ghost is without error. That is no question; and as little there is, that a council hath it. But the doubt that troubles is, Whether all assistance of the Holy Ghost be afforded in such a high manner as to cause *all the definitions* of a Council in matters fundamental in the Faith, and in remote deductions from it, *to be alike infallible.*"

On examination, he indicates that it is so only in "all truth absolutely necessary to salvation, and this, when they suffer themselves *to be led by the Blessed Spirit, by the Word of God*; and all truth which Christ had before, at least fundamentally, declared unto them." It will be noted that this resembles very closely the Venice Statement (19) and Laud drives it home as he links the Spirit's abiding in the Church with the Scriptural criterion in the conciliar process. Thus he concludes: "all necessary to salvation; in which I shall easily grant a General Council cannot err, *suffering itself to be led by this Spirit of Truth in the Scripture*, and not taking upon it to lead both the Scripture and the Spirit."[37] In fact, the Commission came increasingly to feel that this was the real context in which to investigate further the problem of papal infallibility as noted in VS (24). Accordingly, in the course of its work on that paragraph, subsequent to the

---

[37] All quotations from Archbishop WILLIAM LAUD are taken from: A Relation of the Conference (1639), Sect. XXXIII.

publication of the Venice Statement, the Rev. Herbert Ryan S.J. and Archbishop Henry McAdoo were requested to prepare papers on this subject, from
the Roman Catholic and the Anglican standpoints, under the heading "The
Spirit's Abiding in the Church."

(d) In view of some simplistic head-lines which appeared at the time of
publication, it is not otiose to emphasise once again what precisely the Venice
Statement says about a universal primacy. It did not announce agreement on the
Roman primacy as it now is and in the context of the separated Churches. as
they now are. The key phrase is the final sentence in VS (23): "It seems appropriate that in any future union a univeral primacy such as has been described
should be held by that see."

The primacy "such as has been described" is one in which "primacy and
conciliarity are complementary elements of *episcope*" (VS, 22) and the Statement
categorizes as "serious imbalance" a situation in which one element is over-
emphasised "at the expense of the other." The practical implications of this for
both Communions were enlarged upon in the Co-Chairmens' Preface to the
Venice document. This links up with the Anglican reservations on features of
the Roman primacy which are tabulated in VS (24).

The setting of such a reconstituted universal primacy is that of a "future
union" and the siting of such a primacy in the See of Rome is described as
"appropriate." The adjective conveys overtones of the historical factors involved
in the development of the Roman primacy (cf. VS (12) and (17) and of the conviction that acceptance of such a primacy is not essential to the fulness of
authentic ecclesiality (cp. VS [24], b).

The following paragraph (24) of the Venice Statement sets out four
problem areas for Anglicans in respect of the Roman primacy as it now is and
has developed, namely, the basing of papal claims on the Petrine texts; the use
of "divine right" language as applied to the popes seen as successors of Peter;
the question of papal infallibility as defined in 1870 and that of the universal
immediate jurisdiction claimed for the pope. These have been recurring themes
over the centuries and it remains to be seen whether they are final obstacles,
irremovable, or whether new thinking on the nature and purpose of authority in
the Church will oblige them to take what many to-day believe to be their proper
place in the "hierarchy of truths," thus allowing "action to bring about a closer
sharing between our two Communions in life, worship and mission." (VS, 26).

At the time of writing (1981) the Commission is engaged on a further explication of VS (24) in which it will endeavour to see how much closer to one
another the Churches may be brought through a rigorous analysis of terms and
meanings. An 'Elucidation', by way of response to critics and correspondents as
in the case of the Windsor and Canterbury documents, is also to be prepared as
a companion to the Venice Statement. Furthermore, a general introduction to
the three Agreed Statements (which will include material on ecclesiology) is
planned and the volume will be presented as ARCIC's final report to its appointing authorities in Rome and in Lambeth. It is to be hoped that both will see in it
a basis for a favourable decision conerning movement towards a new stage of
ecclesial relationships, such as is foreshadowed in Resolution 33 of the Lambeth

Conference of 1978. This report would be the Commission's final bow, having worked during some thirteen years of concentrated joint investigation, and it will be replaced in due course by another possibly smaller body the terms of reference of which are still to be spelt out.

Whatever the immediate and the ultimate outcome may be, the documents stand — the product of the first officially-sanctioned dialogue in four centuries between Rome and Canterbury — and history will judge them and "if it seems good to the Holy Spirit and to us" (Acts 15:28), the Church of the future may well use them to help repair the breaches of the past, so "that they may be one" (John 17:11).

So, as of now, we may ask — Where does the Roman Catholic assertion of papal infallibility in 1870 and Anglican rejection of it, as by Lambeth 1968, leave the dialogue? If, as seems probable, Anglicans and Roman Catholics are unlikely to achieve a verbal agreement on infallibility acceptable to both Churches, is a doctrinal pluralism on the meaning of the papal office (a teaching after all peculiar to the Roman Catholic Church) something which can be encompassed within the legitimate limits of diversity in a united Church?

Yarnold and Chadwick in their commentary on the Venice Statement ('Truth and Authority' 1977 — note the title) wrote:

"The Roman Catholic tradition has seen the Bishop of Rome as possessing by God's will a unique function in the Episcopal College, taking different forms at different times in history, but possessing the duty and the right to invite the following of all the faithful, and therefore being also the focus of teaching authority with a safeguarding power of definition in matters structural to Christian faith and ethics. This Roman Catholic tradition can be presented in brief and perhaps oversimplified terms as a belief that the Son of God founded His Church on Peter and the Apostles, that the Pope and bishops are to the end of time the juridical inheritors of the powers the Lord entrusted to His Church on earth; and that these powers include not only primatial leadership but also a prophetic teaching office (commonly called 'infallibility') inherent in Christ's promise to be with His Church always.

The Anglican tradition has regarded this doctrine of authority in the Church as one-sided and as needing to be qualified by (a) appeal to the sources of apostolic faith and life in the scriptures, (b) the ancient catholic tradition, especially as enshrined in the decisions of the ecumenical councils of the undivided Church, (c) reason. Accordingly, the Anglican tradition has seen the problems of authority in the Church in terms of a need to preserve a balance between several elements, and has therefore felt that a true and proper understanding of truth and teaching authority in the Church is unlikely to be found centred upon one particular bishop, whose judgement can at times be coloured by his background and national culture and who, because of this concentration of authority in a single person, can escape the checks and balances provided by other norms of authority."

Anglicans would hold, with Archbishop Wake, that "the chair of Peter is preserved in all Catholic Churches," a view already expressed in the third century by St. Cyprian of Carthage. Roman Catholics would hold that it is to be identified with the See of Rome. One side may regard the other's view of the Spirit's guidance and abiding in the Church as far too localised and particularised. The other may regard the view of the first as too diffused and lacking a point of application. But the question is, should these two understandings of how the Spirit keeps the Church faithful to the Gospel allow themselves to be polarised to the extent that each side misses the real point, that the other is concerned with and striving to ensure that the truth of the Gospel is faithfully transmitted so that the Church remains in that truth?

Given the large area of full agreement, outlined in the 'Malta Report' ([3], [7] and cp. [4]), and given the Windsor and Canterbury Agreed Statements, the proper context for an assessment is that provided by the concept of "sister-churches." This was elaborated by Cardinal Willebrands in 1970, at a service in Great St. Mary's, Cambridge, and in the same year, on 25th October, at the canonisation of the Forty Martyrs, Pope Paul VI referred to the Anglican Church as an "ever beloved sister" of the Church of Rome. There is no reason to take this as the language of ecclesiastical hyperbole since the Pope explicitated the phrase: "There will be no seeking to lessen the legitimate prestige and the worthy patrimony of piety and usage proper to the Anglican Church when the Roman Catholic Church — this humble 'servant of the servants of God' — is able to embrace her ever-beloved sister in the one authentic communion of the family of Christ: a communion of origin and faith, a communion of priesthood and of rule, a communion of the Saints in the freedom of love and of the Spirit of Jesus."

It will be recalled that this particular vocabulary of ecumenism had been developing before this between Rome and Orthodoxy. The letter 'Anno ineunte' of Pope Paul VI to the Patriarch Athenagoras I on 15 July 1976 had made use of the term 'sister Churches' and explained its context. In 1971, the Pope declared that "between our Church and the venerable Orthodox Churches there already exists an almost total, though it be not yet perfect, communion." In the following year, the Pope affirmed "We are in almost complete communion with the Orthodox Churches." It is clearly relevant that the latter do not accept papal primacy as expressed since 1870, or papal infallibility, for as J. Meyendorff has said, "The question of authority has stood for centuries in the very centre of the issues between East and West."[38] Yet Vatican II has permitted a limited *communicatio in sacris* between the Roman Catholic and the Eastern Orthodox Churches.

It is at this point that, in the context of the concept of sister churches, the Malta Report's concept of unity by stages needs to be remembered. It is a realistic concept, building as it does upon the existing measures of full agreement, of substantial agreement, and of convergence. Instead of an all-or-nothing approach, it says that growth together upon this basis and under the leading of the Spirit is a real possibility and could open up further possibilities through

---

[38] In: A Pope for All Christians (London 1976, ed. PETER J. McCORD), p. 142.

degrees of shared life which could never emerge from paper agreements or union plans which seek to prescribe everything beforehand.

If Anglicans and Roman Catholics can agree, as in the Venice Statement, that the purpose of authority in the Church is to maintain the Church in the truth, but if the two communions differ in the methods by which they seek to achieve this purpose, must this preclude a stage of closer fellowship? Or does the degree of agreement outlined in VS argue for "greater communion between our churches?" Is such a new stage in the inter-church relationship not possible on the basis of the extensive agreement so far achieved and on the analogy of the Rome-Orthodoxy situation, without Roman Catholics giving up the doctrine of papal infallibility, or Anglicans accepting it?

VS looked forward in (22) and (23) to a future union in which the primatial and conciliar aspects of *episcope* would come to be complementary. Can this ever begin to come about outside a living situation of growth in a new relationship of sister-churches living and learning together? Was Karl Rahner prophesying to us when he said that the only and right way out of the present ecumenical stagnation was to reverse the process and proceed in the opposite direction: "Could we not consider full unity of faith and theology as a consequence of institutional unification, particularly since the latter need not mean institutional uniformity based on dogma as hitherto envisaged by the Code of Canon Law?"[39] He considers that the theologians have more or less done their work and that it is now over to the office-holders. In this, and in what he has to say about a "Petrine ministry" in a re-united Church, Rahner is speaking to the present situation. Is the Malta Report not doing the same thing? Is it only in a measure of shared life that unity will grow and bear fruit unexpected and unforeseen by all of us?

(e) One may round off this assessment of the main thrust of the Venice Statement by referring briefly to paragraph 24. After noting the establishing of a consensus on the nature of authority in the Church, the statement enumerates four Anglican objections both to the concept and to the manner of the exercise of this authority by a papal primacy and to the claims on its behalf which are involved. Here familiar themes reappear and the question for separated Christians seeking unity in truth is how best to handle them with integrity at the present time. Are these problems of such a nature as to preclude completely any substantial change in ecclesial relationships? Underlying these matters is for many the deeper question as to whether or not the papacy is an object of faith.

It is the Commission's hope to produce for its final report some further work on, and elucidations of, these four aspects of papal primacy, namely, the use in this connection of 'Petrine' texts, the use of 'divine right' language in 'Pastor Aeternus', the affirmation of papal infallibility and the claim that the pope possesses universal immediate jurisdiction. The Venice document indicates how and to what several extent these constitute real difficulties for Anglicans. Problems arise in that, for instance, while the New Testament records indicate

---

[39] The Shape of the Church to Come (English ed. 1974), pp. 104–107.

18*

that Peter had a special position among the Twelve, there is no record of any explicit transmission of this special position. This ties in with the question of 'divine right' as applied to the claim for a universal primacy of the bishop of Rome. Even if, by analogy with the position of Peter, the Roman See is regarded as exercising a 'Petrine' ministry, this for Anglicans would have to be on the basis that authentic ecclesiality does not depend on communion with that See. This theme has appeared from Wake onwards, and before that, and its sensitive handling is important as the Churches consider the implications for a reunited Church of a primacy in which "this general pattern of the complementary prim-atial and conciliar aspects of episcope serving the *koinonia* of the churches needs to be realized at the universal level." (VS, 23).

Similarly, the affirmation of papal infallibility and universal immediate jurisdiction raises problems not only by definition but also in respect of the nature and exercise of such a teaching authority and the scope of its jurisdiction. For Anglicans, the concept of papal infallibility is particularly called in question by "the recent Marian dogmas, because Anglicans doubt the appropriateness, or even the possibility, of defining them as essential to the faith of believers." (VS, 24 [c]). The basis of the rejection is, of course, that it is not possible to define as binding that which is not supported by or follows necessarily from revealed truth. As to the exercise of this authority, the Venice document notes that "the claim that the pope possesses universal immediate jurisdiction the limits of which are not clearly specified, is a source of anxiety to Anglicans who fear that the way is thus open to its illegitimate or uncontrolled use." (24 [d]). Par-allel to this is another anxiety about the mode or manner in which the teaching authority can be exercised, as in the recent condemnation of the views of Hans Küng. Doubtless the matter is complex in that it involves the degree of freedom of the theologian, the parameters within which divergence is allowable, and the delicate area of the relation of the truth of the Gospel to the interpretation of it in contemporary thought forms. But what is noted is the action and the manner of it, suggesting a more authoritarian approach than that of Anglicanism which, while credally firm on the fundamentals, tends to hold that the truth has strength to stand on its own feet and to allow a greater latitude for its explora-tion. This is doubtless more in the realm of psychology than of theology but the anxiety is there and has been expressed.

As we pass in review these areas of disagreement as outlined in VS (24), it must surely be apparent that genuine movement and real advance can only come about by taking into consideration the saving rubric set out in the 'Malta Report' (6). This passage advocates the use of "the Anglican distinction of fundamentals from non-fundamentals and the distinction implied by the Vatican Council's reference to a 'hierarchy of truths' (Decree on Ecumenism, 11), to the difference between 'revealed truths' and 'the manner in which they are formulated' (Pastoral Consitution on the Church in the Modern World, 62)." It is indeed, as Wake and Du Pin discovered, a basic and liberating theme.

Whatever the history of the next couple of decades may hold for the quest for unity in truth, it is the conviction of many that at this time in history the Churches, given the wide areas of credal agreement and of convergence on eucharist, ministry and the nature and purpose of authority, must now on this basis conclude what are the legitimate limits of diversity which will make possible a new ecclesial relationship capable of growing into an ever deepening *koinonia*.

(f) Finally, the last word of the previous sentence leads to emphasis on a theme which has undergirded the work of the Commission since its inception — the concept of *koinonia* as the key to understanding the meaning of the mystery of the Church. During the Malines conversations Halifax perceptively commented that the fundamental question was "What is the Church?" and an agreement between Wake and his French correspondents as to a definition of the Church resembled closely the conclusions of the Venice papers published earlier by the Commission. From the beginning of its work ARCIC has seen the apostolic Church as the living context of its investigation of the three areas outlined in the 'Malta Report'. It will be remembered that, at the Commission's first meeting in Windsor (1970), the subject matter was divided into 'Church and Eucharist', 'Church and Ministry' and 'Church and Authority'. As that work developed over the following decade, the members' early conviction that the reality of *koinonia* was of the greatest importance grew and developed and it is hoped to include some material on this in the final report. The Agreed Statements themselves however sufficiently indicate that a key-concept to their understanding is *koinonia*, involving both men's fellowship in Christ with God and with one another and its manifestation through the means of grace.

This theme of the nature of the Church leads directly to the present. On 4th September 1980, Pope John Paul II received the members of the Commission at Castelgandolfo and welcomed them with cordiality. In the course of his address of welcome, published the following day in 'Osservatore Romano', he referred appreciatively to the Commission's method of going behind the polemics of the past "to scrutinize together the great common treasure." He spoke of the three agreed statements: "This effort calls for warm appreciation." Referring to the approaching end of the Commission's work he said "Now the time is approaching when you will make a final report, which the respective ecclesiastical authorities must assess." Thanking the members for their work and pledging his concern for it and his support of those who may continue it, the Pope said: "But you yourself realize that much remains to be done. To understand the mystery of Christ's Church, the Sacrament of Salvation, in its fullness is an abiding challenge. Many of the practical problems which still face us (questions of order, of mixed marriages, of shared sacramental life, of Christian morality) can only move towards solution as our understanding of that mystery deepens."

From what we have seen in the course of this study, the theme of "the mystery of Christ's Church" has never been far from the surface. It is apparent that, in accordance with the formularies of their Church, countless Anglican writers during the centuries have seen the tests of authentic ecclesiality in the entire profession of the Christian faith, the use of the Sacraments and an apostolic ministry. These were the elements constitutive of the Church which is One, Holy, Catholic and Apostolic. Successive Lambeth Conferences from 1888 onwards have re-emphasised this. The Church is a divine society and a fellowship of those who, being incorporated into Christ by baptism, profess the Christian faith of the New Testament summarised in the Creeds and lived in the fellowship of this new community. Their growth in the life of this family is nourished by union with Christ, through eucharist and prayer, and formed by grace as the law of Christ becomes life for the individual. Christ is therefore both the law and the life of the Christian. Because he is a member of Christ, whose Body the Church is, the imitation of Christ and incorporation in Christ are two aspects of one thing, discipleship.

As we pass all this in review, what verdict can be given particularly in the light of the Agreed Statements? Have they or have they not revealed a substantial agreement on the mystery of the Church? Is it the case that the remaining disagreement in ecclesiology lies in the area of the nature and claims of the papal office and the way in which its authority is exercised within the community of the faithful, or is there something further, as yet uncovered by joint investigation? As has often been remarked, this area of disagreement has not, in the case of the Eastern Orthodox Churches, ruled out the permissibility of a closer relationship. Time will tell how valid or how inadequate such an assessment of the position may be and whether it is an over-simplification.

In 1981, during what seems likely to be its final plenary meeting, the Commission is to be received by the Archbishop of Canterbury at Lambeth.

Conclusion

What then can be said by way of conclusion at this stage when possible and actual development still lies veiled in the future? For two hundred and fifty years certain themes have been at once both the key to understanding the problems of Anglican/Roman Catholic relations and the substance of the problems themselves. Some themes have been modified in their divisive effects by a growing process of mutual questioning and answering and by changing climates in theology and inter-Church attitudes. Others have been hardened by dogmatic formulations and by differing emphases in ecclesiology. Some have yielded to convergence while others seem to remain intractable. But in the face of full agreement in some central areas of doctrine and of substantial agreement in others, the separated Churches will sooner or later have to evaluate formally the recommendations of their officially-appointed Commission and decide whether its work is of a sufficiently serious calibre to warrant forward steps on an institutional basis. Recognising a new and unprecedented situation, they must ask what degree of communion fits this situation and by what steps can it be inaugurated, for as Karl Rahner has pointed out, the initiative must now pass from the theologians to the office-holders. Only history will tell whether or not the present enterprise, launched by the Common Declaration of a Pope and a Primate, will have advanced the "communion of 'sister-churches'." But comparing the present state of affairs with that of ten years ago, not to mention that of Halifax's and Portal's generation, who can assert what the situation will be a decade hence? In the meantime there is the sustaining hope of those who, like

Archbishop Laud, could not see catholicity in a "narrow conclave" and who sought "to lay open those wider gates of the Catholic Church, confined to no age, time or place; not knowing any bounds but that faith which was once (and but once for all) delivered to the saints."[40]

Appendix A

Anglican Theologians and the Concept of a Roman Primacy

In setting out the views of some of Wake's Anglican predecessors it will become clear that for them the possibility that a ministerial primacy could in certain defined circumstances be regarded as at least not contrary to Scripture was very different from the developed claims for the papal primacy as they understood them. Hans Küng pin-pointed the problem when he wrote "The real question is not the mode of exercising this primacy, or its actual limitations, but the very existence of papal primacy in the first place. This is where the real difficulties begin. . . . All the difficulties are centred on three questions; the second and third questions depend on a positive answer being given to the preceding one. Are there grounds for assuming the primacy of Peter? Was the primacy of Peter something that was to continue? Is the Bishop of Rome the successor of the primacy of Peter?"[1] Küng was faithfully reflecting a basic concern of Anglicans (and others) constantly expressed, and with a greater degree of historical criticism in modern times than in the seventeenth century, as for example by George Salmon in 1888: "And first we have to consider the Scripture argument, resting on a supposed transmission to the Pope of certain prerogatives of St. Peter. In order to make out the theory by this process four things ought to be proved — (1) that Christ gave to St. Peter a primacy over the other Apostles not merely in dignity and precedence, but in authority and jurisdiction, constituting him their guide and teacher and ruler; (2) that this prerogative was not merely personal but designed to be transmitted to successors; (3) that Peter was Bishop of Rome and continued so to his death; and (4) that those who succeeded Peter in this local office were also the inheritors of his jurisdiction over the whole Church."[2]

Today there is a trend towards modifying these questions and shifting the emphasis as in the Lutheran/Roman Catholic statement on 'Papal Primacy:

---

[40] From the preface to WILLIAM LAUD's 'A Relation of the Conference between William Laud and Mr. Fisher the Jesuit' (1639).

[1] The Church (English Trans. 1967), pp. 455–456 and cp. p. 462 "The difficulties of the argument about primacy can . . . be graded: before proving *perpetuitas*, it is essential to prove *petrinitas*; and before proving *romanitas* it is essential to prove *perpetuitas*."

[2] GEORGE SALMON, The Infallibility of the Church (London 1888 and subsequent editions), Lecture XVIII.

Converging Viewpoints'[3] just as there is a tendency to interpret *de jure divino* in this connection as meaning a divinely-willed sequel or a providentially-guided development in history. Yet it is neither naive nor uneirenic to indicate that the underlying question remains, for Anglicans and Orthodox alike, as to whether or not the concept of a papal primacy is integral to a true ecclesiology and whether such a primacy and its exercise are essential to the true being of the Church.

Richard Field, whose one book 'Of the Church' (1606, 1610) was in many ways as important as that of his friend Richard Hooker, also a man of one great book, makes his comment and it is noticeable how the theme of collegiality runs through the writings of the period on this subject. Field wrote:

"We deny not but that blessed Peter has a kind of primacy of honour and order, that in respect thereof, as all metropolitans do succeed him, as being greater than other bishops in honour and place; so the patriarchs yet more specially; and amongst them the Roman bishops in the first place. We will not therefore put our adversaries to so much pains, as some other have done, to prove, that Peter was at Rome; that he died there, and that the Bishop of Rome succeeded him. But this is it which we say, that he succeeded him in the bishopric of that city, and in the honour of being one of the prime bishops of the world, as the bishops of Alexandria and Antioch likewise did: but not in the condition of being universal bishop, that is, such a one in whom all episcopal power and authority is originally invested: from whom it is derived to others: and who may limit and restrain the use of it in other, as seemeth good unto himself. For Peter was not such an apostle, but had only a joint commission with the rest, who were put into it immediately by Christ as well as he, though he were in some sort the first man in it.

We deny not therefore to the Roman bishop his due place among the prime bishops of the world, if therewith he will rest contented: but universal bishop in sort before expressed, we dare by no means admit him to be, knowing right well, that every bishop hath in his place, and keeping his own standing, power and authority immediately from Christ, which is not to be restrained or limited by any, but by the company of bishops: wherein though one be chief for order sake, and to preserve unity, and in such sort, that all things must take their beginning from him, yet he can do nothing without them."[4]

This statement, which in some respects parallels the Lambeth Report of 1968, can be matched at any rate in part from the writings of other seventeenth-century Anglicans, notably from those of Cosin, Laud and Bramhall, all of whom were actively engaged in the theological conflicts of their time with the Roman Catholic Church. In the midst of his controversy with the Jesuit Fisher, Wake's predecessor, Archbishop Laud, had been able to concur that "the Roman patriarch, by ecclesiastical constitutions, might perhaps have a primacy of order; but for principality of power, the patriarchs were as even, as equal, as the apostles were before them," and he added "A primacy of order was never

---

[3] Published in 1974 by the Lutheran/Roman Catholic Dialogue in the United States.
[4] Loc. cit., Chapter 32 (Second ed. 1628, p. 518).

denied him by the Protestants; and an universal supremacy of power was never granted him by the primitive Christians."[5] Likewise John Cosin, whose path had lain through the Anglican/Roman Catholic polemics of the day, could still write that Anglicans might agree "in acknowledgment of the Bishop of Rome, if he would rule and be ruled by the ancient canons of the Church, to be the Patriarch of the West, by right of ecclesiastical and imperial constitutions . . . without any necessary dependence upon him by divine right."[6] Most interesting of all was John Bramhall, not simply because the circumstances of his life as well as the atmosphere of the times had obliged him to be active in the controversy between the two Churches, but also because, in spite of this, his theological assessment of the matter was deeper.

Denying that primacy and universal jurisdiction are by divine right,[7] Bramhall distinguishes between primacy of order and supremacy of power – "A primacy of order may consist with an equality of dignity; but a supremacy of power taketh away all parity. He is blind who doth not see in the history of the Acts of the Apostles, that the supremacy or sovereignty of power did not rest in the person of any one single Apostle, but in the Apostolical College."[8] As to the position of Peter, the English Church has "no controversy with St. Peter, nor with any other about the privileges of St. Peter. Let him be 'first, chief or prince of the Apostles', in that sense wherein the ancient Fathers styled him so. Let him be the first ministerial 'mover'. And why should not the Church have recourse to a prime apostle or Apostolical Church in doubtful cases." The point is, continues Bramhall citing Lancelot Andrewes, that while we agree St. Peter had a primacy, the real question is what that primacy was and whether it is the same as that claimed by the popes.[9] "St. Peter never enjoyed or exercised any greater or higher power in the Church than every one of the apostles had, either extensively or intensively, either in relation to the Christian world or the apostolical college; except only that *primordium unitatis* or primacy of order . . ."[10] He is prepared to say that Anglicans need not find such a primacy unacceptable in itself: "And although we know no Divine right for it, yet, if he would be contented with it, for peace' sake we could afford the Bishop of Rome a 'primacy of order' by human right, which is all that antiquity did know."[11] Looking

---

[5] A Relation of the Conference between William Laud and Mr. Fisher the Jesuit (1639), Sect. XX.

[6] Works (ed. L.A.C.T.), Vol. IV, pp. 332–336.

[7] Works (ed. 1844), Vol. III, pp. 551–552.

[8] Works (ed. 1844), Vol. II, p. 469 and cp. ib. 321, 372, 387, 496.

[9] Ib. II, p. 371 and cp. II, pp. 468–469.

[10] Ib. II, p. 483 and cp. II, pp. 609. 612.

[11] Ib. II, p. 495 and cp. II, p. 357: "Yet the main controversy, *I might say the only necessary controversy*, between them and us, is about the extent of papal power . . . If the pope would content himself with his *exordium unitatis*, – which was all that his primitive predecessors had, and *is as much as a great part of his own sons will allow him at this day*, – we are not so hard hearted and uncharitable, for such an innocent title or office, to disturb the peace of the Church; nor do envy him such a preeminence among patriarchs as St. Peter had (by the confession of his own party) among the apostles."

ahead to the unity of Christians, he could see no other way but that, as he wrote in his answer to De La Milletière, "If you could be contented to wave your last four hundred years' determinations; or, if you liked them for yourselves, yet not to obtrude them upon other Churches; if you could rest satisfied with your old patriarchal power, and your *principium unitatis*, or primacy of order, much good might be expected from free Councils, and conferences from moderate persons; and we might yet live in hope to see an union, if not in all opinions, yet in charity and all necessary points of saving truth, between all Christians."[12]

Some may regard this as visionary while others will look on it as prophetic. Speculation may be idle, but since Vatican II structures have become less pyramidal with the growing emphasis on collegiality. *We may therefore add to the catalogue of themes recurring from Wake to the present dialogue that of collegiality.*

Interestingly, Bramhall refers to others who take the same view of the primacy. One of these was Richard Montague, successively bishop of Chichester and of Norwich, who wrote "Let the Bishop of Rome have delegated unto him (that is, by the Church) a power of order, direction, counsel, consultation, conclusion (or pronouncing sentence) and putting in execution; but let that power be subject to the Church, let it be in the Church's power to take it away, seeing it is not instituted in the Holy Scriptures, nor tied personally unto Peter."[13]

Lancelot Andrewes is also cited: "Neither is it questioned among us whether St. Peter has a primacy, but what that primacy was; and whether it be such an one as the Pope doth now challenge to himself, and you challenge to the Pope; but the king doth not deny Peter to have been the prime and prince of the Apostles."[14] The reference in the quotation is to King James I who, in his 'Apology for the Oath of Allegiance' had expressed his support for the institution of patriarchs "for order sake", with the exclusion of supremacy and jurisdiction, and wrote, "I would with all my heart give my consent that the Bishop of Rome should have the first seat; I, being a western king, would go with the Patriarch of the West."[15] Casaubon, in his epistle to Perron, quoted James in a comment on the way to concord which bears directly on the first theme uncovered in the Gallican correspondence, the distinction between fundamentals and non-fundamentals, and the terms of definition are of interest.[16]

---

[12] Ib. I, p. 80.

[13] The quotation is from MONTAGUE's 'De Originibus Ecclesiasticis Commentationes' (1636, 1640). The words in brackets are BRAMHALL's glosses.

[14] The reference is to LANCELOT ANDREWES's 'Responsio ad apologiam Cardinalis Bellarmini' (1610).

[15] The english edition was in 1609, and the Latin version (part of the exchange with Bellarmine) had appeared previously in 1607.

[16] "The King calleth those things simply necessary, which either the Word of God commandeth expressly to be believed or done, or which the ancient Church did draw out of the Word of God by necessary consequence . . . If this distinction were used to decide the present controversies, *and Divine right were ingenuously distinguished from positive or ecclesiastical right,* it seemeth not, that the contention would be long or sharp, between

For Bramhall, the immediate essential context of such a primacy of order is collegiality,[17] and ultimately it cannot be separated from the question of General Councils and their authority.[18] Finally, while "the sovereign power over the universal Church was ever in an Oecumenical Council" he concedes that a primacy of order might, though not necessarily, help to prevent schism.[19] Having glanced at examples of the Anglican tradition in respect of the papal office, primacy, jurisdiction and infallibility and collegiality, it may fairly be claimed that Wake, in what he wrote to Du Pin and Girardin, was solidly within that tradition.

Appendix B

Extracts from the Report of the Lambeth Conference, 1968

The Lambeth Conference of 1968 passed the following resolution: "*Collegiality* 55. The Conference recommends that the principle of collegiality should be a guiding principle in the growth of the relationships between the provinces of the Anglican Communion and those Churches with which we are, or shall be, in full communion, and draws particular attention to that part of the Section III report which underlines this principle." See 'The Lambeth Conference 1968: Resolutions and Reports' (London 1968), p. 44.

The part of the Section III report (The Renewal of the Church in Unity) to which resolution 55 refers reads as follows:

"EPISCOPACY, COLLEGIALITY, PAPACY

The Anglican tradition has always regarded *episcopacy* as an essential part of its Catholic inheritance. We would regard it as an extension of the apostolic office and function both in time and space, moreover, we regard the transmission of apostolic power and responsibility as an activity of the college of bishops and never as a result of isolated action by any individual bishop.

In the discharge of his episcopal responsibility, the bishop is the guardian of the faith, the father of his people, and the driving force of mission in his area.

Traditionally the bishop is father in God to the clergy and laity of a territorial diocese, and part of his vocation is to represent the Catholic Church in his diocese and, conversely, to represent his diocese within the councils of the wider Church.

While we have no wish to diminish the importance of this traditional pattern, the demands of a new age suggest the wisdom of also consecrating bishops without territorial jurisdiction but with pastoral responsibility, directly of indirectly, for special groups such as the armed forces, industry, and particular

---

pious and moderate men, about things absolutely necessary" (BRAMHALL, Works, III, pp. 568–569).

[17] Works, II, pp. 371–372, 468–469, 483.

[18] Ib. II, pp. 609, 612.

[19] Ib. II, pp. 155–156.

areas of concern within the mission of the Church. This principle would simply be the extension of the widespread current practice of appointing suffragans, auxiliaries, and assistants. We submit that all such bishops, by virtue of their consecration as bishops in the Church of God, should have their due place in episcopal councils throughout the world.

The principle underlying *collegiality* is that the apostolic calling, responsibility, and authority are an inheritance given to the whole body or college of bishops. Every individual bishop has therefore a responsibility both as a member of this college and as chief pastor in his diocese. In the latter capacity he exercises direct oversight over the people committed to his charge. In the former he shares with his brother bishops throughout the world a concern for the wellbeing of the whole Church.

Within the college of bishops it is evident that there must be a president. In the Anglican Communion this position is at present held by the occupant of the historic see of Canterbury, who enjoys a primacy of honour, not of jurisdiction. This primacy is found to involve, in a particular way, that care for all the Churches which is shared by all the bishops.

The renewed sense of the collegiality of the episcopate is especially important at a time when most schemes for unity are being developed at a national level, because the collegiality of the episcopate helps to stress the worldwide and universal character of the Church. This collegiality mut be a guiding principle in the growth of the relationships between the provinces of the Anglican Communion and those Churches with which we are, or shall be, in full communion. Within this larger college of bishops, the primacy would take on a new character which would need to be worked out in consultation with the Churches involved.

As a result of the emphasis placed on collegiality at the Second Vatican Council, the status of bishops in the Roman Catholic Church was in great measure enhanced, though the teaching of the First Vatican Council on the infallibility and immediate and universal jurisdiction of the Pope was unaffected. We are unable to accept this teaching as it is commonly understood today. The relationships between the Pope and the episcopal college, of which he is a member, are, however, still being clarified, and are subject to development. We recall the statement made in the Lambeth Conference of 1908, and repeated in 1920 and 1930, 'that there can be no fulfillment of the Divine purpose in any scheme of reunion which does not ultimately include the great Latin Church of the West, with which our history has been so closely associated in the past, and to which we are still bound by many ties of common faith and tradition'. We recognize the Papacy as a historic reality whose developing role requires deep reflection and joint study by all concerned for the unity of the whole Body of Christ.

Although the declaration and guardianship of the faith has traditionally been regarded as belonging fundamentally to the episcopal office, the collegiality of the episcopate must always be seen in the context of the conciliar character of the Church, involving the consensus fidelium, in which the episcopate has its place." See 'The Lambeth Conference 1968: Resolutions and Reports' (London 1968), pp. 137–8.

Appendix C

The Eucharist: Du Pin and Anglican Teaching Compared

It is informative to compare Du Pin's thinking in the extract quoted in the text with traditional Anglican beliefs as expressed, for example, in the last six questions and answers in the Church Catechism and in the Articles. There is in these formularies a balanced emphasis on the objectivity of the gift, "The Body and Blood of Christ, which are verily and indeed taken and received by the faithful in the Lord's Supper", and on the role of faith, "the mean whereby they are taken and received is Faith." Article 28 sums it up, "to such as rightly, worthily and with faith, receive the same, the Bread which we break is a partaking of the Body of Christ; and likewise the Cup of Blessing is a partaking of the Blood of Christ.' The manner of the taking and receiving is described as a 'heavenly and spiritual manner." By its assertion that sacraments are "effectual signs of grace", Article 25 rejects a merely symbolic or figurative view of the Eucharist. Similarly, by rejecting the theory of transubstantiation on theological and philosophical grounds and as the only and obligatory explanation of the how, Article 28 asserts that Scripture furnishes no revealed explication of this, and therefore none such could be required as *de fide*. It is the fact of the Eucharist and its reality in the *koinonia* which are given. Lancelot Andrewes is typical: "Christ said, This is my Body. He did not say, This is my Body in this way. We are in agreement with you as to the end; the whole controversy is as to the method . . . and because there is no word, we rightly make it not of faith; we place it perhaps among the theories of the Schools, but not among the articles of the faith . . . we believe no less than you that the presence is real. Concerning the method of the presence, we define nothing rashly."[1]

Bishop Guest, who was the author of the third paragraph of Article 28, expressly stated that it was drawn up not to "exclude the Presence of Christ's Body from the sacrament, but only the grossness and sensibleness in the receiving thereof."[2] John Overall (1560–1619) who probably wrote the catechism of 1604, comments: "In the sacrament of the Eucharist or the Lord's Supper the body and blood of Christ, and therefore the whole Christ, are indeed really present, and are really received by us, and are really united to the sacramental signs, as signs which not only signify but also convey" and he adds that this is not "in a carnal, gross, earthly way" but "in a way mystical, heavenly and spiritual, as is rightly laid down in our Articles."[3]

Even more interesting is the reformer, Nicholas Ridley, who wrote: "In the Sacrament there is a certain change, in that that bread, which was before

---

[1] Responsio ad Apologiam Cardinalis Bellarmini (1610), C. I, 1.
[2] Quoted in E. J. BICKNELL's 'A Theological Introduction to the Thirty-Nine Articles' (1936), p. 480.
[3] Quoted in C. W. DUGMORE's 'Eucharistic Doctrine in England from Hooker to Waterland' (1942), p. 40.

common bread, is now made a lively presentation of Christ's body, and not only a figure, but effectuously representeth his Body" and adds "Such a sacramental mutation I grant to be in the bread and wine, which truly is no small change but such a change as no mortal man can make, but only the omnipotency of Christ's word."[4] Bearing in mind the phrasing of the Windsor Statement on sacramental presence,[5] and the thinking which understands this in terms of appropriation and relationship,[6] it is possible to discern not only a theme but an approach to a theme, and links between past and present. In these formularies, the fact of the presence is affirmed and the assertion is rejected that there is only one conceptual framework within which to explain the manner of Christ's presence and that this explanation is revealed and *de fide*.

Appendix D

Extract from the Roman Catholic Memorandum,
'The Conversations at Malines' (1927), pp. 78—83

"1. Baptism constitutes the means of entry into the Church, and the initiation which baptism inaugurates ought to develop within an organized life.

2. The social life of Christians is organized round an episcopal hierarchy.

3. This social and organized life finds expression within the Church in the existence and the use of the sacraments.

4. In the Eucharist the Body and Blood of our Lord Jesus Christ are verily given, taken, and received by the faithful. By consecration the Bread and Wine become the Body and Blood of Christ.

5. The Sacrifice of the Eucharist is the same sacrifice as that of the cross, but offered in a mystical and sacramental manner.

On the subject of eucharistic doctrine the Anglicans made particular reference to the letter published by the English Archbishops in reply to the Encyclical letter of Leo XIII on Anglican Orders: we give below[1] the pas-

---

[4] Quoted in J. M. R. TILLARD's 'Roman Catholics and Anglicans; the Eucharist', in: One in Christ, Vol. IX, 1973, No. 2, p. 173.

[5] E. g. "his true presence, effectually signified by the bread and wine which, in this mystery, become his body and blood" (6), "gives himself sacramentally in the body and blood of his paschal Sacrifice" (7), "offers to his Church, in the eucharistic signs, the special gift of himself" (7), "the sacramental body and blood of the Saviour are present as an offering to the believer awaiting his welcome" (8).

[6] Cp. Aquinas, "When we say that He is under this Sacrament, we express a kind of relationship to this sacrament", S.T. Part III, 3rd Number, Q. 76, A. 6.

[1] "Further we truly teach the doctrine of Eucharistic sacrifice, and do not believe it to be a 'nude commemoration of the Sacrifice of the Cross', an opinion which seems to be attributed to us by the quotation made from that Council. But we think it sufficient in the Liturgy which we use in celebrating the holy Eucharist — while lifting up our hearts to the Lord, and when now consecrating the gifts already offered that they may become to us the Body and Blood of our Lord Jesus Christ — to signify the sacrifice which is offered at that

sage which they state to be a specially authoritative expression of their real belief.

6. Communion in both kinds was once the practice of the whole Church, but in the West communion came to be limited to one kind for practical reasons dependent upon circumstances. Consequently, in our view, communion in both kinds is not a matter of doctrine, but one of ecclesiastical discipline.

7. In both Churches provision exists for a ministry and a discipline of penitence, whereby the sinner is reconciled to God through the sacramental absolution whith the priest pronounces upon the sinner.

   Although the use of the Sacrament of penance and of sacramental absolution is much more wide-spread in the Roman Catholic Church, yet the formulae given in the Prayer Book for the Order of Communion and for the Visitation of the Sick leave no doubt as to the belief of the Anglican Church in this respect, or as to the opportunity given to its members of having recourse to sacramental absolution for the purpose of their reconciliation with God, if they have fallen into any grave sin.

8. In regard to the anointing of the sick, it is true that there is less agreement; but it is to be noticed that there is a tendency among Anglicans to revive the ancient custom of anointing the sick.

Further meetings between Anglicans and Roman Catholics are much to be desired in order to elucidate further these general statements, and to secure that there should be no ambiguity or misunderstanding with regard to their deepest significance. In any case the result of this interchange of explanation is a very hopeful impression that a satisfactory accomodation may be reached with regard to the doctrine of the sacraments regarded as means of grace and of spiritual life."

point of the service in such terms as these. We continue a perpetual memory of the precious death of Christ, who is our Advocate with the Father and the propitiation for our sins, according to His precept, until His coming again.

For first we offer the sacrifice of praise and thanksgiving; then next we plead and represent before the Father the sacrifice of the cross, and by it we confidently entreat remission of sins and all other benefits of the Lord's Passion for all the whole Church; and lastly we offer the sacrifice of ourselves to the Creator of all things which we have already signified by the oblations of His creatures. This whole action, in which the people has necessarily to take its part with the Priest, we are accustomed to call the Eucharistic sacrifice."

sion appointed by Michael Ramsay and Paul VI in 1970, and an official visit of archbishop Donald Coggan of Canterbury to Pope Paul VI in 1977 (cf. McADOO, above pp. 224ff., 253f.). This dialogue will be given a new impetus by the mutual upgrading of diplomatic representatives and by the pastoral visit of Pope John Paul II to Britain planned for April, 1982[3].

The three essays which form this book have different themes and adopt various methodological approaches. The first two are written by historians (D. M. LOADES, Professor of History, University College of North Wales, Bangor, and J. C. H. AVELING, M. A., Chairman of Social Sciences Faculty, Garth Hill Comprehensive School, Bracknell, Berkshire)[4] and deal exclusively with conditions of the past, of the sixteenth and seventeenth centuries. The last one which has a Church leader as author (The Most Reverend Dr. H. R. McADOO, Archbishop of Dublin)[5], begins in chronicle form with the early years of the eighteenth century. Finally, however, from the open perspectives of present-day attempts at agreement between the two Churches the author, who has been active in shaping these attempts (cf. below pp. 287f.), points towards a path of coexistence and cooperation for the future.

D. M. LOADES' contribution on 'Relations between the Anglican and Roman Catholic Churches in the 16th and 17th Centuries' (above pp. 1–53) describes the first two centuries of the separation by means of the history of personalities and events as reflected in the political and reduced diplomatic relationship between the respective heads of the two Churches, the Pope and the English monarch. As the author notes (above p. 1), the theme has received little attention in the research of the last decades, in contrast, for example, to the history of the English Catholics generally, the attitudes of the English to the Papacy, and the social history of the Puritans on the one hand and the Roman Catholic "recusants" in England on the

---

[3] Cf. Orientierung Ökumene. Ein Handbuch, hrsg. v. H.-M. MODEROW u. M. SENS, Berlin 1979, p. 221. – L'Osservatore Romano 1982, No. 14 (January 18), pp. 1f.

[4] Important earlier publications of these authors include: D. M. LOADES, Two Tudor Conspiracies, Cambridge 1965; The Oxford Martyrs, London – New York 1970; Politics and the Nation 1450–1660. Obedience, Resistance and Public Order, Brighton–London 1974; The Reign of Mary Tudor. Politics, Government, and Religion in England, 1553–1558, London 1979; also: The Bibliography of the Reform, 1450–1648, relating to the United Kingdom and Ireland for the years 1955–1970, edited by D. BAKER, compiled by D. M. LOADES, J. K. CAMERON, D. BAKER for the British Sub-Commission, Commission Internationale d'Histoire Ecclésiastique Comparée, Oxford 1975. – J. C. H. AVELING, Post-Reformation Catholicism in East Yorkshire, York 1953; Catholic Recusancy in the West Riding, 1558–1791, Leeds 1963; Northern Catholics: Recusancy in the North Riding, 1558–1791, London 1966; Catholic Recusancy in the City of York, 1558–1791, London 1968; The Handle and the Axe: The Catholic Recusants in England from the Reformation to Emancipation, London 1976; The Jesuits, London 1981.

[5] Of his work the following examples may be listed: The Structure of Caroline Moral Theology, London – New York – Toronto 1949; John Bramhall and Anglicanism, 1663–1963, Dublin 1964; The Spirit of Anglicanism. A Survey of Anglican Theological Method in the Seventeenth Century, London 1965; Modern Eucharistic Agreement, London 1973; Modern Ecumenical Documents on Ministry, 1975; Being an Anglican, Dublin 1977.

other. Its present treatment is distinguished from comparable earlier work by the
relative breadth of its chronological framework, while keeping within a restricted
space, and by the impartial balance of its judgement. In its condensed form it
differs also from the corresponding chapters of the well known book by B. and
M. Pawley entitled 'Rome and Canterbury through four centuries'[6]. As a consequence of the European involvement of the Papacy and of the English Crown,
this contribution throws light not only on a phase of English political history and
of Church history, but also touches on simultaneous developments in the history
of other countries, in particular of France, the Netherlands, Spain and the Holy
Roman Empire (cf., e.g., above pp. 8, 10ff., 24f.).

Of a different type is the essay by J. C. H. Aveling on 'The English Clergy,
Catholic and Protestant, in the 16th and 17th Centuries' (above pp. 55–142).
Although proceeding chronologically by chapters, in each chapter its author
does, by means of a cross-sectional view, present a structural analysis of material
which covers periods of several decades. The questions of social history which he
raises relate to education, origin, function and position of all the Anglican and
Roman Catholic clergy in England. Thus, to an extent, he develops systematically
motifs which had already occurred peripherally with a political accent in D. M.
Loades' contribution (cf., e.g., above pp. 24f., 27, 32f., 40f., 46f.). Aveling
expressly says (above p. 56) that when he joins both sides, the Anglican and the
Roman Catholic, in one study, this has nothing to do with ecumenical, but purely
with historical and comparative aims. Regarding its theme and methodological
approach, one may characterize this piece of work, though the author does not
emphasize the fact himself, as an important contribution to the research into elites
or leadership strata and groups and their mentalities[7], an area which stands so
prominently in the fore of current historical interest. The Anglican clergy of the
early modern period is, of course, to be regarded as being associated with leadership to a greater extent than its Catholic equivalent; for it is a fact, as, for example,
G. R. Elton says of the period of Elizabeth I, that "the Church appeared as the
spiritual manifestation and organization of the state" and the monarch "governed
in ecclesiastical affairs through archbishops, bishops, and the rest of the clergy"[8].
In this respect the English clergy as a whole has so far never been dealt with so

---

[6] B. and M. Pawley, Rome and Canterbury through four Centuries. A Study of the Relations
between the Church of Rome and the Anglican Churches, 1530–1973, London – Oxford
1974 (idem, with an American Epilogue by A. A. Vogel, New York, N. Y. 1975) pp. 1 –
ca. 50. In the present volume this work is expressly cited only by H. R. McAdoo, above
pp. 146, 190 n. 65, 193f., 196ff.

[7] As a recent introduction and research report see R. Reichardt, «Histoire des mentalités»,
Internationales Archiv f. Sozialgeschichte d. deutschen Literatur 3 (1978) pp. 130–166, esp.
the chapters on 'Zum Begriff der Mentalität' (pp. 131ff.), 'Historische Religionssoziologie'
(pp. 142ff.) and 'Sozialgeschichte der Bildung' (pp. 149ff.). Cf. also M. Erbe, Zur neueren
französischen Sozialgeschichtsforschung. Die Gruppe um die 'Annales' (= Erträge der Forschung CX), Darmstadt 1979, pp. 110ff.

[8] G. R. Elton, England under the Tudors (= A History of England, ed. C. Oman, IV),
London ²1974, p. 421. Cf. E. W. Zeeden, Hegemonialkriege und Glaubenskämpfe 1556–
1648 (= Propyläen Geschichte Europas II), Frankfurt a. M. – Berlin – Wien 1977, pp. 130ff.

thoroughly across the confessional divides, nor chronologically so extensively[9]. The enquiry into the sixteenth and seventeenth century period, at the beginning of which the institutional and confessional division and differentiation took place, is also illuminating in so far as it covers a period in which a certain 'modernization' of the clergy occured by means of an internal structural development from an 'estate' to a profession, even if this came about more slowly and less clearly than has commonly been assumed (cf. J. C. H. AVELING, above pp. 140f.). The English example of two centuries can for that branch of social history which is increasingly taking as its subject, besides the political elites as primary leadership strata, other, secondary, strata and groups, thereby not ignoring the spiritual and religious leadership[10], be instructive in a comparison of similarities and differences within a European context. The present contribution from J. C. H. AVELING, then, may as an advanced synthesis be profitably compared with recent works in

---

[9] In addition to G. R. ELTON, op. cit., pp. 420–429 cf. IDEM, Reform and Reformation in England 1509–1558 (= The New History of England II), London 1977, passim, esp. pp. 118f., 123f., 240f., 248ff. and Bibliography pp. 398f., 404ff.; A. GOODMAN, A History of England from Edward II to James I, London 1977, pp. 340–356 and Bibliography pp. 445f.; H. J. COHN, Reformatorische Bewegung und Antiklerikalismus in Deutschland und England, in: Stadtbürgertum und Adel in der Reformation. Studien zur Sozialgeschichte der Reformation in England und Deutschland (= Veröffentlichungen d. Deutschen Historischen Instituts London V), Stuttgart 1979, pp. 309–329, here 312ff. Introductory comments especially for German readers are given by H. LEHMANN, Das Zeitalter des Absolutismus. Gottesgnadentum und Kriegsnot (= Christentum und Gesellschaft IX), Stuttgart – Berlin – Köln – Mainz 1980, pp. 72–83. To recent literature cited by J. C. H. AVELING in the course of his study may now be added F. HEAL, Of Prelates and Princes. A Study of the Economic and Social Position of the Tudor Episcopate, Cambridge 1980; A. T. HART, Some Clerical Oddities in the Church of England from Medieval to Modern Times, Bognor Regis, W. Sussex (GB) 1980, pp. 39–102 with Select Bibliography pp. 289ff., and Princes and Paupers in the English Church, ed. by R. O'DAY and F. HEAL, Leicester 1981.

[10] See most recently TH. SCHIEDER, Zur Theorie der Führungsschichten in der Neuzeit, in: Deutsche Führungsschichten in der Neuzeit. Eine Zwischenbilanz. Büdinger Vorträge 1978, hrsg. v. H. H. HOFMANN u. G. FRANZ (= Deutsche Führungsschichten in der Neuzeit XII), Boppard am Rhein 1980, pp. 13–28; also generally, e. g., W. DOYLE, The Old European Order 1660–1800, Oxford 1978, pp. 151–173.
In 1972 still B. MOELLER rightly found it necessary to say: „Die soziale Stellung der christlichen Geistlichen in der Geschichte – das ist ein ungemein weitläufiges Thema . . . . Andererseits aber ist das Problem auf weite Strecken ganz unerforscht" (Pfarrer als Bürger, Göttinger Universitätsreden LVI, Göttingen 1972, p. 6). So in the late sixties and early seventies a collection of studies like 'Beamtentum und Pfarrerstand 1400–1800'. Büdinger Vorträge 1967, hrsg. v. G. FRANZ (= Deutsche Führungsschichten in der Neuzeit V), Limburg/Lahn 1972, could be regarded as something of a pioneer undertaking though the trend of research of which it was to be an expression had already been envisaged in the late fifties (cf., e. g., H. RÖSSLER, Elite, in: Führungsschicht und Eliteproblem [Jahrbuch d. Ranke-Gesellschaft III], Frankfurt a. M. – Berlin – Bonn 1957, pp. 136–143, esp. 139, 141).
The notion of 'secondary leadership' is here used in the sense of, e. g., G. HEINRICH, Amtsträgerschaft und Geistlichkeit. Zur Problematik der sekundären Führungsschichten in Brandenburg–Preußen 1450–1786, in: Beamtentum und Pfarrerstand 1400–1800 (op.cit.).

which research is advanced or critically reported on religious leadership strata and groups of the early modern period for Germany or France[11].

In contrast to the two first contributions of this volume, in the third and last essay by H. R. McADOO on 'Anglican/Roman Catholic Relations, 1717–1980. A Detection of Themes' (above pp. 143–281) the ecumenical point of view plays a central role beside the historical. Accordingly here we find, in addition to themes of a political, personal and institutional nature, a greater concentration on aspects of dogma. With regard to the last decade of inter-Church dialogue this richly-documented account gains in value by the fact that its author has been able to

[11] For Germany, where in consequence of the territorial fragmentation there is, of course, a dearth of syntheses, see the diverse research reports by V. PRESS, Führungsgruppen in der deutschen Gesellschaft im Übergang zur Neuzeit um 1500, in: Deutsche Führungsschichten in der Neuzeit etc. (above n. 10) pp. 29–77, esp. 44, 67ff. (cf. the programmatic remarks in P. MORAW – V. PRESS, Probleme der Sozial- und Verfassungsgeschichte des Heiligen Römischen Reiches im Späten Mittelalter und in der Frühen Neuzeit (13.–18. Jahrhundert). Zu einem Forschungsschwerpunkt, Zeitschrift f. Historische Forschung 2 [1975] pp. 95–106, esp. 105); R. ENDRES, Die deutschen Führungsschichten um 1600, ibid. pp. 79–109, esp. 86ff., 96f.; J. KUNISCH, Die deutschen Führungsschichten im Zeitalter des Absolutismus, ibid. pp. 111–141, esp. 134ff.; W. ZORN, Deutsche Führungsschichten des 17. und 18. Jahrhunderts. Forschungsergebnisse seit 1945, Internationales Archiv f. Sozialgeschichte d. deutschen Literatur 6 (1981) pp. 176–197, esp. 189f. (cf. also M. L. BAEUMER, Sozialkritische und revolutionäre Literatur der Reformationszeit, ibid. 5 [1980] pp. 169–233, esp. 186f.); in detail the following which are not taken into account in the aforementioned: Stadt und Kirche im 16. Jahrhundert, hrsg. v. B. MOELLER (= Schriften d. Vereins f. Reformationsgeschichte CXC), Gütersloh 1978, passim; H. J. COHN, Reformatorische Bewegung und Antiklerikalismus etc., in: Stadtbürgertum u. Adel etc. (above n. 9); V. PRESS, Adel, Reich und Reformation, ibid. pp. 330–383, esp. 337ff.; H. LEPPER, Reichsstadt und Kirche im Späten Mittelalter und der Frühen Neuzeit, in: Voraussetzungen und Methoden geschichtlicher Städteforschung, hrsg. v. W. EHBRECHT (= Städteforschung. Veröffentlichungen d. Instituts f. vergleichende Städtegeschichte in Münster, Reihe A: Darstellungen VII), Köln – Wien 1979, pp. 28–46, esp. 32ff.; Kirche und gesellschaftlicher Wandel in deutschen und niederländischen Städten in der werdenden Neuzeit, hrsg. v. F. PETRI (= Städteforschung etc., A: X), Köln – Wien 1980, passim, in which, e. g., pp. 252–296: V. PRESS, Stadt und territoriale Konfessionsbildung, esp. pp. 255ff., 290, 292; H. KRAMM, Studien über die Oberschichten der mitteldeutschen Städte im 16. Jahrhundert. Sachsen, Thüringen, Anhalt (= Mitteldeutsche Forschungen LXXXVII), Köln – Wien 1981, I pp. 355ff. together with II pp. 769ff. (notes); cf. S. OZMENT, The Social History of the Reformation. What can we learn from Pamphlets?, in: Flugschriften als Massenmedien der Reformationszeit. Beiträge zum Tübinger Symposion 1980, hrsg. v. H.-J. KÖHLER (= Spätmittelalter u. Frühe Neuzeit XIII), Stuttgart 1981, pp. 171–203, esp. 189ff. – For France see R. MANDROU, La France aux XVIIe et XVIIIe siècles (= Nouvelle Clio. L'histoire et ses problèmes XXXIII), Paris ³1974, pp. 104f., 168–177, 294ff.; P. GOUBERT, L'Ancien Régime II. Les pouvoirs, Paris 1973, pp. 68f., 164–179; R. BRIGGS, Early Modern France 1560–1715, Oxford – London – New York 1977, esp. pp. 167–183, 188f.; M. C. PERONNET, Les évêques de l'ancienne France, Thèse Paris 1976, I. II, Lille – Paris 1977; further references to important case studies in F. RAPP, Les nouvelles orientations de l'histoire religieuse II. Du XIVe au milieu du XVIe siècle, in: Tendances, perspectives et méthodes de l'histoire médiévale (= Actes du 100e Congrès National des sociétés savantes, Paris 1975, Section de philologie et d'histoire jusqu'à 1610, I), Paris 1977, pp. 113–135, esp. 122ff.

report not only from written sources but also as an engaged eye-witness to the events, having been, as Bishop of Ossory, Ferns and Leighlin, since 1967 a member of the 'Joint Preparatory Anglican/Roman Catholic Commission' (JPARC) which worked between January 1966 and January 1967 (cf. above pp. 215ff.) and, from 1969/70 to 1981, first as Bishop of Ossory, then (since 1977) as Archbishop of Dublin, Co-chairman (with the Roman Catholic Bishop A.C. Clark, Auxiliary Bishop of Northampton) of the 'Anglican/Roman Catholic International Commission' (ARCIC) (cf. above pp. 224ff.) to the members of which he dedicates his present essay "in grateful remembrance of work done together" (above p. 143).

All three contributions in this book were originally written in connection with the international cooperative project 'Aufstieg und Niedergang der römischen Welt. Geschichte und Kultur Roms im Spiegel der neueren Forschung' (ANRW). In the planned third part of this work[12], which will have the subtitle 'Spätantike und Nachleben' ('Late Antiquity and Heritage') there is to be a category on 'Religion'[13], spanning several volumes, which will also contain a series of contributions dealing with the external and internal history of the Church in the post-antiquity period. The Church — above all the West Roman-Latin-Catholic and the East Roman-Greek-Orthodox — is here seen as a sphere in which ancient tradition from the Roman world has been more or less continuously transmitted through all periods of history. Furthermore not only the ancient Church centres, above all Rome and Constantinople, still continue to exist as such, but also the ancient Church traditions from the New Testament to the teachings of the Fathers and the Councils of Late Antiquity have an undiminished actuality[14]. Among works stimulated in the context of the relationship of the Churches of the First and Second Rome (Constantinople) to churches separated from them there

---

[12] Cf. the general Preface to ANRW by H. TEMPORINI in vol. I 1, Berlin — New York 1972, pp. XIIf., XVIf.

[13] The category 'Religion' of Part II ('Principat'), edited by W. HAASE, has been in print since 1978. It comprises volumes II 16—II 28, of which II 16—II 18 are dedicated to paganism, II 19—II 21 to Judaism, II 22 to Gnosticism and related phenomena, II 23—II 28 to early Christianity. Cf. the present editor's prefaces to voll. II 16, 1 (1978) pp. VIIf., II 19, 1 (1979) pp. Vff., II 23, 1 (1979) p. V, and II 25, 1 (1982) p. V.

[14] See under various historical perspectives: Latein und Europa. Traditionen und Renaissancen, hrsg. v. K. BÜCHNER, Stuttgart 1978; H. RAHNER, Vom Ersten bis zum Dritten Rom, in: IDEM, Abendland. Reden und Aufsätze, Freiburg — Basel — Wien 1966, pp. 253—269; E. v. IVANKA, Rhomäerreich und Gottesvolk. Das Glaubens-, Staats- und Volksbewußtsein der Byzantiner und seine Auswirkung auf die ostkirchlich-osteuropäische Geisteshaltung, Freiburg — München 1968; C. ANDRESEN, Antike und Christentum, Theologische Realenzyklopädie (TRE) III, Berlin — New York 1978, pp. 50—99; and H. LUTZ, Rom in der Neuzeit — Perspektiven und Methodenfragen, in: Rom in der Neuzeit. Politische, kirchliche und kulturelle Aspekte, hrsg. v. R. ELZE — H. SCHMIDINGER — H. SCHULTE NORDHOLT, Wien — Rom 1976, pp. 9—18, esp. 10f.; from a specifically theological point of view, e.g., Y. M.-J. CONGAR, La tradition et les traditions I. Essai historique, Paris 1960, II. Essai théologique, Paris 1963, and more briefly IDEM and A. BENOÎT, Tradition, in: Vocabulaire œcuménique, sous la direction de Y. CONGAR, Paris 1970, pp. 307—328.

emerged at an early stage a group of essays on the relationship between Rome and the Anglicans which were so comprehensive and related that it appeared advisable to bring out a separate publication, especially as this would become possible now at a time when particular interest in its theme seemed assured. The common aim of the editor, authors and publishers was to reach a broad audience of interested readers sooner and more easily than would have been possible in the larger context of the collective project of ANRW. Thanks to the agreement of the authors and the cooperation of the publishers Walter de Gruyter & Co., Berlin— New York, represented by the director of their Arts Department (Abteilung Geisteswissenschaften), Prof. HEINZ WENZEL, this volume can now be given over to the public.

The origin of the plan for this volume from a context in which Rome is the central theme has led to the name of "Rome" standing at the beginning of the title. This should not suggest a "pro-Roman" attitude on the question of primacy, nor, by contrast, should the fact that two of the three authors have their roots in the Anglican Church and that the editor is a Lutheran Protestant be thought to have caused even a hint of any "anti-Roman complex". Both would have been quite inappropriate to historical sense and to the positive atmosphere in the relationship between 'Rome and the Anglicans'[15]. If a second Roman Catholic voice in addition to that of J. C. H. AVELING is missing from the small chorus of contributors, this has but one historical, biographical reason. JOSEPH Cardinal RATZINGER, the present Archbishop of Munich and Freising, as a result of his work for the central direction of his church (which was, indeed, already a preliminary notice of his future Roman office at the head of the 'Sacra Congregatio pro Doctrina Fidei') was unfortunately not in a position to write the preface, which he would, with a scientific theological and an ecumenical intention[16], have liked to send with this book on its way.

Tübingen, January 1982   WOLFGANG HAASE

---

[15] On the good climate which has existed since the sixties and seventies of this century in the dialogue between the two Churches see the comments, independent of both sides, by GÜNTHER GASSMANN, Research Professor at the 'Centre d'Études Œcuméniques' at Strasbourg, who as Observer of the World Council of Churches participated in the work of the 'Anglican/Roman Catholic International Commission' (cf. H. R. McADOO, above pp. 226, 234 n. 9), in: Vom Dialog zur Gemeinschaft. Dokumente zum anglikanisch-lutherischen und anglikanisch-katholischen Gespräch. Mit einer historischen und vergleichenden Einführung von G. G. (= Ökumenische Dokumentation II), Frankfurt a.M. 1975, esp. pp. 29 ff.

[16] See the basic remarks in J. RATZINGER, Das neue Volk Gottes. Entwürfe einer Ekklesiologie, Düsseldorf 1969, pp. 319 ff.; IDEM, Der Primat des Papstes und die Einheit des Gottesvolkes, in: Dienst an der Einheit. Wesen und Auftrag des Petrusamtes, hrsg. v. J. R. (= Schriften d. Katholischen Akademie in Bayern LXXXV), Düsseldorf 1978, pp. 165– 179, esp. 178 f., and IDEM, Europa — verpflichtendes Erbe für die Christen (Tagung der Katholischen Akademie in Bayern „Europa und die Christen" 28./29. April 1979, Straßburg), München 1979, pp. 3–13, esp. 10.

Index

Aufstieg und Niedergang der römischen Welt (ANRW)

Geschichte und Kultur Roms im Spiegel der neueren Forschung

Herausgegeben von Hildegard Temporini und Wolfgang Haase

3 Teile in mehreren Einzelbänden und Gesamtregister
Groß-Oktav. Ganzleinen

RUBRIK »RELIGION«

Herausgegeben von Wolfgang Haase

In allen drei Teilen von ANRW soll eine Übersicht über den gegenwärtigen Stand der Forschungen zu den Religionen der antiken römischen Welt und ihrer Nachbargebiete gegeben werden. Die einzelnen Beiträge sind ihrer Form nach, dem jeweiligen Thema entsprechend, entweder zusammenfassende Darstellungen oder Problem- und Forschungsberichte oder exemplarische Untersuchungen.

Im I. Teil des Werkes („Von den Anfängen Roms bis zum Ausgang der Republik") besteht die Rubrik „Religion" nur aus einer kleinen Gruppe von Beiträgen in Bd. I 2 (Berlin–New York 1972) über wichtige Aspekte der älteren römischen Religion. Im II. und III. Teil („Principat" bzw. „Spätantike und Nachleben") wird sie dagegen jeweils mehrere Bände umfassen und dem Charakter einer handbuchartigen enzyklopädischen Übersicht näherkommen. Hier wie in den anderen Rubriken werden Lücken und Ungleichmäßigkeiten des Programms zumeist Tendenzen der aktuellen Forschung widerspiegeln.

Im II. Teil behandelt die Rubrik „Religion" außer den sog. heidnischen Religionen griechisch-römischen, orientalischen und sonstigen regionalen Ursprungs (Bde. II 16 – II 18) auch das späthellenistische, das „intertestamentarische" und das rabbinische Judentum im Blickfeld der römischen Welt (Bde. II 19 – II 21), Gnostizismus und verwandte Erscheinungen (Bd. II 22) und das frühe Christentum vor Konstantin (Bde. II 23 – II 28). Im III. Teil wird das spätantike Christentum etwa von der Zeit Konstantins an Hauptgegenstand der Rubrik sein. Darüber hinaus werden aber mehrere Beiträge auch dem byzantinischen und dem römisch-katholischen Christentum des Mittelalters und der Neuzeit bis hin zum 2. Vatikanischen Konzil hinsichtlich ihrer Beziehungen zum Alten und Neuen christlichen Rom der Antike gewidmet sein.

Walter de Gruyter Berlin · New York